JUVENILE CRIME
AND
DELINQUENCY

JUVENILE CRIME AND DELINQUENCY
- SHOOTOUTS IN SCHOOL

By
Anju Khosla

2009

SBS Publishers & Distributors Pvt. Ltd.
New Delhi

ISBN 13 : 9788189741846

First Published in India in 2009

© Reserved

Published by:

SBS PUBLISHERS & DISTRIBUTORS PVT. LTD.
2/9, Ground Floor, Ansari Road, Darya Ganj,
New Delhi - 110002,
INDIA
Tel: 0091.11.23289119 / 41563911 / 32945311
Email: mail@sbspublishers.com
www.sbspublishers.com

Printed in India by Chaman Enterprises, New Delhi.

Preface

VIOLENCE LIKE ANY OTHER SOCIAL BEHAVIOR IS PART OF A SOCIAL SYSTEM. Many aspects of society promote or inhibit violence. LEGITIMATE VIOLENCE INCREASES ILLEGITIMATE AND CRIMINAL VIOLENCE.

Studies of school shootings have been conducted in a variety of disciplines, including sociology, psychology, and media studies. Despite the widely diffused recognition and fear associated with violence in schools, empirical evidence indicates that schools are among the safest places for children, compared to their homes and neighborhood environs.

People automatically assume that these killers are evil and twisted and they are thankful that they are either dead or locked up, when in fact most of these people who have done this were people who reached out and were never seen or heard. It is very necessary that every school has an in-house counselor who can talk to children whenever they are disturbed by any issue.

School shootings can happen at any school at any time. Lack of security is only a small part of the problem. The major issue lies in the low morality of students and warning signs overlooked by administration. Not all, but a majority of the students are cold-blooded killers. And shooting fellow students is often not their first choice. In fact, most school shooters are victims themselves, and shooting fellow students was a last resort. They feel as if no one is listening and this is their only way of getting their voice heard. The shooter has more and likely made many attempts to solve this problem.

Gun control laws focus on making guns more difficult to obtain, as well as easier to trace; it also means constitutionality of gun control, the effectiveness of gun ownership, and measures to reduce gun violence.

The new generation resorts to violence over trivial issues or for no apparent reason. This is because many youths, particularly those in major urban centers, are "beset with idleness" and that a "growing number of teens see few attractive alternatives to violence, drug use, and gang membership."

Contents

1

Student Teacher and Tradition

The dictionary defines education as to develop the knowledge, skill or art... The Greek philosopher Socrates argued that education was about drawing out what was already within the student. Though India is a modern nation, the thread of Indian civilization has more than a 5000, year-old historical legacy.

India's history begins not with independence in 1947, but more than 4,500 years earlier, when the name *India* referred to the entire subcontinent, including present-day Pakistan and Bangladesh. The earliest of India's known civilizations, the Indus Valley civilization (about 2500 to 1700 BC), was known for its highly specialized artifacts and stretched throughout northern India. Another early culture—the Vedic culture—dates from approximately 1500 BC and is considered one of the sources for India's predominantly Hindu culture and for the foundation of several important philosophical traditions. India has been subject to influxes of peoples throughout its history, some coming under arms to loot and conquer, others moving in to trade and settle. India was able to absorb the impact of these intrusions because it was able to assimilate or tolerate foreign ideas and people. Outsiders who came to India during the course of its history include the Greeks under Alexander the Great, the Kushânas from Central Asia, the Mongols under Genghis Khan, Muslim traders and invaders from the Middle East and Central Asia, and finally the British and other Europeans. India also disseminated its civilization outward to Sri Lanka and much of Southeast Asia. Buddhism, which originated in India, spread even farther. India's official goal for *education* since independence in 1947 has been to ensure free and compulsory education for all children up to age 14. At independence 25 per cent of males and 8 per cent of females were literate.

Education for the Elite

Education for the elite has been a tradition in India since the beginnings of its civilization. Great Buddhist universities at *Nalanda* and *Taxila* were famous far beyond India's borders. Withholding education from the no elite, including women, has also been a tradition. The lowest caste members, including the Harijans and non-Hindu tribal groups, were denied the right even to hear the *Vedas*, sacred Hindu texts, recited.

"Veda"

The word *"Veda"* is a Sanskrit word which means *"knowledge"* or *"wisdom"*. There are in fact four Vedas: the Rig Veda" or "Veda of Hymns", the Sama-Veda or the "Veda of Chants", the Yajur-Veda or the "Veda of sacrifice" and the Artharva-Veda, which is later in date than the earlier three. The roots of Hindu Dharma lie in the Vedas, considered as their supreme scriptures. Vedas were the sacred scriptures of the *Aryans*. Aryans were a nomadic and pastoral tribe from Central Asia who came to India during the second millennium BC, and eventually settled here and made it their home. Indus Valley Civilization is a connecting link to the history of ancient India.

The period during which the sacred Vedic texts were written is known in the Indian history as the Vedic period, which lasted from 1800-500 BC. Sanskrit was the language of the intelligentsia during the Vedic period, though common people of those times were largely unfamiliar with it. Vedic hymns do not advise that education should be under state control or supervision of the government. Schools should be in the natural surroundings either in the outskirts of towns or away from there. The male and female students are described therein as *Brahmachari and Brahmacharni*, as they acquire the knowledge of Brahma- the formless and ineffable God (R.V. 1-XL1-4). The boys and girls should stay separately in their respective hostels under the supervision of *rsis and rsikas*-male and female preceptors. Children of all four divine *Varna* should join these schools (*Vidayalayas*), which are mostly the *asharams* of the *gurus*. The mother is the teacher until the age of 5 years of the child. Between the age of 5 to 8 years, father is the teacher. He should teach further what mother has already taught with certain practical illustrations from animate and inanimate life/things. The child should be encouraged for sports, games etc.; till the age of 8 years.

The students of Brahma's knowledge are advised to participate daily in such *Yajnas* performed by their preceptors. By this method, all the students' daily learnt the spiritual and material significance of the Vedic hymns and performance of their noble duties for the welfare of society and not for their personal benefits. This method also helped in memorizing the Vedic hymns by the students until the printing material became available. Prakrti has thousands of attributes, for easy understanding by the students, these attributes were divided into 33 parts, like selfless service, light, energy, power, strength, discipline, stability etc. For each set of attributes a formless deva like, Surya, Agni, Indra, Varun, Usha, Prithvi and others was made in-charge. The word deva is from the root *divu*, which means having ten attributes and meanings and so applied to forces of Nature.

Early Vedic Period

In the early Vedic period (beginning c. 1200 B.C.E.), an elite controlled the teaching of the four Vedas, the hymns and ritual practices of Aryan people who had migrated into north India in the previous century. Daughters as well as sons of higher-status families probably memorized these hymns and learned their meanings and associated ritual practices. *Rishis,* sages or seers who mostly belonged to the Brahman *varna* or caste, produced, transmitted, and controlled access to this knowledge. The Sanskrit of the Vedas was the language of classical learning.

Respected teachers (gurus) taught apprentices pronunciation of the Vedas and all that it implied, as well as phonology, metrics, elementary grammar, and etymology, in return for the students' mundane services. This education was extra-institutional and closed to people of low status before the end of the Vedic period. In the modern era, nineteenth-and twentieth-century Hindu teachers of indigenous curricula frequently looked back to an idealized Vedic model for pedagogical inspiration.

Heterodox Belief Systems

In the sixth and fifth century B.C.E., historical founders Nigantha Nataputta (or Mahavira, the "Great Hero" of Jainism), and Siddhartha Gautama (the Buddha, the "Enlightened One") created heterodox belief systems that monks elaborated, preserved, and taught to initiates. Buddhist monks congregated in monasteries (*viharas*), and provided itinerant teaching for laypeople. Elder monks taught the disciplines of the *Sangha* (the monastic order) as well as discourses on doctrine, spiritual exercises, and advanced philosophical ideas. Female converts created nunneries with similar practices. The Nalanda Mahavihara in Bihar and other great monasteries were centers of learning that included secular arts and sciences as well as theology. Mahaviharas flourished in northeastern India with royal support until they were destroyed at the beginning of the thirteenth century. In southern India, education was likewise linked to the ideas of Buddhist, Jaina, and Hindu teachings. Itinerant teachers carried ideas and the Sanskrit language to the south, where a Tamil prose and poetry tradition flourished from around 100 C.E. onwards.

Arab and Central Asian peoples brought Muslim educational models to the subcontinent in both the medieval and early modern periods. Within decades of the Prophet Muhammad's death in 632 C.E., Arab mariners began to trade, reside, and intermarry with local women in south India. Turkic peoples and other Central Asians raided northern India around 1000 C.E. and thereafter established several foreign-conquest empires. Muslim rulers promoted urban education by endowing libraries and literary societies. They also founded primary schools (*maktabs*) in which students learned reading, writing, and basic Islamic prayers, and secondary schools (*madrasas*) to teach advanced language skills, Koranic exegesis, prophetic traditions, Islamic law (*shari a*), and related subjects. Often attached to mosques, Islamic schools were open to the poor but were gender segregated, often only for boys. Muslim girls of affluent families studied at home, if they received any education beyond learning to recite the Koran. From the beginning of the Mughal empire in India in 1526 until the end of Mughal political presence in 1848, Persian was the court language, and elite boys could attend Persian schools to learn literature, history, ethics, law, administration, and court protocol. Subjects such as medicine, mathematics, and logic also formed an important part of the curriculum in centers for Islamic learning. More intimate settings for the spread of ideas were the retreats (*khanqah*) of famous Sufis (Muslims who professed mystic doctrines). These new educational models did not necessarily displace older ones, although state patronage patterns shifted. Sanskrit academies continued to teach young male Brahmans literature and law; apprenticeship and commercial schools taught boys the skills needed for business. Education for girls was the exception rather than the rule.

Present Education System

In India, education is the joint responsibility of the centre and the states, State governments control their own school systems, with some assistance from the central government. The federal Ministry of Education directs the school systems of centrally administered areas, provides financial help for the nation's institutions of higher learning, and handles tasks such as commissioning textbooks. The Indian education system is based on 12 years of schooling, which generally begins at age 6 and includes 5 years of primary school, 3 years of middle school, 2 years of secondary school, and 2 years of higher secondary school.

On the one hand a section of its educated and highly skilled manpower is highly coveted by west; on the other hand the country has the dubious distinction of having the largest number of illiterates in the world. On the one hand, powered by its IT revolution, India is emerging in the global map as one of the foremost knowledge economies, on the other hand, many of its children are not fortunate enough to get even a basic education; instead they sell their childhood for a pittance as their child labor contributes to the marginal income of their impoverished families.

According to the 2001 census, India's literacy rate is 64.8 percent, with literacy rate for males being 75.3 percent, and the literacy rate for females at 53.7 percent. The adult literacy rate is only 61.3 percent, which is way behind the global average of 81.7 percent. Though the 86th Amendment of the Indian Constitution has made education a fundamental right for all children aged 6-14 years, but still that fundamental right is not accessed by many Indian children, and a major chunk of those getting inducted into elementary education are translated into alarming drop outs. The figures are dismal to say the least. Though India has come a long way from 12.2 per cent literacy rate in 1947, or for that matter from 52.2 per cent literacy rate in 1991, but still lots of grounds need to be covered before we reach a truly educated India. Some states in India have attained a high degree of literacy, while most have failed in that effort.

Nearly 60 per cent children in India drop out from school by the eighth standard, and 11 per cent from the age group of 17-23 have access to higher education. Though the Union Government has decided to spend 5.1 per cent of its budget expenditure on education in 2007-08, as compared to 4.1 per cent in the previous fiscal, but still it is far from enough. More critical is in which areas the outlay on education is being made. Presently, approximately 97 per cent of the Union Government's expenditure on elementary education in India goes in paying teachers' salaries, which leaves very little scope for infrastructure developments in the elementary education sector.

Demography

The 1991 census enumerated 846,302,688 residents, including 407,072,230 women, and 217 million people defined as urban dwellers. However, with a population growth rate estimated at 17 per one thousand in 1998, by May 2000 the national figure reached one billion. Life expectancy in the 1991 census was sixty years, and in 1997 it was estimated that almost 5 per cent of the population was age 65 or older. The population is still primarily rural, with 73 per cent of the population in 1997 living outside the cities and towns. In 1991, the largest urban centers were Bombay or Mumbai (12,596,243), Calcutta or Kolkata (11,021,915), Delhi (8,419,084), Madras or Chennai (5,421,985), Hyderabad (4,253,759), and Bangalore (4,130,288).

Linguistic Affiliations

There are four major language families, each with numerous languages. Indo-Aryan, a branch of Indo-European, covers the northern half of the country, and the Dravidian family covers the southern third. In the middle regions a number of tribal languages of the Munda or Austroasiatic family are spoken. In the northeastern hills, numerous Tibeto-Burman languages are spoken.

Institutional form of Imparting Learning

India has a rich tradition of learning and education right from the antiquity. These were handed over generations to generations either through oral or written medium. The highly esteemed Vedas have come to down to us. They existed for nearly 2000 years before they were known in India. It was the knowledge of acoustics that enabled ancient Indians to orally transmit the Vedas from generation to generation. Institutional form of imparting learning came into existence in the early centuries of the Christian era. The approach to learning was to study logic and epistemology. The study of logic was followed by Hindus, Buddhists and Jains, one of the most important topics of Indian thoughts was pramana or means of reliable knowledge. The Nyaya schools upheld four pramanas—perceptions of are liable by analogy or comparison, word (Sabda), and pronunciation of a reliable authority such as the Vedas. The Vedanta school added one more to it i.e. intuition. It is probably while studying the process of inference that the schools of true logic arose. Ancient Indian postulated syllogism though not as accurate as that of Aristotle.

Guru-Sishya System

Regarding institutional form of education the first was the *guru-sishya system*. According to sacred texts, the training of the Brahmin pupil took place at the home of a Brahmin teacher. In some texts the guru is depicted as the poor ascetic and it is the duty of the student to beg for his teacher. The first lesson that was taught to the student was the performance of sandhya and also reciting of gayatri. The family functioned as a domestic school, an ashrama or a hermitage where the mental faculties of the pupils were developed by the teacher's constant attention and personal instruction. Education treated as a matter of individual concern, did not admit of the method of mass production applicable in industry. The making of man was regarded as an artistic and not a mechanical process. Indeed, the aim of education was the developing of the pupil's personality, his innate and latent capacities. This view of education as a process of one's inner growth and self-fulfillment evolved its own technique, its rules, methods and practices

The primary subject of education was the mind itself. According to the ancient Indian theory of education, the training of the mind and the process of thinking, are essential for the acquisition of knowledge. The chase counts more than the game. So the pupil had mainly to educate himself and achieves his own mental growth. Education was reduced to the three simple processes of Sravana, Manana and Nidhyasana. Sravana was listening to the truths as they fell from the lips of the teacher. Knowledge was technically called Sruti or what was heard by the ear and not what was seen in writing. The second process of knowledge called Manana implies that the pupil has to think out for himself the meaning of the lessons imparted to him orally by his teacher so that they may be assimilate fully. The third step known as Nidhyasana means complete comprehension by the pupil of the truth that is taught so that he may live the truth and not merely explain it by word. Knowledge must result in realization. The admission was made by the formal ceremony Upanayana or initiation by which the pupil left the home of his natural parents for that of the preceptor. In this new home he had a second birth and was called Dvijya or twice-born. Besides these regular schools of instructions, there were special institutions for the promotion of advance study and research. These are called in the Rig Veda as Brahmana-Sangha, Academies of learned most its discussions hammered into shape the very language of the country, the refined language of Sanskrit (Samkrata) as the Vehicle of highest thought. These Academics were called parisads, there is a reference to the Pancala parisad in the Upanishads, in whose proceedings even kings participated, learning was also prompted by discussions at public meetings which were a regular of rural life, and were addressed by wandering scholars known as Carakas, These scholars toured the country to deliver public discourses and invite discussion.

Equality of Sexes

A lady-philosopher named Gargi was a prominent participant beside men like Uddalaka Arni. Obviously, in those days women were admitted to the highest knowledge and did not suffer from any education disabilities. There was equality between the sexes in the filed of knowledge. The Rig Veda mentions women Rais called Brahmanavadinis. To begin with, in ancient India; the main subject was the Veda. The teacher would instruct handful of students seated on ground. For many hours daily they would repeat verses after verses of the Vedas till they attain mastery of at least one of them. To ensure correctness of memory, the hymns were taught in more than one way. Soon the curriculum was expanded. The limbs of the Veda or the six Vedangas were taught—the performance of sacrifice, correct pronunciation, knowledge of prosody, etymology, grammar, and jyotisha or the science of calendar. Also in the post-Vedic era, teachers often instructed their students in the six schools of Philosophy.

The writers of Smritis maintain that young women of upper class under went this kind of training. This is a doubtful contention. Princes and other leading Kshatriyas were trained in all the manifold sciences to make them fit for government. Most boys of the lower orders learnt their trades from their fathers. Some cities became renowned because of their teachers. Chief among them were—Varanasi, Taxila from the day of Buddha and Kanchi in the beginning of the Christian era. Varanasi was famous for its religious teachers. Taxila was known for its secular studies. Among the famous men connected with Taxila was Panini, the grammarian of the fifth or fourth century B.C.: Kautilya, the Brahmin minister of Chandragupta Maurya and Charaka one of the two leading authorities of Indian medical sciences. The institutions imparting Vedic knowledge that exists even today. There were also universities like Taxila and Ujjain for medicine and learning including mathematics and astronomy respectively. In the south Kanchi became an important center of learning. Hiuen Tsang remarks that Vallabhi was as great as Nalanda and Vikramashila.

Nalanda and Vikramashila

Although the Smritis maintained that a small number of students study under a single teacher, university turned towns came into existence like Varanasi, Taxila etc. At Varanasi there were 500 students and a number of teachers. The whole establishment was maintained by charitable people. Ideally, the teacher asked no fee, but the students repaid his debt by their service to the teacher. A Jataka story tells of how a teacher of Taxila treated well the students who paid him money while keeping other waiting. It is also interesting to note that in Taxila even married people were admitted as students.

Out of all the Universities, Nalanda and imposed structures. Eight Colleges were built by different patterns including one by the king of Sri Vijaya (Sumatra). One of the colleges was four strayed high as stated by Hiuen-Tsang. Every facility existed for studying various kinds of subjects in the University. There were three great libraries as per Tibetan records. Nalanda attracted students not only from different parts of India but also from Tibet and China. The standards of examination were stiff, and only those who could pass the test prescribed by the dvarapandita or the scholar at the gate were admitted to this university. Also, for being admitted to the university, candidates were required to be familiar with old and new books. Nalanda was one of the earliest examples of residential cum-teaching institutions which housed thousands of monks devoted to learning, philosophy and meditation. Over 10,000 students including teachers lived and studied at the university. They came from various parts of the world apart from India, Central Asia, China and Korea.

Though Nalanda was primarily a Buddhist university its curricula included Hindu scriptures, philosophy and medicine as recorded by Hiuen-Tsang. Logic and exegetics were pre eminent because these students were expected to enter into dialogue with visiting doctors of all schools. This compulsion of public debate made both teachers and students become familiar with all systems of thought in accurate summary. The university had also succession of brilliant teachers. Dharmapala was a Tamil noble from Kanchi in the south. Janamitra come from another country. Silabhadra, the saintly guru of Hiuen-Tsang, came from Assam and he was a converted Brahmin. A great achievement of the University was that it was able to continuously rejuvenate Buddhism in far off countries. Tibetan records mention a succession of learned monks who visited their country. It is also said that Sudhakara Simha went to China and worked there on the translation of Buddhist texts.

The Education System in Ancient India: Gurukulas

The Gurukula System was an important concept associated with pursuit of studies in ancient India. A gurukula was a place where a teacher or a guru lived with his family and establishment and trained the students in various subjects. The gurukulas usually existed in forests.

Admission into the gurukula was not an easy process. A student had to convince his guru that he had the desire, the determination and the required intelligence to pursue the studies and had to serve him for years before he was admitted into the school and initiated into the subjects. Students in the gurukulas were subjected to rigorous discipline. They had to live in a very austere environment and practice yoga and meditation under the supervision of the master and also perform many menial jobs for the master's household. On specific occasions they had to undergo fasting as a necessary means of purification and mastery of the body and mind.

Sometimes if the Guru traveled to other places, the students accompanied him. Girls were not admitted to the Gurukulas. They were not even allowed to study like the boys. Ancient India had some educated women, like Maitreyi, wife of Yajnavalkya, who were generally related to some seers and sages or wives of some great kings. But it is doubtful if ordinary women in ancient India had any role other than performing household duties and procreation.

Lower caste people were not permitted to study any subject outside their occupation. In the early Rigvedic period, some gurus were broadminded enough to admit some low caste children as their students, as is evident from the story of Satyakama Jabala who was born to a free woman and Yajnavalkya who came from a very humble background. But the trend changed completely during the later Vedic period, so much so that even the mere act of hearing the Vedic hymns by low caste men was declared a sacrilege and great crime.

Ancient India had a number of universities and centers of education, where not one guru but several lived together and taught to groups of students different subjects. The emergence of Buddhism and the migration of gurus to towns and cities contributed to this new movement.

Wisdom of the Ages

Hinduism emphasizes the importance of verification of truth through personal experience. It regards the external world as a great illusion, but does not discourage those who want to study it in order to realize the nature of external reality. In ancient India a number of subjects other than religion were taught to students as a part of their occupational study or even general study. These included subjects such as mathematics, medicine, metallurgy, magic, music, art of warfare, sculpting, temple building, commerce, pottery, weaving and so on. Since the occupations were based upon castes, children were initiated into the secrets of their traditional vocations from a very early age.

Hinduism recognizes the importance of knowledge in the spiritual progress of man, but at the same time it is wary of the fact that you cannot teach everything to every one. Knowledge should be imparted only to those who are interested, who are mentally disposed, who are qualified by virtue of their evolution or current knowledge and who knows the true value of knowledge.

Aim of Education Worldwide

All over the world educationists are grappled with one central and all-encompassing question; what kind of education is needed for what kind of society of tomorrow? They are conscious of the new role of education and the new demands made on educational systems in a world of accelerating economic, environmental and social change and tension. They have come up with some of the underlying principles which are universal and common to the aims of educators, citizens, policy-makers, and other partners and participants in the process of education at all levels.

According to them education, formal and non-formal, must serve society as an instrument for fostering the creation of good citizens. All approaches to redesign the educational processes must take into account the basic and agreed-upon values and concerns of the international community and of the United Nations system such as human rights, tolerance, and understanding, democracy, responsibility, universality, cultural identity, the search for peace, the preservation of the environment and the sharing of knowledge.

The cultivation of a global outlook, a love of nature and a concern for fellow human beings and environment should be part of the scheme of education. In order to achieve this, education has to cover the four distinct dimensions of the human personality beginning with the physical body, the development of intellectual and aesthetic sensibilities, the development of socially desirable moral values and finally, the inner dimension of spiritual growth.

Education should be understood as the art of cultivating the moral, emotional, physical, psychological, artistic, and spiritual—as well as intellectual—dimensions of the developing child. Robin Ann Martin (2002) describes holistic education further by stating, "At its most general level, what distinguishes holistic education from other forms of education are its goals, its attention to experiential learning, and the significance that it places on relationships and primary human values within the learning environment."

Ultimacy

1. *Religious*: As in becoming "enlightened". Spirituality is an important component in holistic education as it emphasizes the connectedness of all living things and stresses the "harmony between the inner life and outer life"
2. *Psychological*: As in Maslow's "self-actualization". Holistic education believes that each person should strive to be all that they can be in life. There are no deficits in learners, just differences.
3. *Undefined*: As in a person developing to the ultimate extent a human could reach and, thus, moving towards the highest aspirations of the human spirit

Sagacious Competence

1. Freedom (in a psychological sense).
2. Good-judgment (self-governance).
3. Meta learning (each student learns in their "own way").
4. Social ability (more than just learning social skills).
5. Refining Values (development of character).
6. Self Knowledge (emotional development).

In holistic education, the teacher is seen less as person of authority who leads and controls but rather is seen as "a friend, a mentor, a facilitator, or an experienced traveling companion" Open and honest communication is expected and differences between people are respected and appreciated. Cooperation is the norm here, rather than competition. The reward of helping one another and growing together is emphasized rather than being placed above one another. Teachers help young people feel connected by fostering collaboration rather than competition in classrooms. They encourage reflection and questioning rather than passive memorization of "facts".

Purpose of Ancient Indian Education

The direct aim of ancient Indian education was to make the student fit to become a useful and pious member of society (Rangachar S, 1964). Inculcating the civic and social duties among the students was also a part of ancient Indian educational system. The students were not to lead a self-centred life. They were constantly reminded of their obligations to the society. Convocation address to the students as found in Upanishads show how they were inspired to be useful members of the society (Radha Kumood Mookerje, 1989). The most important idea governing the ancient system of education was that of perfection, for developing the mind and soul of man. Ancient Indian education aimed at helping the individual to grow in the power and force of certain large universal qualities which in their harmony build a higher type of manhood. Ancient Indian educational system focused on building a disciplined and values-based culture. Human values such as trust, respect, honesty, dignity, and courtesy are the building blocks of any free, advanced society (Markandan N, 2005). The convocation address found in *Taittiriya Upanishad* throws significant light on the qualities required to be developed in the students which are not very different from the qualities that modern educational systems are trying to impart and hence we quote a few lines from it here:

"Speak the truth. Practice righteousness. Make no mistake about study. There should be no inadvertence about truth. There should be no deviation from righteous activity. There should be no error about protection of yourself. Do not neglect propitious activities. Do not be careless about learning and teaching. There should be no error in the duties towards the gods and manes. Let your mother be a goddess unto you. Let your father be a god unto you. Let your teacher be a god unto you. Let your guest be a god unto you. The works that are not blameworthy are to be resorted to, but not the others. The offering should be with honour; the offering should be in plenty. The offering should be with modesty. The offering should be with sympathy. Then, should you have any doubt with regard to duties or customs, you should behave in those matters just as the wise men do, who may happen to be there and who are able deliberators, who are adepts in those duties and customs, who are not directed by others, who are not cruel, and who are desirous of merit. This is the injunction. This is the instruction. This is the secret of the scriptures. (*Taittiriya Upanishad*, I. xi. 1-4).

This convocation address outlines some of the domestic and social duties of students in very clear terms. Accordingly students are: to honour father, mother, teacher, and guest as gods; to honour superiors; to give in proper manner and spirit, in joy and humility, in fear and compassion. Lastly, the pupil is also asked not to neglect his health and possessions. This convocation address is very important in understanding the role of ancient Indian education in building a values-based culture. It tried to inculcate in the students the following qualities (Ramajois M, 1987):

❖ Social consciousness based on love for the humanity,
❖ Character, honesty based on moral law,
❖ Discipline based on the sense of duties and responsibilities of an individual.

Discipline like character is an essential quality for personal as well as social life. It consists in obedience to laws, rules and decisions. In this regard we must admit that ancient Indian system of education played a major role in making students realize their duties and responsibilities and emphasized on the necessity of discipline for an orderly social life. Character and discipline cannot be imparted to an individual by preaching or through speeches. While students can be imparted with the knowledge of what is moral and what is immoral, what is discipline and what is indiscipline what is character and what is characterless, they can be made to act in conformity with the required standard of behaviour, only through personal example. These qualities are acquired by emulation in addition to education.

It is only by generating these qualities in individuals the ancient Indian educational system prompted the students to utilize their educational attainments and capacities for the benefit of society restricting their own selfish desires and prevented them from acting in a manner harmful and detrimental to the common good (Ramajois, 1987). Mere knowledge of what is virtue and what is not does not enable an individual to be virtuous.

This aspect is forcefully brought forth in the character of Duryodhana in the epic *Mahabharata*. He says:

"I know what righteous conduct is, but I have no inclination to act accordingly. I know what unrighteous conduct is, but I cannot abstain from doing it".

Just as an ordinary stone requires a beautiful design and long and continued effort of an expert sculptor in chiseling and engraving in order to make it a beautiful idol, a proper blueprint or scheme and a constant and vigilant and untiring efforts of all those concerned are necessary, to make a child into a worthy individual. A very useful observation has been made by Swami Vivekananda in this context:

"The character of any man is but the aggregate of his tendencies, the sum total of the bent of his mind. We are what our thoughts have made us. Thoughts live: they travel far. Every work that we do, every movement of the body, every thought that we think, leaves an impression on the mind stuff. What we are every moment is determined by the sum total of these impressions on the mind. Every man's character is determined by the sum total of these impressions. If good impressions prevail, the character becomes good, if bad, it becomes bad. When a large number of these impressions are left on the mind they coalesce and become a habit. The only remedy for bad habit is counter habits; all the bad habits that have left their impressions are to be controlled by good habits" (Ramajois, M, 1987).

Many rites and rituals were developed in order to infuse piety and religiousness in the students. The rituals that a student had to perform at the beginning of his educational career, the religious observations that he had to observe during the educational course, the daily prayers that he offered morning and evening, the religious festivals that were celebrated very often in the school or the preceptors house-all these tended to foster piety and religiosity in the mind of the young learner (Rajbali Pandey, 1994). Ancient education system aimed at character formation through proper development of moral feelings to make the students really learned, pure in their life, thoughts and habits (Biswanath Ghosh, 2005). Teaching of values, ideal life led by teachers, and examples of extraordinary personalities cited from the epics, poetry, literature and history-all these helped to mould the character of students (Altekar, A.S., 1943). Ancient Indian educational system also aimed at the development of personality by eulogisinig the feeling of self-respect, by encouraging the sense of self-confidence, by inculcating the virtue of self-restraint and fostering the powers of discrimination and judgement.

Ancient Indian thinkers fixed for education certain life-long objectives that require life-long effort to achieve and realize (Kireet Joshi, 1992). These objectives were summarized in triple formula which gave a wide and lofty framework to the ancient system of education.

> *asato ma sadgamaya*
> *tamaso ma jyotirgamaya*
> *mrityorma amritam gamaya*
>
> (Lead me from falsehood to truth
> Lead me from darkness to light
> Lead me from death to immortality)
> (Brihadaranyaka Upanishad, I.3.28)

To them the ideals of truth, light and immortality constituted a triune unity, each subsisting in the other. The students were not allowed to forget that they had within them a higher self beyond their little personal ego, and that numerous ways and disciplines were provided by which they could realize the higher self. The holistic education of ancient India involves a harmonious blending of the knowledge of the outer world (*avidya*) and that of the inner-world (*vidya*). The former, as it were, enables a man to keep his body and soul together and the later, i.e. *vidya*, the wisdom, leads him to immortality, freedom from all sufferings of the world of change (Kunhan Raja C., 1950).

It may be noted here that the Lord Buddha preached middle path which lies between the two extremes, viz, gross sensualism or vile pleasure-seeking on the one hand and the extreme asceticism or the severest self-mortification on the other hand. Buddha laid stress on purity of conduct, truthfulness, love and benevolence, obedience to parents and respect for the elders, non-drinking, charity and kindness and mercy to all living beings (Hajimi Nakamura, 1991). Ahimsa non-violence towards life is recognized as an integral principle of his practical morality. The spirit of Buddhism was very liberal and accommodating. These values have become very essential for survival of human race in the present day situation.

The ancient Indian thinkers felt that a healthy society was not possible without educated individuals. They framed educational set up carefully and wisely aiming at the harmonious development of the multiple dimensions of the human personality. This is an essentially a universally applicable educational framework highlighting the purpose of human life and interconnectedness at all levels of existence as a basis of human values. In this system understanding oneself (self-knowledge) is as important as understanding the world. According to them without a deep understanding of one's relationship with nature, with ideas, with fellow human beings, with society, and a deep respect for all life, one is not really educated (Ramachandra Rao S.K., 1992).

Another unique feature of this educational system is that it aims at creating a mind that is both scientific and spiritual at the same time-one that is enquiring, precise, rational and sceptical but at the same time has sense of beauty, wonder, aesthetics, sensitivity, humility, and an awareness of the limitations of the intellect (James Moffett, 1994). It also aims at developing a mind, which is rational, flexible and not dogmatic, open to change and not irrationally attached to an opinion or belief should. In this system of education both scientific and spiritual quests are the complementary quests (J. Krishnamurti, 1981), one for the discovery of the order that manifests itself in the outer world of matter, energy, space and time and the other for discovering order (peace, harmony, virtue) in the inner world of human consciousness. Actually they are both quests for truth into two complementary aspects of a single reality which is composed of both matter and consciousness.

For an ordered, gradual and holistic development of human personality and to secure a progressive balance and harmony of growth, the ancient educational thinkers developed another unique concept viz. the *"Purushartahs"*. *Purushartha* is translated to mean a human goal, an object of desire, consciously pursued. This significant concept of development upholds the legitimacy of man's desire for economic security (*artha*) and sensuous aesthetic satisfaction (*kama*) and spiritual welfare (*moksha*). This scheme is further elaborated in the following:

- ❖ Human Needs/Pursuits
- ❖ Material well-being
- ❖ Bodily needs (Kama)
- ❖ Needs of material well-being (Artha)
- ❖ Need for social and moral order (dharma)
- ❖ Spiritual well-being
- ❖ Need to overcome suffering and realize one-self (Moksha)

But it does not support the insatiable greed which could destroy the possibility of realizing them. Both wealth and pleasure are goals only pursuable in society, but they can be successfully pursued only if society has at least some amount of stability and harmony. Dharma is claimed to be an important factor in the maintenance of social stability and harmony. Therefore, the observance of dharma, in virtue of its being a necessary condition of social stability and harmony, is insisted upon as an indispensable ethic for the pursuit of wealth and pleasure. Dharma is an ethical law which prevents human beings from falling into crooked ways of the ordinary and unbridled demands of impulses, desires, ambitious and egoism.

Dharma denotes that morality and those values which are founded upon higher, i.e. metaphysical and cosmic principles and they appeal to the highest goals and yet they are related to the common life and social processes.

Dharma is learning (*vidya*), in a broader sense, which can enlighten the human beings to understand the subtle niceties of living a dignified life. The values inculcated through education included a rule of prohibition regarding acquisition of wealth or securing or fulfilling of pleasures and desires of an individual. The rule is: Reject the wealth, pleasure and desires which are inconsistent with moral law (dharma). This may be termed as strategic pursuit of human needs for developing a holistic personality and the same is illustrated in the following:

- ❖ Strategic Pursuit of Human Needs
- ❖ Dharma (Moral and Social Order)
- ❖ Artha (Material needs)
- ❖ Moksha (Spiritual (Well being)
- ❖ Kama (Bodily needs)

Ancient Indians also developed the concept of Yoga for disciplining the mind and the body. Without the practice of the principles of *yama* and *niyama*, which lay the firm foundation for building character, there cannot be an integrated personality (BK Iyengar, 2005). In Yoga Sastra the" Right Living" is based on *yama* and *niyama*. Very simple ethical disciplines of "dos and don'ts". Sage Patanjali in his authoritative Treatise *Yoga Sutras* builds his entire Eight-fold path of Yoga on the foundation of *yama* and *niyama*. Practice of *asanas* without *yama* and *niyama* is mere acrobatics. Discipline does not arise from one's own mind. It has to be learned from outside. The word *Yama* can be broadly translated as "Self Restraints". They are five in number as shown in the following diagramme:

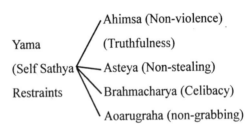

The following table provides more details on this topic:

- ❖ *Ahimsa*—Non-violence. Restraint from harming other living beings. Extending love affection to all other creations of nature. Compassion, mercy and gentleness towards every other living being.
- ❖ *Sathya*—Truthfulness, Restraining from falsehood, in thought, word and deed.
- ❖ *Asteya*—Non-stealing. Restraining from desire to take what is

not belonging to oneself.
- ❖ *Brahmacharya*- Literally means "moving towards realization of Brahman". Restrain from waste of energy in body, mind and speech.
- ❖ *Aparigraha*—Non grasping (coveting). Restraint from hoarding and greed. Holding things which are not needed in the modern parlance "consumerism".

The word *niyama* refers to internal restraints and they are also five in number as shown in the following diagramme:

Niyama (Internal Restraints)
- Saucha (Cleanliness)
- Santosha (Contentment)
- Tapas (Hard Work)
- Swadhyaya (Self-study)
- Ishwarapranidhana (Surrender to God)

The following table provides further details on this topic:

- ❖ *Saucha*—Cleanliness and Purity of body, mind and thoughts. This will bring orderliness, punctuality and clarity in one's living.
- ❖ *Santosa*—Meaning Contentment within. True happiness in life lies in accepting the way of things that the life offers. Then Peace and tranquility will follow with patience.
- ❖ *Tapas*—Burning desire for spiritual path.
- ❖ *Swadhyaa*—Self study. Broadening of intellect through serious study of known (physical world) and unknown (spiritual world).
- ❖ *Iswara Pranidana*—Surrender to the Lord. Accepting the fact that noting is in our hands. All that happens are fro the good. Its Lord's Will.

In Hindusiam education is an important means to achieve the four aims of human life, namely dharma (virtue), artha (wealth), kama (pleasure), and moksha (liberation). Also, it is vital to the preservation and propagation of Dharma, without which, declares Vedic dharma, we cannot regulate our society or families properly or live in peace. Vidya or education is the means by which an individual can gain right knowledge, control his desires and learn to perform his obligatory duties with a sense of detachment and devotion to God, so that he can overcome the impurities of egoism, attachment and delusion and achieve liberation. In Hindu tradition, an illiterate person is considered to be equal to an animal (pasu), because without education he will not be able to rise above his physical self. Hence the belief that a person who is initiated into education is twice born, first time physically and second time spiritually. Knowledge is a double edged sword. In the hands of an immoral or evil person it can become a destructive force. With knowledge comes power and if it falls into the hands of an ill equipped person who is bereft of morality and sense of responsibility, he may misuse the power and bring misery to himself and others. The basic difference between a god and an asura (demon) is that the former uses his knowledge for the welfare of the world and the latter for his own selfish and egoistic aims. Hence as a part of their education, in ancient India, students were advised to follow the path of gods and cultivate virtue under the careful and personal guidance of their teachers, so that they would remain on the path of righteousness for the rest of their lives and contribute to the welfare of society. The believed that if students were grounded in dharma, they would become its upholders and take care of its survival and continuity.

Guru, God in Human Form

Central to the traditional educational system of Hinduism is the concept of guru or teacher as a remover of darkness. A teacher is a god in human form. He is verily Brahman Himself. Without serving him and without his blessings, a student cannot accomplish much in his life. In imparting knowledge, the teacher shows the way, not by trial and error, but by his own example and through his understanding of the scriptural knowledge, gained by his own experience, sadhana (practice) and deep insight. In ancient India, while the parents were responsible for the physical welfare of their children, a guru was responsible for their spiritual welfare. It was his moral and professional responsibility to subject them to rigorous discipline and shape them into responsible adults. By keeping a close watch on his students and by not giving them any scope for leniency or carelessness, he ensured that they learnt by heart each and every subject he taught them. Till a student mastered a scripture completely and recited all the verses from memory without fault, he would not teach him another. In ancient India students were required to spend several years in completing their education, as they were required to learn every subject by heart and understand each and every verse thoroughly. Once they mastered all the subjects to the satisfaction of their gurus, they were allowed to leave. After a student completed his education, his teacher had a right to demand a gift (gurudakshina) from him either in kind or in cash.

In ancient India, two types of teachers taught children, namely acharyas and the upadhyayas. An acharya was considered superior to the upadhyaya for two reasons. He had both theoretical and practical knowledge, while an upadhyaya had only theoretical knowledge. Secondly, an acharya lived in a gurukula and taught his students for free, besides undertaking the responsibility of looking after them by keeping them in their household. Thus he was both a father figure and a venerable teacher. An upadhyaya usually collected fee for his services, either working for an acharya or working.

For himself. Society therefore showed more respect to acharyas and their students, because they valued the acharyas for not trading their knowledge for money and trusted their knowledge and experience more.

In the Gurukul system that India had, there was a very peculiar practice—at least in the Takshshila gurukul. From the passing out students, one or two students—those which were the top of the class—were retained to teach at the Gurukul. Others could go home and indulge themselves in whatever other profession they cared for.

Student Life

Student life for boys of the second caste (warriors/leaders caste) begins with the *Upanayana* or *sacred thread ceremony* about the age of nine or before adolescence. It marks the beginning of the study of Vedas, or holy books. This stage is said to be the second (but spiritual) birth for him. He will wear a sacred thread to show his status. "Upanayana" means to take or lead the child near the Guru, or teacher. He is initiated into the stage of "student bachelorhood". He must be celibate (not have sex), concentrate on his studies, and respect his elders.

A Brahmin child's sacred thread ceremony must be performed earlier, when he is seven years and two months old. A merchant caste boy is to be initiated between the ages of twelve and sixteen.

The boys learn mantras (chants or prayers repeated over and over). The mantras give the boy mental strength and health. It will increase the child's power of concentration, sharpen his intelligence, make him physically strong. Later in life, when he feels the urge of kama (sexual desire) the mantras will prevent him from being dragged downwards and be a protective shield for his body and mind. Those who wear the sacred thread say the mantras up to a thousand times daily. "The mantra is the hypnotic means of liberating ourselves from worldly existence as well as controlling desire and realizing the goal of our birth."

Originally girls could also have their sacred thread ceremony performed, with two options. They could have the complete ceremony performed, just as boys did. Or, if their Upanayanam was not performed in their youth, it could be done just before the marriage ceremony. However, by the time of the 8th century, the ceremony became exclusively for males. By the 8th century way of thinking, caring for the home and husband were duties equivalent to those performed by a student for his guru. Therefore, women were not required to go through the ceremony. In time, the Upanayanam lost its original significance. Initially supposed to mark the beginning of a child's student hood, it became a process of initiation into one's caste. The beginning of Vedic study, performed during the "student-bachelor" stage of life is at the home of the guru (teacher).

The first shave; This ceremony is performed for a boy at the age of 16. It marks the beginning of his adolescence. The end of student-hood; this ceremony marks the end of the student-bachelor stage of life. The boy returns to live at home after living in his guru's home. Ritual bathing is an important part of this ceremony, symbolizing the crossing of the ocean of learning. This happens about the age of 20 for the two higher castes. They are ready to get married and start a family

Modern India

Approximately one fourth of all Indians live in urban places. Of these, more than half live in settlements of more than 100,000 people, officially defined as cities. The 2001 census listed 27 cities with more than 1 million people. The two largest—Bombay (Mumbai) and Delhi (including the capital, New Delhi)—had populations of more than 9 million each.

Culture of poverty theorists contend that the marginal socio-economic position occupied by many minority groups within our society is the result of a self-perpetuating poverty "way of life," which includes certain characteristic personality attributes such as a tendency to live for the moment rather than to plan ahead, fatalism, and a lack of ambition.

Our current education system has unwittingly contributed to the slow demise of values in our society. This is also the direct fallout of the politicization, commercialization and criminalization of education. The rampant student unionism has only fostered disrespect for the teaching community. The students who humiliate the teachers and professors are very much a product of our own education system. So, on the one hand, we have a section of misguided students resorting to abhorrent practices, holding the majority to ransom. On the other hand, the majority has been reduced to being a mute spectator in this unabashed display of muscle power and disdain. The silent majority is unable to speak out due to fear. Sadly, education has failed to mould the character of the students, both the strident minority as well as the silent majority. Today, our education system has been reduced to mastering the three R's. It is seen as a means of earning one's livelihood. It has become an instrument for going up the social ladder, an instrument that has been much abused than used. The focus has shifted radically from character building to making the student more marketable in the job market. Learning by rote has more emphasis than overall student development. If education was mere mastering of the physical and social sciences, why is there so much disharmony and unrest in society today? Why is there widespread disillusionment? Why is there no clarity about the path to be taken? Are we teaching our children to be upright citizens who have the moral courage to uphold their values in the face of a crisis? The answer would be an emphatic no! Obviously, there is no connection between our present day education and culture. The fallout of all this is a section of freshly graduated students simply ill equipped to face the school called LIFE.

Redefine Aim of Education

Education isn't mere textbook knowledge. Real education goes beyond that. It should encompass the habits that one imbibes from one's atmosphere and from the friends one keeps. Wisdom would be in maintaining a healthy atmosphere and a healthy friends circle. The more important aspect of education should be to impart humanity to the taught. This is where the teacher plays a prominent role of inculcating these values amongst his/her wards; As Aristotle has said: "Virtue is not learnt by reading big volumes". True education should impart empathy and social awareness.

Education should also impart the fortitude to act righteously upon the knowledge that one has gained. As the Thirukkural says: "Let a man learn thoroughly whatever he may learn and let his conduct be worthy of his learning" *Kural* Chapter 40 verse 1.

True education would be one that moulds one's character to perform one's duties without fear or favour, and to observe ethics in one's conduct and behaviour. The test would be whether such education lays a strong foundation for a moral path. Gandhiji said: "…learning without courage is like a waxen statue, beautiful to look at but bound to melt at the least touch of a hot substance." An unwavering moral standard would liberate the mind from fear. A fearless mind should be the benchmark of good education. What is the use of an education system that doesn't rid the mind of fear? What good is an education that doesn't teach us to follow the path of truth?

Character formation should have priority over knowledge of the alphabet. Education without character is like a flower without fragrance. An education system that doesn't recognize this can be self-defeatist at the best.

Professor Huxley has thus defined education:

That man, I think, has had a liberal education .... whose intellect is a clear, cold, logic engine with all its parts of equal strength and in smooth working order;.... whose mind is stored with a knowledge of the fundamental truths of nature;...whose passions are trained to come to heel by a vigorous will, the servant of a tender conscience;.... who has learnt to hate all vileness and to respect others as himself. Such a one and no other, I conceive, has had a liberal education, for he is in harmony with nature. He will make the best of her and she of him.

In essence, good education is that which will help one in using one's senses positively and creatively. Any education that doesn't achieve this end is no education. Good education would be one that helps the child know right from wrong, make the right choices, stand for truth, and reject the bad and the untrue. Education should impart self-discipline. Good education is one that leads to wholesome development of the body, mind and spirit. True education is one that is successful in opening the eye of reasoning and inquiry.

2

Gun Culture in India

It has shocked all of us to learn that shoot outs have started happening in Indian schools! It saddens us very much that school students, instead of enjoying learning and playing with each other, have started killing each other! What has gone wrong and where???

It has been the perception that school shootings or violence have only been prevalent in American schools. Yet the Erfurt shooting (Germany) has been somewhat of a rude awakening to the extent violence has increased in European schools. Well India is also not lagging behind.

Time Line

On Dec. 11: 14 yr. student of Euro International school was shot dead by two of his classmates. reason, the victim used to bully. They used the gun .32 automatic and that according to the sources belonged to the father of one of the shooters. On Dec 25: An engineering student at GNIT was shot dead by three of his friends. On Jan 3: The most recent incident where a class 10th student of a village government school shot dead 15 year old with his fathers country made Pistol.

A First of Its Kind in India

The incident comes as a reality check for those who believe that shootout in schools and among the very young is something that plagues the western world alone.

Earlier this year, even as the first videos of the Virginia Tech shooting in the US played out across computer and television screens, back in India it moved us as much as to look for Indian names in the list of those missing. The culture of hate has entered our society. There is aggression in video games, playgrounds, movies. Our children are witness to this aggression in society. Psychologists, stumped by the excessive intolerance among kids; Children these days are not prepared to hear no for an answer. This needs to change arid despite hectic schedules parents must make it a point to spend time with their kids

First Person Account

I thought it was loud metal work going on," says the student of the private Euro International school in Gurgaon, a thriving info-tech and property market town. But as Karan approached the dank ground floor stairwell, he stopped in his tracks and froze. Lying on the floor near a rubbish bin was the blood splattered body of fellow school pupil, Abhishek Tyagi, 14, with whom he had played a game of cricket in the school playground a few hours earlier on Tuesday.

'Body Downstairs!'

Two students had allegedly pumped in bullets from an imported. 32 Harrison pistol—which one of them had apparently picked up from home— into Abhishek's head and chest. They had allegedly smuggled the tiny pistol into the school and hidden it in the toilet, before retrieving it when the classes were over. I and my friends panicked. Then we all ran back up to take the other stairway shouting, 'Run, run, there is a body lying downstairs!'," says Karan. Downstairs, near the stairwell, all hell was breaking loose. Karan's elder sister, Nitu, who goes to the same school, had also stumbled upon the body and was trying to keep everybody calm.

"I herded some of the younger children into classrooms. The kids were wailing and crying," says the 12-year-old girl. Then, she says, she saw the boys who allegedly killed Abhishek—one 13, the other 14 years old—quietly entering their class room and packing their bags. "There was no remorse, no emotion on their faces. They sat in their classroom till the police came and picked them up," says Karan. In the playground, Karan and Nitu's youngest sibling, Arjun, was playing on the swing when he heard the shots and the commotion. By the time the six-year-old boy ran out of the ground and up into the school, he saw Abhishek's body being wheeled out. Since then, Arjun has been feverish, refusing to sleep or step out of home muttering that he can "see the body everywhere", his siblings say.

India's first school shooting has left 550 students and 38 teachers shaken at this five-year-old private school which claims, on its website, to "accentuate on the safety of every child with cameras set up throughout to better monitor each activity in and outside the classrooms".

It is another matter that the close circuit cameras were scrapped more than a year ago after teachers complained that they were too intrusive. Tax consultant Anil Sharma, who sends his two children to Euro International, says he will pull them out if the school does not step up its security. Nine-year-old Mayur and seven-year-old Ashwin have already told their parents that they don't want to go to the school any longer.

Totally Clueless

"They should have metal detectors at the gate, and more security guards to check on students," says their father. Rakesh Sharma, father of Karan, Arjun, and Nitu, says his wife is so upset that she wants to take the children out of the school and relocate to some other place.

"My children knew Abhishek, and one of them played with him. They have seen such a bloody death that they are rattled," he says.

School authorities say they are shocked by the incident, but totally clueless about why it happened.

The kids had fought over trivial incidents in the past. And children are never checked in our schools. I put it down to the need for proper parenting, the need to keep your firearms away from your children," says school Chairman Satya Vir Yadav.

But several parents say privately that the two boys who allegedly killed Abhishek had recently threatened him after a fight, and even sped around the school in a motorcycle a few days ago.

They also speak about a rumour that spread in the school a few months ago that somebody was carrying a gun.

Symbol of Power

Like most schools in India, school bags are rarely checked here, and there is no frisking of students. Regular meetings are held between parents and teachers. School authorities point to the fact that one of the alleged killers picked up his father's licensed gun easily from home and bought it to school. Though gun control laws are strict in India, more and more people in places like Gurgaon own guns because they are a symbol of power and prestige in caste-ridden and feudal northern India.

The number of gun licenses in the suburb, according to a report, has shot up from 95 in 2005 to nearly 300 already this year. The four-storey, bright looking school is one of the many private schools with sometimes pretentious names that have mushroomed in suburbs like Gurgaon and attract children of some of India's new rich—property agents, developers, traders, transporters, a section of farmers—who are prospering by selling land and running small businesses.

The police came out with the names of the two accused boys to the media immediately after the killing, contravening laws about identification of juvenile law breakers. Back at the school, the school bag of one the boys who the police are questioning still lies on the classroom table, raising questions about the quality of investigation.

The Fate of a Bully

The two 8th graders, who later claimed that the victim used to bully them and his other classmates, planned the crime as if it were a godfather-style mafia execution plan. One of them stole his father's gun from the TV trolley, and brought it to the school. They then hid the gun in the school toilet. At the end of the day, one of them fetched the gun from the toilet, and shot the victim at close range, then handed the gun to the other student so he could shoot at the victim as well.

Two aspects of the case are even more troubling. The victim as well as the main shooter are the sons of real estate dealers in the Gurgaon area (The shady nature of that profession explains why the shooter's father had a gun at home). Only a few days ago, both these students had had a fight on the school premises, a fact well known to the school authorities who probably did nothing hoping for the animosities to just disappear.

In its website this particular school claims it as one of the top boarding schools of the area and has CCTV cameras all through the campus to monitor each and every activity of the students in and outside the classroom. But Abhishek's shootout in broad daylight itself describes how much the school authority is concerned about the students.

Interestingly, the school management had recently decided to remove the CCTVs installed at various places in the school after the teachers and the staff complained about the presence of these intruding electronic gadgets. This incident is a rising alarm for the increasing instances of juvenile crimes across the country. We require urgent move to control such juvenile crime because it may become fatal for society. Need of the hour is that the parents, wards, school authority and teachers should at least wake up now to avoid such unpleasant circumstances. They should focus more on student-teacher relationship rather than electronic gadgets.

Satvir Yadav has objected to media for printing stories without verifying them. "My school is not a day boarding school. It is a normal school," he said. Yadav is the only person from the school's board of directors who has been interacting with the media; even the school principal has been barred from talking to the media. "The institution is run by the Satya Education Society. We have built the Euro International School over one and a half acres of land," he said.

"We have 500 students and 35 staff members to run the school. In addition to that, there is a board of directors comprising 17 people including me, who look after the day to day running of the school. Principal Mamata Sharma has an experience of 25-30 years in various prestigious schools. But she has never come across such an incident," said Yadav. The school has been closed for two days and the classes will resume only on Friday, to give enough time to the teachers and students to cope with the tragic incident. According to Manoj Tyagi, a family friend of the Tyagi's, the deceased boy's family had moved to Gurgaon six months ago from Badshahpur village as Abhishek's father Ravinder wanted to keep his son away from the village atmosphere. "Abhishek was his only son. Look at the irony of life, the more he protected his son the more death came closer to him," said another friend of the Tyagi's.

"Ravinder had a flourishing transport business which is good for nothing now," Manoj Tyagi.

Eyewitness Account

Then, she says, she saw the boys who allegedly killed Abhishek—one 13, the other 14 years old—quietly entering their class room and packing their bags. There was no remorse, no emotion on their faces. They sat in their classroom till the police came and picked them up.

Two students had allegedly pumped in bullets from an imported. 32 Harrison pistol—which one of them had apparently picked up from home—into Abhishek's head and chest. They had allegedly smuggled the tiny pistol into the school and hidden it in the toilet, before retrieving it when the classes were over. The two boys who shot their classmate dead have confessed that they have no remorse about their deed as the other boy was bullying them to no end. That it was brought to the school authority's notice, but went ignored, made the boys take this extreme step!

Why do children bully others? We understand that the bullies are themselves victims first and then they perpetrate it on some body weaker than them. Many a times, we find the elders aggressing on the children severely, disproportionate to the mistakes that they may commit. Parents or teachers do not always give explanation to the child why he/she was punished. The elders, most often target the children to vent out their own frustrations caused by various life events. This kind of continued targeting makes the child very hard within. Also, the increased depiction of violence on TVs and Computer/Video games make the children lose sensitivity to others' pain. They look upon violence as bravery and fun! Their values get mixed up and there is no one to give them proper guidance. The one who is severely punished at home may look out for someone who is weaker than them, who can easily become their target. In the current case, the children decided to take the law into their own hands to punish the bully. This chain continues and many children become emotionally scarred for life.

Here both the victim of bullying and the bully himself need counseling. We need to find out what is bringing about such a behavior in the child. Who could be causing it—at home or at school or outside? It is very necessary that every school has an in-house counselor who can talk to children whenever they are disturbed by any issue. Just listening patiently to their grievances lifts the burden off their hearts. Counselors can remain objective and non-judgmental about any of the confessions people make. Counselors keep up the confidentiality of the matter. They try to help the client sort out his/her emotions and help them to think in positive direction. They teach assertive skills to the victims to stand up for their rights. This can go a long way in reducing many of the ills that are cropping up among student community.

The Police Statement

Tuesday, December 11, 2007 (Gurgaon): It's a parent's worst nightmare come true. A class 8 student at the Euro International School in Guragaon, on the outskirts of Delhi, was shot dead by two of his classmates after school hours on Tuesday. Abhishek Tyagi was found dead in his school corridor with 3 bullets in his body. At 2 pm (IST), a bus driver heard gunshots and raced to find a 13-year-old he often brought to school, lying in a pool of blood. Abhishek Tyagi, a class 8 student, was shot five times at close range over a disagreement. The two accused allegedly took turns shooting him with the same gun.

One of the students reportedly smuggled the weapon into the school by hiding it in his socks. They hid it in the school toilet before using it on Abhishek. Both the accused have been arrested by the Police. The Police Commissioner of Gurgaon described what led to the shooting.

"Akash Yadav took his father's revolver, hid it and carried it to school. He then put it in the school bathroom. In the evening when everyone left he fired at Abhishek. He fired four rounds and then he gave the pistol to his friend. He too fired a bullet. "They had a fight sometime back. The matter was taken to the Principal but perhaps the matter wasn't resolved completely," said Mohinder Lal, Police Commissioner, Gurgaon.

Abhishek Tyagi, who was walking in the corridor soon after school closed for the day, was accosted by Akash Yadav and Vikas Yadav over an old grudge. Akash pulled out his father's licensed revolver and allegedly shot Abhishek four times, handed the gun to Vikas who fired another bullet. Of the bullets fired, one struck Abhishek in his temple and two in the chest, killing him immediately. School chairman Satbir Singh said the authorities had not yet been able to talk to the principal and class teacher to learn the details of the incident. The Euro International School, in its website, claims to be one of the top boarding schools of the area and has set up cameras throughout the campus to monitor each and every activity in and outside the classroom. Meanwhile, At abhishek's home a sense of disbelief prevails over a senseless loss that could have been averted. The recent incident lays claim to the rising instances of juvenile crime in the national capital region.

Parents Reaction

Parents of one of the teenagers, accused in the *shocking school shooting* **case**, on Thursday claimed that their son was innocent and that they were not aware of him being involved in any quarrel with the victim.

Surfacing before the media for the first time after their son along with his classmate allegedly killed a co-student, the parents said they had no enmity with anyone and had never met the victim or the other accused or their families. The parents of the other accused are still absconding.

A case has been registered against Azad Yadav, the absconding father whose gun was used in the murder, under the Arms Act for alleged negligence. "Our child is innocent. We do not have a revolver or any other firearm. I am a responsible person," said the father of the teenager, who allegedly shot Class VIII student Abhishek Tyagi of Euro International School in Gurgaon. Another student had allegedly fired four shots at the victim. He said his son was an 'obedient' boy, who was interested in sports and games. "We are sad about the boy who was killed. I was shocked when I heard about the incident. I do not believe that my son did it," he told television *NDTV*, claiming that that he was at his farm in Rajasthan at the time of the shooting and denied reports that he was a property dealer. "They might have fought. But we never had any information about it. The school authorities never informed us about anything," he claimed.

The teenager's mother claimed that he was being framed and that the family came to know about the incident only from the school bus driver. The teenager's mother claimed that he was being framed and that the family came to know about the incident only from the school bus driver. "As I could not find him in the bus, I asked the driver who told me that he was involved in this incident. School authorities did not even bother to inform us. Why did not they inform us that our child was involved in such an act," the mother said. She said none of his friends used to visit him at his house and he would tell her about everything that happened in school. "He was interested in computer games and cricket. He used to tell me and his elder sister about everything," she said. The mother claimed that she sent the boy's uncles to the police station to enquire about the case as the father was away in Rajasthan at the time of the incident. "But the police never called us," she claimed.

Teacher's View

Punam Gupta, Principal, BGS International Public School, and Delhi: The task is to identify hostile tendencies. Every school should encourage a democratic set-up and an open-door policy. Concerted efforts should be made to increase student-teacher interaction.

Appointing a Discipline-in-charge is one of the measures a school can take to identify unruly behaviour. In co-ed schools, for instance, it is not unlikely to find girls and boys seeking their moments of solitude in corridors. It is only natural for the school authority to object to such rendezvous. Some students may obey. Others may retort with an "It's my life". It is the latter group that the school, perhaps, needs to keep a watch on

Blame Game

1. Was it because of the negligence of the school authorities?

❖ Teachers have big classes to deal with.
❖ They have an incredible load of lessons to complete as the curriculum is horrendous.
❖ They are harassed and overworked with the school management riding heavy on their backs.
❖ The kids are unruly and uncooperative and cannot be strictly disciplined because of backlash from parents.

❖ Teachers used to be on corridor and grounds duty during recess and were on the lookout for trouble between kids, gangs etc. Now they have time only to scurry from classroom to staffroom with their focus entirely on the timetable.

❖ The teachers are also ineffective in controlling bullies because inevitably they come from powerful families who have clout in the school.

❖ The role of the teacher as protector has been greatly diluted.

2. Are parents unable to keep track of their kids and what they are undergoing in the school like being bullied or threatened into unsociable behaviour?

❖ The mantra is a lack of communication between kids and parents.

❖ Schools claim that parents have to know more about the kids as they spend more time with them. Yet the interaction between kids takes place in the school and parents are not physically there to take note of problems. Any problems between kids should be visible to the school authorities first.

❖ Parents too should be able to find out if their ward is being victimised and take note of it and make discreet enquiries without making an issue of it at the school.

3. Are kids afraid to confess to being victimised to either both or one set of authority—school or parental?

❖ From time immemorial bullying and fagging has been part of growing up pains of most kids.

❖ Peer pressure is horrendous and kids are vulnerable and afraid to ask for adult intervention.

❖ Aggressive behaviour is learnt from the home, from school and from entertainment –media, movies and computer games.

❖ Aggression is glorified and kids begin to think that power is the only way to in, so they zone in on weaker kids and establish control.

4. Can the media be held accountable?

❖ Maybe, TV news channels can stop repeatedly broadcasting the issue as it only hammers in the event into kids' minds.

❖   Violence in movies and especially on TV should be controlled.
❖   Maybe it is time that TV censorship should come into force as
      unsociable behaviour is shown in most serials and comes into
      the homes and can be imbibed by vulnerable minds.

Finally the kids are the losers, unable to cope with pressures that
come from various quarters. They will carry the onus into adult lives and
this will have a ripple effect on society as well.

This is not an exhaustive analysis of the situation. This is just a blog
to start us communicating and to discuss various ways of preventing
copycat crimes from happening.

In Nutshell

SINCE TIME immemorial schools are considered as temples of knowledge
and a place of learning basic manners of civilized society. What happened
yesterday in a Gurgaon school shocked everyone and it became the worst
nightmare of the parents came true.

Abhishek Tyagi, a VIII class student of a school in Gurgaon, was
shot dead by two of his classmates after school hours. 13 year old
Abhishek is son of a city based property dealer. According to Abhishek's
classmates he had a fuss with the two accused three days ago and the
shootout is the result of that disagreement. As per media reports one of
the accused brought his father's revolver from his home by hiding it in
his socks. Before the commencement of the classes he hid the weapon
in the school toilet. Soon after the close of the school for the day,
Abhishek was walking in the corridor. The accused first pulled out the
licensed revolver of his father and shot at Abhishek four times and handed
it to the other accused who fired another bullet. Of the five bullets fired,
one hit Abhishek in his temple and two in his chest. After hearing the
gunshots, a bus driver raced towards the school corridor where Abhishek
was lying in a pool of blood. Abhishek was brought to hospital where
the doctors declared him dead. Meanwhile the two accused students
have been arrested by the police and later sent to 14 days in judicial
custody by a local court. Both the accused will be kept at a juvenile
home in Faridabad.

According to Mahender Lal, police commissioner of Gurgaon, "Amit
(name changed) has told the police that Abhishek had been harassing him
and Sumit (name changed), for a long time. They had a fight sometime
back. The matter was taken to the principal but perhaps the matter wasn't

resolved completely." The police commissioner also said the revolver belonged to Sumit's father, also a property dealer.

Yesterday's incident raises many questions. First regarding today's education system and the safety measures taken by private schools. Secondly, there is the question about basic teachings given in the rich families by parents. Of course, today with the latest technologies, sky is the limit but at the same time we are losing the ground. Today we can see the adverse affect in our education system. Money is a big factor and the relation of teacher-student has changed totally. Only a few students pay respect to their teachers nowadays. But on the other hand, teachers too show signs of a change in their attitude towards students.

There was a time when teachers were highly respected in the society and teachers were also dedicated to enlighten the pupil with his knowledge. However with the changing time the concept changed gradually and today the world has become very much professional. Now that rapport between teachers and students is missing.

Every year, private schools are mushrooming across the country but they lack basic facilities. Most of the schools claim to have computer facilities, CCTV cameras for monitoring the activities of students. However, very few schools talk about providing any teaching for discipline or manners. In its website this particular school claims it as one of the top boarding schools of the area and has CCTV cameras all through the campus to monitor each and every activity of the students in and outside the classroom. But Abhishek's shootout in broad daylight itself describes how much the school authority is concerned about the students.

Blame the parents, especially the upper class for such unpleasant incidents. After enrolling their children they forget to monitor their daily activities, about their study, the persons with whom they interact. For the sake of showing off in the society and in the name of glamour they provide all the luxurious amenities like mobile and I-pods to their children. These electronic gadgets cause more negative effect on their education.

Moreover, yesterday's incident is a rising alarm for the increasing instances of juvenile crimes across the country. We require urgent move to control such juvenile crime because it may become fatal for society. Need of the hour is that the parents, wards, school authority and teachers should at least wake up now to avoid such unpleasant circumstances. They should focus more on student-teacher relationship rather than electronic gadgets. Who shares the blame of this tragedy along with the 8th-grade shooters?

On one side we are adopting foreign foods, jobs, culture and see their serials in TV. Our channels are also showing those school related serials where all kind of politics shows which is worst than our national politics. There is no escape rule these kind of incidences will be common after few years. Today's urban India has lost the values of our Indian culture. With the glossy media promoting 'stylish' lifestyles, Bollywood movies which take Indian audience to a trance for 2 hours seducing them with limitless possibilities in luxury, empty fun, enjoyment, daredevil attitude to life etc. They are blindly and selfishly showing the unimaginative audience the glitter and bad things that happen in the West and people think that is their lifestyle of the population in general in the West.

How many media endorse the good things that happen in the West? Like punctuality, volunteerism, keeping one's health till very old age by physical activities, keeping the neighborhoods clean and selfless work spirit to continue with that, recycling and caring for nature

It is not a shootout -but a shooting -shootout is when shots are exchanged between two or more groups.

1. *The shooter's parents* who could have locked his gun securely and could definitely have prevented the tragedy? The two shooters would probably have chosen a more conventional way to deal with the classroom bully.
2. *The principal* who having known about the fight on the school premises, could have taken a few more precautions and was certainly in a position to avert the tragedy. He could have heeded some warnings, could have punished the classroom bully, thus calming some of the shooters' anger towards him.
3. *The victim's parents* who having known his son's nature, could have prevented his son from being a victim by educating him more about not bullying other kids in the class.
4. *The rest of the parents* who, having known about a student bully, could have done some more towards raising a red flag.
5. *The teachers*, who must have known about the classroom bully, but surely did nothing to educate him more about the tensions and ill vibes his actions would produce.
6. *Television and Bollywood*, who glorify and romanticize crime and violence, making it look like an unreal comic-book, on-the-screen video-gamish thing, without any real-life consequences.
7. *The real estate mafia*, who seem to devour properties left and right, making millions a day, turning a once-uncomplicated

profession into an organized-crime enterprise that requires its members to carry guns or gunmen at all times.

8.   *The society and community* of the India, Inc who now live in a televised version of 21st century community that has little time for its kids and is busy making money, eating out, watching reality dramas, and swapping partners.

9.   *Two little stupid kids*, who couldn't deal with a class bully as probably everyone else has, at least once, in their lifetimes.

10. *The damn gun*, the wicked mechanical contraption that kills.

No Repentance

Still simmering with resentment, the Class VIII student, who allegedly fired four shots at his colleague, seems unrepentant about the killing. "Yes, I killed Abhishek," the 14-year-old said without a trace of remorse or hesitation, when he was produced at Sector 40 police station after the shooting at Euro International School. The two boys allegedly killed Abhishek Tyagi as 'he was physically stronger than both of them and been beating them up for the past two months', Gurgaon Police Commissioner Mohinder Lal said. The boys told police that the three of them were not 'enemies' as they used to meet only during recess and when school closed for the day. "We are students of Class VIII Section B on the ground floor, while Abhishek was in Section A on the second floor," Lal said, quoting the boys who have been sent to a Juvenile court in Sonepat. Their last meeting proved fateful, when the two accosted Abhishek in the school premises and fired five shots at him. Two bullets hit him in the chest and one in the head, the CP added.

Evaluation

This incident raises many questions.

- ❖   Regarding today's education system,
- ❖   The safety measures taken by private schools, and
- ❖   The question about basic teachings given in the rich families by parents.

Of course, today with the latest technologies, sky is the limit but at the same time we are losing the ground. Today we can see the adverse affect in our education system. Money is a big factor and the relation of teacher-student has changed totally. Only a few students pay respect to their teachers nowadays. But on the other hand, teachers too show signs of a change in their attitude towards students.

There was a time when teachers were highly respected in the society and teachers were also dedicated to enlighten the pupil with his knowledge. However with the changing time the concept changed gradually and today the world has become very much professional. Now that rapport between teachers and students is missing.

Every year, private schools are mushrooming across the country but they lack basic facilities. Most of the schools claim to have computer facilities, CCTV cameras for monitoring the activities of students. However, very few schools talk about providing any teaching for discipline or manners.

In its website this particular school claims it as one of the top boarding schools of the area and has CCTV cameras all through the campus to monitor each and every activity of the students in and outside the classroom. But Abhishek's shootout in broad daylight itself describes how much the school authority is concerned about the students.

Blame to the parents is not unwarranted, especially the upper class for such unpleasant incidents. After enrolling their children they forget to monitor their daily activities, about their study, the persons with whom they interact. For the sake of showing off in the society and in the name of glamour they provide all the luxurious amenities like mobile and I-pods to their children. These electronic gadgets cause more negative effect on their education.

Moreover, Euro incident is a rising alarm for the increasing instances of juvenile crimes across the country. We require urgent move to control such juvenile crime because it may become fatal for society. Need of the hour is that the parents, wards, school authority and teachers should at least wake up now to avoid such unpleasant circumstances. They should focus more on student-teacher relationship rather than electronic gadgets.

Television content, from cartoons to movies to *neta*s, portrays a lot of violence. Kids see politicians getting elected to the parliament; they see gangsters glorified in movies; and they see easy money and power. All this cultivates in them a 'Nuke-them' attitude and contributes to making violence attractive and heroic. A gang war can keep a whole theatre entertained. They see candidates with criminal background win elections. They see people getting away with crime. In such a set-up, it is easy for a teenager to assume that might is right.

Appointing a Discipline-in-charge is one of the measures a school can take to identify unruly behaviour.

In co-ed schools, for instance, it is not unlikely to find girls and boys seeking their moments of solitude in corridors. It is only natural for the school authority to object to such rendezvous. Some students may obey. Others may retort with an "It's my life". It is the latter group that the school, perhaps, needs to keep a watch on.

Bullying

Having a fight in school is not new; a lot of students get bullied at some point of time in the premises. And, this phenomenon occurs frequently anywhere between the sixth and eighth standard students. Boys indulge more in bullying than girls. This kind of occurrence is widespread in American schools, such as the Virginia Tech massacre. But a murder in an Indian school due to bullying is probably the first of its kind.

Bullying can occur in any settings, where human beings interact with each other. And, schools are notoriously famous for it. However, a lot depends on the kind of bullying that takes place. When it is done in a playful and friendly way, it is not hurtful and both the bully and the bullied end up finding the incident funny.

But, when bullying becomes intentionally physically hurting, verbally abusive, psychologically excruciating and nerve-racking, it becomes unbearable. Mocking, threatening, extorting, ridiculing on appearance or lack of talent becomes constant, it leaves a deep emotional scar in the mind of the victim.

The reason for the killing in the Euro International School, Gurgaon, Haryana, is reported to be bullying by the deceased. For the two boys, taking revenge became unavoidable and an easy access to a gun precipitated matters. On December 12th evening, 14-year-old Abhishek Tyagi was shot dead by two gun-totting classmates in the middle of the school corridor. The boy was shot five times from close range on his forehead, chest and shoulder and was declared dead at a hospital. One of the boys had brought his father's licensed pistol and the two culprits took turns to shoot Abhishek!

Today's children, less involved in physical activities, are constantly viewing negative news and violence being featured on television regularly. Thus, perhaps becoming prone to abuse and violence in their childhood. Those who bully have personalities that are authoritarian with an urge to control or dominate others. And envy and resentment are known motives for bullying.

For observant parents, it is not very difficult to figure out signs of bullying. Children on their own are often hesitant to tell their parents about the harassment faced. They would tend to worry that their parents would be affected. However, visible signs of the child becoming a victim of bullying could be all there—such as bruises or injuries on the child's body, torn uniforms, missing school, avoiding the school bus and increasing demand for more pocket money.

Besides, if a child is acting in a different way or appears seemingly anxious, moodier, easily upset, or not eating enough or not sleeping well, or not doing things he enjoyed doing, it could well be because of a getting bullied in school.

Can bullying hurt so much that its victims are driven to take a gun in hand and shoot the bully at point blank many times besides taking turns too? Strangely, the killers (victims of bullying) feel no remorse. According to reports available, the deceased had threatened to kill the two boys and this probably was the last straw to break the camel's back.

If a scrappy child's aggressive behavior is not curbed at the early stage the danger is that he or she may take it to adulthood and exhibit strange violent or socially unacceptable behavior. This is what 16-year-old Brenda Ann Spencer of Cleveland elementary school did. She did not like Mondays. Just to liven up the day, she opened fire with a .22 rifle and wounded 8 children and killed two adults. In yet another case, six-year-old Dedrick Owens of Mount Morris in Michigan has taken a .32 caliber pistol of his uncle to school and shot dead another six-year-old. In a parallel case of Gurgaon school incident, two students were fatally shot by a 14-year-old student, claiming to be a victim of bullying, at the Raumanmeri Secondary School in Rauma, Finland. In another case, 15- year-old Brian Head of Cherokee County, Georgia, US, shot himself dead in his classroom. He too had been a target of bullies because of his overweight and thick glasses. Brian's father lobbied hard for the enactment of a law for criminalizing bullying that required schools to alert parents of bullied children. Given the above scenario, it is time that our schools pay greater attention to reducing violence and aggression in their institutions. It should not be difficult for school authorities to identify bullies and devise ways to intervene and check them. They should be constantly watched and repeatedly advised that their behavior could land them into serious trouble. Increased parent-teacher supervision, making bullying a punishable offence in schools, providing protection to the bullied and counseling to the bullies will go a long way in preventing the spread of this menace.

However, never ever advise your child to bully back. It will cause more suffering and more violence. It is best to advise the child to avoid the bully by walking away from a problematic situation created by the latter, and to learn to ignore hurtful remarks. This is bound to get the desired result—the intimidator will in all probability lose interest and stop the harassment. And, perhaps we will be spared another Gurgaon incident.

Time Line USA

Schoolyard Shoot Out in America

1992-93	—	55	deaths
1993-94	—	51	deaths
1994-95	—	20	deaths
1995-96	—	35	deaths
1996-97	—	25	deaths
1997-98	—	40	deaths

January 1979—Brenda Spencer, 17, got a rifle for Christmas and used it to shoot into an elementary school across the street from her home in San Diego, California. Eight children and a police officer were injured, and two men lost their lives protecting the kids. When the six-hour standoff finally ended, Brenda explained with a shrug, "I don't like Mondays."

March 2, 1987—Nathan Ferris, 12, was an honor student in Missouri, where he finally got tired of being teased. He brought a pistol to school and when a classmate made fun of him, he killed the other boy. Then he turned the gun on himself. He had warned a friend not to attend school that day, signaling his plans, but no one had listened to this overweight loner.

November 15th, 1995—Jamie Rouse, 17, dressed in black, went into Richland School in Giles County, Tennessee, with a .22-caliber Remington Viper. He shot two teachers in the head, one of them fatally. Then with a smile, he took aim at the football coach, but a female student walked into his path and was killed with a shot to the throat. Rouse had told five friends exactly how he had planned this killing, but no one had called for help.

February 2, 1996—Barry Loukaitis, 14, dressed up like a gunslinger from the Wild West and went into his algebra class in Moses Lake, Washington. Concealed in his long duster were two pistols, seventy-eight rounds of ammunition, and a high-powered rifle. His first victim was 14-year-old Manuel Vela, who later died. Another classmate fell with a bullet to his chest, and then Loukaitis shot his teacher in the back as she was writing a problem on the blackboard. A 13-year-old girl took the fourth bullet in her arm. Then the shooter took hostages, allowing the wounded to be removed, but was stymied by a teacher who rushed him and put an end to the irrational siege. In all, three people died, and Loukaitis blamed "mood swings." A classmate claimed that Loukaitis had thought it would be "fun" to go on a killing spree.

February 2, 1996—David Dubose, Jr., 16, killed a teacher in a school hallway in Atlanta, Georgia.

January 27, 1997—Tronneal Mangum, 13, shot and killed another student in front of their school.

February 19, 1997—Evan Ramsey, 16, went to Bethel High School in Alaska with a shotgun. This is the place where other kids called him "retarded" and "spaz." He killed a boy with whom he'd argued and then injured two other students. Then he went to the administration office and shot the principal, Ron Edwards, killing him instantly. Police came quickly and ended the rampage, which appeared to be motivated only by some amorphous rage. Two fourteen-year-old friends who had discussed Ramsey's plan with him were arrested as accomplices.

October 1, 1997—Luke Woodham, 16, worshipped Adolph Hitler, perhaps because it made him feel powerful in light of the bullying he received from classmates in Pearl, Mississippi. When his girlfriend broke up with him, he went into a rage. He slashed and stabbed his mother that morning, then went to school with a rifle and a pistol. Right away he killed his former girlfriend and then another girl. Yet he didn't stop there. Seven other students were wounded before he ran out of ammunition. He returned to his car for his other gun, and that's where the assistant principal disarmed him. He complained that the world had wronged him and he just couldn't take it anymore.

"I killed because people like me are mistreated every day," he said. "I did this to show society: Push us and we will push back."

Two members of his group devoted to Hitler were charged as accessories to murder, and others were arrested on the basis of a conspiracy, but those charges were later dismissed. Woodham claimed at trial that he'd been possessed by demons that were manipulated by a member of his group.

December 1, 1997—Michael Carneal, 14, liked to wear black and was thought by classmates in Paducah, Kentucky, to be a Satanist. That morning, he brought a gun to school and opened fire on a small prayer group. Three girls died and five other students were wounded. Another student tackled him, and it was soon revealed that Carneal had a pistol, two rifles, and two shotguns, along with 700 rounds of ammunition, all of it stolen. He'd threatened earlier to "shoot up" the school, but no one had taken him seriously.

March 24, 1998—Andrew Golden, 11, and his gun buddy, Mitchell Johnson, 13, dressed in camouflage fatigues and then gunned down fifteen people at the Westside Middle School playground in Jonesboro, Arkansas. Five died, all of them female and four were children. The boys had a van stocked full of ammunition and guns, which they took from their kin. Golden went into the school and set off a fire alarm, then ran to where Johnson lay in position with the rifles. As people filed out for the fire drill, the boys began shooting.

April 24, 1998—Andrew J. Wurst, 14, liked to threaten other people and then laugh it off. However, no one was laughing when he took a pistol into the eighth-grade graduation dance in Edinboro, Pennsylvania, and killed a popular teacher. Then he opened fire into the crowd, wounding another teacher and two classmates before he ran out. The banquet hall owner went after him, disarmed him, and held him for police, but the boy acted as if the whole thing was a big joke.

May 21, 1998—Kipland Kinkel, 15, had just been expelled from school in Springfield, Oregon, for carrying a gun to class. He returned with a semiautomatic rifle and went into the cafeteria, where he started shooting. He killed one student and wounded eight others, one of whom later died, and he also caused a stampede that resulted in more injuries. He was disarmed and taken to the police station, where he withdrew a hidden knife. He claimed he wanted to die. Police officers who went to his home discovered that he'd killed both of his parents and had booby-trapped the house with five homemade bombs—one of which he'd placed underneath his mother's corpse. His classmates had once dubbed him the student "most likely to start World War III."

Other Countries also have Problems with School Violence

An arson fire at Kyanguli secondary school in Kenya killed 62 students. Two students were charged with murder.

On April 29th, 2002 Dragoslav Petkovic opened fire with a handgun at his high school in Vlasenica, Bosnia-Herzgovina, killing one teacher and wounding another before taking his own life.

On April 26th, 2002 Robert Steinhauser who was expelled from high school in Erfurt, Germany returned to the school shot to death 13 teachers, two students, and a police officer before killing himself.

In Munich, Germany on February 19th, 2002 a 22 year old gunman killed his former boss and a foreman at the company that fired him, then went to a high school and killed the schools headmaster when he could not find a teacher. After that he shot a teacher in the face and set off multiple homemade bombs before he killed himself.

Mamoru Takuma forced his way into Ikeda elementary school to stab eight students to death and wounding 13 others on June 8th, 2001 He had a long history of mental illness.

3

Trigger Happy

There are some who believe that the only difference between the two greatest democracies USA and India is India's better gun laws. There are more than 223 million firearms in the United States. Guns are unique weapons, highly lethal, and easily available. Their use by and against children and youth has exacted an enormous toll on American society. There are so many guns distributed in America now that it would be too late and time consuming to get rid of all of them in our households. It is possible to issue more gun control with penalties, but it's hard to do when many Americans abide by the first Amendment of "rights to bare arms". Although there are some gun restrictions now, people still find a way to get them and use them when they feel is needed.

How the U.S. Compares to the Rest of the World?

The United States is home to a tremendous number of guns. Current estimates place the number of guns in the United States at between 200 million and 250 million. In the period between 1968 and 1992, gun ownership in the U.S. increased 135 percent—and during that same period, handgun ownership increase 300 per cent. The 17 million residents of Texas alone own 68 million guns. The United States has one of the highest murder rates in the world, and leads western nations in homicides. More Americans are shot in one day than Japanese are shot in an entire year. Whereas other nations, such as Great Britain, have moved to ban handguns and assault rifles after shooting incidents, the United States has not done so. In Australia, just two weeks after a shooting at Port Arthur that killed 35 people, the nation's various levels of government agreed to ban weapons like those used in the attack. Similarly, Great Britain banned handguns after a man broke into a Scottish school and opened fire, killing 16 children.

Other nations treat gun control as a public health issue, Robert Spitzer of the State University of New York at Cortland, told ABC News. "There is general agreement in other nations that the government has the right to engage in regulation that is good public policy protecting the health and safety of the populace," he said.

However, in the United States, strong political interest groups such as the National Rifle Association oppose gun control and say that the Second Amendment guarantees the rights of Americans to own weapons.

History of the Issue

Americans are fiercely protective of their right to own guns. The founders of this country believed that this "right to bear arms" was so important that they made it the Second Amendment to the United States Constitution. "A well-regulated Militia, being necessary to the security of a free state, the right of the people to keep and bear Arms, shall not be infringed," the founders wrote.

Today there is considerable argument over just what the founders intended by their words. Did they mean to provide only for armed units, such as the Army and National Guard, to protect us from invasion, or did they mean that each individual has a right to a gun? Both gun-control supporters and gun-rights advocates have their legal arguments to support their side, but the federal courts have upheld all laws regulating gun ownership when the laws have been challenged on the basis of violating the second amendment.

In the early days of the American colonies, nearly every settler owned a gun; guns were a more obvious necessity for members of an expanding nation. However, as the European population became more settled here, as the frontier was driven westward and the native populations driven out, fewer people owned guns. As historian Michael Bellesiles notes, during the time between the American Revolution and the Civil War, no more than one-tenth of the American population owned guns. They became more a part of American culture due to the marketing efforts of gun manufacturer Samuel Colt, who played on the fears of them idle-class to sell weapons for "self-defense"; the end of the Civil War also played a role in the increase of gun ownership, as many soldiers returned home with their weapons in hand.

In 1876, the Supreme Court ruled, in *United States v. Cruikshank,* that neither the Constitution nor the Second Amendment grant the right to bear arms; rather, the Second Amendment restricts the power of the federal government to control firearms. Several other Supreme Court cases (notably *U.S. v. Miller,* 1939) spoke to gun control during the late 1800s and first half of the 1900s; but overall, gun control was not a major issue or concern.

However, that all changed in the 1960s. After the assassinations of John F. Kennedy and Martin Luther King, Congress passed the 1968 Gun Control Act, which banned mail-order gun sales and instituted more stringent licensing requirements for dealers.

After John Hinckley attempted to assassinate President Ronald Reagan in 1981, gun control became the hot issue it is today. Congress passed several laws concerning armor-piercing bullets and automatic weapons. In 1993, President William J. Clinton signed the Brady bill, which requires a five-day waiting period for all handgun purchases. The following year, Congress and President Clinton passed a ban on assault-style weapons and a number of semiautomatic weapons.

What role does unfettered access to guns and the mass media's depiction of gun use as exciting and a good thing have in contributing to the breakdown of inhibitions against gun use. Do other countries' gun restrictions and cultural animus towards guns reduce gun violence?

You are right that depictions of gun use and mass violence are sadly inspirational many of these angry, deranged killers.

What is usually going in on in a person's mind that leads them to do something like this? And is suicide usually part of the plan?

Suicide is often part of the plan, indeed the seedbed for the irrational thinking that leads to violence. Suicidal persons lose perspective on reality, see no hope for themselves, and develop tunnel vision that there is nothing else they can do. We have to more to identify and intervene with persons who are depressed like this. There are too few mental health resources, and too much stigma against mental health treatment, in our society.

Gun Advocacy

Tragic events involving guns rarely seem to speak for themselves or to point directly to the effectiveness or ineffectiveness of firearms; rather, what the incident "proves" depends largely on the speakers and whether gun control or gun advocacy is their primary agenda.

We have the right to life, liberty, and the pursuit of happiness. All of this is endangered more than it is protected if millions of people are carrying firearms. Look at other countries around the world. How many have applied the principal of no gun regulation? Let me emphasize that guns are not the sole problem, and regulated access to guns is feasible and still protects our constitutional rights.

We don't have to go so far as completely banning guns. We still have a constitutional issue. But we can regulate guns in ways similar to how we regular automobiles without losing our basic right to own and drive cars. Pick almost any modern country in the world and you will find handgun regulation and much lower rates of violence. Again, the issue is more complicated and there are other factors than just guns in understanding violent crime, but guns are a critical factor.

What does it take to get a handgun in USA? Let's take a look at the requirements:

First, you must not belong to any of the following categories:

❖ Persons under indictment for, or convicted of, any crime punishable by imprisonment for a term exceeding on year;

❖ Fugitives from justice;

❖ Persons who are unlawful users of, or addicted to, any controlled substance;

❖ Persons who have been declared by a court as mental defectives or have been committed to a mental institution;

❖ Illegal aliens, or aliens who were admitted to the United States under a nonimmigrant visa;

❖ Persons who have been dishonorably discharged from the Armed Forces;

❖ Persons who have renounced their United States citizenship;

❖ Persons subject to certain types of restraining orders; and

❖ Persons who have been convicted of a misdemeanor crime of domestic violence.

Curtailing gun ownership, to curb violent crime, through denying licenses or making legal arms & ammunition ridiculously expensive is based on flawed reasoning. The fact is that licensed firearms are found to be used in a statistically insignificant number of violent crimes. Most violent crimes involving firearms are committed using untraceable illegal guns. Terrorists or the mafia are not going to be deterred by gun-control laws, they will be willing and able to procure arms of their choice and use them to commit crimes irrespective of any laws. Ironically in India it is cheaper (by several times) to buy the same gun in the black market than it is to buy it legally!

"If someone has a gun and is trying to kill you, it would be reasonable

to shoot back with your own gun."—The Dalai Lama, (May 15, 2001, The Seattle Times) speaking at the "Educating Heart Summit" in Portland, Oregon, when asked by a girl how to react when a shooter takes aim at a classmate

Closer home take the case of the Godhra carnage and the anti-Sikh riots of 1984. Would wanton mobs have slaughtered so many innocent people with such disregard to consequences if their potential victims had been armed and ready to defend themselves? A serious consideration should be given to an armed civilian population as a solution to religious and racial riots as well as other crimes. Since all criminals are instinctively driven by self-preservation allowing legal ownership of firearms by law abiding citizens would act as a serious deterrent. This will make sure that if the Govt. fails to do its duty to protect the life and liberty of its citizens, citizens will be able to protect themselves.

Laws are only a concern for law-abiding citizens who would abide by them. It would be impossible to erase guns from our world.

For millions of people modern life is increasingly like a waking dream. The stereotypical school shooting event has permeated cultural consciousness to such an extent that it has become a symbolic act, a reflexive action even that plays out in the subconscious mind of millions— the school shooting dream—and if the connection to waking reality is broken such an event can be acted out for real by the mentally unstable

Knifes and Guns

Many chief police officers say guns are more easily available for less money each year. The fact is young people may not be buying them with the intention of using them. Fear forces young people to carry a knife in the belief they will be protected from attack. They think that if they carry knives and are threatened, all they will have to do is show their knife for the attacker to back off.

The reality is completely different. Carrying a knife only increases the chances of being attacked. But it doesn't feel that way to a teenager. Many I interviewed seemed to have been quite unrealistic about carrying knives and guns, believing everything would turn out as it does in films and music videos. Guns and knives were carried for protection and respect, if you have to use one, well it's just a jab in the thigh, it doesn't go very deep, it's not very serious. Almost all stopped carrying knives when one of their friends was killed or seriously wounded. They spoke of how naive they had been about the injuries that a small blade could cause.

The same naivety is now at play with guns. They are carried or kept for similar reasons and there is the same belief that using a gun will be just as it appears on television or music videos; cartoon-like violence where you can duck behind a car door during a drive-by like Snoop Doggy Dogg or 50 Cent. Guns and knives are becoming a part of growing up for children in a few countries. They are already a reality for school heads and teachers. And they are an issue for many parents, even well-off middle-class parents.

Gun in Different Countries

It has seemed as if Americans have always had an obsession with owning guns. With the laws allowing U.S. citizens the right to bear arms, they have always been quick to take advantage of it and scoff at anyone who tries to interfere. England has completely illegalized the ownership or usage of guns except for the military and occasionally the police.

The population of Japan is 127,463,611; the number of children killed by guns in Japan every year: 0. When a group of people, be they a law enforcement agency or an entire state, go rogue, people under their control are in great danger. No one, and certainly no group of people, can be trusted with a monopoly on force in the long run. Historic evidence shows clearly what happens when government agencies are permitted to abuse defenseless individuals.

Every year, throughout the world, it is estimated that more than half a million people are killed by small arms and light weapons (SALW) in violent and conflict situations, and the deaths occur predominantly in the developing world. Small arms and light weapons (SALW), or "conventional weapons", are those that can be operated by one or two individuals and include handguns, assault rifles, machine guns, grenades and landmines. Small arms are used for killing not only in times of armed conflicts/war but even in their absence. One might remember the shooting incident at the Virginia Polytechnic Institute, US in April 2007, described as one of the bloodiest campus killing in US history in which a 23-year-old Virginia Tech student killed 27 other students and five faculty members in the rampage before fatally shooting himself.

In Switzerland where every man of military age is required to keep a gun at home as part of the country's civil defence policy, the number of deaths per 10,000 population was 0.05. In South Africa it was 7.1 for every 10,000 people. In India too, country made guns, pistols, etc. are plenty in the market for a price that is affordable by many. In the North East of India, small arms are used as weapons of intimidation and violence by militant outfits to further their cause at the expense of the common people and the region's development.

Children, including adolescents, are the most vulnerable populations in situations of armed conflict and many are actually involved in the conflict both as combatants and victims. Recruitment of children to be combatants is common in many strive torn countries/regions around the world as seen in Africa, the Middle East, Afghanistan, Sri Lanka, etc. There are an estimated 120,000 child soldiers in Africa alone. Displacement, injury and death due to armed conflicts have ravaged countless innocent lives and entire generations of children grow up without getting proper schooling or education. Many become malnourished, missed vaccination doses and fall prey to illness and disease (including vaccine preventable diseases). Landmines are also a particular threat to children; more than 50 per cent of landmine victims are children. Children suffer a range of physical, emotional and psychological conditions –disability, inability to cope, sleep deprivation, depression, post-traumatic stress disorder, psychosis (particularly those who had witness and/or inflicted extreme violence), etc. Even in India the situation is worsening every day. Over the last four or five decades, the country has witnessed a series of gun violence all across the country. Hundreds of small arm weapons have been penetrating in India's northeast and Jammu and Kashmir region

North East India, comprising the seven states of Assam, Arunachal Pradesh, Manipur, Meghalaya, Mizoram, Nagaland, Tripura, and 7.6 per cent of the land area and 3.6 per cent of the total population of India. The fire of insurgency has long engulfed this strategic region for the last half a century or more, making it one of South Asia's most disturbed areas. There are human rights abuses by both the insurgent groups and security forces in Manipur, Assam and other areas in the North East.

According to Binalakshmi Nepram, secretary general of the Control Arms Foundation of India (CAFI), states like Uttar Pradesh and Bihar, who have not seen much violence like in northeast and Jammu and Kashmir, have also become prone to violence.

And now these two states top the list of states with the maximum number of licensed arms. India has emerged as the second most heavily armed country in the world. An estimated 40 million firearms in India are in civilian possession. There are 9,00,000 arms license holders in Uttar Pradesh alone, she added.

Though we have seen enormous gun violence over the last few months if not years, taking hundreds of innocent lives, maiming thousands of people, the country has not been able to curb the spiraling situation.

The intriguing question that remains to one's guess is that how many of us are aware of the fact that over three lakh people are killed every year by guns. It's not the responsibility of a particular country or region that has been affected by gun culture. In fact no country is immune.

Leaving aside for a while of what happened in Gurgaon, ten and thousands of soldiers in the armed forces of over 60 countries, between 2001 and 2004, were children and at least 10 of those countries have used these child soldiers during the conflict.

In the U.S. there are approximately 200 million privately owned guns, which is statistically close to a gun per person and places more than one gun per home on average. The children that live within a gun infested society are going to suffer the consequences. In fact, kids between the ages 16 and 19 have the highest handgun victimization rate among all age groups.

Gun and Sports

As mentioned earlier, crime is not the only issue related to firearms ownership. Hunting is a popular sport and, in some parts of the country, an important source of food. On the surface, it might appear that hunting is harmful to wildlife and the environment. The fact is that the opposite is true. Wildlife biologists have found that well managed and regulated hunting programs are beneficial to wildlife. If the wildlife population becomes too large, food becomes scarce and the population starves to death. Wildlife biologists take counts of game animals in a given area and study the habitat to determine the population level it can support. Then they make recommendations to State Game and Fish officials who set hunting seasons and bag limits. Hunting is a tool used by these officials to manage the wildlife under their care.

Non-game wildlife is also protected by hunters, and even by firearms owners who do not hunt. Approximately 77 per cent of the funds used to operate state Fish and Game and other wildlife agencies are derived from the sales of hunting licenses, excise taxes levied on sales of firearms and ammunition, and the sale of federal duck stamps. More than three billion dollars have been raised from these sources and used to protect both game and non-game animals. Firearms ownership is clearly beneficial to the environment and a good environment is beneficial to everyone.

Firearms are also used in competitive sports. The Olympic Games include competitions with pistols, rifles, and shotguns. Shooting is also part of the biathlon and has been part of the Olympic pentathlon since

1912 ("Pentathlon"). There are also many competitions throughout the country in bull's eye, bench rest, silhouette, practical pistol, trap and skeet, and other shooting sports. Men, women, older children, and even individuals with certain disabilities can enjoy these sports since shooting does not require much agility or physical strength.

Even without formal competition, shooting can be enjoyed as a hobby. Recreational shooting may involve paper targets, tin cans, or other suitable targets. This hobby can be enjoyed at indoor target ranges, but is usually practiced outdoors. In fact, shooting can often be combined with other enjoyable outdoor activities, such as hiking, camping, and sight seeing.

Shooting is a relatively inexpensive activity which the entire family can enjoy. With close supervision, children can be taught to shoot. Learning how to shoot safely means learning about responsibility, and the time spent teaching a child to shoot is quality time. When a child is ready, they may be allowed to shoot with less supervision. When this time comes, the child knows they have earned their parent's trust and they gain a sense of self-confidence. Sharing a hobby like shooting can bring a family closer together, teach children responsibility, and promote trust between parents and children. This is definitely good for society.

Throughout history violence has plagued the human race. Since ancient times the strong have preyed on the weak and the meek. We have passed laws to protect society, but the violence continues. Laws attempt to change human behavior, but laws are not able to change human nature. Laws are not enough to protect people from aggression. We must allow people the means to protect themselves. Protection is a major reason that about half of all Americans own a firearm (Lester 30).

It is a fact that not all people are the same size or possess the same amount of strength. Sometimes people must defend themselves from stronger aggressors, or sometimes from multiple aggressors. This is especially true for women since they are, on average, smaller than men. Also, older people are generally less able physically to defend themselves than young adults are. Everyone deserves to be safe, but not everyone has the physical ability to defend themselves. Firearms are the most effective tools used today for self-defense, but they are only useful if they are available.

In certain regards, Canada and the United States share a similar culture, which can be defined as "North American." Canadians are exposed to much American culture, due to the proximity of the United States, a common linguistic bond shared between majorities of Canadians. Despite the close ties, Canadian culture can also sometimes seek to differentiate itself from that of the United States. The fact of the matter is Canada's overall crime rate is now 50 per cent higher than the crime rate in the United States, all involving guns. Gun control doesn't seem to be taken seriously by our government, the law is making matters worse for schools and Canadians can get their hands on gun from wherever they can get them. The question comes, should Canada take the ban on gun ownership a step further?

Cash for Guns' Campaign

'Cash for Guns' campaign and concurrent amnesty program; the response has been outstanding and police could not be happier. The two-month program has seen 246 firearms turned in or seized. Approximately 1/3 of the firearms taken in were handguns. This program has been such a success, that serious consideration is being given to making this an annual event. Now-a-days it's easy for Canadians to even get an AK-47 from the black market. The price of an AK-47 is a barometer of social stability. Although the diffusion of small arms has drawn less attention than the spread of heavy armaments and weapons of mass destruction, it is nonetheless significant. More than 80 per cent of the violent conflicts of the past decade made use of small arms alone. Black-market gun prices can be one of the best indicators of looming—or ebbing-conflict. Recent black-market prices of AK-47 assault rifles, whose killing power and widespread avail

Legal and Illegal Gun Markets

A gun is a tool that is used to fire ammunition. A gun is simply a device that stores, aims and launches a small piece of metal called a bullet. A bullet is made from lead, copper or steel or a combination of these metals depending on the bullet's purpose. The gun was invented around the early 1280's. There are many types of firearms. Generally, they are divided into three categories.

- ❖ Rifles,
- ❖ Shotguns, and
- ❖ Handguns.

Guns merit special attention; the lethality and widespread availability of guns have worsened youth violence in this country. Gun violence is a significant cause of death and injury among young people, and imposes serious psychological, economic, and social consequences on children, families, and communities.

The increase in youth gun violence in the late 1980s coincided with the diffusion of high-powered semiautomatic pistols into the legal and illegal gun markets. These pistols had higher calibers (the higher a gun's caliber, the higher its destructive potential and held more ammunition than their predecessors. Semiautomatic pistols, particularly inexpensive ones, quickly became weapons of choice for criminals, including young people; by 1999, these pistols accounted for one-half of all guns traced by the U.S. Bureau of Alcohol, Tobacco and Firearms (ATF) after being recovered by law enforcement following a crime. With the increasing use of these guns came increases in rates of firearm violence, the average number of bullet wounds per person injured, and the proportion of victims who died before reaching the hospital.

U.S. Department of Education Reports

The U.S. Department of Education reports that during 1997, nearly 6,300 students were expelled from American schools for carrying firearms. Fifty-eight per cent of the expulsions were for handguns and 17 per cent for shotguns. As evidenced in many of the recent reports about school violence, many students have chosen to express their anger in destructive ways. Renate Caine, former educational psychology professor at California State University at San Bernardino, states that when students feel threatened, their brains shift into primitive, instinctive states for defending themselves (Easterbrook, 1999).

We can learn from these school shootings because they reflect factors not typical of the antisocial offenders. They challenge our stereotypes and force us recognize violent influences we otherwise might overlook. They were committed by white, middle class youth who had many social and economic advantages. Many of them came from good homes where they were loved, not abused, by their parents. Many of their parents were well-respected citizens and good role models for their children. Although it is common to blame the parents in these cases, this cannot explain what their children did. At worst, we can say that these parents failed to recognize what was happening to their children, not that they caused it to happen. A breakdown in parental supervision is a serious problem, but it is not the full explanation. Instead, we have to recognize the role of broader cultural factors affecting children outside the home.

According to one Web site, every hour in the United States someone under the age of 25 dies from a gunshot wound. There are also nearly 200 million firearms in this country and a new one is produced every eight seconds gun culture entered INDIA gun culture entered INDIA centuries back along with europeans, That was for different purpose. that was to fight the out siders who have occupied INDIA and treated INDIANS as slaves. But not shoot or kill fellow citizen just to show their muscle power. It can be stopped only if it is proved and made clear in the minds of people that possessing and/or using unauthorized weapons is treated with corporal punishment by the judiciary & executives (politicians) with out any bias by punishing people who have already committed the crime.

Gun a Mechanical Device

A gun is a mechanical device that expels a projectile. In most cases the projectile is a gyroscopically stabilized bullet which can accurately travel a large distance. Most guns burn solid propellants to produce high-pressure gas, which drives the projectile through the barrel. Guns have been used for hundreds of years in the history of our world and nation; guns inflict more damage than other instruments, they can be fired multiple times with little effort, firearms have a greater range, and assailants intending to kill choose the most efficient instrument. Whatever the impact of these different factors, it is clear that the fatality rate from gun assaults is much higher than that from other weapons. Gun violence also is frequently more random than other types of criminal victimization. One participant noted that "bullets don't always have a name on them. You can be shot from a great distance even with a bullet meant for someone else." The gun, as an instrument of both power and detachment, allows the shooter to remain physically and emotionally distanced from his or her victims.

The participants who work with adolescents spoke of the pessimism and despair, particularly in the inner cities, where communities are losing children to gun violence daily. Youngsters whose relatives and friends have been shot automatically think that sooner or later it will happen to them. They plan their funerals, write their obituaries, and specify the clothing in which they want to be buried. Studies of urban youth show a high correlation between exposure to violence and depression.

Gun control has been a major debating issue during the past few decades. On one side there are those who completely agree with the control laws and on the other there are those who oppose gun control laws.

Guns make it easier to kill and injure people. You've likely heard or read that having a gun in the home causes a risk of death or injury, and maybe that the risk is greater than the probable benefits of having that gun. If your family is mentally/emotionally healthy and learns about and practices safe handling, however, the gun will be of essentially zero danger to you or your family. If you get a gun for protection but have not learned about protective use of the gun, and have not decided that you are willing to kill someone rather than let that someone harm you or someone in your family, your risk may be a little higher than if a criminal comes to your home and you didn't have the gun. One of the many things a person must learn for her own safety is that one does not grab for a gun when the criminal already has one trained on you, except as a last resort. A person with a gun for protection doesn't necessarily get to use it when a need arises.

Gun Possession: A Liability or Blessing

The bad side of gun possession is supposed to be that:

* Guns cause murder, suicides, accidental deaths, injuries from suicide attempts, and accidental injuries.
* Guns cause these things among good normal people "just like us" and among "helpless" children, especially in the home.
* Guns cause or facilitate crime and violence, and (publicly, at least) some guns do so more than others.
* Many people who have never owned or used a gun feel afraid because others do, even though about half of U.S. citizens have always had guns (including during periods of low violent crime).
* On the other side of the ledger.
* Guns are used for sport.
* Guns are used to stop crime and violence, and to deter criminal activities, victimization and oppression.

Internal Conflict of India and Gun Circulation

Exposed to unending armed conflict, children in states like Chhattisgarh, Jharkhand, Andhra Pradesh, Jammu and Kashmir, Manipur, Nagaland and Assam get drawn into fighting both with rebel groups as well as security forces. What was considered a problem in Sudan, Libya, Sierra Leone, Sri Lanka and Nepal has become a reality for India too.

These children—exposed to war and conflict—are one of the most vulnerable groups, often forced to witness or perpetrate atrocities. They are scarred for life, their childhood shattered. A UNICEF estimate says about 2.50 lakh children have been recruited as soldiers in various capacities worldwide. In India, no studies have been conducted to even document the number of children involved in combat. "Rebels are inaccessible and security forces don't want to own up to employing children. Explaining the reasons why children get sucked into rebel activities, a human rights activist based in North-east India says, "The situation lures them. They are fascinated by the gun and its power." Another activist said, "On the one hand children see the extreme poverty their families live in, and on the other they see rebels leading well-off lives. To them, joining the rebels seems like an opportunity to get out of their misery." A child soldier told a Nagaland-based activist that he had joined rebels because he did not have money to pay the fees for his class VIII examination. Also, when the child soldier learns the tricks of the trade and starts getting money, the parents also enjoy a better life style. "While the government is not giving enough support and compensation for victims, rebel groups are willing to step in to act as guardians,

Self Psychology

Weapons have been objects of fascination throughout history and have had highly symbolic meanings for many cultures, including our own. Their significance has been examined from a variety of theoretical orientations and by a number of disciplines. Self psychology provides valuable insights into the importance of weapons. Children exposed to gun violence may experience negative short- and long-term psychological effects, including:

- ❖ Anger,
- ❖ Withdrawal,
- ❖ Posttraumatic stress, and
- ❖ Desensitization to violence.

All of these outcomes can feed into a continuing cycle of violence. Certain children may be at higher risk for negative outcomes if they are exposed to gun violence.

Groups at risk include children injured in gun violence, those who witness violent acts at close proximity, those exposed to high levels of violence in their communities or schools, and those exposed to violent media. Parents, school administrators, and mental health workers all can play key roles in protecting children from gun violence and helping them overcome the effects of gun-related trauma. Remember that a gun is only a device that launches a small piece of metal at very high speed. That is all a gun does. A gun does absolutely nothing by itself. A gun all by itself is nothing that should be feared. It is only a tool in someone's hand. Don't let anyone tell you that guns are bad. Guns are neither bad nor good. The truth is that loaded guns can hurt people if they are mishandled. A gun is simply a device that can launch a small piece of metal at very high speed. They are neither good nor bad. They are just a tool or machine that can be dangerous, just like a chainsaw or other power tool. Guns are not dangerous if they are handled properly and all safety rules and precautions are followed.

Safe Gun Handling Rules

Always Point the Barrel in a Safe Direction!!!

This is the Golden Rule of Gun Safety. If a gun's barrel never gets pointed at another child, there will never be another injury to children due to the mishandling of guns. (Unless you drop it on your toes, of course.)

Don't Touch the Trigger Until You are Ready to Fire

There is a natural tendency for people to place their trigger finger inside the trigger guard when they handle a gun. This impulse must be avoided. The person handling the gun has to condition themselves to place their trigger finger alongside the frame of the gun, just above the trigger guard. The gun will ONLY fire, if your finger is on the trigger. Most times, when an accident happens, the shooter does not even realize that their finger is on the trigger.

Never touch the trigger until you have cleared the range, the range officer tells you it is ok to shoot, you have acquired your target in the sights and you are ready to fire.

There is no other reason for you to touch the trigger until then.

Never load the gun until you are ready to use it.

This is the third and final rule of safe gun handling. *Do not Load Cartridges into a Gun Unless You are About Ready to Use it.*

A fully loaded gun, just laying there on the shooting bench, is a possible accident waiting to happen. *ONE MORE TIME:*

Do not load the gun, until you are about ready to fire it.

That's all three rules of safe gun handling. Please repeat them as many times as you can without getting too bored.

Are Bullets Dangerous?

❖ Do you think that bullets can be dangerous all by themselves?
❖ Bullets are really only one of the four (4) components of a cartridge.
❖ If you find a cartridge for a gun outside your home or in the home of a friend, you really should treat them as if they are a real gun.
❖ You should not touch it, walk away and tell an adult that you found a "bullet" or cartridge.
❖ If a cartridge is found and tossed into a fire, it can explode and may injure you or someone around you.
❖ A cartridge is not as dangerous outside a gun as it is when it is fired from inside a gun, but the bullet still may shoot out of the cartridge case a ways and harm you.
❖ Never toss a cartridge into a fire.
❖ Never bang on a cartridge.
❖ Never squeeze a cartridge with a vice or pliers.

Guns and Laws

Everyone in the United States of America has an opinion on gun control regardless of their age, race, or religion. From within those opinions arguments are formed. People are arguing about gun control at their jobs, at their schools, and sometimes at their places of worship. On one side of things there are the people that support gun control like certain politicians or political organizations, teachers, police officers, and so on. On the other side of things there are the people that are against gun control, people such as hunters and various types of criminals. When it comes down to sensitive topics like gun control, there are very few people that do not choose a side. Of the many pieces of colonial legislation that still stay with India today, the Arms Act is one that is perhaps most "colonial" in nature. In its present form, the Arms Act of 1959, which is pretty much a copy of the older Raj—era legislation, prohibits the possession, acquisition and bearing of guns without a license.

A proud firearm owner is an exception not the norm, an odd situation in a country with a proud martial heritage and a long history of firearm innovation. This is not because the people of India are averse to gun ownership, but instead due to anti-gun legislation going back to colonial times.

Roots of India's Anti-gun Legislation

To trace the roots of India's anti-gun legislation we need to step back to the latter half of the 19th century. The British had recently fought off a major Indian rebellion (the mutiny of 1857) and were busy putting in place measures to ensure that the events of 1857 were never repeated. These measures included a major restructuring of administration and the colonial British Indian Army along with improvements in communications and transportation. Meanwhile the Indian masses were systematically being disarmed and the means of local firearm production destroyed, to ensure that they (the Indian masses) would never again have the means to rise in rebellion against their colonial masters. Towards this end the colonial government, under Lord Lytton as Viceroy (1874 -1880), brought into existence the Indian Arms Act, 1878 (11 of 1878); an act which, exempted Europeans and ensured that no Indian could possess a weapon of any description unless the British masters considered him a "loyal" subject of the British Empire.

An example of British thinking in colonial times:

"No kingdom can be secured otherwise than by arming the people. The possession of arms is the distinction between a freeman and a slave. He, who has nothing, and who himself belongs to another, must be defended by him, whose property he is, and needs no arms. But he, who thinks he is his own master, and has what he can call his own, ought to have arms to defend himself, and what he possesses; else he lives precariously, and at discretion. "—James Burgh (Political Disquisitions: Or, an Enquiry into Public Errors, Defects, and Abuses) [London, 1774-1775]

And thoughts (on this subject) of the man who wanted to rule the world:

"The most foolish mistake we could possibly make would be to allow the subject races to possess arms. History shows that all conquerors who have allowed the subject races to carry arms have prepared their own downfall by so doing. Indeed, I would go so far as to say that the supply of arms to the underdogs is a sine qua non for the overthrow of any sovereignty. "—Adolf Hitler (H.R. Trevor-Roper, Hitler's Table Talks 1941-1944)

The leaders of our freedom struggle recognised this, even Gandhi the foremost practitioner of passive resistance and non-violence had this to say about the British policy of gun-control in India:

> *"Among the many misdeeds of the British rule in India, history will look upon the Act depriving a whole nation of arms, as the blackest."*—Mahatma Gandhi (An Autobiography OR The story of my experiments with truth, by M.K. Gandhi, p. 238)

Post Independence

India became independent in 1947, but it still took 12 years before this act was finally repealed. In 1959 the British era Indian Arms Act, 1878 (11 of 1878.) was finally consigned to history and a new act, the Arms Act, 1959 was enacted. This was later supplemented by the Arms Rules, 1962. Unfortunately this new legislation was also formulated based on the Indian Government's innate distrust its own citizens. Though somewhat better than the British act, this legislation gave vast arbitrary powers to the "Licensing Authorities", in effect ensuring that it is often difficult and sometimes impossible for an ordinary law abiding Indian citizen to procure an arms license.

> *"A system of licensing and registration is the perfect device to deny gun ownership to the bourgeoisie."*—Vladimir Ilyich Lenin

Also the policy of throttling private arms manufacturing was continued even after independence. Limits on the quantity and type of arms that could be produced by private manufacturers were placed—ensuring that the industry could never hope to be globally competitive and was instead consigned to producing cheap shotguns, of mostly indifferent quality, in small quantities. A citizen wishing to purchase a decent firearm depended solely on imports, which were a bit more expensive but vastly superior in quality.

In USA the school's "gun-free zone" laws in particular create an atmosphere of false security, and prevent adults in the schools—who may be extremely responsible individuals very capable of carrying a weapon—from being able to provide an extra level of protection for the most vulnerable of potential victims—the children they are entrusted with on a daily basis. Indeed, laws preventing guns in the schools in the hands of capable adults create a huge population of defenseless possible victims who are at the mercy of those who would commit these crimes. Laws only apply to those who respect them in the first place—not criminals.

More Recently

This changed towards the mid to late 1980s, when the Government, citing domestic insurgency as the reason, put a complete stop to all small arms imports. The fact that there is no documented evidence of any terrorists ever having used licensed weapons to commit an act of terror on Indian soil seems to be of no consequence to our Government. The prices of (legal & licensed) imported weapons have been on an upward spiral ever since—beating the share market and gold in terms of pure return on investment. Even the shoddy domestically produced guns suddenly seem to have found a market. Also since the Government now had a near monopoly on (even half-way decent) arms & ammunition for the civilian market, they started turning the screws by pricing their crude public sector products (ammunition, rifles, shotguns & small quantities of handguns) at ridiculously high rates—products that frankly, given a choice no one would ever purchase.

> *"That rifle on the wall of the labourer's cottage or working class flat is the symbol of democracy. It is our job to see that it stays there."*— George Orwell, the author of Animal Farm and 1984, himself a socialist

Lessons from Gurgaon School Shoot-Out

On the face of it, it seems a fairly reasonable thing. Who can possibly argue that we need to de-regulate the possession, acquisition, etc of arms? Close on the heels of incidents of campus shootings in various schools across the country, experts on Thursday stressed on making the gun legislation more stringent. "We want to make the Indian Arms Act of 1959 more stringent. Everyone should not be allowed to possess arms. Those provided license for possessing weapons should be accountable for their use," Lt Gen (retd) B S Mallik, president of Control Arms Foundation of India, an organization spearheading the movement against misuse of arms, said at a seminar. He said children should not be allowed to use these weapons at all. "Children should be denied access to arms," he said at the seminar on 'Lessons from Gurgaon school shoot-out: Call for redrafting India's gun legislation'.

The issue assumes significance in view of recent incidents of children resorting to shooting their friends in schools. A boy was shot dead by his classmates in a Gurgaon school in December last year, while another student in Satna district in Madhya Pradesh was shot dead by a fellow student last month. Jasjit Singh, Director, Centre for Air Power Studies, said the Constitution allows somebody to defend himself, not to carry weapons. "The licenses for weapons are given for three reasons—hunting, display and protection. It shows the state is failing to provide security to its people that is why people are opting for arms for their security," he said. India's former ambassador to the US, Arundhati Ghose, emphasised on conducting research to know the details of arms use and taking up awareness programme against the misuse of arms.

State Control of Gun Ownership

Police officers know that they cannot protect us at all times. That is why most of them recommend that people get the training and the tools for protecting their own lives.

Gun control is not a single issue. There are numerous gun control issues. The issues are highly emotional and the antagonists are deeply committed to their views, resulting in irrational, hateful dialog and the country being deeply divided. This situation is causing the country to waste huge resources that we should be committing to solving our problems, like crime and violence.

Laws are not very effective in preventing possession. If we examine major events in Indian history after the experience of the 1857 Revolt, the colonial regime obviously did not want us natives to get our hands on too many weapons which we could use to threaten the regime. The Arms Act of 1878 was one way of depriving Indians the means to attack and challenge an oppressive and exploitative regime. This becomes even more obvious when we see that the same restrictions do not apply to "Europeans" living in India. This was not a unique Indian experience as the native populace was routinely disarmed by the victorious colonizers.

When we attained Independence, through mostly peaceful means, the Government thought it fit to continue this colonial policy, albeit without the discrimination between Indians and Europeans. The Indian state was supposed to be the sole wielder of violent force, and would use it to come to the defense of the weak and oppressed against their enemies.

The issue of gun control has been debated for a long time, probably ever since they were invented. The gun is a small, rather easy to obtain, weapon that is lethal if used in the right (or wrong) way. This makes the gun an extremely dangerous factor in our lives. If used improperly, a gun could be lethal to not only the target, but the user as well. The availability of guns has sky rocketed in the past decade or so, and the immense populatiHon of guns in society make it a dangerous place to live.

Why do you Need Guns when you Got the Police?

Unfortunately, we have seen that it is not so. We have seen the State take the side of the oppressors against the oppressed. We have seen the State actively disarm threatened minorities (Sikhs in Punjab, Muslims in Gujarat,), and idly stand by as atrocities are committed by a rampaging mob (against Dalits).

Generally, violence of any sort in India is almost inevitably mob violence. It is rarely, if ever, the single maniac, or a single serial killer. Generally, it is not even called "violence" until the other side hits back. That is when "agitations", "movements", etc become "warfare", "riots" and the like.

Guns are a great "force multiplier", to use military terms. As we have repeatedly seen, a single volley of bullets is usually enough to disperse an otherwise dangerous and angry mob.

India is still developing as a "rule of law" society. The revolutionary sparks are no longer nascent—Naxalism, religious fundamentalism, illegal mining, looting of forest/wildlife wealth, linguistic chauvinism, destruction of public/private property, bullying of rural populations, etc. These are all serious challenges to the rule of law. Allowing free gun ownership would do more bad than good in this situation.

A gun without licence is like a license to kill. If the intention is to use it as a deterrent against violence, a person can take the trouble to get a license. Free access may encourage actual use... I mean unwarranted use. A mob usually does not think straight... it merely acts and that too in frenzy. If guns become common place, they (mobs, violence perpetrators) will come prepared with bombs.

Micro-Stamping

Micro-stamping is a proposed means for imprinting unique serial numbers onto cartridges fired from a gun. Similar to "ballistic fingerprinting," it allegedly helps police identify what firearm might have been used in a crime. Micro-stamping uses precision equipment to remove microscopic amounts of metal from the tip of the firing pin.

Gun Registration in Different Countries

Some countries like New Zealand feel Gun registration does not work. They repealed their gun registration law in the 1980s after police acknowledged its worthlessness. In Canada More than 20,000 Canadian gun-owners have publicly refused to register their firearms. Many others are silently ignoring the law. The Federal Republic of Germany began comprehensive gun registration in 1972. The government estimated that between 17,000,000 and 20,000,000 guns were to be registered, but only 3,200,000 surfaced, leaving 80 per cent unaccounted for. Criminals don't register their guns.

Registration is required in Hawaii, Chicago, and Washington D.C. Yet there has not been a single case where registration was instrumental in identifying someone who committed a crime. Criminals very rarely leave their guns at the scene of the crime. Would-be criminals also virtually never get licenses or register their weapons.

It did in Canada. The handgun registration law of 1934 was the source used to identify and confiscate (without compensation) over half of the registered handguns in 2001. It did in Germany. The 1928 Law on Firearms and Ammunition (before the Nazis came to power) required all firearms to be registered. When Hitler came to power, the existing lists were used for confiscating weapons.

It did in Australia. In 1996, the Australian government confiscated over 660,000 previously legal weapons from their citizens.

It did in New York City. In 1967, New York City passed an ordinance requiring a citizen to obtain a permit to own a rifle or shotgun, which would then be registered. In 1991, the city passed a ban on the private possession of some semi-automatic rifles and shotguns, and "registered" owners were told that those firearms had to be surrendered, rendered inoperable, or taken out of the city. It did in Bermuda, Cuba, Greece, Ireland, Jamaica, and Soviet Georgia as well.

Who Possess Guns?

A 1998 survey found that 31 per cent of family homes kept guns. 40 per cent of guns in homes are left unlocked and sometimes loaded! Even if there are no guns in their own home they can steal one or borrow from a friend. There are almost 7,000 violent crimes committed a year by juveniles using guns found in their own home.

During the 1999-2000 academic year in California schools showed 2/3 of cases showed kids got their gun from a relative or friend. A study at Alfred University showed 24 per cent of kids could easily get a gun. Guns are exceptionally lethal weapons, and they are easily available to young people. In the late 1980s and early 1990s, the lethality and availability of guns, particularly handguns, fueled a youth gun violence epidemic that peaked in 1994, when nearly 6,000 young people under age 20 died from firearm injuries. Guns cause deaths and severe injuries more frequently than knives, clubs, or fists, and with guns, even transitory violent impulses can have lethal consequences.

Imagine enjoying a movie at Cinema 10, eating a meal, or even sitting in a history class at School while people all around you are carrying loaded guns! Although this may seem unbelievable, it is possible because the second amendment of the United States Constitution gives citizens the right to possess and carry guns. It is understandable that Americans would want to possess guns such as shotguns and rifles for the popular sport of hunting. However, it is ridiculous that government would allow people to carry handguns. Handgun possession should be strictly limited, because they are made solely to kill people, they have increased the murder rate in the U.S., and they have even allowed children to easily kill other children.

Currently it is so easy to get a gun, that people with criminal records and mentally unstable individuals can gain access to such a dangerous tool. Handguns can easily get into the hands of little children. For example, about one and a half years ago, a six year old boy in the Beecher School District took a loaded handgun to school and shot and killed a six year old female classmate. This young boy may not have understood the concept of death. However, because he had easy access to a handgun, he was able to hurt someone he didn't like. Though gun control laws are strict in India, more and more people in places like Gurgaon own guns because they are a symbol of power and prestige in caste-ridden and feudal northern India. The number of gun licenses in the suburb, according to a report, has shot up from 95 in 2005 to nearly 300 already this year. The mafia, and corrupt people have had guns for quite some time in India and have used it very often on innocent people as well as cops and in gang wars. The parents of these kids were property dealers, one of the categories having strong links with mafia and corrupt babus. So the culture has been there now it seems these guys have started giving guns to kids. Northern India has more such problems compared to south. People there seem to get the evil of politics much faster.

The Easy Availability of Guns

The increased lethality of guns, particularly handguns, coincided with their increasing availability to and use by young people. The epidemic of violence from 1983 to 1993 in USA does not seem to have resulted from a basic change in the offending rates and viciousness of young offenders. Rather, it resulted primarily from a relatively sudden change in the social environment—the introduction of guns into violent exchanges among youth. The violence epidemic was, in essence, the result of a change in the presence and type of weapon used, which increased the lethality of violent incidents. An estimated 34 per cent of children in the United States live in homes with firearms. A 1999 national survey estimated that 833,000 American youth between the ages of 12 and 17 had carried a handgun at least once in the previous year; many teens that carry guns cite the need for self-protection as their primary reason for doing so. A February 2002 study found that children ages 5 to 14 were more likely to die from gunshot wounds if they lived in states where firearm ownership was more common. Children and youth are perpetrators as well as victims of gun violence. In 1998, juveniles and youth under age 25 committed 54 per cent of gun homicides in which the offender was known; juveniles under age 18 alone accounted for 12 per cent of gun homicides in which the offender was known even without firearms, American children are more likely to die in homicides than their counterparts in other industrialized nations. However, guns worsen the violence.

Illegal Guns

Youth obtain illegal guns. The gun traces have revealed that between 25 per cent and 36 per cent of traced guns that were used by youth to commit crimes are new guns (less than three years old), often sold illegally to youth by corrupt licensed firearms dealers, or illegally bought for youth by adult purchasers (called "straw" purchases).

Toy Gun

Toy guns are more common with boys than girls. This is not a debated issue, what is, is if they reinforce the aggressive nature of males, or if they allow the child a device in the development of rational thinking associated with the images produced by Hollywood and real life. Boys are more likely to play with a toy gun as well as being the protagonist in a school shooting. Without structure nothing can stand, our society must come to a realization of this simple but fundamental idea once again, if they have forgotten it. Boys pretend to be the hero while girls pretend to be the damsel, boys play with guns and girls don't. They have dolls. It's a stereotype. A gun will give any person the feeling of empowerment making that gun wielding person more inclined to act in a hostile fashion. Also a toy gun during a role-playing event can strengthen those thoughts about using it as a weapon on other people. Given the right situation every young boy has the chance of becoming a murder if he hasn't been taught properly about gun safety; this is just likely in girls as well.

Fun, but are they safe to give children? Do toy guns increase violence or make them immune to it? Information parents need to know. In the past a game of cowboys and Indians or cops and robbers was seen as harmless fun, but in the wake of changing attitudes to war and the escalating level of gun crime and accidental deaths, seeing a child running around with a realistic toy gun chills most parents. It has been a long standing argument with doctors, psychologists, behavioural scientists, parents, law enforcement and politicians all weighing in with their opinions.

Parents should be concerned, guns are frightening, guns kill and maim that is what they are for. That is their express purpose. They are not made for target shooting, they are not made to play games with, they are made to kill and injure. The big questions are: Do toy guns make children immune to the reality of guns? Do toy guns make children more violent? Do toy guns give children an unreal sense of the power of violence? Do toy guns affect how children see violence? Are toy guns worse than computer games and violent films? Is there a scale of suitability with toy guns?

Should a Child be Given a Toy Gun?

This really depends on how much parental guidance is given and what type of toy gun is given to a child. It is true that children especially boys will make a gun out of anything, a banana, a stick or a finger. The thing is these are imaginary guns and the child usually recognises this, even pop guns and water pistols are recognisable as fakes, but it seems with the proliferation of violent crime, the proliferation of look alike weapons has gone hand in hand. To see a child running around with a realistic semi-automatic gun is horrifying to most parents. They look so real. The ultimate decision in whether a child should have a toy gun is entirely in the hands of parents. The decision should be taken carefully and with several arguments in mind.

Toy Guns and the Real Thing

As to whether toy guns make a child immune to real guns, there is a distinct possibility that the look of toy guns has an impact on this. Some children are in no real position to judge the difference between a plastic gun that looks like the real thing and an actual gun. This may be due to age, developmental level, or emotional/behavioural personality. This is distinctly different from the idea that a banana will be used as a gun and a child recognising it is actually an imaginary gun. The realistic toy guns can lead to serious accidents. A child may also believe that their familiarity with the toy gun means that they are capable of handling the real thing without problems or repercussions. Buying realistic toy guns for a child is probably foolhardy and a child having any toy gun without accompanying adult input could also be extremely detrimental. Parents need to step up and make an educated decision about whether a child should be allowed toy guns, what types should be allowed and how to communicate the pitfalls of real guns and their dangers. Remember more than one child dies every day in the USA from gun related violence and accidents. The argument about toy guns and children include aspects of parental guidance with toy guns, whether toy guns make children more violent and if banning toy guns would be beneficial as well as whether toy guns contribute to a child's level of violence as much as TV, video games and movies.

Real Gun Or Toy Gun?

- ❖ Do you think it is easy to tell a real gun from a toy gun?
- ❖ Don't answer so quickly.... Many models of handguns that are intended for carrying are very small and could be easily mistaken for a toy.
- ❖ If you find a gun outside or in a friend's home NEVER assume that the gun is a toy. Some models of small caliber handguns like the .25 ACP can weigh much less than a pound.
- ❖ If you are not ABSOLUTELY CERTAIN, that the gun is a toy, you should not handle it at all.
- ❖ If the gun looks like it is mostly made of metal, it is probably real.
- ❖ If it has an orange or red plastic stopper, in the end of the barrel and is made of plastic, it is probably a toy.
- ❖ If you are not certain that the gun you found is a toy, you should not pick it up. However if some child hands one to you and it feels heavier than a toy should be, it is probably real.
- ❖ If another child hands you a gun which is heavier than you think a toy gun should be, and it does not have an orange or red plastic stopper in the end, you should place the gun carefully right back where it was found and you should leave the area immediately, then tell a parent what you found.

Teach your children the difference between a real gun and a toy gun. Make sure they understand that real guns can seriously hurt or kill someone. Never point a firearm at anything you are not prepared to destroy. This includes real guns and toy guns that shoot projectiles.

With today's realistic versions of video games, it can be difficult for children to tell the difference between fantasy violence and real violence. You should determine if "shooting" video games are appropriate for your child. You then must make sure they understand that a gun used in real life has very different consequences than one on a video screen.

Fatal Accidents or Intentional; Two Sides of the Coin

Bang! Death can happen just like that. That is exactly how guns work; as deadly as they can be. The New York Times states that "Everyday in the United States fourteen children are killed with guns in accidents, suicides and homicides. The hotly debated topic represents two evenly endorsed sides: those who want guns removed from society at all levels beyond law enforcement, and the other side who says the right to bear arms is everyone's right.

Some in support of gun control support a limited control which focuses on laws meant to restrict ownership to dangerous persons or end the ownership of automatic or assault weapons while others wish to control all gun ownership among all citizens. Issues

Gun control issue ranges from those which are concerned with constitutional rights and the values of citizens to those which relate to the types of policy, if any, which should be in place. Opponents of gun control, including the most influential National Rifle Association (NRA) argue that the constitutional "right to bear arms" is an absolute right and should have no limitations.

Both the pros and cons are considered. It is true that gun control in and of itself will not curb the violent streak that lives within an individual, nor will it lessen the number of violent acts committed on a daily basis. It will, however, serve to deter the level of fatalities as a result of gunshot wounds.

Law in USA

❖ Federal law 18 USC Section 922 generally prohibits anyone under 18 from possessing a handgun. It also prohibits licensed firearm dealers and collectors from selling handguns to anyone under 21 years of age.

❖ Laws in the United States generally prohibit the sale, possession, or use of cocaine. About 200,000 American children, age 12-17 used cocaine in 1997. About 2.5 million 12-17 year olds (11.4%) used an illicit drug in 1997.

❖ Federal law 18USC Section 922 generally prohibits civilians from having guns in school zones.

❖ Seven days after the 1999 Columbine school massacre in which 12 students and a teacher were murdered, Bill and Hillary Clinton held a press conference on gun control legislation. Bill Clinton stated:

"Do we know for absolutely certain that if we had every reasonable law and the ones I'm going to propose here that none of these school violence things would have happened? No. But we do know one thing for certain; we know there would have been fewer of them, and there would have been fewer kids killed in the last several years in America. We know that for certain. We know that." (Applause)

❖ In about 5 years since enactment of the Brady Bill and Assault Weapons Ban in 1993, there have been 9 "school massacres."

❖ About 6,000 children were caught with guns at school in 1997 and 1998. Out of these, 13 were prosecuted by the Clinton administration Justice Department.

In October of 1997, sixteen-year-old Luke Woodham stabbed his mother to death and then went to school with a rifle where he shot 9 students, killing 2 of them. Assistant Principal Joel Myrick raced to his car, retrieved a .45 caliber handgun, and used it to subdue Woodham until police arrived.

The Arguments for and Against Gun Control

Advocates of gun control maintain that by making firearms—especially handguns—more difficult to obtain, the number of shootings (both accidental and deliberate) will be reduced. They also support licensing all persons who own firearms and registering each gun as well.

However, just because a gun is registered does not mean that it won't be used in an illegal act. For example, Buford O. Furrow, the man who opened fire at Los Angeles Jewish community center in 1999, was armed with seven guns, including a Clock 9 mm automatic handgun and a custom-made assault rifle—and every one of his guns was registered.

Similarly, Bryan Uyesugi, the man who shot and killed seven employees of the Xerox Corporation in Hawaii on November 2, 1999, had 17 firearms registered. Between June 18, 1990 and November 3, 1999, workplace shootings caused the deaths of 116 people.

Just registering a gun does not guarantee that its owner will not use it to commit a crime. Advocates of gun registrations say that by having to register their weapons with the federal government, gun owners will be more careful in making sure that their guns do not become stolen, or that they do not sell or trade their guns to a criminal. Opponents fear that one day the federal government may use gun registrations against gun owners and confiscate all registered weapons. As mentioned previously, Americans vary widely in their attitudes toward gun control. According to various polls and studies, residents of New England and the mid-Atlantic states tend to be strongly in favor of gun control; they are far less likely to have ever owned a gun than are other Americans. While two out of five Southerners and one out of three Westerners have owned guns, fewer than one in seven residents of the Northeast have. Meanwhile, Southerners are more likely to have a gun at home and elsewhere (such as in the car), and they are more likely to shoot to kill. Westerners are most likely to hear gunshots. As a group, residents of the mountain states are the most certain that guns deter crime. Midwesterners are most concerned about crime. As might be expected given these regional variables, gun control laws vary from state to state. For example, Arizona residents are not required to register their weapons, and they may carry concealed weapons. (A concealed weapon is one that is hidden from view, such as under a shirt or in an ankle holster.) In Massachusetts, it is illegal to carry a concealed weapon, and gun owners must be licensed and their weapons registered, even if the gun is used solely for target shooting.

There is great debate as to whether allowing concealed weapons decreases or increases crime. Some supporters of concealed weapons reason that people are less likely to attempt to commit a crime when they face the possibility that the potential victim may be armed. Detractors say that carrying a weapon makes person more likely to use it—particularly in anger, such as after being cut off in traffic.

Currently, there is no nationwide law that requires gun owners to be licensed. The federal government has left that up to the individual states.

Self-Defense or Self-Destruction?

Supporters of guns maintain the need for the weapons as a means of self-defense. Through surveys of jailed criminals, sociologists have found that 40 per cent of criminals say they would not commit a crime they were considering if they thought the potential victim was armed. In addition, criminals who attempted break-ins of occupied homes succeeded only 14 per cent of the time when the homeowner was armed—compared to 33 per cent of the time when the homeowner was not armed.

Researcher Gary Kleck of Florida State University has done a number of surveys regarding the successful use of guns in self-defense, and he estimates that American use guns for self-defense between 800,000 and 2.45 million times each year. They fire less than one-quarter of the time.

However, figures from the Census Bureau maintain that the numbers of Americans defending themselves with guns is much lower—closer to 80,000 times per year.

And while having a gun in the house may make the gun owner feel more secure and safe, the problem with having guns in the home, argue gun control supporters, is that they are a temptation both for children and adults. Children die every year by being accidentally shot while playing with guns, or by being nearby when someone else is playing with them. Such tragedies can occur when the parents keep a loaded gun in the house—particularly in a night-table drawer—for self-defense. The child finds the gun, and tragedy follows.

In such cases, it is important that the gun be stored unloaded, with a trigger lock, and with its ammunition stored separately from it.

Guns are also often used in domestic squabbles. Prompted by the 1984 shooting death of singer Marvin Gaye (who was killed by his father after a family argument), researcher Arthur Keller Mann began studying the role of the firearm in domestic incidents. His results, which appeared in the *New England Journal of Medicine,* found that for each homicide that was committed in self-defense in the home, there were 37 suicides, 1.3 accidental deaths, and 4.6 criminal homicides. Another of his studies, which tracked domestic homicides in three cities over a five-year period, found that a home that contained guns were three times more likely to be the site of a homicide than a home without guns.

Under the influence of strong emotions, alcohol, or drugs, people often do things they might not normally do otherwise—including drawing a gun on a family member and pulling the trigger. Experts note that it's important to recognize the social influences that may drive people to gun violence. For example, Eric Harris and Dylan Klebold, the two teens who opened fire at Columbine High School, were described as outsiders. Michael Carneal, who opened fire on prayer group at his West Paducah, Kentucky, high school, killing three and wounding five in 1997, was similarly described. In cases like these, or those of Buford Furrow or Bryan Uyesugi, there is rarely a single cause. It would behave to say that Harris and Klebold and Carneal shot 16 people in their separate rampages solely because they had guns; they shot those people because something inside them that would normally have prevented such an occurrence, broke down.

Experts on both sides of the gun control issue urge people to consider their personal situation when thinking about bringing a gun into the home. Are there children or young people in residence who may find the gun a temptation? Is there someone living in the house who has problems controlling his or her temper? Someone who has been depressed and may be suicidal? In any of these cases, experts urge potential gun owners to think twice before introducing a weapon into the equation.

Controversial Measures for Control

Numerous laws and regulations have been passed in an effort to control guns. In June 1999, Connecticut legislators passed a bill that allows police to seize the weapons of anyone whom they believe presents a threat to him- or herself and others. The law went into effect October 1, and on November 1, police in Greenwich, Connecticut, made the first seizure under the new law, raising a house and taking 11 guns—six handguns, two rifles, a shotgun, an assault rifle, and a submachine gun—from a 45-year-old man. The man, Thompson Bosee, told the *Hartford Courant* newspaper that he would challenge the seizure and the law's constitutionality.

Part of controlling where guns go is controlling the people who sell them. Massachusetts recently enacted a law that requires gun dealers to maintain their businesses in separate buildings from their homes—no longer allowing "kitchen table" gun sales.

Possible Solutions

It seems unlikely that the United States will ever ban firearms. However, there are measures that both gun supporters and gun detractors do agree on that may help cut down on gun violence.

- ❖ *Trigger locks*: Trigger locks are small, inexpensive devices that fit over a gun's trigger and make it impossible to fire. As the *St. Louis Post-Dispatch* reported, "Mandating locking devices for each firearm owned is a logical first step in controlling guns by limiting who has access to firing them."
- ❖ *Education*: Just as people aren't allowed on the road until they have been taught to drive a car, so people should not be allowed

to own a gun until they successfully complete a gun education course, say supporters. Besides courses that teach adults the rules of handling and storing guns, so too are there courses that teach children that guns are not toys. Gun education programs are taught by such diverse groups as the National Rifle Association and the Boy Scouts of America, and more than 10 million children have completed the NRA's Eddie Eagle safety course. By teaching kids a healthy respect for guns and the damage they can do, perhaps the number of accidental shootings that claim so many young lives can be reduced.

❖ *Background checks*: The Brady bill, the national gun-control legislation named for James Brady, the presidential assistant wounded in the attack on President Reagan, requires instant background checks on all purchasers. To date, this system has prevented more than 200,000 gun purchases by people who had been in mental institutions, been dishonorably discharged from military service, were fugitives, or had a history of domestic abuse.

The main drawback to this system is that all police records are not yet available in a nationwide database, making it possible that someone will fall through the cracks. It also does not cover the "secondary" market of private sales at gun shows and flea markets, where guns can be bought without a mandatory waiting period or a background check.

Legislation controlling guns bought by legitimate people—hunters or enthusiasts—does not reach such private-deal gun sales. Nor does it control stolen guns, or guns purchased by licensed owners for resale to anyone—including criminals. How can this aspect of the gun issue be dealt with? Some have suggested that tougher enforcement of existing weapons laws is needed. For example, it is illegal to possess drugs and a weapon. For years, authorities did not enforce this law. But Richmond, Virginia, started using these laws to crack down of people apt to be involved in criminal acts. The apparent result has been that the homicide rate fell by nearly a third; 215 violators are in jail, and 512 guns have been seized.

Technology may be able to help, too. Scientists are working on developing a so-called "smart gun." This gun would be able to be fired only by its owner. Two means of recognition are currently being tested. One method uses biometric technology to recognize the fingerprints of the authorized user. The gun would recognize the fingerprints of the person holding it, and if the prints did not match the ones in its memory, it would not go off. The other uses a device called a radio transponder that allows the gun to be fired only within a given distance of the device; if a criminal should wrest a police officer's gun away and try to fire it, the smart gun would not go off because it was too far from the device. A prototype model had the radio transponder in a wristband; plans are to make it small enough to be worn as a ring. Research on smart guns began in the early 1990s, and the weapons may be available in 2001.

For the time being, however, it looks as if the debates over gun control will continue. America may never become an unarmed nation, but with stronger enforcement of criminal laws, education of new gun owners, and responsible care and storage of their weapons by gun owners, perhaps the current death toll of almost 100 Americans a day will one day fall.

Costs on Society

Exposure to gun violence at home, at school, in the community, or through the media all can cause harm.

Economic Costs

The most obvious economic costs associated with gun violence in the general population are health-related, in the form of increased medical costs due to injury and death. Other economic costs include those associated with strengthening law enforcement to combat gun crime, and prosecuting and incarcerating gun offenders. Other, less tangible costs related to gun violence—such as higher taxes to ensure public safety, higher housing costs as families move to areas that are perceived as safe from gun violence, and the psychological costs associated with fear—make up most of the costs of gun violence. Such costs affect not only the families of gun violence victims, but all Americans, through increased taxes, decreased property values, limits on choices about where to live and work, and concerns about safety, particularly children's safety. A 1998 national survey that asked people about their willingness to pay for policy interventions to reduce gun violence found that the average American household was willing to pay $239 a year to reduce the threat of gun violence in its state by 30 per cent.

Psychological Costs

Just as the economic costs of gun violence are substantial, so are the psychological costs. Children exposed to gun violence, whether they are victims, perpetrators, or witnesses, can experience negative psychological effects over the short and long terms. Psychological trauma also is common among children who are exposed to high levels of violence in their communities or through the media. Common effects associated with exposure to gun violence, including sleep disturbance, anger, withdrawal, posttraumatic stress, poor school performance, lower career aspirations, increased delinquency, risky sexual behaviors, substance abuse, and desensitization to violence. All of these effects can make children and youth more prone to violence.

Every child in the United States is exposed to gun violence through media coverage of shootings, films and television shows, and violent video games that allow young people to shoot lifelike targets on the screen. More than 1,000 studies have documented a link between violent media and aggressive behavior. Children exposed to media violence have been shown in experimental studies to become more aggressive, to view more favorably the use of aggression to resolve conflicts, to become desensitized to violence, and to develop a belief that the world around them is a frightening place.

However, the children and youth at highest risk for psychological trauma from gun violence are those exposed to it directly: children who are injured, who witness gun violence at close proximity, or who are exposed to high levels of gun violence in their homes, schools, or communities. School and community violence are particularly worrisome because they can affect large numbers of children at one time.

Despite widespread recognition of the psychological costs to children and youth associated with gun violence, physicians and mental health professionals have been slow to develop treatments that help young people cope with gun-related trauma. Even children and youth who are injured often go without psychological help. Government, schools, and health care practitioners should work together to ensure that children and youth who are exposed to gun violence get the psychological help they need.

Strategies: Reduction in Youth Gun Violence

Key strategies that may reduce youth gun violence include:

* Reducing unsupervised exposure to guns among children and youth;
* Rtrengthening social norms against violence in communities;
* Enforcing laws against youth gun carrying;
* altering the design of guns to make them less likely to be used by children and youth; and,

❖ Perhaps most importantly, implementing new legal and regulatory interventions that make it more difficult for youth to obtain guns.

Parents, community leaders, policymakers, and researchers all have vital roles to play in implementing these strategies.

Community Leaders

Community leaders should take steps to change this expectation. They can promote young people's safety by sending unequivocal messages to youth that gun violence is not an acceptable way to resolve conflict. Elected officials, faith leaders, and educators all can play key roles in enforcing social norms against youth gun use. Because many youth who carry guns report obtaining them from family members and friends, community leaders also should send messages to adults that it is dangerous—to youth and to the broader community—to allow young people unsupervised access to guns.

Youth as Agents for Change

Engaging youth themselves as agents for change in their neighborhoods also may be a promising strategy for reducing gun violence, and is being tried in some communities.

Strengthening Law Enforcement against Youth Gun Violence

Stronger enforcement of existing laws against youth gun carrying is another strategy to reduce gun violence. Beginning in the early 1990s, some police departments adopted an aggressive approach toward identifying and punishing youthful gun offenders. Supporters of this approach argue that punitive law enforcement against the criminal use of guns is an effective way to deter gun violence.

Community-based policing strategies, which emphasize close collaboration between police and citizens to prevent crime before it occurs, may reduce youth gun violence more effectively over the long term.

Changing the Design of Guns

Rather than focus on changing the behavior of parents and young people through education, community efforts, or law enforcement, some injury prevention experts suggest that it might be easier to reduce youth gun violence by changing the design of guns themselves.

Childproof

Requiring product safety features on guns, such as child safety grips (which make it difficult for young children to fire guns), magazine disconnect devices (which prevent guns from being fired when their magazines are detached, even if a round of ammunition remains in the gun), and loaded chamber indicators (which indicate whether guns are loaded), could reduce unintentional shootings among children and youth.

Emerging technologies would enable manufacturers to personalize guns, which could prevent unauthorized users such as teenagers or thieves from operating the weapons. Personalized guns, referred to as "smart" guns, hold promise for preventing intentional as well as unintentional shootings.

In USA Guns are not regulated for safety by the Consumer Product Safety Commission, ATF, or any other federal agency. The federal government requires that imported guns meet a few basic safety standards (which do not include child safety features), but Congress has exempted domestically manufactured guns from these standards.

Limiting the Flow of Illegal Guns to Youth

Youth can obtain guns from family or friends, from corrupt dealers or straw purchasers, through theft, or on the street from private sellers or illegal dealers. Because private sales of guns in the United States are largely unregulated, it is all too easy for guns—especially handguns—to flow illegally into the hands of young people, even though federal law prohibits most young people from owning or possessing them.

Youth can obtain guns illegally from licensed dealers or in private transactions. Although licensed firearms dealers are regulated by the federal government (and by many states) and are required to conduct criminal background checks on all purchasers, some dealers do sell illegally to youth, often by turning a blind eye to straw purchases, in which youth ask older acquaintances to buy guns for them. It appears that only a small minority of licensed gun dealers are involved in illegal activity.

Case History of Gun Control Advocates

Behind the heated arguments surrounding gun control are motivations rising from very personal experiences with guns. For example, Carolyn McCarthy became an activist for stricter gun control laws after tragedy forever altered her life. In 1994, a gunman shot at twenty-five people inside a crowded Long Island Rail Road commuter train, killing six people including McCarthy's husband and leaving her son partially paralyzed. Grief over the loss of her husband and the pain of struggling with her son in his recovery propelled her on a mission to prevent similarly devastating tragedies by curtailing the availability of assault weapons.

Others who have experienced tragedies emerge with very different attitudes toward guns. After suffering a violent attack by a rapist, Nancy Bittle founded Arming Women Against Rape and Endangerment, which advocates women's gun ownership as a form of self-protection. "I was raised to view guns as symbols of evil," says Bittle, "but now I look at them as tools—like fire extinguishers."

Gun lobby groups, such as the National Rifle Association, have claimed the stories of people like Bittle to build their case to protect gun ownership. Women especially have been recognized as a group whose safety could be ensured most effectively by responsible gun use.

Personal experiences have acted as motivations behind gun advocacy but the "evidence" needed to further the passage of pro-gun policies comes from statistics- based studies by criminologists and social scientists.

Research on Gun Control

A 1996 study by John R. Lott and David B. Mustard, presented in the *Journal of Legal Studies'* article, "Crime, Deterrence, and Right-to-Carry Concealed Handguns," provided the "proof" for which gun advocates had been waiting. According to Lott and Mustard's study, states that allowed citizens to carry concealed handguns showed a marked decline in violent crimes. Furthermore, concealed handguns did not result in more gun accidents but deterred potentially violent incidents and prevented future crimes.

While gun lobbyists embraced Lott and Mustard's study, others criticized it, pointing out that unreliable statistical methods ultimately invalidated the study's pro-gun evaluations and, therefore, should not be employed in making policy decisions. Franklin Zimrig and Gordon Hawkins, authors of a critical analysis, "Concealed Handguns: The Counterfeit Deterrent" in *Responsive Community* assert, "The benefits and costs of permits to carry are marginal to the tremendous costs we already pay for the high ownership and use of handguns in the United States."

Education is No Guarantee of Safety

43 per cent of households in USA that have children also have handguns in them 10 children are shot and killed every day 1 child will die every day from an accidental gun shot.

43 per cent of households have guns. Just think about that number for a moment. Let's say your young son has 10 friends that he regularly plays with. At least 4 of those friends live in a house with a gun. Some may say that it does not sound like a large number; after all, just because there is a gun there does not mean that the child knows where it is right? WRONG.

The ABC network conducted an experiment a couple of years ago. They went to a child care centre, and put the kids through a gun safety talk. Then, a couple of days later, they hid a couple of guns in the centre, all totally disabled of course. These kids, aged 4 to 8 years, found the guns easily enough, and then proceeded to do all things imaginable with them; looking down the barrel, waving them around the room, pointing them at their friends, getting involved in the old "cops and robbers" games. There was even one kid who said to his friend with the gun, "shoot me".

Some of these kids were not well educated in guns, that are true, but some of them have parents who would swear black and blue that their child would never, EVER touch a gun, let alone play with it. Yet one of those well educated kids found the gun and said "Ohh, a gun. I'm not allowed to touch guns". He then picked the gun up and waved it around the room proclaiming "I'm touching a gun, I'm touching a gun". The boys mother was absolutely horrified when she saw the footage. Education is no guarantee of safety.

The debate in USA is on the constitutionality of gun control, the effectiveness of gun ownership, and measures to reduce gun violence.

4

Violence

Meaning of Violence

There is a tendency, at present, towards viewing aggression, bullying and violence as being synonymous. While few will disagree that bullying and violence are sub-sets of aggressive behavior, disagreements are encountered, especially in respect of what constitutes bullying and violence.

The Concise Oxford Dictionary defines violence as unlawful exercise of physical force; Olweus (1999), also confines violence to the use of physical force. He defines violence/violent behavior as aggressive behavior where the actor or perpetrator uses his or her own body as an object (including a weapon) to inflict (relatively serious) injury or discomfort upon an individual. With such a definition there is an overlap between violence and bullying, where bullying is carried out by physical aggression.

However, violence has been defined in a broader sense to include behavior by people or against people liable to cause physical or psychological harm (Gulbenkian Foundation, 1995).

Aggression and Its Development

What is Aggression?

❖ Aggression is hurting others on purpose. The problem is deciding when this is the case—sometimes it is hard to know whether a child intended to cause harm.
❖ Hostile aggression is the impulsive, angry form.
❖ Instrumental aggression is calculated and has a goal.

Developmental Trends and Changes in Aggression

❖ Aggression decreases during first few years, and then increases (Holmberg, 1980; *see* PIP p.572).

❖ This is noted particularly in boys (Cairns, 1986; *see* PIP p. 572).

Changes in Expression / Type

❖ Aggression becomes more verbal than physical as children get older (Schaffer, 1996; *see* PIP p. 572).
❖ There is a decrease in instrumental aggression from 4 to 7 years, but anger-based aggression remains the same (Hart-up, 1974; *see* PIP p. 572).

Stability

❖ However, many children show reasonable stability in their levels of aggression. If they were aggressive at 8 years, they are also aggressive at 18 (Eron, 1987; *see* PIP p. 572) and they are more likely to show criminal behavior/domestic violence by 30.

Risk Factors

❖ Patterson *et al.* (1989; *see* PIP p. 572) found that a lack of parental discipline led to behavior problems, which led to academic failure, which led to identification with deviant group.
❖ Farrington (1995; *see* PIP p. 573) found there were seven factors involved in delinquency:

1. Hyperactivity
2. Poor concentration
3. Low intelligence and school performance
4. Family poverty
5. Poor parenting
6. Family criminality
7. Trouble at school.

Cultural Cariations

Research Evidence

❖ Chen *et al.* (1998b; *see* PIP p. 580) found there were similar amounts of misconduct in American and Chinese 13/14-year-olds but that Americans are more influenced by their peers.
❖ Feldman et al. (1991; *see* PIP p. 580) found there was less misconduct in Chinese than Australian and American adolescents (they studied older adolescents than Chen's group).

❖ Genta *et al.* (1996; *see* PIP p. 580) found there was more bullying in Italy than in Norway, Japan, Spain, and England.

In conclusion, there are developmental changes and cultural differences demonstrated; some factors identified.

Influences on Aggression

Media and Video Games

Basic idea:

❖ Watching violent TV/playing violent video games makes children more aggressive.

Research Evidence

❖ Eron (1987; *see* PIP p.573) conducted a longitudinal study showing that violence watched by 8-year-olds predicted aggression at 18 (but also depended on aggression at 8).

❖ Anderson et al. (2001; *see* PIP p.574) conducted a longitudinal study showing that violence watched by 5-year-olds predicted adolescent aggression in girls.

❖ Leyens *et al.* (1975; *see* PIP p.574) showed that delinquents exposed to violent films showed increased aggression.

❖ However, Charlton (1998; *see* PIP p. 574) carried out a study in St Helena, which found that the introduction of TV had no adverse effects on children.

❖ Hennigan *et al.* (1982; *see* PIP p. 574) found no differences in crime rates in US states with/without TV from 1949 to 1952.

❖ Comstock and Paik (1991; *see* PIP p. 575) reviewed more than 1000 findings and found that there were strong effects short term, but minor effects long term.

❖ Griffiths (2000; *see* PIP p. 575) found that violent video games have small effects on older children, but larger effects on younger children.

Influential Factors

Research Evidence

❖ Comstock and Paik (1991; *see* PIP p. 575) found that five factors were influential:

Factor	Description
Instrumentality	Presenting violent behavior as a way of getting what you want
Similarity	Of actor to viewer
	Realism More realistic, greater effects
Suffering	The less obvious this is, the greater the effects
Emotional arousal	Greater arousal produces more effects

❖ Josephson (1987; *see* PIP p.575) noted the importance of *cognitive priming* (presenting cues associated with violence). The walkie-talkie study confirms this.

❖ Wiegman and van Schie (1998; *see* PIP p.575) studied Dutch children and found that those that preferred aggressive video games were more aggressive. This indicates a reduced emotional responsiveness—being used to seeing violence makes it more likely to occur.

Evaluation

❖ The effects are mostly weak. They may be caused by observational learning and cognitive priming, and affect those already predisposed. Those already aggressive may choose to watch violence.

Theories

Social Learning Theory

Basic idea (Bandura, 1973;): Aggression is learnt through observation, imitation, and subsequent reinforcement.

Research Evidence

❖ Bandura *et al.* (1963;) in the Bobo doll study, found that children attacked the doll if the model did.

❖ Bandura (1965 ;) found there was less aggression if the model had been punished, but children still remembered the behavior.

❖ Huesmann *et al.* (1984;) found that aggression levels were similar in parents and children at the same ages.

❖ Eron *et al.* (1991;) found a similarity in aggressive behavior across three generations.

Evaluation

❖ Most research is supportive of the social learning theory.
❖ However, Bandura's work involved play-fighting rather than real aggression, and was based on a doll rather than a person. Children may have hit the doll because of the novelty of it bouncing back. This theory ignores the internal factors in aggression.

Biological Theory

Basic idea: There is a genetic predisposition to aggression and differences between the sexes due to testosterone.

Research Evidence

❖ Rhee and Waldman (2002) carried out a meta-analysis of 51 twin/ adoption studies which showed that 41% of variance in anti-social behavior was due to genetic factors.
❖ Eley *et al.* (1999; *see* PIP p. 577) conducted a twin study that showed aggressive anti-social behavior was influenced more by genetic factors than non-aggressive anti-social behavior.
❖ Miles and Carey (1997)—conclusions are not confirmed when observational ratings are used to measure aggression in children.
❖ Eagly and Steffen (1986) carried out a meta-analysis, which showed only a small tendency for males to be more aggressive, mainly in physical aggression.
❖ Tieger (1980) found few sex differences in aggression below the age of 5 years.
❖ Bjorkqvist *et al.* (1992) found that males show more physical aggression, females more indirect (e.g., gossip).
❖ Olweus (1985) found a correlation between high aggression and high testosterone in adolescent boys.
❖ Condry and Ross (1985) found that adults are more tolerant of aggression in boys.

Evaluation

❖ Genetic factors have an important role and testosterone is possibly implicated.

❖   However, the small sex differences observed may be learnt, rather than innate.

Family Dynamics

Basic idea: Patterson (1982) suggested that a coercive family cycle (where matching or topping aggression is shown) may lead to increases in aggression.

Research Evidence

❖   Eron and Huesmann (1984) found that aggressive children are often physically punished.
❖   O'Connor *et al.* (1998) found that adopted children of anti-social parents received more negative control (hostility) from adoptive parents than others did, so an aggressive child may produce aggression in parents.
❖   Patterson *et al.* (1989) carried out observational studies, which showed escalation of anger and lack of affection/encouragement in parents.

Evaluation

❖   Focusing on family dynamics has proved useful.
❖   However, how cycles develop is unclear. Genetic factors may be of importance in explaining aggression in families.

Bullying as a Behavior

Basic criteria of bullying:

❖   Includes verbal, psychological and physical aggression.
❖   That the behavior is repeated over time.
❖   That there is an imbalance of power between victim and bully.
❖   That the behavior is intentional.

Violence is aggressive behavior that may be physically, sexually or emotionally abusive. The aggressive behavior is conducted by an individual or group against another, or others. Physically abusive behavior, is where a child, adolescent or group directly or indirectly ill treats, injures, or kills another or others. The aggressive behavior can involve pushing, shoving, and shaking, punching, kicking, squeezing, burning or any other form of physical assault on a person or on property. Emotionally abusive behavior is where there are verbal attacks, threats, taunts, slugging, mocking, yelling, exclusion, and malicious rumors. Sexually abusive behavior is where there is sexual assault or rape.

TV—Good Guy Verses Bad Guy

To give you perspective on just how much violence kids *see* on TV, consider this: The average American child will witness 200,000 violent acts on television by age 18. TV violence sometimes begs for imitation because violence is often demonstrated and promoted as a fun and effective way to get what you want.

Many violent acts are perpetrated by the "good guys," whom children have been taught to emulate. Even though children are taught by their parents that it's not right to hit, television says it's OK to bite, hit, or kick if you're the good guy. And even the "bad guys" on TV aren't always held responsible or punished for their actions.

The images children absorb can also leave them traumatized and vulnerable. Children ages 2 to 7 are particularly frightened by scary-looking things like grotesque monsters. Simply telling children that those images aren't real won't console them, because they can't yet distinguish between fantasy and reality. Kids ages 8 to 12 are frightened by the threat of violence, natural disasters, and the victimization of children, whether those images appear on fictional shows, the news, or reality-based shows. Reasoning with children this age will help them, so it's important to provide reassuring and honest information to help ease your child's fears. However, you may want to avoid letting your child view programs that he or she may find frightening.

The word "society" comes from the French société, which is based on the Latin words, "societas," meaning "a friendly association with others, and "socius," meaning "associate or companion.

Organization of Society

Within the discipline of social sciences, the term "society" refers to a group of people who together make up a semi-closed social system, meaning that most interactions occur among people within the group. Some sociologists consider any interdependent community to be society. Others argue that there's a difference between a community and a society because society includes social structure with roles and ranks, where a community can be made up of equals.

Societies also form and regulate in accordance with their food sources, available shelter and modes of safety. There are nomadic (pastoral) societies, who move according to where food is available, hunter-gatherer societies, which hunt and gather food to bring back home, horticulturist, farming and larger agricultural societies, all of which rely on planting and cultivating. The largest of these are referred to as civilizations. Societies also serve to keep individuals safe, and to help them in times of crisis. Traditionally, when a member of society needed aid, while giving birth, when injured or sick, after a family death, or a disaster, other members of the community would step in to help, rally the help of others and render aid, be it physical, symbolic, mental, linguistic, financial, emotional, religious, spiritual or medical. But societies are not always all love and helpfulness. They can also outcast and scapegoat some of their members, either fairly or unfairly. Societies often have ranks and classes. In some cases these are more pronounced than in others. Some grant public assistance to the underlings, and prestige, honor and special privilege on those they admire and recognize as particular contributors to the society, whether it be in the form of politics, military battle, finances, knowledge, entertainment, or some other value to the society. Some societies are organized largely around a political structure. In order to remain organized, orderly, powerful and well protected, and to grow, they have bands, tribes, chiefs, and a hierarchy of political positions with checks and balances. Such societies, when competing with societies at their same level of technological and cultural advancement, are more likely to be the surviving society should battles over geography and other societal elements arise.

Culture

Culture is the totality of learned and socially transmitted behavior from one generation to the next. It includes symbols, signs and language, besides religion, rituals, beliefs and artifacts. In fact, culture is a guiding force in everyday life. It is the culture that distinguishes one society from the other. Elements of one culture may migrate to another culture, but they get properly assimilated in the receiving culture, and are at times given a different meaning or role. In that sense, each society has a culture that is historically derived and passed on from one generation to another and constantly enriched by those who live it.

Social Structure

Social structure refers to the pattern of interrelations between individuals. Every society has a social structure, a complex of major institutions, groups, and arrangements, relating to status and power. It is said that the study of social structure is comparable to the study of human anatomy and that of social organization to that of physiology. But this is only a partial and not a complete analogy.

Social Institutions

A social institution is a procedure, practice and an instrument; hence an ensemble of a variety of customs and habits accumulated over a period of time. According to Malnowskiwork in every society, people create social institutions to meet their basic needs of survival. Institutions are instruments and tools of human transactions. An institution is, thus, a stable cluster of norms, values and roles.

Anomie

ANOMIE is a state of normlessness in society According to Durkheim. The loss of direction felt in a society when social control of individual behavior has become ineffective.

The Study of Deviant Behavior

Sociology divides deviance into two distinct categories:

❖ Informal deviance, and
❖ Formal deviance.

Informal Deviance

Informal deviance refers to the fact that an individual (or group of individuals) may be slightly non-conformist to the general trend of society; however, his/her/their behaviour does not constitute an illegal act. Informal deviants are people/groups of people therefore whose behaviour might raise an eyebrow but will not encourage a person to call the police. Informal deviants are people who are simply "different" for some reason or another. In effect, it is fair to say that we are all informally deviant to some degree or another. In Sociology, there is a fascination with young people because of their informally deviant tendencies—particularly when looking at youth subcultures.

A subculture: A group of people in society whose behaviour (and sometimes style of dress) is significantly different from wider society—so much so that they have a unique culture (away of life). However, because they still exist within our society they are called sub cultures.

Formal Deviance

Formal deviance, quite simply, describes an act committed by a person or group of persons that contravenes (goes against) the established laws of society. A formal deviant is therefore a criminal.

Hagan (1984), a Canadian Criminologist, outlined how society constructs our notion of deviance. He argued that society tends to use three measures of seriousness when judging the degree of deviance of an act.

These are:

❖ The degree of agreement about the wrongfulness of the act—This may range from confusion/apathy to total agreement
❖ Severity of the social response elicited by the act; this can range from life imprisonment to polite avoidance,
❖ Societies evaluation of the harm elicited by the act; this looks at the degree of victimisation—the degree of personal and social harm.
❖ Deviant behavior refers to actions that transgress commonly held norms. What is regarded as deviant can shift from time to time and place to place; "normal" behavior in one cultural setting may be labeled "deviant" in another.

Sanctions, formal or informal, are applied by society to reinforce social norms. Laws are norms defined and enforced by governments; *crimes* are acts that are not permitted by those laws.

Biological and psychological theories have been developed claiming that crime and other forms of deviance are genetically determined. They see crime as caused by factors outside the individual's control. For the most part, these have been largely discredited.

Conformity, Deviance and Crime

Society and Crime: Sociological Theories

Sociologists argue that conformity and deviance intertwine in different social contexts. Divergences of wealth and power in society strongly influence opportunities open to different groups of individuals and determine what kinds of activities are regarded as criminal. Criminal activities are learned in much the same way as are law-abiding ones and in general are directed toward the same needs and values.

Functionalist theories see crime and deviance as produced by structural tensions and a lack of moral regulation within society. Durkheim introduced the term *anomie* to refer to a feeling of anxiety and disorientation that comes with the breakdown of traditional life in modern society. Robert Merton extended the concept to include the strain felt by individuals whenever norms conflict with social reality. Sub cultural explanations draw attention to groups, such as gangs, that reject mainstream values and replace them with norms celebrating defiance, delinquency, or nonconformity.

Interactionist theories focus on deviance as a socially constructed phenomenon. Sutherland linked crime to differential association, the concept that individuals become delinquent through associating with people who are carriers of criminal norms. *Labeling theory*, a strain of interactionist theory that assumes that labeling someone as deviant will reinforce their deviant behavior, is important because it starts from the assumption that no act is intrinsically criminal (or normal). Labeling theorists are interested in how some behaviors come to be defined as deviant and why certain groups, but not others, are labeled as deviant.

Conflict theories analyze crime and deviance in terms of the structure of society, competing interests between social groups, and the preservation of power among elites.

Control theories posit that crime occurs when there are inadequate social or physical controls to deter it from happening. The growth of crime is linked to the growing number of opportunities and targets for crime in modern societies. The theory of broken windows suggests that there is a direct connection between the appearance of disorder and actual crime.

Victims and Perpetrators of Crime

The likelihood of someone being a victim of crime is linked to where they live; people in poor inner-city neighborhoods face a greater risk than do residents in affluent suburban areas.

Rates of criminality are much lower for women than for men, probably because of general socialization differences between men and women, and the greater involvement of men in non-domestic spheres. Unemployment and the "crisis of masculinity" have been linked to male crime rates.

Popular fear about crime often focuses on street crimes—such as theft, burglary, and assault—that are largely the domain of young, working-class males. Official statistics reveal high rates of offense among young people, yet we should be wary of moral panics about youth crime. Much deviant behavior among youth, such as antisocial behavior and nonconformity, is not in fact criminal.

White-collar crime and corporate crime refer to crimes carried out by those in the more affluent sectors of society. The consequences of such crime can be farther-reaching than the petty crimes of the poor, but there is less attention paid to them by law enforcement.

Organized crime refers to institutionalized forms of criminal activity, in which many of the characteristics of orthodox organizations appear but the activities engaged in are systematically illegal.

Deviance

In everyday language to deviate means to stray from an accepted path; many sociological definitions of deviance simply elaborate upon this idea. Thus deviance consists of those areas which do not follow the norms and expectations of a particular social group. Deviance may be:

- ❖ Positively sanctioned (rewarded),
- ❖ Negatively sanctioned (punished), or
- ❖ Simply accepted without reward or punishment.

In terms of the above definition of deviance, the soldier on the battlefield who risks his life above and beyond the normal call of duty may be termed deviant, as the physicist who breaks the rules of his discipline and develops a new theory. Their deviance may be positively sanctioned; the soldier might be rewarded with a medal, the physicist with a Noble prize. In one sense, though, neither is deviant since both conform to the values of society, the soldier to the value of courage; the physicist to the value of academic progress. By comparison, a murderer deviates not only from society's norms and expectations but also from its values, in particular the value placed on human life. His deviance generally results in widespread disapproval and punishment. A third form of deviance consists of acts which depart from the norms and expectations of a particular society but are generally tolerated and accepted. The little old lady with a house full of cats or the old gentleman with an obsession for collecting clocks would fall into this category. Usually their eccentricities are neither rewarded nor punished by others. They are simply defined as a 'bit odd' but harmless, and therefore tolerated.

Collective Sentiments

Deviance is relative. This means that there is no absolute way of defining a deviant act. Deviance can only be defined in relation to a particular standard, but no standards are fixed or absolute. As such deviance varies from time to time and place to place. In a particular society an act which is considered deviant today may be defined as normal in the future. An act defined as deviant in one society may be seen as perfectly normal in another. Put another way, deviance is culturally determined and cultures change over time and vary from society to society. The following examples will serve to illustrate the above points. Sometimes ago in Western society it had been considered deviant for women to smoke, use make-up and consume alcoholic drinks in public. Today this is no longer the case. In the same way, definitions of crime change over time. Homosexuality was formerly a criminal offence in Britain. Since 1969, however, homosexual acts conducted between consenting adults in private are no longer illegal. A comparison of modern Western culture with the traditional culture of the Teton Sioux Indians of the USA illustrates how deviance varies from society to society. As part of their religions rituals during the annual Sun Dance Ceremony Sioux Warriors mutilated their bodies, leather thongs were inserted through strips of flesh on the chest and attached to a central pole, and warriors had to break free by tearing their flesh and in return they were granted favors by the supernatural powers. Similar actions by members of Western society may well be viewed as masochism or madness. In the same way behaviour accepted as normal in Western society may be defined as deviant within primitive society. In the West the private ownership of property is an established norm; members of society strive to accumulate wealth and substantial property holding brings power and prestige. Such behaviour would have incurred strong disapproval amongst the Sioux and those who acted in terms of the above norms would be regarded as deviant. Generosity was a major value of Sioux culture and the distributed rather than accumulation of wealth was the route to power and prestige. Chiefs were expected to distribute gifts of horses, beadwork and weapons to their followers. The norms of Sioux culture prevented the accumulation of Wealth. The Sioux had no conception of the individual ownership of land; the produce of the hunt was automatically shared by all members of the group. Emile Durkheim developed his view on deviance in his discussion of crime in The Rules of Sociological Method. He argues that crime is an inevitable and normal aspect of social life; it is an integral part of all healthy societies. It is inevitable because not every member of society can be equally committed to the 'collective sentiments, the shared values and beliefs of society. Since individuals are exposed to different influences and circumstances, it is impossible for all to be alike. Therefore, not everybody shares the same restraints about breaking the law.

Yesterday's Deviance must Become Today's Normality

Crime is not only inevitable, it can also be functional. Durkheim argues that it only becomes dysfunctional when its rate is unusually high. He argues that all social change begins with some form of deviance. In order for change to occur, Yesterday's deviance must become today's normality. Since a certain amount of change is healthy for society, so it can progress rather than stagnate. So for change to occur, the collective sentiments must not be too strong, or too hostile. In fact, they must have only moderate energy' because if they were to strong they would crush all originality both of the criminal and of the genius. Thus the collective sentiments must not be sufficiently powerful to block the expression of people like Jesus, William Wilberforce, Martin Luther King and Mother Teresa. Durkheim regarded some crime as and anticipation of the morality of the future. Thus heretics who were denounced by both the state and the established church may represent the collective sentiments of the future. In the same way terrorists of freedom fighters may represent a future established order. If crime is inevitable, what is the function of punishment. Durkheim argues that its function is not to remove crime in society. Rather it is to maintain the collective sentiments at their necessary level of strength. In Durkheim's words, punishment 'serves to heal the wounds done to the collective sentiments'. Without punishment the collective sentiments would lose their force to control behaviour and the crime rate would reach the point where it becomes dysfunctional. Thus in Durkheim's view, a healthy society requires both crime and punishment, both are inevitable, both are functional.

Following Durkheim, Merton argues that deviance results not from pathological personalities but from the culture and structure of society itself. He begins from the standard functionalist position of value consensus, that is, all members of society share the same values. However, since members of society are placed in different positions in the social structure, for example, they differ in terms of class position; they do not have the same opportunity of realizing the shared value. This situation can generate deviance. According to Merton's the social and cultural structure generates pressure for socially deviant behavior upon people variously located in that structure.

Normlessness or 'Anomie'

Using USA as an example, Merton outlines his theory as follows. Members of American Society share the major values of American culture. In particular they share the goal of success for which they all strive and which is largely measured in terms of wealth and material possessions. The 'American Dream' states that all members of society have an equal opportunity of achieving success, of owning a Cadillac, a Beverley Hills mansion and a substantial bank balance. In all societies there are institutionalized means of reaching culturally defined goals. In America the accepted ways of achieving success are through educational qualifications, talent, hard work, drive, determination and ambition. In a balanced society an equal emphasis is placed upon both cultural goals and institutionalized means, and members are satisfied with both. But in America great importance is attached to success and relatively less importance is given to the accepted ways of achieving success. As such, American society is unstable, unbalanced. There is a tendency to reject the 'rules of the game' and to strive for success by all available means. The situation becomes like a game of cards in which winning becomes so important that the rules are abandoned by some of the players; When rules cease to operate a situation of normlessness or 'anomie' results. In this situation of anything norms no longer direct behavior and deviance is encouraged. However, individuals will respond to a situation of anomie in different ways. In particular, their reaction will be shaped by their position in the social structure. Merton outlines five possible ways in which members of American society can respond to success goals. The first and most common response is conformity. Members of society conform both to success goals and the normative means of reaching them. A second response is 'innovation'. This response rejects normative means of achieving success and turns to deviant means, crime in particular. Merton argues that members of the lower social strata are most likely to select this route to success.

Merton uses the term 'ritualism' to describe the third possible response. Those who select this alternative are deviant because they have largely abandoned the commonly held success goals. The pressure to adopt this alternative is greatest on members of the lower middle class. Their occupations provide less opportunity for success than those of other members of the middle class. However, compared o members of the working class, they have been strongly socialized to conform to social norms. This prevents them from turning to crime. Unable to innovate and with jobs that offer little opportunity for advancement, their only solution is to scale down or abandon their success goals. Merton terms the fourth and least common response, 'retreatism'. It applies to psychotics, artists, pariahs, drug addicts. They have strongly internalized both the cultural goals and the institutionalized means but is unable to achieve success. They resolve the conflict of their situation by abandoning both the goals and the means of reaching them. They are unable to cope with challenges and drop out of society defeated and resigned to their failure. They are deviant in two ways: they have rejected both the cultural goals and the institutionalized means. Merton does not relate retreatism to social class position. Rebellion forms the fifth and final response. It is a rejection of both the success goals and the institutionalized means and their replacement by different goals and means. Those who adopt this alternative want to create a new society. Thus urban guerillas in Western European capitalist societies adopt deviant means- terrorism- to reach deviant goals such as a communist society. Merton argues that it is typically members of a rising class rather than the most depressed strata who organize the resentful and rebellious into a revolutionary group.

To summarize, Merton claims that his analysis shows how the culture and structure of society generates deviance.

Crime Reduction Strategies

Prisons have developed partly to protect society and partly with the intention of reforming the criminal. Prisons do not seem to deter crime, and the degree to which they rehabilitate prisoners to face the outside world without relapsing into criminality is dubious.

Only a fraction of what modern police forces do involves controlling crime. Today, police officers spend much of their time detecting and managing risk; in particular, policing is about communicating knowledge about risk to other institutions in society that demand that information.

Alternatives to prison, such as community policing and community-based punishment, have been suggested.

School Violence

School violence is a serious problem, especially in public schools. Improving the quality of American education is difficult without also addressing school violence, since regardless of how good the teachers or curriculum are, violence makes it difficult for students to learn.

School violence wears many faces. It includes gang activity, locker thefts, bullying and intimidation, gun use, assault—just about anything that produces a victim. Violence is perpetrated against students, teachers, and staff, and ranges from intentional vendettas to accidental killings of bystanders.

"school violence," is a broad term, which includes, but is not limited to, assault (with or without weapons), threats of force, bomb threats, sexual assault, bullying or intimidation, arson, extortion, theft, hazing, and gang activity.

Copy Cat Effects

Unfortunately, it is possible that there will be copy cat effects. There will be false threats and pranks, expressions of anger, and perhaps, even an actual attempt at violence. Most of the copycats are false threats, but we have to take them seriously because one of them might be real. This creates a tremendous dilemma for school authorities and communities in general.

School violence is a subset of youth violence, a broader public health problem. Youth violence refers to harmful behaviors that may start early and continue into young adulthood. It includes

❖ bullying,
❖ slapping,
❖ punching,
❖ weapon use, and
❖ rape.

Victims can suffer serious injury, significant social and emotional damage, or even death. The young person can be a victim, an offender, or a witness to the violence-or a combination of these.

Reasons for Violence

What causes someone to punch, kick, stab or fire a gun at someone else or even him/herself? There is never a simple answer to that question. But people often commit violence because of one or more of the following:

❖ *Expression*: Some people use violence to release feelings of anger or frustration. They think there are no answers to their problems and turn to violence to express their out of control emotions.
❖ *Manipulation*: Violence is used as a way to control others or get something they want.
❖ *Retaliation*: Violence is used to retaliate against those who have hurt them or someone they care about.
❖ *Violence is a Learned Behavior*: Like all learned behaviors, it can be changed. This isn't easy, though. Since there is no single

cause of violence, there is no one simple solution. The best you can do is learn to recognize the warning signs of violence and to get help when you see them in your friends or yourself.

Factors that contribute to violent behavior include:

❖   peer pressure,
❖   need for attention or respect,
❖   feelings of low self-worth,
❖   early childhood abuse or neglect,
❖   witnessing violence at home, in the community or in the media
❖   easy access to weapons, and
❖   poverty, discrimination, and violence are often linked.

Gun violence in America crosses the demographic lines of age, race, ethnicity, religion, gender, and class. Gun violence corrodes the fabric of communities, traumatizing victims, witnesses, families, communities, and even our Nation. To understand and respond effectively to violence in society, a country must build on many disciplines, including the victim assistance and criminal justice fields, health care, social services, education, and the clergy. While we typically think of gun violence victims as victims of homicide, we must remember that there are many more victims who survive their injuries, often with long-term physical and psychological disabilities. Addressing the needs of secondary victims, including children and adults who witness violence, is another challenge for practitioners. Secondary victims also include those who are touched by or witness gun violence in their homes, schools, or workplaces or on the street.

Bullying

However, less than a month later another incident of schoolboy shooting hit the media. This time in Satna district of Madhya Pradesh, where a boy was shot dead by fellow students, aged 15 and 13 years, of a village school.

Having a fight in school is not new; a lot of students get bullied at some point of time in the premises. And, this phenomenon occurs frequently anywhere between the sixth and eighth standard students. Boys indulge more in bullying than girls. This kind of occurrence is widespread in American schools, such as the Virginia Tech massacre. But a murder in an Indian school due to bullying is probably the first of its kind.

Bullying can occur in any settings, where human beings interact with each other. And, schools are notoriously famous for it. However, a lot depends on the kind of bullying that takes place. When it is done in a playful and friendly way, it is not hurtful and both the bully and the bullied end up finding the incident funny.

But, when bullying becomes intentionally physically hurting, verbally abusive, psychologically excruciating and nerve-racking, it becomes unbearable. Mocking, threatening, extorting, ridiculing on appearance or lack of talent becomes constant, it leaves a deep emotional scar in the mind of the victim.

The reason for the killing in the Euro International School, Gurgaon, Haryana, is reported to be bullying by the deceased. For the two boys, taking revenge became unavoidable and an easy access to a gun precipitated matters. On December 12th evening, 14-year-old Abhishek Tyagi was shot dead by two gun-totting classmates in the middle of the school corridor. The boy was shot five times from close range on his forehead, chest and shoulder and was declared dead at a hospital. One of the boys had brought his father's licensed pistol and the two culprits took turns to shoot Abhishek! Today's children, less involved in physical activities, are constantly viewing negative news and violence being featured on television regularly. Thus, perhaps becoming prone to abuse and violence in their childhood. Those who bully have personalities that are authoritarian with an urge to control or dominate others. And envy and resentment are known motives for bullying. For observant parents, it is not very difficult to figure out signs of bullying. Children on their own are often hesitant to tell their parents about the harassment faced. They would tend to worry that their parents would be affected. However, visible signs of the child becoming a victim of bullying could be all there—such as bruises or injuries on the child's body, torn uniforms, missing school, avoiding the school bus and increasing demand for more pocket money.

Besides, if a child is acting in a different way or appears seemingly anxious, moodier, easily upset, or not eating enough or not sleeping well, or not doing things he enjoyed doing, it could well be because of a getting bullied in school. Can bullying hurt so much that its victims are driven to take a gun in hand and shoot the bully at point blank many times besides taking turns too? Strangely, the killers (victims of bullying) feel no remorse. According to reports available, the deceased had threatened to kill the two boys and this probably was the last straw to break the camel's back.

If a scrappy child's aggressive behavior is not curbed at the early stage the danger is that he or she may take it to adulthood and exhibit strange violent or socially unacceptable behavior. This is what 16-year-old Brenda Ann Spencer of Cleveland elementary school did. She did not like Mondays. Just to liven up the day, she opened fire with a .22 rifle and wounded 8 children and killed two adults. In yet another case, six-year-old Dedrick Owens of Mount Morris in Michigan has taken a.32 caliber pistol of his uncle to school and shot dead another six-year-old.

In a parallel case of Gurgaon school incident, two students were fatally shot by a 14-year-old student, claiming to be a victim of bullying, at the Raumanmeri Secondary School in Rauma, Finland. In another case, 15-year-old Brian Head of Cherokee County, Georgia, US, shot himself dead in his classroom. He too had been a target of bullies because of his overweight and thick glasses. Brian's father lobbied hard for the enactment of a law for criminalizing bullying that required schools to alert parents of bullied children.

Given the above scenario, it is time that our schools pay greater attention to reducing violence and aggression in their institutions. It should not be difficult for school authorities to identify bullies and devise ways to intervene and check them. They should be constantly watched and repeatedly advised that their behavior could land them into serious trouble. Increased parent-teacher supervision, making bullying a punishable offence in schools, providing protection to the bullied and counseling to the bullies will go a long way in preventing the spread of this menace.

However, never ever advise your child to bully back. It will cause more suffering and more violence. It is best to advise the child to avoid the bully by walking away from a problematic situation created by the latter, and to learn to ignore hurtful remarks. This is bound to get the desired result—the intimidator will in all probability lose interest and stop the harassment. And, perhaps we will be spared another Gurgaon incident—INFA

Researches Views on Bullying

A study conducted several years ago by the U.S. Centers for Disease Control and Prevention revealed that ten thousand children stay home from school at least one day every month because they fear bullies, and fifty per cent of the children surveyed said they were bullied once per week. In addition, sociological research reveals that bullying is the foremost problem in the minds of teenagers, while it is often regarded by many adults and students alike as a way of school life or rite of passage. Psychotherapists and parents of the bullied child, however, continue to bear witness to the damage that bullying has on its victims and on their relationships and emotional well-being in later life.

Regardless of the bullied child's "contribution," here are the psychological facts: Bullying on the playground, in the classroom, in the hallways, *anywhere*, has deleterious effects on the developing psyche of the victim. Children's' reactions to emotional or physical violence, in the form of harassment, intimidation, embarrassment, and fear can be seen through a spectrum of Post Traumatic Stress reactions and behaviors, including a hyper-vigilance to the recurrence of danger, inability to attach with intimacy, irritability, poor concentration, sleep disturbances, alterations in eating, academic difficulties, feelings of shame and hopelessness, fear of connection, malaise and depression.

Victims of school bullying may find themselves embroiled in lengthy and negative legal battles with school personnel, and they may become the focus of neighborhood gossip, both of which may unwittingly stimulate an already hostile and threatening school environment. In addition, the child's sense of self becomes defined more deeply by his status as "victim," a self-image that stays with him sometimes through the remainder of life.

The tragic events that occurred at Columbine High School, Virginia Tech University, and a growing number of other schools, have altered everyone's sense of security. Dealing with emotional violence is thus, for many parents and all school personnel today, a foremost priority.

Parents of the bullied child need to form alliances with other parents to take on the school system; they need to participate in positive activities that help build alliances and create safe places for their children; and they must help more students to develop moral leadership by reaching out to children who are "different" and emotionally vulnerable.

Only once we see ourselves and our children as potential victims of bullying can we begin the next part of the healing process—education, empathy, and action.

Kids are constantly picked on and pushed around for simply being different. The difference nowadays is that bullying is now in discreet forms. You can't recognize a bully right away as one of those big, tough guys shoving puny kids around and demanding lunch money. Bullies today are now disguised as the most popular girl, inviting everyone to her giant sweet sixteen except that one "loser" girl. Although many bullies are formed and brewed through problems at home, society is really what fuels bullying. According to the unwritten rules of society, the most popular girl in school does not and should not associate herself with the "lower orders". We should begin teaching kids at an early age that everyone is equal and that helping other people essentially helps you help yourself. There isn't one drastic fix that will cure bullying right away, but by gradually changing society and teaching kids more selfless values at a younger age, the bullying problem will eventually reach an end.

Bullying can have devastating effects on a child's self image and self esteem. However, unlike drugs and alcohol, in-school bullying can be prevented.

A Conditional Acceptance

Schools must have standards of behavior, and obviously hurtful behaviors will not be tolerated, but there is clearly a difference between standards of behavior intended to prevent chaos and violence, and standards intended to appropriate, control, and breed compliance. It is not enough to say what one parent of a Columbine athlete did with regard to Erik Harris and Dylan Klebold: "They had no school spirit and they wanted to be different. Anyone who shows any kind of school spirit, any pride in the school, they're accepted." Such a statement is indicative of a very constricted and insufficient type of acceptance—a conditional acceptance that rejects personal differences and freedom of choice regarding personal affiliation.

Dealing with Anger

It's normal to feel angry or frustrated when you've been let down or betrayed. But anger and frustration don't justify violent action. Anger is a strong emotion that can be difficult to keep in check, but the right response is always stay cool.

Here are some ways to deal with anger without resorting to violence:

❖ *Learn to Talk About Your Feelings*: If you're afraid to talk or if you can't find the right words to describe what you're going through, find a trusted friend or adult to help you one-on-one.
❖ *Express Yourself Calmly*: express criticism, disappointment, anger or displeasure without losing your temper or fighting. Ask yourself if your response is safe and reasonable.
❖ *Listen to Others*: listen carefully and respond without getting upset when someone gives you negative feedback. Ask yourself if you can really see the other person's point of view.
❖ *Negotiate*: work out your problems with someone else by looking at alternative solutions and compromises.

Anger is part of life, but you can free yourself from the cycle of violence by learning to talk about your feelings. *BE STRONG. BE SAFE. BE COOL.*

Anger management' programs are clearly intended to prevent violent retaliation on the part of angry kids, and do not target those who might have provoked the anger in the first place.

Are you at Risk for Violent Behavior?

If you recognize any of the warning signs for violent behavior in yourself, get help. You don't have to live with the guilt, sadness and frustration that comes from hurting others. Admitting you have a concern about hurting others is the first step. The second is to talk to a trusted adult such as a school counselor or psychologist, teacher, family member, friend or clergy. They can get you in touch with a licensed mental health professional who cares and can help.

Risk Factors

Research on youth violence has increased our understanding of factors that make some populations more vulnerable to victimization and perpetration. Many risk factors are the same, in part, because of the overlap among victims and perpetrators of violence.

Risk factors increase the likelihood that a young person will become violent. However, risk factors are not direct causes of youth violence; instead, risk factors contribute to youth violence (Mercy *et al.* 2002; DHHS 2001). Research associates the following risk factors with perpetration of youth violence (DHHS 2001; Lipsey and Derzon 1998; Resnick *et al.* 2004):

Individual Risk Factors

- ❖ History of violent victimization or involvement
- ❖ Attention deficits, hyperactivity, or learning disorders
- ❖ History of early aggressive behavior
- ❖ Involvement with drugs, alcohol, or tobacco
- ❖ Low IQ
- ❖ Poor behavioral control
- ❖ Deficits in social cognitive or information-processing abilities
- ❖ High emotional distress
- ❖ History of treatment for emotional problems
- ❖ Antisocial beliefs and attitudes
- ❖ Exposure to violence and conflict in the family

Family Risk Factors

- ❖ Authoritarian childrearing attitudes

- ❖ Harsh, lax, or inconsistent disciplinary practices
- ❖ Low parental involvement
- ❖ Low emotional attachment to parents or caregivers
- ❖ Low parental education and income
- ❖ Parental substance abuse or criminality
- ❖ Poor family functioning
- ❖ Poor monitoring and supervision of children

Peer/School Risk Factors

- ❖ Association with delinquent peers
- ❖ Involvement in gangs
- ❖ Social rejection by peers
- ❖ Lack of involvement in conventional activities
- ❖ Poor academic performance
- ❖ Low commitment to school and school failure

Community Risk Factors

- ❖ Diminished economic opportunities
- ❖ High concentrations of poor residents
- ❖ High level of transiency
- ❖ High level of family disruption
- ❖ Low levels of community participation
- ❖ Socially disorganized neighborhoods

Controlling Your Own Risk For Violent Behavior

Everyone feels anger in his or her own way. Start managing it by recognizing how anger feels to you.

When you are angry, you probably feel:

- ❖ muscle tension
- ❖ accelerated heartbeat
- ❖ a "knot" or "butterflies" in your stomach
- ❖ changes in your breathing
- ❖ trembling
- ❖ goose bumps
- ❖ flushed in the face

You can reduce the rush of adrenaline that's responsible for your heart beating faster, your voice sounding louder, and your fists clenching if you:

❖ Take a few slow, deep breaths and concentrate on your breathing.
❖ Imagine yourself at the beach, by a lake, or anywhere that makes you feel calm and peaceful.
❖ Try other thoughts or actions that have helped you relax in the past.

Keep telling yourself:

"Calm down."
"I don't need to prove myself."
"I'm not going to let him/her get to me."

Stop. Consider the consequences. Think before you act. Try to find positive or neutral explanations for what that person did that provoked you. Don't argue in front of other people. Make your goal to defeat the problem, not the other person. Learn to recognize what sets you off and how anger feels to you. Learn to think through the benefits of controlling your anger and the consequences of losing control. Most of all, stay cool and think. Only you have the power to control your own violent behavior, don't let anger control you.

Protective Factors

Protective factors buffer young people from risks of becoming violent. These factors exist at various levels. To date, protective factors have not been studied as extensively or rigorously as risk factors. However, identifying and understanding protective factors are equally as important as researching risk factors.

Most research is preliminary. Studies propose the following protective factors (DHHS 2001; Resnick et al. 2004):

Individual Protective Factors

❖ Intolerant attitude toward deviance
❖ High IQ or high grade point average
❖ Positive social orientation
❖ Religiosity

Family Protective Factors

❖ Connectedness to family or adults outside of the family
❖ Ability to discuss problems with parents
❖ Perceived parental expectations about school performance are high

❖   Frequent shared activities with parents

Consistent presence of parent during at least one of the following: when awakening, when arriving home from school, at evening mealtime, and when going to bed involvement in social activities.

Peer / School Protective Factors

❖   Commitment to school and
❖   Involvement in social activities.

Violence Against Self

Some people who have trouble dealing with their feelings don't react by lashing out at others. Instead, they direct violence toward themselves. The most final and devastating expression of this kind of violence is suicide.

Like people who are violent toward others, potential suicide victims often behave in recognizable ways before they try to end their lives. Suicide, like other forms of violence, is preventable. The two most important steps in prevention are recognizing warning signs and getting help. Warning signs of potential self-violence include:

❖   previous suicide attempts
❖   significant alcohol or drug use
❖   threatening or communicating thoughts of suicide, death, dying or the afterlife
❖   sudden increase in moodiness, withdrawal, or isolation
❖   major change in eating or sleeping habits
❖   feelings of hopelessness, guilt or worthlessness
❖   poor control over behavior
❖   impulsive, aggressive behavior
❖   drop in quality of school performance or interest
❖   lack of interest in usual activity
❖   getting into trouble with authority figures
❖   perfectionism
❖   giving away important possessions
❖   hinting at not being around in the future or saying good-bye
❖   These warning signs are especially noteworthy in the context of:
❖   a recent death or suicide of a friend or family member
❖   a recent break-up with a boyfriend or girlfriend, or conflict with parents

❖ news reports of other suicides by young people in the same school or community

Often, suicidal thinking comes from a wish to end deep psychological pain. Death seems like the only way out. But it isn't.

If a friend mentions suicide, take it seriously. Listen carefully, and then seek help immediately. Never keep their talk of suicide a secret, even if they ask you to. Remember, you risk losing that person. Forever.

When you recognize the warning signs for suicidal behavior, do something about it. Tell a trusted adult what you have seen or heard. Get help from a licensed mental health professional as soon as possible. They can help work out the problems that seem so unsolvable but, in fact, are not.

Take a stand against violence.

Aggression

The child or adolescent:

❖ bullies, threatens, or intimidates others
❖ initiates physical fights
❖ uses a weapon with potential to cause serious harm
❖ is physically cruel to people
❖ is physically cruel to animals
❖ steals while confronting the victim (mugging, extortion, robbery)
❖ forces another person into sexual activity

Destruction of Property

❖ deliberately engages in fire-setting with the intention of doing serious damage
❖ deliberately destroys others' property (other than by fire).

Violence and Aggression

Violence denotes the 'forceful infliction of physical injury' (Blackburn, 1993). Aggression involves harmful, threatening or antagonistic behavior (Berkowitz, 1993). Violent behavior often involves the loss of a sense of personal identity and personal value. A young person may engage in actions without concern for future consequences or past commitments.

Gun violence is an important aspect of the larger problem of aggression among children and youth, mainly because it dramatically increases the seriousness of any specific aggressive act. Unlike other weapons, a momentary aggressive impulse can become lethal with a gun. For example, with fists, blunt objects, and even knives, the process of killing someone typically takes longer than it does with a gun and provides abundant sensory feedback (such as bleeding, screaming, and imploring) that can inhibit aggressive impulses. Research reveals that using a gun indicates. A higher level of violent intent than does using fists to fight.

Second, the consequences are often very different depending on the role the young person plays in an incident of gun violence—perpetrator, victim, or bystander.

Third, relatively little research has focused specifically on the effects of youth exposure to gun violence or on interventions to help youth cope with their exposure.

Research shows that youth can suffer severe and lasting emotional distress from exposure to gun violence, and may become more likely to perpetrate violence themselves.

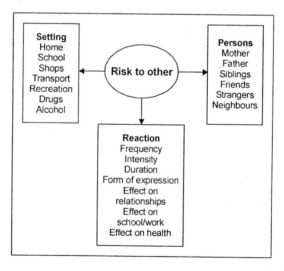

Factors Contributing to Serious Antisocial Behaviour and Violence (Bailey *et al,* 2001; Garborino, 2001)

Family Features

❖   Parental antisocial personality disorder

❖ Violence witnessed
❖ Abuse, neglect, rejection

Personality Features

❖ Callous unemotional interpersonal style
❖ Evolution of violent and sadistic fantasy
❖ People viewed as objects
❖ Paranoid ideation
❖ Hostile attribution

Situational Features

❖ Repeated loss and rejection in relationships
❖ Threats of self-harm
❖ Crescendo of hopelessness and helplessness
❖ Social disinhibition in group settings
❖ Substance misuse
❖ Changes in mental state over time

Predominant factors within families that contribute to longer-term aggressiveness and risk of violence have been clearly identified in child rearing and parenting styles (Farrington, 2000). Three key clusters emerge. The first is the presence of criminal parents and siblings with behavioral problems. In the second, the day-to-day behavior of primary caregivers is one of parental conflict, inconsistent supervision and physical and emotional neglect, with little or no reinforcement of pro-social behaviors. The child learns that his or her own aversive behavior stops unwanted intrusions by the parents/caregivers. Young people who assault others have lower rates of positive communication with their families. A third cluster of family factors linked with later violence in the child include cruel authoritarian discipline, physical control and shaming and emotional degradation of the child.

Where young people live in a culture of violence in their homes and neighborhoods, school has the potential to offer positive outlets to satisfy needs for belonging and recognition and acceptance through non-violent means. Failure to achieve academic success, peer approval and satisfying interpersonal relationships within the school context creates additional stresses and conflicts, with increased likelihood of aggression and violence linked to competition for status and status-related confrontations with peers (Laub & Lauristen, 1998).

Effects of Gun Violence on Children

Exposure to gun violence can traumatize children and youth not just physically, but emotionally as well. Studies have documented that young people exposed to gun violence experience lasting emotional scars. Some children may develop posttraumatic stress disorder (PTSD), which can affect brain development. The psychological trauma of gun violence may lead some children to arm themselves "for protection," or desensitize them so that they feel less hesitation about engaging in violent acts.

Sleep Distortion and Withdrawal

Research shows that exposure to violence can cause intrusive thoughts about the traumatic event leading to sleep disturbances as well. Children experience difficulty concentrating in the classroom, declines in academic performance, and lower educational and career aspirations. The chances of increased delinquency, risky sexual behaviors, and substance abuse increase many-folds. Children withdraw from the very people who may be best equipped to help them—friends and family. many survivors and bystanders agonize during the event about whether to flee from the danger in self-preservation or to stay to aid their victimized friend. Memories of this dilemma can be extremely distressing.

Posttraumatic Stress Disorder

Gun violence can lead in children is typically associated with hyper-vigilance (an overly alert state), an exaggerated startle response, anxiety, and recurring thoughts and dreams associated with the traumatic event. Traumatized children may attempt to avoid people, places, or objects that remind them of the trauma. "Psychic numbing" also can occur, causing children to detach emotionally from others and show decreased interest in activities they once enjoyed. Some trauma witnesses have difficulty expressing their emotions, lose their temper easily, or exhibit outbursts of anger.

Based on studies of how children's brains adapt to trauma, researchers at Baylor Medical College have concluded that a distinctive pattern of brain activity develops in response to exposure to threatening stimuli. The greater the intensity and frequency of stimulation—and thus the distinctive brain activity—the more likely that the brain will form "an indelible impression. Recurrent exposure to the trauma strengthens this response and lowers the child's ability to deal with any type of trauma. The child's brain becomes highly sensitive to threat and trauma-related cues, which in turn can affect his or her emotional and psychological well being. Several studies have documented that child with a history of trauma develop a persistent, low-level fear, and respond to threats either with dissociation (separating certain ideas or emotions from the rest of their mental activity to avoid stress or anxiety) or with an unusually heightened state of arousal. This pattern of brain activity may also affect children's general information processing.

Children do not have to witness gun violence directly to develop symptoms of traumatic stress. After hearing about incidences of gun violence or learning about them on television, children may feel that their safety is threatened.

Risk Heightened by Exposure to Violence in the Community, at School, and in the Media

The degree of exposure, the relationship with the victim, and the presence of other risk factors (such as preexisting mental health problems) influence the severity of the lasting effects of gun violence. The psychological effects of gun violence are especially serious for children and youth who are physically injured. They are left with traumatic memories and feelings of insecurity, as well as physical injuries or scars that remain as permanent reminders of the trauma.

Exposure to Community Violence

Living in communities where violence is common can negatively affect children's development, even if they are not directly exposed to violent activity. The effects of high levels of violence within a community are similar to those associated with direct exposure and can include nervousness, sleep problems, intrusive thoughts, anxiety, stress, loneliness, depression, grief, and antisocial behavior. Violence-exposed children also may show a decline in cognitive performance and school achievement. Repeated trauma can lead to anger, despair, and severe psychic numbing, resulting in major changes in personality and behavior.

Age and social and cognitive development are key determinants of how children respond to community violence. For example, the effects of community gun violence can be particularly severe if exposure occurs during critical periods of neurological growth and development, such as early childhood and early adolescence. Children who are exposed to traumatic events before age 11 are three times more likely to develop PTSD than children over age 12.24 However, adolescents who witness a single episode of violence, such as a school shooting, may experience greater stress than younger witnesses because they feel guilty about surviving and about not being able to help other victims. These feelings of guilt, coupled with anger and the desire for revenge, can make this type of violence exposure particularly difficult for teens.

Media Violence

According to the Center for Media Education USA, by the time children complete elementary school, they will witness more than 100,000 acts of violence on television, including 8,000 murders. These numbers double to 200,000 acts of violence and 16,000 murders by the time they complete high school this bombardment of media violence in television, films, and video games seems to negatively affect some young viewers, priming them to act aggressively. As with direct exposure to violence, exposure to media violence may spur some children and youth to commit violent acts.

Violence in Films and Television

Television and movie violence can affect subsequent displays of aggression by modeling and glorifying violence, triggering aggressive impulses in some people, and decreasing feelings of empathy for victims. Content analyses of prime-time television indicate that perpetrators of gun violence typically are depicted as using guns to protect themselves, which gives the impression that guns are important for self-protection. Furthermore, perpetrators are seldom held accountable for their actions. Death and physical injuries from gun violence are usually glossed over or totally overlooked. Even the mass television coverage of school shootings can contribute to violent behavior, as with copycat shootings. Some highly impressionable youth may see the publicity surrounding a school shooting as exciting and an opportunity for infamy.

Video Games

Another form of popular media entertainment for youth is violent video games. The combination of technological advances and a growing demand for intensity and arousal has substantially altered video game content. The latest generation of games is much more violent and accurate in its depictions of violence than its predecessors were; with many lifelike images of blood, guts, and gore. Data indicate that children and adolescents prefer violent video games to all others. Some scholars suggest that violent video games, because of their interactive and participatory nature, are even worse for children and teenagers than violent television programs. Playing these video games allows young people to practice violence—often gun violence—in ways television does not.

Several studies have demonstrated that teenagers who play violent video games are more likely to engage in aggressive behavior and violence than are children who play nonviolent video games. Much less is known about the link between playing violent video games and later perpetrating gun violence. However, the experience of the military suggests that video games are an effective tool for training people to use firearms.

According to one professor of military science, "first person shooter video games"—which involve firing a lifelike digital gun at human forms that pop up on the television screen—teach children how to kill the same way that flight simulators teach pilots to fly without leaving the ground.

Columbine Shooting: Killer Kids

On April 20th, 1999 two teenagers, Eric Harris and Dylan Klebold walked into their school in Columbine Colorado and began a one-hour long killing spree, which ended in the death of 12 of their fellow classmates and one teacher and left another 28 wounded. The shooters then took their own lives. The two teenage gunmen did not have a previous history of violence but were both enthusiasts of killing-oriented video games. The violence in video games was a major factor in teaching these kids how to shoot other people in real life. Violent video games can and have led children to committing acts of violence against other children and adults.

Growing Children and Role Model

Growing children are easily influenced by the examples laid out before them. A young boy who plays hockey and follows the sport closely is probably more likely to resort to violence to solve a conflict than a boy whose role model is a pacifist folk-singer simply because violence and fighting is a prominent overtone of the sport. The same goes for a child who is very interested in one or more of the numerous video games available that focus on killing as their main theme. A child who plays violent video games will resort to violence more easily when faced with a problem than a child who has never been exposed to such interactive killing. Violent video games do not teach any other way to deal with a conflict. So a young, impressionable youth will be susceptible to resorting to violence if that child has been exposed to violent video games.

Violence in Video Games

Violence in video games can also act as a gateway to more serious forms of violence. If a child who has no interest or knowledge in guns and weaponry begins to play a "shoot-me-up" video game where the sole purpose is to kill other people that child could become interested in guns and move on to something more realistic such as pellet and paint ball weaponry. From there the child could move into actual guns when he/she is able to acquire such weapons and this could lead to an act of violence against another human being. Violent video games can foster an interest in guns and violence in children, which can lead them to more realistic violence.

Video game companies are continuously releasing more and more realistically violent video games onto the market in order to sell more copies, because market statistics clearly show that violence sells: all the most popular video games include a violent main theme. Many games include very real-life scenarios with existing weaponry that were created to be as close to the real thing as possible. This can teach children all about the way a gun works and how to use it. If a child is killing people in an almost perfectly realistic virtual world, it would quickly desensitize that child, making it easier for him/her to commit such acts in real-life. A young boy brought his dad's gun to an American school one day and used it to shoot a boy who had been bullying him. In the video games the boy played, when a person was shot, the person would simply fall to the ground with a quiet grunt or moan, and in some cases a shot with a less powerful gun to a person in a video game is not enough to kill the character so that person will continue doing whatever it was that he/she was doing. In real life the boy's victim moaned and screamed in agony while rolling in a puddle of blood on the ground, leaving the boy who shot him incredibly traumatized by what he had done. As realistic as video games are, they still lack certain aspects of real life; the difference between shooting a video game character and shooting a real living, breathing human being is it is easy to shoot an object you do not even perceive as alive.

Violent video games can teach a person how to aim and use a handgun. In an article of the July issue of Shift magazine, the editors addressed the issue by giving a young man who had played violent arcade games all his life a real handgun at a shooting range where he could test his shooting ability for the first time. Even the young man himself was perplexed when he missed an incredibly low percentage of the shots fired. He was shooting with deadly accuracy and he had never even held a real gun before in his life. Similarly, a man in the United States walked into a church with a Glock. 18 16-shot pistol and killed twelve people with it and injured another two. Twelve of the sixteen shots he had available to him were so accurate, he was able to kill a fleeing person in a single hit—shooting accuracy that many trained law enforcement officers cannot equal. The unsettling part of the story is that the man had never shot a handgun before, not even before he walked into the church that morning. However, for many years he had played arcade games where the player holds an electronic pistol and shoots targets on the screen and was outstandingly good at the game.

Therefore, violence in video games for any medium is a dangerous thing to children who are at an age where they are easily influenced by the subjects around them. Video games promote an interest in guns, present a distorted reality, and may actually train people to be marksmen. Incidents like the Columbine school shooting, the worst school shooting in the history of the United States, are proof of the influence of heavy violence in today's games.

Abuse of Parents by Children

There is remarkably little known or documented on children violent to their parents, which is surprising given the level of knowledge and concern about antisocial and violent behavior committed by children in school or in the community. The abuse of parents can at best be seen as under researched and at worst as a taboo subject associated with a sense of shame that parents cannot protect themselves against the violence of those with whose care and protection they are charged. work by Strauss, Gelles and Steinmetz dating back to 1980 (Strauss & Gelles, 1990) estimated that 18 per cent of children between the ages of 3 and 17 years carried out one or more acts of violence towards parents. The victim was most often the mother; the violence ranged in severity from 10 per cent of children hitting or striking a parent, 7 per cent striking a parent with an object, 1 per cent severely beating a parent to 1 per cent using a potentially lethal weapon.

What is known about children who are violent to parents? Adolescents who have assaulted peers, siblings, teachers and strangers are at increased risk of having assaulted or threatened to inflict physical violence on their parents. Children who inflicted physical violence on parents were described by Harbin & Madden (1979) as more often economically dependent, male and aged between 13 and 24 years. Adolescents who are violent to parents appear to straddle socio-economic groupings. Family dynamics provide the greatest insight into the evolution of this particular form of violence in children (Harbin & Madden, 1983). It is common to find that the parents of such children convey inconsistent values about aggression. Although severe child abuse in this group is unusual, parents who use harsh child rearing techniques are at increased risk of being victims of violence at the hands of their children. Role reversal between parent and child (parentification) takes place, to the extent that parental authority is given over to the child.

Parents tend to deny the seriousness of acts of aggression and violence displayed against them. In the clinical situation when a child is referred because of violent acts occurring in the community or school, parents will not always reveal a preceding or coexisting history of violence in the home. Violent assaults against parents are most likely to occur in the context of parenting stress arising from parent–child disagreement. Failure to set consistent limits on unacceptable behavior produces a dynamic in which the child experiences an evolving sense of empowerment and, indeed, a sense of justification in dealing with increasingly failing attempts at parenting by escalating both the frequency and severity of violent responses. The tyrannical child is rewarded and reinforced in this behavior by the parents giving in to this graded continuum of physical aggression.

The evolution of parental inconsistency and loss of authority that includes fear of the child can be likened to the need to maintain relationships through co-dependency as seen in adult male-to-female domestic violence. In domestic violence, the violence and abusive behaviors are used to control. The abusive behavior is also used to support the sense of entitlement that allows an adult male to see his behavior as reasonable given his partner's 'unreasonable' resistance to his expectation. This further fuels the process of partner blaming (Blacklock, 2001). Whatever other factors place a child at risk of being violent, this sense of entitlement and experience of being in control can lead to aggression and violence becoming the child's normal form of social transaction in the home and then beyond.School shootings are not a simple issue with a single solution. This violence is rooted in psychological imbalances within the students themselves, poor parenting and a decay in significance of traditional institutions along with the guilt forces they rely on for effectiveness—to name a just a few.

Virtual Violence: Newspaper Report

New Delhi: Worried over the growing aggressiveness among kids, schools have started orientation programmes urging children to stop laying violent games and switch over to educational and mythological ones. Even the firms promoting multimedia games have joined hands with the Confederation of Indian Industries (CII) to develop educational games.

"Our counselors have been asking students not to spend hours on play station playing violent games which tends to increase aggressiveness among them. Orientation programmes for parents at least once in a week have been organized asking them to encourage games soccer and cricket. A series of mythological computer games are also available these days," said. Amity International (Saket) principal Bharti Sharma.

"Children are becoming impatient and intolerant these days. Violent games have affected the behavioural patterns of kids besides their language. With parents not being able to spend adequate time with their kids, they tend to compensate by providing them with such computer games. However, we have been conducting special orientation programmes for parents to encourage kids to play traditional games," said DPS (RK Puram) principal Shyama Chona.

TV, Film, Game Violence Threaten Public Health

New York: Violence depicted on television, in films and video games raises the risk of aggressive behavior in adults and young viewers and poses a serious threat to public health, according to a new study.

After reviewing more than 50 years of research on the impact of violence in the media, L Rowell Huesmann, of the University of Michigan, and his colleague Brad Bush-man concluded that only smoking posed a greater danger. "Exposure to violent electronic media has a larger effect than all but one other well known threat to public health. The only effect slightly larger than the effect of media violence on aggression is that of cigarette smoking, a leading cause of preventable death, is linked to lung cancer and other illnesses.

Huesmann said children spend an average of three hours watching television each day and more than 60 per cent of TV programs contain some violence, including 40 per cent showing extreme violence.

"Children are also spending an increasingly large amount of time playing video games, most of which contain violence. Video game units are now present in 83 per cent of homes with children," he added. The findings, which are reported in the 'Journal of Adolescent Health', support earlier research which showed that children who watch violent television shows and who identify with the characters and believe they are real are more likely to be aggressive as adults.

The results were true for both men and women. "The research clearly shows that exposure to virtual violence increases the risk that both children and adults will be have aggressively," said Huesmann, adding it could have a particularly detrimental effect on the well-being of youngsters.

Although not every child exposed to violence in the media will become aggressive, he said it does not diminish the need for greater control on the part of parents and society of what children are exposed to in films, video games and television programs.

5

Parental Responsibility

Family structures and processes affect and are affected by numerous social and cultural trends, and changes in any one of these can lead to new familial functions, forms, and relationships. As mentioned elsewhere, families can be envisioned as society's shock absorbers of change, absorbing, for instance, socio-cultural changes in gender roles, intergenerational relationships, racial relationships, demographics (such as new waves of immigrants), in the division of labor, and shifts in the stratification order. Of course, such broad changes vary in their familial impacts by social class, region of the country, and so forth.

In 2002, Public Agenda released its "*A Lot Easier Said Than Done: Parents Talk About Raising Children in Today's America*" survey. Among the findings:

❖ a large majority of parents say American society is an inhospitable climate for raising children

❖ nearly half the parents said they worry more about protecting their child from negative social influences than they do about paying the bills or having enough family time together

❖ 6 in 10 rate other parents only "fair" or "poor" in raising their children

❖ One of the most far-reaching changes in [moral] norms relates to what parents believe they owe their children and what their children owe them. ...The overall pattern is clear: today's parents expect to make fewer sacrifices for their children than in the past, but they also demand less from their offspring in the form of future obligations than their parents demanded of them....Sixty-seven percent believe that "children do not have an obligation to their parents regardless of what their parents have done for them."

— Daniel Yankelovich, New Rules: Searching for Self-fulfillment in a World Turned Upside Down, 1981:102

❖ *Spending Time with Dad*: The amount of waking time 4-year-old children spend alone with their fathers each day compared with daily waking time in day care, according to a 1986-94 study by the Netherlands-based International Association for the Evaluation of Educational Achievement.

Country	Time with dad	Time in daycare
Belgium	30 minutes	6.8 hours
China	54 minutes	11 hours
Finland	48 minutes	6.8 hours
Germany	36 minutes	5 hours
Nigeria	42 minutes	7 hours
Portugal	24 minutes	8.8 hours
Spain	18 minutes	7 hours
Thailand	12 minutes	11 hours
United States	42 minutes	5.6 hours

when Americans were asked to rate the roles different adults played in the lives of children, fathers came in a poor third—behind mothers and grandparents—scoring roughly in the midpoint between the mean scores given to mothers:

❖ With industrialization and the bifurcation of public and private life, dads' primary (and socially approved) activities were in the public realm of work while the sphere of mothers' control was in the private realm of family life (referred to as the "feminization of the domestic sphere"). Adequacy of one's performance of his father role was largely judged on the basis of his "breadwinner" activities. In 1900, one observer noted how "the suburban husband and father" had become "almost entirely a Sunday institution." To this day, corporate America advises the new father not to take paternity leave if he is to be "taken seriously."

❖ The role of "father" is dialectically related to roles of "mother"—which has changed dramatically over the post-war years, dissolving the males' distinctive (and authority-enhancing) role as primary wage earner —and "children"—whose status in the family historically shifted from being economic assets to economic liabilities as the family transformed from being a unit of production to being a unit of consumption.

❖ Over the postwar era, as families have become increasingly leisure- and child- oriented (at least within the middle-class), instead of serving as a role model in dealing with the public realm, fathers now often sit on the sidelines to view their children's performances in sports and in the arts.

There are, however, signs of change:

❖ nowadays, more than 90 percent of fathers are present in the delivery room, compared to almost none thirty years earlier.

❖ according to a 1993 report issued by the Population Reference Bureau (authored by Martin O'Connell of the Census Bureau), fathers are the primary care givers for one in five preschoolers whose mothers work.

❖ there is a growing market for fathering "self-help" books and websites, with such titles as *How to Father, Expectant Father, Pregnant Fathers, The Birth of a Father, Fathers Almanac, Father Power,* and *How to Father a Successful Daughter>*

❖ Implications of Fatherlessness:
A community that allows a large number of young men to grow up in broken families, dominated by women, never acquiring any stable relationship to male authority, never acquiring any set of rational expectations about the future—that community asks for and gets chaos.   —*Patrick Moynihan, 1965*
What are the consequences of 37% of America's children sleeping in homes where their natural fathers don't live? Department of Health and Human Services Secretary Louis Sullivan observed in 1994 that "Children who do not live with a mother and father are more likely to be high school dropouts, more likely to abuse drugs and alcohol and more likely to be dependent on welfare than children who live with both biological parents." By the mid-1990s, 46% of families with children headed by single mothers were living below the poverty line, compared with 8% of children living with two parents.

❖ Mothers and fathers are complementary and not interchangeable roles. Fathers are not substitute mothers. Among the speculations and findings:
— absence of role modeling for young males;

— higher risks for males of having low esteem and being emotionally rigid;

— in Nancy Gibbs Time magazine cover story "Bringing Up Father" (June 28, 1993:52- 61), it was reported how some researchers find mothers' love to be unconditional while that of fathers is more qualified and tied to performance, and how mothers are more likely to be worried about their children's survival while fathers are more likely to be concerned about their future success.

❖ The Mother Role & The Sibling Bond:
Every mother is a judge who sentences her children for the sins of the father.   —*Rebecca West*

— Often sibling relationship has been described in terms of rivalry, featuring sibling competitions for parental attention and approval. Longitudinal studies indicate that such contests wane after adolescence, with growing adulthood bonds particularly between siblings close in age and of the same sex, and later increases when aging parents need care and disputes over inheritance arise. What needs to be stressed are the cognitive and social skills developed in these relationships.

Among the findings in Klagsbrun's *Mixed Feelings* (1992):

❖ Only 17 percent said that they "weren't close at all" to their siblings;

❖ 84 per cent said one or both of their parents had shown favoritism when they were growing up;

❖ When perceptions were that the respondents' mother had a favorite, two-thirds of the men and slightly more than one-quarter of the women felt favored by her. When respondents believed their father had a favorite, 62 percent of women and 49 percent of the men felt they were the favored one;

❖ Sister-sister relationships were closer to brother-brother and sister-brother relations.

If the parents are not able to provide proper attention and a rational parenthood to the child, what right they have to be parent? Any couple will like to have a healthy, rationally strong and morally able person as their progeny. But if one is not even able to consider and rationalize it that how can the child of him/her achieve those humanistic characters, then what right he/she have to be a parent?

It is much better to **NOT TO BE** a parent if one is not able to provide proper nurture and care and guidance to the child. It is a duty and surely not a way of carnal desires. Parenting is very objectivistic duty, a cause of worth importance. Proper parenting requires imparting a strong set of values, and encouraging the child's confidence in his ability to make wise choices and to attain his goals. It is not at all an easy task. And every couple needs to provide and devote enough time and endeavor to achieve it.

It must not be indoctrination.

The rationales, the morals cannot be indoctrinated. They cannot be taught via some funny religious notes. Proper reasons are to be shown and explained and the child's inner self must be inspired to gather those reasons themselves.

If the parents themselves do not know how to handle the emotions, what they can teach to the child? Many a times, a sort of emotional struggle occurs between parent and child, from the whining and temper tantrums of a toddler to the sulking and angry outbursts of a teenager. It is all a matter of who has the power: you or your child. It becomes a win-lose situation only if the parent is an authoritarian who always wins, or the child knows how to manipulate a parent's emotional responses so that his demands are always met.

This must not be the case.

Ways must be find out so that these distressing events can be avoided or resolved, including teaching a child how to handle emotions, having a parent who enforces standards and giving the parent control while fostering independence in the growing child.

The real power of parents do not lies in being authoritative but it lies in their ability to guide their children toward self-control, which is necessary for self-esteem, maturity and rational independent thinking. There may arise many questions like how to teach children about acquiring reading habits, and to manage money, how to manage anger and enthusiasm and other emotions including lust.

There are very basic and objectivistic duties regarding parenthood and no rationalist can ignore those duties if he/she decides to be a parent. The physical development of child is the responsibility of the parents which includes physical training "Yoga" and introduction to sports and developing habits of health in the child. The environment of intellectual freedom must be provided for the child by providing the sense of "Dignity" in the child by creating an environment of peace and justice in the family and promoting no-fear, no-threat, no-verbal abuse and no discriminatory environment. The child must be taught not only to respect his individual self, but to keep himself away from attacking or encroaching others individual space. Sense of self-worth and self-righteousness is different from sense of arrogance.

Parenthood must be based on set of principles (**DHARMA**). The basic principle of parenthood must be how the parents can help the children become self-confident, self-reliant and happy. A child's mind is his greatest value. A child needs to develop his mind so that he can think rationally and live successfully. Parents must help the child to gain knowledge (not the crap) and help him learn how to use this knowledge effectively and to appreciate the value of their own mind.

Many times in the **ORKUT** forum "Rational Behavioral..." I have stated that the government and the social organizations must stress on providing psychological studies and researches to provide rational ways to help the parents how to raise the kids.

It is very necessary not only for the individual parents but the Society too, to create an environment for the children to adapt rationally with the environment and raise themselves in objectivistic mode. Otherwise such cases will keep on repeating themselves irrespective of arms prohibitions or any other authoritative strict measures.

Work

What Issues Come to Mind When Thinking About Families and the Economic Order?

❖ How, with industrialization, the worlds of work and family were to be bifurcated, contributing to the rise of life's public and private spheres, with the family becoming the realm of the "private self." Nowadays, it supposedly is only here where one's "true self" can be expressed, a shelter from the anomic forces of public world wherein meaning, self- actualization, happiness and leisure can flourish. Indeed, studies consistently show how family life is the chief source overall life satisfactions. In "Marriage and the Construction of Reality" (*Diogenes*, no. 45, 1964:1-25), Peter Berger and Hansfried Kellner write:

The private sphere, this interstitial area created (we would think) more or less haphazardly as a by-product of the social metamorphosis of industrialism, is mainly where he will turn. It is here that the individual will seek power, intelligibility and, quite literally, a name—the apparent power to fashion a world, however Lilliputian, that will reflect his own being: ...a world in which, consequently, he is somebody—perhaps even, within its charmed circle, a lord and master. ... an area of individual choice and even autonomy.

Further, this bifurcation of social realms supposedly leads to a bifurcation of the self: the public and the private.

❖ With both industrialization and the expansion of the service economy, the family system has metamorphosed from being a unit of production to being a unit of consumption (and of therapy). This, in turn, has led to the erosion of many traditional family functions—and their commodification. Consider the rise of such services as:

— procreation, where infertile couples employ high science to perform in vitro fertilization (aka test-tube babies)

— daycare (for both the young and old)—see Lynn Casper's "What does it cost to mind our preschoolers?"; also see Childcare: How does your state rate?

— education (let the teachers handle the "Birds and Bees" lesson);

— restaurants and catering. No longer does one even have to organize birthday parties for the little guys. Check out Birthday Express, which mail orders theme-based party packs, including an outfit for birthday boy or girl; integrated and matching invitations, plates, cups, forks, spoons, napkins, balloons and table cover; game or activity for the party goers; "favor bags" and piñata.

— housecleaning (including "Rent-A-Wife");

— the family counseling, therapy, and social work industries—see, for instance, the Strengthening America's Families conference held in San Antonio in March, 2000, where "family skills training" programs are employed to reduce juvenile delinquency;

— the family advice industries—Miss Abigail's Time Warp Advice: Old Advice on Contemporary Dilemmas features 150 years of etiquette and advice book wisdoms on matters of dating, love, sex and marriage;

— the "family escape" industries, such as Walt Disney World (and note the electronic connection to family.com)

— the "escape from family" industries, such as The Alibi Agency, whose objectives begin: With the pressures of modern life many of us have occasion to stray from our long term partners and dally with a brief sexual or emotional relationship with a third party, this is often a short term affair, inconsequential to our long term plans and relationships, but with modern communications, and media, it has become increasingly difficult to be able to carry on such a temporary dalliance, without risk of detection. ...

— nursing homes

— and the death and grief industries.

— Instead of entertaining each other, family members instead consume the numerous products of the entertainment industries. Another consequence are new bonds between family members, which are decreasingly shaped by working together but rather in sharing each other's leisure or consumptive pursuits (e.g., the parents in the stands at Little League competitions; family summer vacations and trips to the mall).

There is impact on the internal family division of labor, power structure, and distribution of resources (whether economic, social [e.g., "quality time"), emotional, or temporal) when different family members (such as children and/or wives) work and contribute varying proportions to total family (vs. personal) resources. In 1990, it was estimated that one-half of two-income families would drop below the poverty line if the family did not work

Child Abuse and Neglect

Each year, tens of thousands of children are traumatized by physical, sexual, and emotional abusers or by caregivers who neglect them, making child abuse as common as it is shocking. The scars can be deep and long-lasting, affecting not just abused children but society. You can learn the signs and symptoms of child abuse and find out where to get help for the children and their caregivers.

There are four primary types of child abuse:

1. physical abuse

2. sexual abuse
3. emotional abuse
4. neglect

Child Neglect: Types and Warning Signs

Neglect is a pattern of failing to provide for a child's basic needs, to the extent that the child's physical and/or psychological well-being are damaged or endangered. In child neglect, the parents or caregivers are simply choosing not to do their job. There are three basic types of neglect.

Physical Neglect

1. Failure to provide adequate food, clothing, or hygiene
2. Reckless disregard for the child's safety, such as inattention to hazards in the home, drunk driving with kids in the car, leaving a baby unattended
3. Refusal to provide or delay in providing necessary health care for the child
4. Abandoning children without providing for their care or expelling children from the home without arranging for their care

Educational Neglect

1. Failure to enroll a child in school
2. Permitting or causing a child to miss too many days of school
3. Refusal to follow up on obtaining services for a child's special educational needs

Emotional Neglect

1. Inadequate nurturing or affection
2. Exposure of the child to spousal abuse
3. Permitting a child to drink alcohol or use recreational drugs
4. Failure to intervene when the child demonstrates antisocial behavior
5. Refusal of or delay in providing necessary psychological care

Some Signs of Child Neglect

❖ Clothes that are dirty, ill-fitting, ragged, and/or not suitable for the weather,
❖ Unwashed appearance; offensive body odor,

❖ Indicators of hunger: asking for or stealing food, going through trash for food, eating too fast or too much when food is provided for a group,

❖ Apparent lack of supervision: wandering alone, home alone, left in a car,

❖ Colds, fevers, or rashes left untreated; infected cuts; chronic tiredness,

❖ In schoolchildren, frequent absence or lateness; troublesome, disruptive behavior or its opposite, withdrawal,

❖ In babies, failure to thrive; failure to relate to other people or to surroundings.

A single occurrence of one of these indicators isn't necessarily a sign of child neglect, but a pattern of behaviors may demonstrate a lack of care that constitutes abuse.

Physical Child Abuse: Types and Warning Signs

Physical child abuse is an adult's physical act of aggression directed at a child that causes injury, even if the adult didn't intend to injure the child. Such acts of aggression include striking a child with the hand, fist, or foot or with an object; burning the child with a hot object; shaking, pushing, or throwing a child; pinching or biting the child; pulling a child by the hair; cutting off a child's air. Such acts of physical aggression account for between 15 and 20 percent of documented child abuse cases each year.

Many physically abusive parents and caregivers insist that their actions are simply forms of discipline, ways to make children learn to behave. But there's a big difference between giving an unmanageable child a swat on the backside and twisting the child's arm until it breaks. Physically abusive parents have issues of anger, excessive need for control, or immaturity that make them unable or unwilling to see their level of aggression as inappropriate.

Sometimes the very youngest children, even babies not yet born, suffer physical abuse. Because many chemicals pass easily from a pregnant woman's system to that of a fetus, a mother's use of drugs or alcohol during pregnancy can cause serious neurological and physiological damage to the unborn child, such as the effects of fetal alcohol syndrome; mothers can also pass on drugs or alcohol in breast milk. A woman who drinks or uses drugs when she knows she's pregnant can be charged with child abuse in many jurisdictions if her baby is born with problems because of the substance use. Another form of child abuse involving babies is shaken baby syndrome, in which a frustrated caregiver shakes a baby roughly to make the baby stop crying. The baby's neck muscles can't support the baby's head yet, and the brain bounces around inside its skull, suffering damage that often leads to severe neurological problems and even death. While the person shaking the baby may not mean to hurt him, shaking a baby in a way that can cause injury is a form of child abuse. An odd form of physical child abuse is Munchausen's syndrome by proxy, in which a parent causes a child to become ill and rushes the chlld to the hospital or convinces doctors that the child is sick. It's a way for the parent to gain attention and sympathy, and its dangers to the child constitute child abuse.

Is Corporal Punishment the Same as Physical Abuse?

Corporal **punishment**, the use of physical force with the intent of inflicting bodily pain, but not injury, for the purpose of correction or control, used to be a very common form of discipline: most of us know it as spanking or paddling. And many of us were spanked as children without damage to body or psyche.

The widespread use of physical punishment, however, doesn't make it a good idea. Most child-care experts have come to agree that corporal punishment sends the message to children that physical force is an appropriate response to problems or opposition. The level of force used by an angry or frustrated parent can easily get out of hand and lead to injury. Even if it doesn't, what a child learns from being hit as punishment is less about why conduct is right or wrong than about behaving well — or hiding bad behavior — out of fear of being hit.

Signs of physical child abuse include visible marks of maltreatment, such as cuts, bruises, welts, or well-defined burns, and reluctance to go home. If you ask a child about how he or she got hurt and the child talks vaguely or evasively about falling off a fence or spilling a hot dish, think hard before you accept the child's story at face value.

Sexual Abuse in Children: Types and Warning Signs

Sexual abuse, which accounts for about 10 percent of child abuse, is *any* sexual act between an adult and a child. Such acts include:

❖ *Behavior involving penetration:* vaginal or anal intercourse and oral sex.
❖ *Fondling:* Touching or kissing a child's genitals, making a child fondle an adult's genitals.

- ❖ *Violations of Privacy*: Forcing a child to undress, spying on a child in the bathroom or bedroom.
- ❖ *Exposing Children to Adult Sexuality*: Performing sexual acts in front of a child, exposing genitals, telling "dirty" stories, showing pornography to a child.
- ❖ *Exploitation*: Selling a child's services as a prostitute or a performer in pornography.

The adult who sexually abuses a child or adolescent is usually someone the child knows and is supposed to trust: a relative, childcare provider, family friend, neighbor, teacher, coach, or clergy member. More than 80 percent of sex offenders are people the child or adolescent victims know. It's important to understand that no matter what the adult says in defense of his or her actions, the child did not invite the sexual activity and the adult's behavior is wrong. Sexual abuse is never the child's fault.

Children are psychologically unable to handle sexual stimulation. Even toddlers, who haven't formulated the idea that the sexual abuse is wrong, will develop problems resulting from the overstimulation. Older children who know and care for their abusers know that the sexual behavior is wrong, but they may feel trapped by feelings of loyalty and affection. Abusers warn their victims not to tell, threatening children with violence or ostracism, and the shame associated with the sexual activity makes the child especially reluctant to tell. When sexual abuse occurs within the family, children may worry that other family members won't believe them and will be angry with them if they tell — as is often the case. The layer of shame that accompanies sexual abuse makes the behavior doubly traumatizing.

Some Signs of Sexual Child Abuse

Often children who have suffered sexual abuse show no physical signs, and the abuse goes undetected unless a physician spots evidence of forced sexual activity. However, there are behavioral clues to sexual abuse, including:

- ❖ Inappropriate interest in or knowledge of sexual acts
- ❖ Seductive behavior
- ❖ Reluctance or refusal to undress in front of others
- ❖ Extra aggression or, at the other end of the spectrum, extra compliance

❖ Fear of a particular person or family member

Children who use the Internet are also vulnerable to come-ons by adults online. Among the warning signs of online sexual child abuse are these:

❖ Your child spends large amounts of time online, especially at night.
❖ You find pornography on your child's computer.
❖ Your child receives phone calls from people you don't know, or makes calls, sometimes long distance, to numbers you don't recognize.
❖ Your child receives mail, gifts, or packages from someone you don't know.
❖ Your child turns the computer monitor off or quickly changes the screen on the monitor when you come into the room.
❖ Your child becomes withdrawn from the family.
❖ Your child is using an online account belonging to someone else.

Emotional Child Abuse: Types and Warning Signs

Emotional child abuse involves behavior that interferes with a child's mental health or social development: one website calls it "the systematic tearing down of another human being." Such abuse can range from verbal insults to acts of terror, and it's almost always a factor in the other three categories of abuse. While emotional abuse by itself doesn't involve the infliction of physical pain or inappropriate physical contact, it can have more long-lasting negative psychological effects than either physical abuse or sexual abuse.

Examples of emotional child abuse include:

Verbal Abuse

❖ Belittling or shaming the child: name-calling, making negative comparisons to others, telling the child he or she is "no good," "worthless," "a mistake."
❖ Habitual blaming: telling the child that everything is his or her fault.

Withholding Affection

❖ Ignoring or disregarding the child

❖ Lack of affection and warmth: Failure to hug, praise, express love for the child

Extreme Punishment

These are actions that are meant to isolate and terrorize a child, such as tying the child to a fixture or piece of furniture or locking a child in a closet or dark room.

Corruption

This involves causing a child to witness or participate in inappropriate behavior, such as criminal activities, drug or alcohol abuse, or acts of violence. Emotional abuse can come not only from adults but from other children: siblings, neighborhood or schoolyard bullies, peers in schools that permit a culture of social ostracism (the "mean girl" syndrome). The signs of emotional child abuse include apathy, depression, and hostility. If it happens at school, the child may be reluctant to go to school and develop or fake a physical complaint.

Causes of Child Abuse

Why would someone abuse a defenseless child? What kind of person abuses a child? Not all child abuse is deliberate or intended. Several factors in a person's life may combine to cause them to abuse a child:

❖ Stress, including the stress of caring for children, or the stress of caring for a child with a disability, special needs, or difficult behaviors
❖ Lack of nurturing qualities necessary for child care
❖ Immaturity: a disproportionate number of parents who abuse their children are teenagers
❖ Difficulty controlling anger
❖ Personal history of being abused
❖ Isolation from the family or community
❖ Physical or mental health problems, such as depression and anxiety
❖ Alcohol or drug abuse
❖ Personal problems such as marital conflict, unemployment, or financial difficulties.

No one has been able to predict which of these factors will cause someone to abuse a child. A significant factor is that abuse tends to be intergenerational – those who were abused as children are more likely to repeat the act when they become parents or caretakers.

In addition, many forms of child abuse arise from ignorance. Sometimes a cultural tradition leads to abuse. Such beliefs include:

- ❖ Children are property.
- ❖ Parents (especially fathers) have the right to control their children in any way they wish.
- ❖ Children need to be toughened up to face the hardships of life.
- ❖ Girls need to be genitally mutilated to assure virginity and later marriage.

Effects of Child Abuse

Child abuse can produce dire consequences during the victim's childhood and adulthood. Some effects of child abuse are obvious: a child is malnourished or has a cast on her arm; a nine-year-old develops a sexually transmitted disease. But some physiological effects of child abuse, such as cognitive difficulties or lingering health problems, may not show up for some time or be clearly attributable to abuse. Other effects of child abuse are invisible or go off like time bombs later in life.

Emotional Effects of Child Abuse

Just as all types of child abuse have an emotional component, all affect the emotions of the victims. These effects include:

- ❖ Low self-esteem
- ❖ Alienation and withdrawal
- ❖ Depression and anxiety
- ❖ Personality disorders
- ❖ Aggressive behavior/anger issues
- ❖ Clinginess, neediness
- ❖ Relationship difficulties
- ❖ Flashbacks and nightmares

Many adults who were abused as children find it difficult to trust other people, endure physical closeness, and establish intimate relationships.

Behavioral Effects of Child Abuse

Child abuse can play itself out not only in how its victims feel but in what they do years later. Children who suffer abuse have much greater chances of being arrested later as juveniles and as adults. Significant percentages of inmates in U.S. prisons were abused as children. One of every three abused or neglected children will grow up to become an abusive parent.

Other behavioral effects include:

- ❖ Problems in school and work
- ❖ Criminal or antisocial behavior
- ❖ Prostitution
- ❖ Alcohol and drug abuse
- ❖ Teen pregnancy
- ❖ Eating disorders
- ❖ Suicide attempts
- ❖ Spousal abuse

Kids at Risk

No matter how many gun laws are proposed or passed in the next decade, *your* kids are at risk today. The school system steadfastly refuses to teach even the most rudimentary safety measures, prompting some to say that they share blame with.... who?

The playmate?

The parents?

The gun maker?

The gun itself?

Maybe there is no gun in your house and never will be because you hate guns. The fact remains that one out of two American homes has a gun. That means that 50 per cent of the homes your child *visits has* this instantly lethal weapon. Chances are the neighbors on both sides of your home have a firearm.

You can chose to ignore it, and let blind chance control your child's fate or you can act *right now,* educate yourself and your children about gun safety, and give them a fighting chance.

Safe Handling of Guns by Parents at Home

Most fatal firearm accidents and suicides occur when children and teens discover firearms at home that have been left loaded or unsecured. Because of the serious risk of firearm-related death and injury to children and teenagers, experts on all sides of the gun debate agree that the decision to keep a firearm in the home is very serious and one that must not be made lightly. A gun in the home is not appropriate for all homes or individuals. If you are not willing to accept basic responsibilities and adhere to important rules of firearms ownership and storage, parents need not purchase a firearm. It makes no sense to keep a gun at home for "protection," if that same gun puts your family members or visitors at risk.

Tragedies take place daily involving unlocked firearms easily accessible to young people, either at their own homes or the home of a relative or neighbor. These tragedies might very well never have happened if the adults in these children's lives had unloaded and locked their firearms and ammunition, so that the children could not have such easy access to them. USA research shows that 40 per cent of households with children have a firearm in the house, and 1 in 4 of these guns is kept loaded. In addition, in a majority of accidents and suicides and in many of the homicides, the firearms that were used were found at home.

It is vital that guns always be locked up and stored unloaded. Children never should have easy access to guns without parental supervision. This is especially true for handguns, because they are much more likely to be kept where children can get to them. Handguns are likely to be stored in bedrooms where it is easy for children to find them.

Children are naturally curious, especially when it comes to guns. Parents should not lull themselves into a false sense of security on this matter, even if they have spoken to their children about guns; any small child who picks up a gun is going to put a finger on the trigger and click it. All parents must take common sense steps to protect children, both by talking to them about guns and by unloading and locking all guns so that a child or teen cannot access them without direct adult supervision.

To ensure the safety of children, all gun owners should:

❖ unload and lock up their guns;
❖ lock and store ammunition separately; and
❖ hide keys where kids are unable to find them.

There are a variety of devices for securing your firearm. Though safes seem to provide the most security, many people prefer locks, which are often available for free, or at a low cost.

"Troubled Teen" to "Killer Child"

How does someone reach that point, a level of total selfishness and self-interest where they care nothing about other people, society, church or country? It certainly starts with their parents, the original role models for ethics and morality. But everyone is influenced by collective social standards and expectations too.

Parents face some daunting challenges in protecting their children from gun violence, not least of which are social expectations that they bear responsibility for their children's actions. They can address these challenges by closely monitoring their children's behavior, environment, and exposure to violent media.

In USA until the mid-1990s, many parents believed that youth gun violence plagued only inner-city neighborhoods, schools, and communities. But the wave of school shootings that occurred in the late 1990s made many parents realize that no community is free from the threat of youth violence. Although school shootings are rare and account for only a small portion of all youth gun violence, the grisly televised images of wounded children, students barricaded in classrooms or closets, and innocent children being killed by their classmates brought youth gun violence to the forefront of the American consciousness. Parents can acknowledge the danger of gun violence by being alert to signs that their own children might be prone to violent behavior.

Parents may find it difficult to detect a child's impending transition from "troubled teen" to "killer" for many reasons. Teenagers hide many things from their parents, and they act differently around their parents than they do around their peers. Moreover, peers and adults in the school or community often do not share disturbing information about teens with their parents. Finally, it seems disloyal to most parents to "think the worst" of their children

Gun Education to Kids by Parents

It is vital that parents talk to their children about guns, but this can be a difficult conversation to have. The discussion must be age-appropriate and offer children clear instructions about avoiding guns without adult supervision.

- ❖ *Preteens*: This is a good time to begin talking with children about ways to solve problems that do not involve violence. With older children, explain to them the consequences of violence and the dangers inherent in the mishandling of guns. Continue to emphasize to children that they should never touch a gun without adult supervision.
- ❖ *Teens*: This can be a difficult time to maintain open communication with kids as they become more independent and rebellious. However, maintaining dialogue with your children can help you spot any potential problems. The American Academy of Pediatrics suggests that, at this point in a child's life, it is easier to keep guns away from teens than to keep teens away from guns, which are often glamorized in the media. It is important that parents watch for signs of depression or changes in behavior, as teens feeling this way are at an increased risk for suicide.

Don't carry a gun or a weapon. If you do, this tells your children that using guns solves problems.

Monitoring the Environment

Parents who are concerned that their children may become victims or perpetrators of gun violence can alter their parenting behavior to compensate for dangers in the children's social environments. One parenting practice that has been researched extensively is parental monitoring, which involves tracking and attending to the child's activities and whereabouts. Research reveals that well-monitored children and youth are less likely to smoke, use drugs and alcohol, engage in risky sexual behavior, become antisocial or delinquent, and socialize with deviant peers. Though parental monitoring may protect children from many of life's temptations and dangers, can it protect them from gun violence? Closely monitoring children and adolescents is the only way to protect them from the widespread gang activity and gunfire that are characteristic of their community. Similarly, studies indicate that many parents in urban areas try to compensate for the unpredictability of their environment by setting greater restrictions on their children's behavior and using more physical discipline. Parents of the accused in Indian school shoot out are responsible for the incident. They are supposed to keep the weapon beyond the reach of their children under the safe custody. They are negligent in keeping their weapon. The school is not at all responsible for the students. The management cannot keep an eye on each and every student.

Children have to be guided, and it is our most important job as parents to do just that. Parents have to nurture their children and provide them with strong positive guidance and discipline. We have to send our children to school as responsible and respectful young people and we can't expect our sitters or housekeeper to supplant us as parents. Making parents legally accountable for their children and requiring them to assume primary responsibility for the actions and control of their children may be the only way to do this and will ultimately offer the best chance for reducing the violence in our schools.

Monitoring the Media

Defining Moment in the Public's Consciousness

On April 20, 1999, the world watched as two high school students, armed with automatic weapons and shotguns, killed 12 students and a teacher and wounded 23 others before turning the guns on themselves. The tragedy at Columbine High School is considered a defining moment in the public's consciousness about gun violence. The nonstop real-time media coverage of this horrendous massacre, both on the air and in print, was traumatizing to the victims' families and friends, the community, the state of Colorado, the United States, and the world.

School-Phobic Kids

School shootings in particular are traumatizing for children because they all go to school. After Columbine, preschoolers in Colorado began talking about where they would be going to school as the place where they would die. School systems around the country saw the phenomenon of school-phobic kids, as both the news media and talk shows exaggerated a child's risk of being shot at school. The misconceptions about the risk of school shootings are pervasive in all age groups.

Parental interest in regulating the amount of violent imagery children watch has grown in recent years. Complicating matters, the deregulation of children's television programming has increased parents' responsibility for monitoring their children's television viewing. The growing depend for monitoring technology such as the V-chip suggests that American parents are struggling with the task.

Similarly, there are efforts to impose—and, in some cases, enforce—age restrictions or recommendations on certain forms of violent media. Such efforts include restricting admission to R-rated movies, placing warning labels on music with explicit lyrics, and providing recommended audience ages for prime-time television shows. These initiatives are self-imposed and self-regulated by the entertainment industry, but many adults support stricter legal restrictions on children's access to certain forms of violent material.

In addition, many American parents are beginning to limit their children's access to violent video games in response to findings that they have played a role in the proliferation of youth violence, and that children with certain risk factors, especially signs of peer rejection and emotional instability, should have limited exposure to point-and-shoot video games. Some communities also are taking action to restrict children's access to video arcades. The city of Indianapolis, for example, has prohibited children under age 18 from playing violent video games in arcades without a parent present. Distributors of arcade video games have filed lawsuits that may overturn this action, but other cities have expressed interest in imposing similar restrictions. Legislation pending in Congress also would impose greater restrictions on access to violent video games and other types of violent or age-sensitive media.

Children can be exposed to a good amount of violence by the media, especially from TV and movies. It is important to teach children that this is not real and that guns cause real injuries. Emphasize to them that they should never touch a gun and should always tell an adult if they come across one.

Seeing a lot of violence on television, in the movies, and in video games can lead children to behave aggressively. As a parent, you can control the amount of violence your children see in the media.

Here are some ideas:

❖ Limit television viewing time to 1 to 2 hours a day.
❖ Make sure you know what TV shows your children watch, which movies they see, and what kinds of video games they play.
❖ Talk to your children about the violence that they see on TV shows, in the movies, and in video games. Help them understand how painful it would be in real life and the serious consequences for violent behaviors.
❖ Discuss with your children ways to solve problems without violence.

Even more disturbing is the horrific method of these murders. To charge into a building and try to kill as many people as possible is an enactment of video violence. This is the kind of violence you see in the movies and play on video games. Children of today live in a social environment where violence is a primary form of entertainment, and they are exposed to values and ideas which reinforce and glorify violence. In case after case I have observed just how easily the lessons of well-meaning and capable parents are overpowered by the compelling and pervasive messages of violence in our modern video culture. We protect adults from consumer fraud and deceptive advertising better than we protect our children from these salesmen of hate and violence. As a society, we must be more concerned about the daily does of extreme violence administered to our children through television, video games, music, and the internet. Repeated exposure to messages of violence and hatred over time desensitize many young people, distort their perceptions of personal safety, and erode inhibitions against harming others.

Scientific studies provide overwhelming evidence that television violence encourages aggressive behavior and has a long-term effect on children (see reviews in Berkowitz, 1993; Donnerstein, Slaby, & Eron, 1995; Hughes & Hasbrouck, 1996). Yet the entertainment industry cannot accept these findings any more than tobacco industry could accept that cigarette smoking results in cancer. Concern over our children is cunningly transformed into a debate over constitutional freedom. We have trouble appreciating causal effects that are subtle, indirect, and cumulative over long periods of time. What's the harm in one video game or one cigarette.

Children and TV Violence

Television can be a powerful influence in developing value systems and shaping behavior. Unfortunately, much of today's television programming is violent. Hundreds of studies of the effects of TV violence on children and teenagers have found that children may:

- ❖ become "immune" or numb to the horror of violence
- ❖ gradually accept violence as a way to solve problems
- ❖ imitate the violence they observe on television; and
- ❖ identify with certain characters, victims and/or victimizers

Extensive viewing of television violence by children causes greater aggressiveness. Sometimes, watching a single violent program can increase aggressiveness. Children who view shows in which violence is very realistic, frequently repeated or unpunished, are more likely to imitate what they see. Children with emotional, behavioral, learning or impulse control problems may be more easily influenced by TV violence. The impact of TV violence may be immediately evident in the child's behavior or may surface years later. Young people can even be affected when the family atmosphere shows no tendency toward violence.

Parent as Counselor

Take an active role in your children's schools. Talk regularly with teachers and staff. Volunteer in the classroom or library, or in after-school activities. Work with parent teacher- student organizations. Act as role models. Settle your own conflicts peaceably and manage anger without violence.

Listen to and talk with your children regularly. Find out what they're thinking on all kinds of topics. Create an opportunity for two-way conversation, which may mean forgoing judgments or pronouncements. This kind of communication should be a daily habit, not a reaction to crisis.

Set clear limits on behaviors in advance. Discuss punishments and rewards in advance, too. Disciplining with framework and consistency helps teach self-discipline, a skill your children can use for the rest of their lives.

Communicate clearly on the violence issue. Explain that you don't accept and won't tolerate violent behavior.

Discuss what violence is and is not. Answer questions thoughtfully. Listen to children's ideas and concerns. They may bring up small problems that can easily be solved now, problems that could become worse if allowed to fester.

Help your children learn how to examine and find solutions to problems. Kids who know how to approach a problem and resolve it effectively is less likely o be angry, frustrated, or violent. Take advantage of "teachable moments" to help your child understand and apply these and other skills.

Discourage name-calling and teasing. These behaviors often escalate into fistfights (or worse). Whether the teaser is violent or not, the victim may see violence as the only way to stop it.

Insist on knowing your children's friends, whereabouts, and activities. It's your right. Make your home an inviting and pleasant place for your children and their friends; it's easier to know what they're up to when they're around. Know how to spot signs of troubling behavior in kids—yours and others.

Work with other parents to develop standards for school related events, acceptable out-of-school activities and places, and required adult supervision. Support each other in enforcing these standards.

Make it clear that you support school policies and rules that help create and sustain a safe place for all students to learn. If your child feels a rule is wrong, discuss his or her reasons and what rule might work better.

Join up with other parents, through school and neighborhood associations, religious organizations, civic groups, and youth activity groups. Talk with each other about violence problems, concerns about youth in the community, sources of help to strengthen and sharpen parenting skills, and similar issues.

Kids need a safe and comfortable environment to learn to the best of their capabilities. This means they have to feel safe in their school and be able to positively interact with their teachers and classmates. By doing the following, parents and other adults can help make sure children have a positive school experience.

Talk to your children about their day. Sometimes children won't tell you right away if they are having problems at school. Ask your children if they see anyone bullied, if they are bullied, or if anything else makes them feel uncomfortable. Look for warning signs, such as a sudden drop in grades, loss of friends, or torn clothing.

Teach children to resolve problems without fighting. Explain that fighting could lead to them getting hurt, hurting someone else, or earning a reputation as a bully. Talk to them about other ways they can work out a problem, such as talking it out, walking away, sticking with friends, or telling a trusted adult.

Keep an eye on your children's Internet use. Many elementary schools have computers with Internet access. Ask your children's school if students are monitored when they use the Internet or if there is a blocking device installed to prevent children from finding explicit websites. Talk to your children about what they do online—what sites they visit, who they email, and who they chat with. Let them know they can talk to you if anything they see online makes them uncomfortable, whether it's an explicit website or a classmate bullying them or someone else through email, chat, or websites.

Ask about the safety and emergency plans for your children's school. How are local police involved? How are students and parents involved? What emergencies have been considered and planned for?

Reaction Handling

When children see such an event on television or on Web-based news flashes, it is natural for them to worry about their own school and their own safety, particularly if the violence occurred nearby or in a neighboring city or state.

Talk to Your Children

Psychologists who work in the area of trauma and recovery advise parents to use the troubling news of school shootings as an opportunity to talk and listen to their children. It is important, say these psychologists, to be honest. Parents should acknowledge to children that bad things do happen, but also reassure them with the information that many people are working to keep them safe, including their parents, teachers, and local police.

Young children may communicate their fears through play or drawings. Elementary school children will use a combination of play and talking to express themselves. Adolescents are more likely to have the skills to communicate their feelings and fears verbally. Adults should be attentive to a child's concerns, but also try to help the children put their fears into proportion to the real risk. Again, it is important to reassure children that the adults in their lives are doing everything they can to make their environment—school, home, and neighborhood—safe for them.

Parents, teachers, and school administrators also need to communicate with one another not only about how to keep kids safe, but about which children might need more reassurance and the best way to give it to them.

Limit Exposure to News Coverage

Parents should also monitor how much exposure a child has to news reports of traumatic events, including these recent school shootings. Research has shown that some young children believe that the events are reoccurring each time they see a television replay of the news footage.

Know the Warning Signs

Most children are quite resilient and will return to their normal activities and personality relatively quickly, but parents should be alert to any signs of anxiety that might suggest that a child or teenager might need more assistance. Such indicators could be a change in the child's school performance, changes in relationships with peers and teachers, excessive worry, school refusal, sleeplessness, nightmares, headaches or stomachaches, or loss of interest in activities that the child used to enjoy. Also remember that every child will respond to trauma differently. Some will have no ill effects; others may suffer an immediate and acute effect. Still others may not show signs of stress until sometime after the event.

Traveling to and from School

Map out with your children a safe way for them to walk to school or to the bus stop. Avoid busy roads and intersections. Do a trial run with them to point out places they should avoid along the way, such as vacant lots, construction areas, and parks where there aren't many people.

Teach children to follow traffic signals and rules when walking or biking. Stress that they should cross the street at crosswalks or intersections with crossing guards when they can.

Encourage children to walk to school or the bus stop with a sibling or friend, and to wait at bus stops with other children.

Teach children not to talk to strangers, go anywhere with them, or accept gifts from them without your permission. Tell them that if they see a suspicious stranger hanging around or in their school they should tell an adult.

Help children memorize their phone number and full address, including area code and zip code. Write down other important phone numbers such as your work and cell phone on a card for your children to carry with them.

On the Bus

Have your children arrive at the bus stop at least five minutes before the bus is scheduled to pick them up.

Make sure children know to stand on the sidewalk or on the grass while waiting for the bus.

Teach children to make sure they can see the bus driver and the bus driver can see them before crossing in front of the bus. Tell them to never walk behind the bus.

Be aware that often bullying takes place on the school bus. Ask children about their bus—who they sit with, who they talk to, and what the other kids do. Let them know that if they see someone being bullied, or are bullied themselves, they can talk to you, the bus driver, or another trusted adult.

In the family context, corporal punishment is widely used, and widespread anecdotal evidence, both from parents and from adults who were spanked as children, indicate that, at least in some cases—for instance, when the rules applied are seen as fair—it may be effective, especially when the children involved have an imperfectly developed moral sense.

If your child shows signs of disturbed functioning—at home or at school—because of fears of violence, then it's time to seek professional advice. If your child is sleeping poorly, missing school or not playing normally with friends, consult your pediatrician about how you can best handle the situation.

Parents Regulate TV Watching

Parents can protect children from excessive TV violence in the following ways:

❖ pay attention to the programs their children are watching and watch some with them
❖ set limits on the amount of time they spend with the television; consider removing the TV set from the child=s bedroom
❖ point out that although the actor has not actually been hurt or killed, such violence in real life results in pain or death
❖ refuse to let the children see shows known to be violent, and change the channel or turn off the TV set when offensive material comes on, with an explanation of what is wrong with the program
❖ disapprove of the violent episodes in front of the children, stressing the belief that such behavior is not the best way to resolve a problem

> ❖ to offset peer pressure among friends and classmates, contact other parents and agree to enforce similar rules about the length of time and type of program the children may watch

Parents can also use these measures to prevent harmful effects from television in other areas such as racial or sexual stereotyping. The amount of time children watch TV, regardless of content, should be moderated because it decreases time spent on more beneficial activities such as reading, playing with friends, and developing hobbies.

Range of Violent Behavior

Violent behavior in children and adolescents can include a wide range of behaviors: explosive temper tantrums, physical aggression, fighting, threats or attempts to hurt others (including homicidal thoughts), use of weapons, cruelty toward animals, fire setting, intentional destruction of property and vandalism.

Factors Which Increase Risk of Violent Behavior

Numerous research studies have concluded that a complex interaction or combination of factors leads to an increased risk of violent behavior in children and adolescents. These factors include:

> ❖ Previous aggressive or violent behavior,
> ❖ Being the victim of physical abuse and/or sexual abuse,
> ❖ Exposure to violence in the home and/or community,
> ❖ Genetic (family heredity) factors,
> ❖ Exposure to violence in media (TV, movies, etc.),
> ❖ Use of drugs and/or alcohol,
> ❖ Presence of firearms in home,
> ❖ Combination of stressful family socioeconomic factors (poverty, severe deprivation, marital breakup, single parenting, unemployment, loss of support from extended family), and
> ❖ Brain damage from head injury.

What are the "Warning Signs" for Violent Behavior in Children?

Children who have several risk factors and show the following behaviors should be carefully evaluated:

> ❖ Intense anger

- ❖ Frequent loss of temper or blow-ups
- ❖ Extreme irritability
- ❖ Extreme impulsiveness
- ❖ Becoming easily frustrated

Parents and teachers should be careful not to minimize these behaviors in children.

What can be Done If a Child Shows Violent Behavior?

Whenever a parent or other adult is concerned, they should immediately arrange for a comprehensive evaluation by a qualified mental health professional. Early treatment by a professional can often help. The goals of treatment typically focus on helping the child to: learn how to control his/her anger; express anger and frustrations in appropriate ways; be responsible for his/her actions; and accept consequences. In addition, family conflicts, school problems, and community issues must be addressed.

Can Anything Prevent Violent Behavior in Children?

Research studies have shown that much violent behavior can be decreased or even prevented if the above risk factors are significantly reduced or eliminated. Most importantly, efforts should be directed at dramatically decreasing the exposure of children and adolescents to violence in the home, community, and through the media. Clearly, violence leads to violence.

In addition, the following strategies can lessen or prevent violent behavior:

- ❖ Prevention of child abuse (use of programs such as parent training, family support programs, etc.)
- ❖ Sex education and parenting programs for adolescents
- ❖ Early intervention programs for violent youngsters
- ❖ Monitoring child's viewing of violence on TV/videos/movies

Parenting

Why People Commit Crimes: Farringtons claim (social psychological researcher) as to why people commit crimes looks at problem families.

❖ *1st claim*: criminal offenders have a syndrome, a collection of anti social dispositions.

❖ *2nd claim*: early signs of criminal offending predicts a long and potentially serious criminal career. *e.g.* Badly behaved infant → bullying → shoplifting, assault → robbery → child abuse → alcohol abuse, unemployment/early anti social behaviour = underlying criminal behaviour.

Studies by *Farrington* found a strong correlation (relationship) between criminals & certain family experiences:

❖ Criminals exhibit socially unacceptable behavior from a young age within their families.

❖ Criminals may also possess a range of cognitive defects *e.g.* Poor reasoning abilities.

❖ Criminals tend to have a troubled family life, *e.g.* Alcohol/drug abuse, violence.

❖ Within the family, experience poor parenting, failed education, unemployment.

Social problems/criminal careers originate in specific types of:

❖ Personality,
❖ Families, and
❖ Socialization process.

Problem children → problem adults → more problem children

(a) Criminal careers stem from anti-personality syndrome
(b) The syndrome is transmitted by problem families who exhibit poor parenting
(c) Poor parenting is passed from one generation to the next.

There is an interaction is between genes and the environment, but the environment is much more than nurture—the effect of parenting alone. Certainly, in the first two or three years, babies have their first experiences in forming and maintaining relationships, learning the rules of living and the boundaries of behavior.

Growing up in the same home does not make children more like each other. For several decades, socialization researchers had been producing study after study, yet correlations between parents' behavior and children's characteristics were neither strong nor consistent. Children are built to be social beings. The newborn child certainly attaches to its mother, but soon begins to observe others around it. Childhood is a process of growing away from the parents.

The home and the school are two different environments with their different rules, and children adopt different personas for each. Most parents, when they ask their children, "What did you do at school today?" get a mumbled and incoherent reply. Similarly, children at school find it difficult to talk about their home life. They are two different worlds, and they do not necessarily transfer the experience from one context to the other.

Children get their ideas of how to behave by identifying with the group and taking on its attitudes, behaviors, speech and styles of dress and adornment. Most of them do this automatically and willingly. They want to be like their peers, but just in case they have any funny ideas, their peers are quick to remind them of the penalties of being different. Children learn very early to categorize, to look for feelings of group ness, and they categorize themselves "I am an X", "I am not a Y." Within those categorizations they may emphasize their differences. They may the brains of the group (so long as they don't appear too brainy) or the comic (so long as everyone laughs) Children also categorize life in extremes, in a bipolar and authoritarian fashion, especially gender behavior.

Child rearing varies immensely between cultures. In some native cultures, parents are tolerant of misbehavior in a way that would be shocking to us. In others, often the more 'civilized' adult control is extremely rigid. Yet children, who grow up in cultures different to their parents, to the despair, grow up absorbing the new culture, rather than their parent's. Parents as a group do influence children as a group, but indirectly.

You have a kid you can't manage, either in your home or in your classroom or you know someone who does. It's frightening because you wonder if this particular child will wind up harming himself/herself or someone else. The following descriptions may include some of the behaviors you are seeing in your problem child. I have broken these behaviors down into two different types. These descriptions are the extremes and many violent children may fall somewhere in between them.

The Type I child I will refer to as the "under-controlled" child. These children are impulsive, irritable and overly responsive to threats (Megargee, 1971). They are revengeful, spiteful, blame others for their mistakes, are oppositional and argue with adults and peers. They seem overly hostile and may even be paranoid—that is, they think others are out to get them. Of course, in some ways, these kids are right. Their behavior becomes a self-fulling prophecy as the more hostile and paranoid they become, the more others are apt to blame them and accuse them of misdeeds, even if they were not the actual perpetrator. In their view, teachers are always blaming them for things they never did. I find a surefire way to identify these types of children is if they refer to their accusers as "they." "They say I was smoking at school. They say I was in a fight with another kid at school." These children rarely accept that they themselves ever did anything wrong. The slightest provocation may set the child off: another child or a sibling may call a name or you may ask them to take out the garbage or help around the house. Next thing you know, this kid has put a hole through the wall or thrown a chair. You may even be afraid of this type of child and wonder if they might harm you or someone close to you.

The Type II kid is a whole different animal. This type of child keeps everything inside and can be referred to as "over-controlled". This type of child may be anxious and repressed, but very angry (Megargee, 1971). You may never know anything is wrong with this type of child until one day, they blow. These kids never even seemed like a threat. They might be the small bespectacled young man with the beady eyes in your daughter's classroom or your son's chemistry partner. They may not look like a threat, but listen carefully and you will find that they often talk like one. Several of the kids who were involved in the school shootings last year fit this type of description. When Michael Carneal, the fourteen-year-old who opened fire at his Paducah, Kentucky school told classmates he had a gun days before the shooting, no one said anything because they thought, "no way, he doesn't seem like anyone who would do anything like that, because of his personality." Kip Kinkel (the Springfield Oregon school shooter) had classmates who voted him "most likely to start World War III." Yet, no one thought him much of a threat. Unfortunately, they were wrong.

What can you do as a parent or teacher if you think a child is violent or potentially violent? Following are some suggestions that will focus on those kids who have homicidal revengeful feelings towards others or harbor angry feelings towards others that you feel may one day escalate into a tragedy:

Practical Tips for Parents Only

1. The first thing you must do is to look at your problem child realistically. It's always hard to hear negative feedback from teachers and other adults about your child. Many times I have seen parents who can not accept that anything is "wrong" with

their child. Take for example, a case where a school counselor told a boy's parents that he had been writing odd notes about "microwaving gophers to death just to watch them die." This same boy had been observed by the counselor to be rolling around in manure laughing hysterically in the back of the school building. His parent's diagnosis? He was going to be a screen play writer. Unfortunately, this potential Stephen Spielberg ended up in police custody for writing death threats over the Internet for a number of his teachers and other students. So, remember—take seriously others' concerns about your child, especially if you hear the same one again and again. It might possibly have some validity to it.

2. Many parents see their children's shortcomings as a reflection of themselves or poor parenting skills. Try to frame constructive criticism about your child in a different manner. Here is an opportunity for you to get to know your child better or address a problem behavior before it becomes serious. Try to put your personal feelings aside and focus on what would be best for your child. Remember that your ultimate goal as a parent is to help your child to grow up to live an independent satisfying life. Children cannot go on to do this if 1) they end up in jail and/or 2) they cannot get along with others and/or 3) they do not have the self-control to fulfill their dreams and goals. You are in the best position to help them learn these skills.

3. So the daycare worker (if your child is very young) or a teacher has told you your child is having problems in the classroom. Now what do you do? First, analyze what the problem is and how extreme the behavior is. Is it something simple like he or she is disruptive in class or is it something more serious like hitting others, making threats or even carrying a weapon?

4. Next, determine what you can do and what support you will need to manage your child. If the problem is at school, call a meeting with the school counselor or M-team (multidisciplinary team) if your child is in special education. Listen carefully to what teachers and staff say to you about your child. Try to be as cooperative as possible, even if you feel that what is being said about your child is incorrect or unfair. Bring up your concerns and try to elicit the staff's help. After all, if you become angry and/or belligerent to school staff, the outcome will not be good for your child, no matter what happens next. Stay calm.

5. If the problem is mainly in your home, you need to decide where

to turn for help. Determine whether your child fits one of the descriptions mentioned earlier. Is he/she having problems with being under-controlled (impulsive, aggressive, irritable) or over-controlled (repressed, keeps things to himself/herself, internalizes problems, and has fits of anger that are random). You might even keep a record of your child's incidents at home so you will be able to provide a mental health professional with a detailed description.

6. Contact a licensed psychologist or psychiatrist who is recommended by your school or someone whose judgement you trust. You can even go online on your computer to find out about mental health professionals in your state. Many states now require mental health professionals to have their qualifications and specialties posted as well as whether or not they have had malpractice charges against them.

7. If your child is aggressive or depressed, consider removing all dangerous chemicals and guns from your home. I have met many parents who tell me they believe their child is so angry and revengeful that they believe he/she would harm others or themselves with a weapon or concoct a bomb. Some parents say their children even start fires. Yet these same parents will continue to keep guns and dangerous chemicals such as gasoline around the house. I recently talked with one mother whose twelve year-old was unruly and "on the edge." During our session, his mother commented to me, "My son could very well be one of those school-shooters you see on TV one day." Amazingly, this woman and the boy's father were allowing this boy to shoot rifles and even lock them up in the gun safe at night. Naturally, I told her this was a very bad idea. Guns certainly have their place in the hands of a responsible adult or teen, but for a child who is unstable or impulsive, they can result in tragedy. So, if you have a potentially violent child, you must weigh the advantages of having guns or chemicals in your home (e.g. self-protection, need gasoline to run your lawnmower) against the disadvantages (your kid could get their hands on them and harm himself or someone else). If you fear that your child is potentially dangerous, even if it is just a "gut" feeling—remove the dangerous chemicals and guns from your home. Also, remember that children and teens are very good at finding guns that are hidden. I have talked with many young people who tell me that their parents hide guns from

them but they usually know where to look. Don't get me wrong; I am not against guns as they are useful tools for sport and self-defense, but only in responsible hands.

8. Finally, try to talk with your teen about his/her difficulties or at least be available if she/he wants to talk and really listen. There may be situations and feelings that your child has that you were not even aware of. Of course, talking does not always help. Your child may have extreme emotional problems that need to be addressed.

6

School Responsibility

Primary and Secondary Education in India

India has large number of govt. schools across the country. In different regions of the country, there exist various methods of school information management. The school system in India is composed of primary, upper primary and high schools. A collection of schools forms a cluster, clusters form a block, blocks are under a district, districts form a state and states form the country. Such hierarchy is useful in decentralizing the management of schools.

Current System

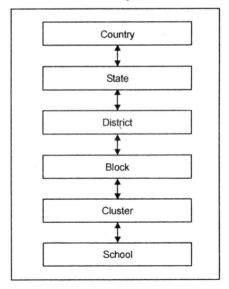

Human Resource at School

- ❖ Headmaster,
- ❖ Teaching Staff,
- ❖ Ministerial staff and
- ❖ Menial staff, etc.

Universal Education in India

Several factors work against universal education in India. Although Indian law prohibits the employment of children in factories, the law allows them to work in cottage industries, family households, restaurants, or in agriculture. Primary and middle school education is compulsory. However, only slightly more than 50 per cent of children between the ages of six and fourteen actually attend school, although a far higher percentage is enrolled. School attendance patterns for children vary from region to region and according to gender. But it is noteworthy that national literacy rates increased from 43.7 per cent in 1981 to 52.2 per cent in 1991 (male 63.9 percent, female 39.4 percent), passing the 50 per cent mark for the first time. There are wide regional and gender variations in the literacy rates, however; for example, the southern state of Kerala, with a 1991 literacy rate of about 89.8 percent, ranked first in India in terms of both male and female literacy. Bihar, a northern state, ranked lowest with a literacy rate of only 39 per cent (53% for males and 23% for females). School enrollment rates also vary greatly according to age. (*see* table 9, Appendix)

To improve national literacy, the central government launched a wide-reaching literacy campaign in July 1993. Using a volunteer teaching force of some 10 million people, the government hoped to have reached around 100 million Indians by 1997. A special focus was placed on improving literacy among women.

A report in 1985 by the Ministry of Education, entitled *Challenge of Education: A Policy Perspective,* showed that nearly 60 per cent of children dropped out between grades one and five. (The Ministry of Education was incorporated into the Ministry of Human Resources in 1985 as the Department of Education. In 1988 the Ministry of Human Resources was renamed the Ministry of Human Resource Development.) Of 100 children enrolled in grade one, only twenty-three reached grade eight. Although many children lived within one kilometer of a primary school, nearly 20 per cent of all habitations did not have schools nearby. Forty per cent of primary schools were not of masonry construction. Sixty per cent had no drinking water facilities, 70 per cent had no library facilities, and 89 per cent lacked toilet facilities. Single-teacher primary schools were commonplace, and it was not unusual for the teacher to be absent or even to subcontract the teaching work to unqualified substitutes.

Education Since Independence

The improvements that India has made in education since independence are nevertheless substantial; from the first plan until the beginning of the sixth (1951-80), the percentage of the primary school-age population attending classes more than doubled. The number of schools and teachers increased dramatically. Middle schools and high schools registered the steepest rates of growth; The number of primary schools increased by more than 230 per cent between 1951 and 1980. During the same period, however, the number of middle schools increased about tenfold. The numbers of teachers showed similar rates of increase. The proportion of trained teachers among those working in primary and middle schools, fewer than 60 per cent in 1950, was more than 90 per cent in 1987 (see table 11, Appendix). However, there was considerable variation in the geographical distribution of trained teachers in the states and union territories in the 1986-87 school year. Arunachal Pradesh had the highest percentage (60 percent) of untrained teachers in primary schools, and Assam had the highest percentage (72 percent) of untrained teachers in middle schools. Gujarat, Tamil Nadu, Chandigarh, and Pondicherry (Puduchcheri) reportedly had no untrained teachers at either kind of school.

Private Schooling

Various forms of private schooling are common; many schools are strictly private, whereas others enjoy government grants-in-aid but are run privately. Schools run by church and missionary societies are common forms of private schools. Among India's Muslim population, the *madrasa*, a school attached to a mosque, plays an important role in education (*see* Islamic Traditions in South Asia, chapter 3). Some 10 per cent of all children who enter the first grade are enrolled in private schools. The dropout rate in these schools is practically nonexistent.

Traditional notions of social rank and hierarchy have greatly influenced India's primary school system. A dual system existed in the early 1990s, in which middle-class families sent their children to private schools while lower-class families sent their children to under financed and under-equipped municipal and village schools. Evolving middle-class values have made even nursery school education in the private sector a stressful event for children and parents alike. Tough entrance interviews for admission, long classroom hours, heavy homework assignments, and high tuition rates in the mid-1990s led to charges of "lost childhood" for preschool children and acknowledgment of both the social costs and enhanced social benefits for the families involved.

The government encourages the study of classical, modern, and tribal languages with a view toward the gradual switch from English to regional languages and to teaching Hindi in non-Hindi speaking states. As a result, there are schools conducted in various languages at all levels. Classical and foreign language training most commonly occurs at the postsecondary level, although English is also taught at the lower levels.

Spare the Rod and Help the Child Grow

Corporal punishment in government schools defeats the purpose of education, causing children to drop out There is a lack of accountability towards children in government schools, and that allows teachers to make use of corporal punishment. Also, due to lack of trained teachers, the number of students allotted to each teacher is overwhelming

However, corporal punishment is an everyday phenomenon in India, particularly in government schools. Children in several schools in India have reported that the teachers regularly hit them hard with their hand or a ruler, pinch them or make them stand or kneel outside the classroom. A study conducted with support from UNICEF revealed that a high percentage of children in Maharashtra reported that their teacher regularly hit them in class; the figure for Tamil Nadu was even higher. The prevalence of corporal punishment against children in rural schools was found to be similar.

Unfortunately, in government schools, corporal punishment is deemed as an indispensable means to in still discipline in children. There are a variety of reasons behind this assumption. Firstly, there is a lack of accountability towards children, and that contributes to violence in schools and allows the teachers to make use of corporal punishment. Also, due to the lack of trained teachers, the number of students allotted to each teacher is overwhelming. The inadequate infrastructure and insufficient learning tools in government schools further contribute to the stress levels of teachers, which subsequently lead them to frequently resort to corporal punishment. Another secondary factor is that since government schools cater to the poorer sections of society. The children who attend these schools frequently face violence at home as well. Hence the immorality of the act of hitting them would seem to be of a lesser magnitude, since these children "are beaten up at home anyway".

The effect corporal punishment has on children is devastating, not only to the child itself, but to society as well. On the child itself, some of the effects are: ¦ Physical pain, injury and in some cases permanent disability and even death. ¦ Humiliation, anger, vindictiveness that may have long-term psychological effects. ¦ The child's sense of worth is severely damaged, which makes him more vulnerable to depression Child abuse and physical violence in the early years contribute significantly to a higher risk of children turning violent themselves, as they learn that violence is acceptable behaviour. Sometimes the child may not clearly understand the reason for the punishment, or the punishment is inconsistently given. In these cases, corporal punishment can lead to passivity or strong feelings of helplessness.

Apart from these disturbing effects on the child itself, children who witness fellow students being beaten and humiliated by teachers are emotionally affected as well.

Socially, a consequence of corporal punishment is that it leads to a fear of the teacher and the school, causing children to drop out of school. Unfortunately, most parents of these children are not averse to the idea of the children absenting themselves from school, as it then provides them with an extra source of income.

The magnitude of the problem is larger than what immediately seems apparent. Illiteracy and all related issues such as unemployment and poverty are extremely serious issues for a country like ours. Hence, any factor that has an impact on the literacy levels of our country warrants detailed investigation. According to Maslow, an eminent psychologist, there exists a hierarchy of needs. One level needs to be fulfilled to reach the other. The topmost level, which symbolises holistic and healthy development, is Self-actualisation. Only a handful of individuals accomplish the final level. Most individuals attain and then remain on the third or fourth level. In this hierarchy, the first two levels, that is, the need for physiological fulfillment and safety, are alpha or primary needs. The third and fourth levels are secondary needs. Unless the two primary needs, the need for physiological fulfillment and the need for safety and security, is fulfilled one cannot possibly grow, and there is an absence of the capacity to expand one's capabilities and improve one's present circumstances. This hypothesis derives support from Henry Shue in Basic Rights Subsistence, Affluence and US Foreign Policy (1980), where he puts forth a similar argument, wherein he says that subsistence and security are both basic needs. When seen in the context of government schools, the mid-day meals scheme is an excellent initiative made by the government in order to ensure the first (and according to Maslow, most basic) need, that is physiological fulfillment. Also, it acts as an incentive for parents to send their children to school, there being one less mouth to feed.

However, the prevalence of corporal punishment does not allow students to climb to the second level of growth. In spite of the ratification of the United Nations Convention on the Rights of the Child, the government has failed to ensure the primary need for the child to feel safe and secure in the school-environment. What needs to be appreciated is that in order to ensure results, both the primary needs have to be guaranteed.

What are the Solutions?

The first step that needs to be taken is to bring corporal punishment in schools, under the Indian Penal Code. Currently, there is no national law prohibiting corporal punishment in schools. Also, the implementation of the law has been very half hearted, even in those states where corporal punishment has been banned.

A child cannot possibly strive for higher goals in life without having his primary needs fulfilled. Growth is seen as a function of the fulfillment of the primary needs and refers to the capability of an individual to rise above his present situation. Unemployment is a direct consequence of illiteracy, and hence an illiterate has no means to combat poverty. This corresponds to Amartya Sen's theory of capability expansion, according to which poverty is seen in the light of one's capacity to expand one's capability: "The 'capability approach' sees human life as a set of 'doings and beings'—we may call them 'functioning'—and it relates the evaluation of the quality of life to the assessment of the capability to function." Therefore a clear pattern emerges. Corporal punishment discourages attendance and consequently leads to a lack of education and literacy, hindering socio-economic growth. It is therefore absolutely crucial to ensure a secure environment for children in schools.

Personality Traits in Teacher

This profession requires dedication, perseverance and patience. Knowledge of the subject one is teaching as well as a rich experience in co-curriculars; keenness to take on responsibility; tact; patience and the ability to get along with all kinds of people are essential. A teacher must always remember that apart from teaching, it is he/she who shapes a child's character. Teacher has to be a friend, philosopher and guide to his wards.

Almost all great visionaries saw this great potential of teaching. They experimented with learning and pedagogy; they wanted new teachers capable of radicalising our ways of experiencing the world. The teacher, Leo Tolstoy imagined, should have sufficient sensitivity to enter into the mind of the child, and to invite him to the vast domain of learning. Tagore wanted the teacher to bring the child nearer the vastness of nature and enable him to feel its rhythm and beauty. For Tagore, the teacher should make the child realize that one learns not just through intellect, but also through intuition and imagination, and the domain of knowledge has diverse manifestations: science and music, or agriculture and aesthetics. Likewise, Paulo Freire saw teaching as a revolutionary practice that unites the teacher and the taught, and involves them in collective project; A project that fights hierarchies and divisions, and seeks to create a just world. In other words, in their perceptions we see the affirmation of a great ideal: a teacher as an intelligent being filled with extraordinary life energy! It is desirable to see the worth of this ideal in the specific context of India, because, if practiced, it can contribute to the process of social reconstruction. For instance, a good teacher of culture/history may help the learner evolve a new sensitivity to the civilization strength of

India—its cultural diversities and its philosophic depth. This sensitivity can create a new generation capable of fighting the authoritarian trends prevalent in contemporary Indian society. Likewise, a good teacher of science can enable the child to see the meaning of empirical observation and deductive reasoning, and how clear ideas can fight superstitions and prejudices. A good teacher can inspire the student to see science as a social movement, not just a lucrative career in the techno-corporate world.

But this great potential of teaching is seldom realized. We live in a society that shows terrible indifference to teaching and education. Barring elite institutions, our schools and colleges do not have adequate infrastructural facilities—satisfactory teacher-taught ratios, laboratories, libraries and other educational materials—to promote a healthy culture of learning. Moreover, here is a state that is not willing to respect the teaching community. Teaching as a vocation is degraded, and school teachers are forced to confront miserable life situations.

What further adds to the crisis is an extremely low level of self-esteem on the part of the teaching community. With a wounded consciousness, many of them refuse to see the worth of their vocation, and, therefore, fail to unfold their potential. The absence of good, self-confident teachers is felt everywhere. More often than not, the teaching community, because of this defeatism, fails to inspire the younger generation.

Indian culture says that Guru (teacher) should be respected as God. This culture continued for many thousands of years. Teacher is the giver of knowledge. They impart wisdom into the young generation for the better future of the country and society

School Responsibility

Parents will forgive school officials if test scores drop, but they are much less forgiving if something happens to their children that could have been prevented or better managed, especially when it comes to school crises. Parents want their school's administrative team and staff to take all possible steps to reduce the risks of an act of crime or violence from occurring at their school. They also expect school staff to be well-prepared for responding to events ranging from student suicides and natural disasters to school shootings and acts of terrorism.

For most of the year, children spend more time at school than anywhere else other than their own home. At school, children need a secure, positive, and comfortable environment to help them learn. Overall, schools are one of the safest places children can be. However, some schools have problems, such as bullying and theft, which make them less secure. These problems make students and educators feel less safe, and it makes it harder for students to learn and for teachers to do their jobs.

School Counselors

School counselors play a vital role in school safety and emergency preparedness planning. School counselors are increasingly looked upon as proactive players in the school safety planning process and should be an integral part of the school's safety and crisis teams.

It is very necessary that every school has an in-house counselor who can talk to children whenever they are disturbed by any issue. Just listening patiently to their grievances lifts the burden off their hearts. Counselors can remain objective and non-judgmental about any of the confessions people make. Counselors keep up the confidentiality of the matter. They try to help the client sort out his/her emotions and help them to think in positive direction. They teach assertive skills to the victims to stand up for their rights. This can go a long way in reducing many of the ills that are cropping up among student community.

Schools need to view school safety planning as an ongoing process, not a one-time event, although there will always be new issues to consider and established plans to revisit. Be sure to include students in your safety-planning process through focus groups, anonymous surveys and other methods.

We can divide school violence-prevention methods into three classes—

❖ Measures related to school management (that is, related to discipline and punishment),
❖ Measures related to environmental modification (for instance, video cameras, security guards, and uniforms), and
❖ Educational and curriculum-based measures (for instance, conflict-resolution and gang-prevention programs).

All methods have their advantages and disadvantages.

1940	1990
❖ Talking out of turn	❖ Drug abuse
❖ Chewing gum	❖ Alcohol abuse
❖ Making noise	❖ Pregnancy
❖ Running in the hall	❖ Suicide
❖ Cutting in line	❖ Rape
❖ Dress code violations	❖ Robbery
❖ Littering	❖ Assault

1940	1990
Defiance	06–Physical sexual harassment, molestation
01–Failure to follow specific instructions by a person in authority	07–Sexual assault, including attempted and completed rape
02–Arguing beyond acceptable limits	08–Assault with a gun
03–Raising of voice beyond acceptable limits	09–Assault with knife
04–Use of profane language	10–Assault with weapon other than gun or knife
05–Display of an obscene gesture	11–Other
06–Refusal to follow a school rule	*Fighting Between Students*

(Contd.)

(*Contd.*)

1940	1990
07–Dishonesty in dealing with another person	01–Hitting, punching, kicking, choking, etc.
08–Creating a disturbance	02–Making verbal or gestural threats
09–Leaving the classroom without permission	03–Verbal tuning
Defacing School Property	04–Slapping, poking, pushing
01–Littering	05–Other
02–Creating graffiti	*Activities Interfering with School Performance*
03–Throwing books	01–Not completing assignment, homework, etc.
04–Purposely destroying school property	02–Excessive talking in class
05–Accidentally destroying school property	03–Inattentiveness in class
06–Throwing other objects	04–Not prepared for activity
07–Pulling fire alarm	05–Failure to return to/from parent
08–Setting a fire	06–Creation of disturbance
09–Other	07–Leaving classroom without permission
Illegal Activities	08–Carrying a beeper
01–Stealing	09–Other
02–Trespassing	*Breaking Miscellaneous School Rules*
03–Possession of weapon	01–Smoking
04–Extortion	02–Leaving school grounds without permission
05–Gambling	03–Making excessive noise
06–Possession or use of drug	04–Tardiness
07–Selling drugs	05–Truancy
08–Other	06–Cutting class
Assault or Abuse	07–Loitering
01–Hitting, punching, or kicking	08–Use of profane language
02–Making verbal or gestural threats	09–Use of obscene gesture
03–Reckless endangerment	10–Dishonesty in dealing with another person
04–Unnecessary use of force	11–Other
05–Verbal sexual harassment	

Source: Thomas Toch, Ted Gest, and Monika Guttman, "Violence in schools," *U.S. News & World Report*, vol. 115, no. 18 (November 8, 1993), p. 30, citing data from Congressional Quarterly Researcher.

Students Characteristics

Student Characteristics	Total Number of Students	Percent of Students Reporting Victimization at School		
		Total	Violent	Property
Sex				
Male	11,166,316	9	2	7
Female	10,387,776	9	2	8
Race				
White	17,306,626	9	2	7
Black	3,449,488	8	2	7
Other	797,978	10	2*	8
Hispanic Origin				
Hispanic	2,026,968	7	3	5
Non-Hispanic	19,452,697	9	2	8
Not Ascertained	74,428	3*	—	3*
Age				
12	3,220,891	9	2	7
13	3,318,714	10	2	8
14	3,264,574	11	2	9
15	3,214,109	9	3	7
16	3,275,002	9	2	7
17	3,273,628	8	1	7
18	1,755,825	5	1*	4
19	231,348	2*	—	2*
Number of times family moved in last 5 years				
None	18,905,538	8	2	7
Once	845,345	9	2*	7
Twice	610,312	13	3*	11
3 or More	1,141,555	15	6	9
Note Ascertained	51,343	5*	5*	—
Family Income				
< $7,500	2,041,418	8	2	6
$7,500—$9,999	791,086	4	1*	3
$10,000—$14,999	1,823,150	9	3	7
$15,000—$24,999	3,772,445	8	1	8
$25,000—$29,999	1,845,313	8	2	7
$30,000—$49,999	5,798,448	10	2	8
$50,000 and over	3,498,382	11	2	9
Not Ascertained	1,983,849	7	3	5
Place of Residence				
Central City	3,816,321	10	2	8
Suburbs	10,089,207	9	2	7
Non-Metropolitan Area	5,648,564	8	1	7

Source: Bastian and Taylor, School Crime, p. 1.

	% of Student Victims	% of Student Perpetrators	Perpetrators' Gender	
			Male	Female
Verbal insults	60	50	60	40
Threats	26	23	34	12
Pushing, shoving, grabbing, slapping	43	42	54	30
Kicking, biting, hitting with a fist	24	26	37	15
Threats with a knife or gun	4	5	8	3
Using a knife or firing a gun	2	3	6	1
Theft	43	1	2	1
Other	2	14	18	9

Source: The Metropolitan Life Survey of the American Teacher: Violence in America's Public Schools (1993), conducted for Metropolitan Life Insurance Company by Louis Harris and Associates, Inc., pp. 71-72.

	Occurred	Witnessed	Worried About	Happened to Students
Bulling, Physical Attack, or Robbery	71%	56%	25%	12%
Bullying	56%	42%	18%	8%
Physical Attack	43%	33%	10%	4%
Robbery	12%	6%	6%	1%

Secondary Effects of School Violence

The effect of school violence is broader than actual victimization statistics suggest. Violence, in any setting, is a problem. The problem is compounded when it pertains to schools, because violent behavior and actions take away from the educational process. Moreover, violence affects the behavior of students, who act differently to avoid the threat of violence. Some students take a special route to get to school; some stay away from certain places in the school or on school grounds; some stay away from some school-related events; some deliberately stay in groups; and some sometimes stay home.

The cost of violence in society at large (*i.e.*, purchases of security systems, carrying of guns, enrollment in self-defense classes, and avoidance of certain streets at certain times) is measured not only by actual harm, but by expenditures to avoid harm, and by the general disruption of people's lives. Students, who spend their time thinking about violence, and rearranging their life to avoid violence, are spending valuable "brain cells," which could otherwise be spent on learning or fun, and are foregoing the pleasure that they would have gotten by frequenting the places that they now avoid. Many students believe restrooms are unsafe, and some have persistent health problems because they are afraid to use restrooms.

American schools, historically, have also had their share of violence, sex, drugs, and gambling. In colonial times, students mutinied at over 300 district schools every year, chasing off or locking out the teacher. It is hard to trace the evolution of school violence, since reporting procedures have never been consistent.

The Extent of Weapon Possession

According to the national MetLife survey in 1993, teachers, on average, believed that three per cent of students regularly carried weapons to school. Students carry guns both for protection and for self-esteem and peer acceptance.

Some schools have dealt with the problem of guns in schools through

❖ punitive means (by suspending or expelling students for carrying a weapon),
❖ by heightening security (e.g., metal detectors), or
❖ by educating people on how to react to gun crimes in such a way as to produce a minimum of bloodshed—for instance, lecturing teachers on guns and violence and telling them what to do if a student pulls a gun in class (don't make any fast moves and follow the student's orders).

The Main Cause of Shot-Out

Students say revenge is clearly the major reason for school shootings.
The top four reasons are:

❖ Other kids pick on them, make fun of them or bully them.
❖ They want to get back at people who have hurt them.
❖ They don't value life.
❖ They have been a victim pf physical abuse at home.

There were some variations in ranking based on gender.
The top five reasons endorsed by boys were:

❖ Getting back at those who hurt them;
❖ Other kids pick on them, make fun of them or bully them;

- ❖ They don't value life;
- ❖ They have mental problems; and
- ❖ They have been a victim of physical abuse at home.

For girls, the top reasons were:

- ❖ Other kids pick on them, make fun of them or bully them;
- ❖ They want to get back at those who have hurt them;
- ❖ They have been a victim of physical abuse at home;
- ❖ They don't value life; and
- ❖ They have witnessed physical abuse at home.

Warning Signs

Schools in USA face the difficult task of preparing for the possibility of school violence without creating a climate of fear. Nonetheless, prevention may be the best alternative to inaction or hysteria. An essential aspect of school violence prevention is performing an effective and in-depth assessment of threats of violence. To avoid "profiling" potential school shooters, the Federal Bureau of Investigation (FBI) has developed a guide for teachers and school administrators to use after a student has made threats of violence.

The FBI urges school administrators to watch for warning signs that can include a low tolerance for frustration, depression, lack of empathy, exaggerated sense of entitlement, excessive need for attention, inappropriate humor, rigid views, and fascination with violent entertainment, access to guns or weapons, and high exposure to violent media.

To help reduce the risk of violent incidents in schools, the FBI suggests that school administrators provide guidance to parents on issues such as the importance of restricting exposure to violent media, and on the need to be aware of their children's peer group and activities, to seek active involvement in their children's life, and to avoid giving children an inordinate amount of privacy. Beyond educating the family, the FBI recommends that administrators evaluate their school's culture and its contribution to the potential threat of gun violence. Indicators that could be monitored include the prevalence of bullying or social cliques, the level of comfort that students feel in sharing concerns with teachers and administrators, and even the physical layout of the school. For example, researchers at the University of Michigan have studied "un-owned places":

undefined territories within schools that are associated with violence and crime. According to this research and similar studies, hallways, dining areas, bathrooms, and parking lots are often centers for school violence because they are "un-owned" and frequently unoccupied by school personnel.

However, some school efforts to prevent gun violence on campus may foster more fear rather than a sense of security. Metal detectors, bars on windows, and surveillance cameras may make students feel unsafe or that they are not trusted. Similarly, emergency drills may send the message to expect a shooting, creating a climate of suspicion and anxiety among students and faculty.

"Zero Tolerance Policies"

Furthermore, some experts note that if schools rely on "zero tolerance policies" and simply expel students who make threats, such practices may actually exacerbate the danger by inflaming students who are already at risk for violent activity. Rather, they suggest, administrators should make a careful assessment of potential risks (including access to weapons in the home or community) and direct these students toward mental health services if necessary

Parental Supervision

Teachers perceive that the major factors contributing to student violence are lack of parental supervision at home (71%), lack of family involvement with the school (66%), and exposure to violence in the mass media (55%) (taken from The American Teacher, 1993).

This new educational environment, which in some respects often resembles a war zone, has created a need for society to develop programs that will offer a safe learning environment for all children and the teachers who teach them. Since laws demand that children attend school, schools have the inherent responsibility to provide them with a safe place where they can learn. To reach this goal most schools have taken technological steps (such as metal detectors and/or police guards) to try to stop some of the more violent acts from happening. While those steps may prevent students from conducting violent acts at school, they will not root out the more basic behavioral problems. And schools can't do it alone. Parents have to get involved and it may take enacting strict laws to get parents to the table. Is it legal to create a law that would hold parents (criminally) responsible for their children's actions? Maybe not, but it sure would get their attention. If the law were enacted, what would the punishment be? Would you take the child away and put them in a home where it could end up being worse to their development than staying with their parents? Fine the parents? That could ultimately cause them to have to work more and further neglect their children. Parents often have to concentrate more on their economic survival than the attitudes and behavior of their children. They do not have the quality time to spend with their children because of job responsibilities and ultimately rely on others to raise their children. While student violence is an enormous problem for our society and there is no simple remedy to fix it, something has to be done.

As reported in the Indian papers the boys had complained regarding the bully. Since no action was taken against the bully these two boys seem to have been 'pushed' into this action. The world is getting progressively 'smaller'. You cannot isolate yourself and follow only 'Indian culture' and avoid 'Western Culture'. What needs to be followed is the best of each culture. In the blame game—the school mainly, for not taking action against the bully and also the parents for making a gun along with the ammunition available to a boy of such tender age.

Schools should have metal detectors at the gate, and more security guards to check on students, most schools in India, school bags are rarely checked, and there is no frisking of students. Regular meetings are held between parents and teachers.

The way some schools have responded to the threats for greater violence has been tighter security. A few of the violence prevention measures include spiked fences, motorized gates, bulletproof metal-covered doors, metal detectors, and security guards who search student desks and lockers. Some complain that this only makes prisons out of the schools. Other schools have hired more counselors and violence prevention coordinators

A Psychologist or Counselor at School or a Religious Leader

Psychologists feel that exposure of kids to the violent characters on T.V. or their favorite cartoons sets a certain kind of mental image in their minds that they hardly know how serious the Gun Play is. But, the children who are taught about guns by their peers are more likely to be involved in various kinds of misbehavior, including gun crime.

Sometimes children cannot avoid seeing violence in the street, at school, or at home, and they may need help in dealing with these frightening experiences. A psychologist or counselor at school or a religious leader is among those who can help them cope with their feelings.

Several states in USA have enacted legislation that makes it easier for schools to share student information with law enforcement agencies and others who are trying to determine whether a student might be moving toward a school-based attack.

Educators can play a part in prevention by creating an environment where students feel comfortable telling an adult whenever they hear about someone who is considering doing harm to another person, or even whether the person is considering harming themselves. Once such an environment is created, it will remain important that the adults in that environment listen to students and handle the information they receive in a fair and responsible manner.

Tips

Enforce zero-tolerance policies toward the presence of weapons, alcohol, and illegal drugs. In an effort to stem this rising tide of school violence, many schools in USA have implemented Zero Tolerance policies. These policies vary widely, but most are based on the principle that violence or even a threat of violence has no place whatsoever in schools and will not be tolerated in any form. Under such policies, students who threaten or commit acts of violence have been punished, often suspended from school, and sometimes expelled. In a small percentage of these cases, school-based sanctions have been followed by juvenile or criminal court prosecutions.

Under most Zero Tolerance policies, each of these students would be suspended from school. Any further action against them would likely depend on the facts of the case, including any mitigating evidence.

Sensible application of a Zero Tolerance policy in all schools is warranted for a number of reasons. First and foremost is the need to at least temporarily separate a dangerous or potentially dangerous student from the rest of the school population. Where a student has acted in a violent manner, as in assaulting another or carrying a truly dangerous weapon to school, removal of the offender from the school setting is necessary for the physical protection of other students. An assessment of the offending student, the reasons for the infraction, and the need for additional sanctions, if any, should be undertaken, but only after this concern for the safety of other students is given paramount importance.

Beyond immediate safety concerns, however, this application of Zero

Tolerance appropriately denounces violent student behavior in no uncertain terms and serves as a deterrent to such behavior in the future by sending a clear message that acts which physically harm or endanger others will not be permitted at school under any circumstances.

More difficult is the application of Zero Tolerance to cases in which violence has been threatened but not carried out. Here, as well, both safety and deterrence warrant at least a brief suspension from school, with any additional action to be determined later. While the vast majority of student threats prove to be idle, in virtually all jurisdictions even threatening to harm another person is a crime. Beyond the law, however, common sense dictates that all student threats must be taken seriously and investigated so as to protect the safety of others in the school environment. Suspending a threatening student provides school and law enforcement authorities the time to conduct a thorough assessment of the threat and to make an informed decision regarding the needs of the school and community, as well as those of the threatening student.

Finally, as for the so-called "joking" threats that are also raised by some critics of Zero Tolerance, it should first be noted that it is often not easy to determine whether a student is joking or serious when making a threat. School officials who attempt to make that distinction do so at their own risk, as well as the risk of others.

- ❖ Establish and enforce drug- and gun-free zones.
- ❖ Establish policies that declare that anything that is illegal off campus is illegal on campus.
- ❖ Engage students in maintaining a good learning environment by establishing a teen court.
- ❖ Develop protocols between law enforcement and the school about ways to share information on at-risk youth.
- ❖ Develop resource lists that provide referral services for students who are depressed or otherwise under stress.
- ❖ Involve teens in designing and running programs such as mediation, mentoring, peer assistance, School Crime Watch, and graffiti removal programs.
- ❖ Insist that all students put outerwear in their lockers during school hours.
- ❖ Require all students to tuck in their shirts to keep them from hiding weapons.
- ❖ Develop and enforce dress codes that ban gang-related and gang-style clothing.

❖ Establish a policy of positive identification such as ID badges for administrators, staff, students, and visitors.
❖ Deny students permission to leave school for lunch and other non-school-related activities during school hours.

Society and School

The literature on school violence is rife with complaints that "this is society's entire problem" and that society is so violent that much school violence is merely expected. In a society where violence is a pervasive part of life, the schools bear less blame for school violence, and in such a society, the schools would probably not be seen as the primary place to stem violence. On the other hand, in a generally peaceful society where schools are violent, schools would both bear more of the blame and be expected to solve the problem to a greater extent.

One must realize the diversity of types of school violence. Some schools are located in violent, economically depressed neighborhoods. The following possible sources of school violence have been suggested:

❖ Poverty, which lays a foundation of anger and discontent;
❖ Illegitimacy and the breakdown of families, which lead children to seek the stability and caring environments of gangs;
❖ Domestic violence and child abuse, which foster learning and behavior problems, frustration, and retaliation;
❖ Society-wide violence rates and juvenile violence rates, which spill over into the school;
❖ The drug culture and its violent distribution network, which encourage students to arm themselves;
❖ Immigration, especially from countries where formal education is less valued;
❖ Population mobility, which creates an atmosphere of anonymity;
❖ Discrimination, which exacerbates the frustration and anger of minority students;
❖ Violent cultural imagery, from TV shows to sympathetic news coverage of militaristic foreign policy, which numbs children to the effects of violence;
❖ Materialism and advertising, which creates a culture where children are manipulated and feel exploited;
❖ Competitiveness and high parent expectations, which make children lose the identity and uniqueness of childhood before their time.

Criminal Penalties

Much school violence—such as theft, assault, on-campus possession of guns and drugs, setting fires—is also criminal in the "real world." Many schools have avoided the use of the police, preferring to rely on their own, internal, disciplinary procedures. But schools are now more likely to treat whatever is a crime outside school as a crime in school, and less likely to decide that "no one was really hurt." They are making greater use of law enforcement and the criminal justice system. Schools are working together with court officials, probation officers, and other professionals, where court officials give administrators information on convicted criminals returning to school, and probation officers are invited to monitor their charges on campus.

Putting children into the criminal justice system has its advantages; if the school's budget is tight, it may benefit from sending wrongdoers into a system that was explicitly designed to deal with such occurrences. It also accords with many people's moral convictions to treat criminals as criminals, regardless of whether they were in school or not. Juvenile courts often only intervene after serious violence occurs.

Corporal Punishment

The value of corporal punishment as a deterrent to school violence is disputed. Critics charge that "violence breeds violence"; corporal punishment teaches children that violence is an acceptable way to compel behavior, and makes them more likely to be violent themselves. Corporal punishment is often misdirected—while most violence is in higher grades, much corporal punishment occurs at primary and intermediate levels, and is more rarely used against bigger students who might retaliate. Corporal punishment, instead of being used as a last resort, is often used as a first punishment for nonviolent and minor misbehaviors.

Corporal punishment can also, depending on its frequency, duration, and intensity, induce post-traumatic stress disorder in its victims, and the victims themselves may show an increase in absenteeism, apathy, and vandalism.

Parents have been known to sue over instances of corporal punishment.

Alternative Education

Unruly children are often sent to, or required to enroll in, alternative education programs. There are three main categories of education for difficult-to-educate students: special education for students with disabilities, education for at-risk students, and corrections education.

Security-Related Solutions

Metal Detectors

If guns are the problem, metal detectors are one obvious way of solving the problem.

Video Cameras

Several analysts have advocated setting up video cameras (closed circuit television) to reduce violence. The assumption behind video cameras is that violence is less likely to occur if it can be seen. Video cameras have been operating on buses for years, but more recently, they have also been suggested for high-traffic areas, like hallways; and places where fights often happen, like parking lots. Some schools do put up "placebo cameras" to create the illusion of surveillance, but even if these cameras have some deterrent effect.

Security Guards

Limitations of security guards are similar to those of the police. They cannot be everywhere. They are no substitute for voluntary respect for the law, which the students at some schools, with few or no security guards and low violence rates, apparently have.

In the bureaucratic public school system, which is not highly sensitive to the demands of parents (especially in poor, inner-city areas), high rates of violence, instead of provoking massive school flight, provokes additional security expenditures, whether on metal detectors, alarm systems, electromagnetic door locks, or security guards. These tangible "rewards" for schools with high violence can be a disincentive to pursuing other, non-technological, violence-prevention methods. As one boys' dean at a lower-tier New York school is said to have remarked, "If I have a rape in the school this year, I'll get two extra security guards next year."

Reliance on security guards may lull other participants in the school system into a sense that violence prevention is not their responsibility. John Devine points out "the gradual withdrawal of teachers, over the past several decades, from the responsibility for school wide discipline, when the union contract removed this function from their job descriptions or reduced it," and notes that in some ways, this withdrawal of teachers (and their replacement by guards) may have exacerbated disorder, as teachers no longer even try to prevent violence.

Finally, guards cost money, and whether they are the best investment for a particular school depends on that school's resources, violence rates and types of crimes, and feasible alternatives.

Other Security-based Methods

Other methods suggested relieving violence problems vary widely. Some rely on knowing exactly what all students have at all times:

- ❖ Searching lockers;
- ❖ Requiring all book bags to be clear;
- ❖ "Shaking down" students.
- ❖ These methods may work in some cases, but require a large commitment of resources to be effective

Some methods rely on successfully identifying intruders:

- ❖ Mandating picture identification cards for students and staff;
- ❖ Encouraging staff and students to report suspicious people or activities;
- ❖ Fencing in campuses;
- ❖ Conducting "drive-by-shooting drills" in addition to traditional fire drills.

Still other methods limit themselves to producing a physical environment that will make it more difficult to commit crimes:

- ❖ Placing trained parent/community volunteers in hallways, on playgrounds, in study halls, and at extracurricular activities;
- ❖ Monitoring entrances;
- ❖ Limiting the number of potential entrances;
- ❖ Placing concrete barriers;
- ❖ Increasing lighting.

Indirect Behavior-Based Solutions

School uniforms have two justifications. One is to reduce violence, by:

- ❖ Decreasing the probability that students will carry concealed weapons.

- ❖ Decreasing the probability that students will fight over clothing jealousy.
- ❖ Decreasing the probability that students will be victims of robbery and assault because of their expensive jackets or shoes. In Detroit, a 15-year-old boy was shot for his $86 basketball shoes; in Fort Lauderdale, a 15-year-old student was robbed of his jewelry; in Oxon Hill, Maryland, a 17-year-old honor student was killed at a bus stop, in the crossfire during the robbery of another student's designer jacket.
- ❖ Decreasing the possibility that students will be victims of gang violence because they are wearing the colors or clothing associated with a gang.

The School Wide Scale: Addressing Juvenile Violence

The theory behind using school-based after-school activities to stem violence is that if students are in a place where they can be easily observed, violence will be more easily controlled. In some ways, such programs do not really aim at decreasing school violence—what disruptive students do on their own time may contribute to violence as a whole, but perhaps not to school violence.

The School System Scale: School Size

School size has also been offered as an explanation of school violence rates. Smaller schools are said to be more likely to become "communities of learners" where teachers, students, staff, parents, and community feel that they belong and share responsibilities. In a small school, teachers may be more likely to counsel a late or forgetful student instead of relying on discipline. Small schools allegedly provide a "human touch" where "personal relationships flourish" and students succeed, largely because of less bureaucracy and fewer regulations. Some studies indicate that students in small schools have more positive attitudes toward school, feel more deeply attached to their, and are more likely to participate in extracurricular programs such as drama and sports.

The Societal Level: Employers Demanding High-School Performance

Japanese high schools seem immune from many of the discipline problems plaguing American high schools. There is a reason for this; Japanese students have vastly more respect for their teachers than do their American counterparts, and more respect for education in general. They care more about their high-school grades, because colleges and employers carefully scrutinize their grades and their teachers' recommendations. Japanese high school teachers are virtually never assaulted by their students; rather, high school students pay attention to their teachers and graduate from high school in greater proportions (93 percent) than American students. They want to go to school because they are convinced, correctly, that their occupational futures depend on educational achievement. Employers are much more closely connected with high schools in Japan than in the United States. Students Comfortable Level in Reporting Safety Concerns to School Staff? Do students have at least one adult they would feel comfortable talking to about safety concerns at school? Are there other methods, such as hotlines or e-mail tip lines for students to report concerns? Schools must work on creating a climate where students feel comfortable reporting safety concerns and have multiple mechanisms for doing so.

School Policies, Procedures and Emergency/Crisis Guidelines on Security and Emergency Preparedness

Have the school board and administration written policies and procedures related to security, crisis preparedness planning and overall school safety planning? If so, when were they last updated? Are you doing what your plans and policies say you should do?

Oftentimes day-to-day practice does not reflect what schools have put in writing, thereby creating confusion and potentially setting up school leaders for increased liability. Does the school have a school safety committee to develop an overall plan for prevention, intervention and security issues? Are these plans balanced and not just prevention-only or security-only? Do students have a written school emergency and crisis guidelines? Is there a school crisis team to deal with emergency planning? Who are members of the safety committee and crisis team? Do these teams involve counselors, school nurses, custodians, secretaries, bus drivers, security and police staff and other support personnel in addition to teachers and administrators? How often do they meet? What type of training has been provided to these teams? Are these plans and guidelines reviewed regularly—at least once a year? Does the school officials test and exercise written crisis guidelines? What type of tests do they do? DOES SCHOOL EMPLOYEES RECEIVE TRAINING ON CRISIS PREPAREDNESS ISSUES?

Crisis Management

Principal's Role

When any individual within a school becomes aware of the sudden death of a student, be it homicide, suicide, accidental death, or the death of a student following an illness, it should be the responsibility of that individual to immediately call the principal and inform him/her of all the known facts regarding the death. It is important that the principal verify the facts concerning the death; including who has died. (There have, in some instances, been inaccurate accounts of who actually was deceased.) The principal needs to quickly assess the impact this death will have on the school community (i.e., how popular was the person, what extracurricular activities did he/she participate in, etc.) The principal will then take the lead in the activation of the protocol and the process through which students will be notified about the death. If the death occurs outside of school hours, the principal should call members of the Crisis Management Team. The team members notify the entire staff that there will be a change in the procedure of the normal school day and requests them to come to school early the following morning. If help, in addition to the building Crisis Management Team, is needed, the principal should arrange to notify the appropriate people. If the principal is not available, the associate principal or the principal's designee will begin this process.

A phone calling tree should be established each school year in order that school staff may be notified of school-related emergencies in a timely manner.

Pre-Planning Phase

Step One

Appoint members to the building Crises Management Team (typically include counselors, nurse, other building administrators, school social worker, school psychologist, educational consultant, etc.).

Step Two

Organize calling tree.

Step Three

Hold twenty-to-thirty minute staff meeting to review protocol procedures (this needs to be done annually).

Protocol Implementation

Step One

When notified of adult or student death, verify the death with appropriate public officials (if notification was not by family member or public official). Instances have occurred where the notification of who died was incorrect.

Step Two

Notify the school **Crises Team Leader** and assess the expected degree of response from the school community. Factors include groups deceased was involved in, the popularity of the person, etc.

Step Three

If death was not during school hours, activate the pre-arranged calling tree to notify staff of early-morning mandatory meeting. Request that Crises Management Team members meet with principal thirty minutes prior to staff meeting.

Step Four

Designate the Crises Management Team Leader as the person responsible for orchestrating the emotional first aid activities for the next few days. This person will serve as the "hub" of information and will direct the team's daily activities.

Step Five

Direct a staff member to immediately remove contents from deceased student's locker. Hopefully, this can be accomplished discreetly and prior to students returning to school. The personal contents belong to the parents and removal to the principal's office will ensure they are properly presented to the parents.

Step Six

Direct a staff member to pull the deceased student's cumulative folder to determine what other schools the deceased student might have attended. The principal should call the other schools and inform them of the events that have occurred, particularly, if younger siblings are in those other schools. Secondly, the principal should notify the central administration office of the circumstances of the day. It is also helpful, at this point, to assign responsibility to someone to pull the student's name off any mailing lists that would be sent from the school and central administration office.

Step Seven

Identify a support center area in the building where students may come for support and counseling. This area should be close to the guidance office and/or the main office to facilitate communications between guidance and administrative staff.

Step Eight

Prepare an announcement to be read over the P.A. system to the students. *(At the elementary level, it is often best to have the classroom teacher make the announcement.)* Do not announce the death of a student until it has been verified by reliable sources (i.e., police department, hospital, parents, etc.)

NOTE: It is important to have a central spokesperson, usually the principal, for all announcements to students. By the time students reach school following the death of a peer, they will have heard many different versions about what happened. The presence of strong, caring, and supportive authority figure (i.e., the principal) sharing information during this stressful time is important. (In elementary schools, it is equally important for the classroom teacher to be a strong, caring, and supportive presence since the teacher will be looked upon by the students to provide stability during this crisis period.)

Step Nine

Direct a staff member to collect funeral arrangement information and to prepare details for student/faculty attendance at the visitation and funeral. When details are final, an announcement can be made to staff and students.

Note: It is important to have faculty members present during the entire visitation period to assist the funeral home staff in handling children and teens. Designate one secretary who will know how to reach the principal throughout the day so the principal can respond to any emergencies/administrative situations which may develop.

Step Ten

Call and/or visit the parents as early as possible to express the schools and your condolences. Visiting the parents is encouraged, and the principal should take along a staff member who has been well acquainted with the student. Ask the parents about pictures and other school related articles to be used for the student's funeral. Determine with the parents who will be the family contact for the school. Recognize this may be the first of several visits. *(The parents likely will be in a state of shock. If the death was by suspected suicide, the parents may not acknowledge or be in agreement with the coroner's finding which they have a legal right to challenge.)*

Step Eleven

Prepare a letter to be sent to all parents regarding the death of a school community member (Please *see* Appendix for sample letters.)

Step Twelve

Arrange fifteen-minute after-school meeting with entire school staff. Review day's activities and seek names of any student faculty thinks needs additional emotional first aid. After meeting with faculty, meet with Crises Management Team. Review day's activities and plan for the next day.

Step Thirteen

On the second or third day following the deceased student's funeral, begin to bring closure by encouraging teachers to resume regular classroom activities as quickly as is appropriate.

Step Fourteen

On the day following the funeral, the principal should make the following closure statement to all students and faculty: (This is done the day following the funeral because many of the deceased student's closest friends will not return to school the day of the funeral.)

Teacher's Role

Teachers play a vital role in helping students deal with their feelings regarding the death of a fellow student, a parent, or any significant person in the student's life.

Drunk on power, flaunting money and riding high on their father's wealth, there is a section of youngsters, who have earned a notorious name among their friend circle for their explosive temperament. The recent shootout at Euro International School, one of the so-called elite schools in Gurgaon, bears semblance of the fact that kids are growing up too fast for comfort. The shocking incident has led the education pundits running new-age schools to forecast a gloomy scenario if parents and teachers alike don't wake up to the gravity of the situation fast.

Sometimes the students are struggling to get out of a vortex of confounding ideas. "Often the schools might hold their grounds on meting out consequences for misbehaviors, but parents try and annul the punishment. Such rapprochement can mislead the child into believing in the power of money. Thus emerges the growing need for a congruence of the parental and school ideology

For many, education means big bucks, which automatically implies larger numbers. How can teachers be expected to teach 2000-3000 students and then also tender in personal care and counseling? Schools were originally started to inculcate skills of cohabitation and co-operation but in elite schools, all students come from the same background and this lack of disparity inhibits exposure to myriad settings and outlooks making the children intolerant to differences

It is important for teachers to determine if they can teach their class this particular day or will need help to "cover" their class(es) so they have individual time to console distraught students, visit parents with the building principal, etc. Sometimes teachers are also extremely distraught over the death. In these instances, the teacher should request assistance to cover their classes. It is okay for teachers to grieve and seek help with their assigned duties.

Step One

Attend all-staff mandatory meetings and review any available written information.

Step Two

Allow the expressions of grief. Acknowledge and encourage students to express their feelings of loss, anger, sadness, etc.

NOTE: People have different reactions to grief. One way for the teacher to encourage the students' expression of grief is to acknowledge your own feelings immediately following the announcement of the student's death. If you are uncomfortable discussing grief or handling this situation in your classroom today, please ask for assistance from the Crisis.

Management Team Leader

Step Three: Death By Natural Causes, Accident, etc.

If the death was a sudden one following an accident or one following a long-term illness, it may be important to have the students discuss their fears and to talk a bit about funerals. This may be a time when students ask questions. Questions need to be answered honestly but tactfully and simply. The major focus should be on assisting students in expressing their feelings and reactions.

Step Four: Death By Suicide

If death was by suicide, emphasize this tragedy as an error in judgment. Suicide is a permanent solution to temporary problems. Encourage students to talk about ways to cope with stress, loss, and personal problems.

Step Five

Channel names and/or students themselves to the guidance office if they seem high risk now or as the week progresses. (See Appendix) *(At the elementary level, much of the crisis intervention will take place in the student's classroom because that is the location students feel most secure.)*

Step Six

Attend a brief after-school meeting to review the day's events/the principal and Crisis Management Team members will be available to discuss concerns you may have regarding any of your students. It should be noted that teachers need to be taken care of, too. Take breaks and have time away from students during the day. Be sure to eat meals and watch personal nutrition and other health habits. After the students have left the building, give yourself an opportunity to process what has happened during the day.

Step Seven

Attend the mandatory all-staff after-school meeting.

Dealing with Traumatic Event, Death

The death of a school community member can be a crisis event. A crisis is defined as a state of emotional turmoil. Emotional crises have four characteristics:

1. They are sudden.
2. The "normal" method of coping with stress failed.
3. Are short in duration. Most crises last from twenty-four to thirty-six hours and rarely for longer than six weeks.

4.   Have potential to produce dangerous, self-destructive, or socially unacceptable behavior.

Traumatic Event

A death of a school community member is a traumatic event if the impact on the students and staff is sufficient enough to overwhelm the usual effective coping skills. Traumatic events are typically sudden, powerful events which are outside the range of ordinary human experiences. Because of the suddenness of the event, even well-trained, experienced people can experience a sense of strong emotions.

Determining the Degree of Trauma Following a Death

Three variables are generally considered:

1.   Who—The number of people the person who has died knew and his/her length of time at the school.
2.   How—The circumstances of the death (suicide or murder generally result in more trauma than death by natural causes.)
3.   Where—A death at school or to and from school and school-related activities generally results in more trauma.

Post-Traumatic Stress

Some students may experience post-traumatic stress as a result of a traumatic event. Posttraumatic stress is a condition which is precipitated by an event beyond the range of typical experience. A student who has, for example, suffered repeated losses in their life may experience post-traumatic stress upon the death of a friend. Also, students may experience posttraumatic stress if a catastrophe has occurred at school (i.e., shooting of teacher or students, natural disaster, etc.) Symptoms of post-traumatic stress include:

❖   Re-experiencing the traumatic event (flashbacks).
❖   Avoidance of stimuli the person associates with the traumatic event.
❖   Numbing of general responsiveness.
❖   Pattern of distressful behavior which lasts longer than one month.

As with any severe anxiety, the helper can assist by:

❖   Providing a safe and supportive environment.

❖ Reassuring the person that the reaction is a normal reaction to abnormal stress.

❖ Helping the person discharge "pent-up" emotions and pain. Often times, counseling groups provide the most support for the individual, particularly teenagers. The ideal group size is from six to eight members. The group sessions should be time limited with the purpose of providing mutual support and understanding as each group member deals with their reactions to the traumatic event.

Death

The sudden loss of a student or adult in the school system is a tragic event and can be a point of crises for the school system. The school community's response to the death situation will set the stage for how well people cope with the loss. The best approach to a death is to acknowledge the death, encourage people to express their emotions and feelings, and provide adequate supportive assistance and counseling.

Bereavement

Bereavement is the process of grieving. The process is unique for each person and may last from six months to two years.

Grief

Grief is the sorrow, emotions, and confusion we experience as a result of the death of someone important to us. Grief is mourning the loss of that person and mourning for your-self. All people grieve differently, depending upon their own life experiences. However, all grief is painful, and like all other pain, the body's first reaction to grief may be a feeling of numbness as if one were in shock.

Grief and Children

Preschool to Age Nine

This age child usually sees death as temporary and reversible. Between ages of five and nine, children begin to see death more like adults but still believe it will never happen to them.

Age Nine To Eleven

Child begins to understand death can happen to them. Death is becoming more real. This age child may show keen interest in the cause of death, details of the funeral, and in the biological aspects of death.

Adolescents

The adolescent searches for the meaning of life, which includes death. "Why" questions will be asked, many of which have no concrete answers. Often, adolescents' emotional response to death will be very intense and issues of unresolved grief of divorce of parents, etc., will emerge.

The Healing Process

A major part of the healing process is allowing oneself to experience the intense emotions associated with the pain of grief. The emotions typically experienced are:

1. Anger
2. Guilt
3. Depression

Elizabeth Kubler-Ross has developed five stages to the healing process:

1. Denial and Isolation
2. Anger
3. Bargaining
4. Depression
5. Acceptance

Guidelines for Helping Someone

Who Is Grieving

When we are required to respond to a death, we ask ourselves: What should I do? What should
I say? A few suggestions are:

1. The best action is to take some kind of action. Let the students know how you feel, encourage them to express their feelings and provide support to those who are grieving.
   Do not restrict the amount of time for the conversations to be finished so that the student does not sense "urgency" in your conversation.

2. Be a good listener and accept the words and feelings being expressed. Don't minimize the loss and avoid giving clichés and easy answers.
3. Encourage the grieving person to care for themselves.
4. Acknowledge and accept your own limitations. Sometimes you may wish to have the help of outside resources.

Emotional First Aid

During the first few days following the death of a student or adult in the school community, each adult will be responsible for administering emotional first aid to those in distress. The goal of emotional first-aid is to give people permission to express their emotions during this time of acute distress. Emotional first aid is the freely giving of support without becoming invasive. The first stage of emotional first aid is through words. Keep your words simple and be brief.

> *Use simple questions.*
> *"Can I help?"*
> *Use simple suggestions.*
> *"It's okay to let it out."*
> *Use simple comments.*
> *"It must really hurt."*
> *"You must feel very bad."*

During the grief process, a person may quickly switch emotions. The primary switch of emotions while crying is to anger. Encourage the person to express his/her anger without pushing it to the point of rage. The best way to be encouraging is to accept the person's feelings of anger. When administering emotional first aid, don't push the contact with the grieving person. Take "no" for an answer. If you are concerned about the well being of the person, stay nearby, find them something to drink, or make some gesture of caring for his/her well being.

Problematic Expressions of Grief

People grieve in different ways. Occasionally a student or adult may grieve in a manner that potentially could be harmful to the person. When administering emotional first aid, be aware of the following problematic expressions of grief:

1. *Acting Out*: Getting "carried away" by an enthusiastic expression

of grief. Take the person's grief seriously and consult a crises management team member.

2. *Self Pity*: This is a normal part of grief but at times becomes problematic in that it can bring out anger in the helper. The helper needs to restrain his/her emotions but still be guided by his/her feelings.

3. *Freezing*: This can be a serious situation. This is when the grieving person has no affectual response. If attempts to communicate with the person fail, remain with the person and have someone get help.

Endless Hysterical Sobbing

Be patient with the person, the sobbing will stop when the person is exhausted. Make the person as comfortable as possible, usually covering with a blanket.

Self-Destructive Behavior

In rare instances, the person may become self-destructive by running around the room, crashing into objects. You may have to encourage the person to yell, restrain without harming, etc. Do not leave the person, but get additional help as quickly as possible.

Research: Anxiety, Stress and Coping

In America, every school population is different. Very poor student populations have parents who cannot and never do come to school. Many have two jobs and are barely upright. They do no bother teachers, we bother them. Middle class student populations are different, with those student populations it cuts both ways when it comes to parents. Upper-class parents put too much pressure on teachers, often breaking them down. Often school administrations pander to these affluent-powerful parents' whims. On the other hand, at under-resourced schools, the principals' offices, education departments and politicians take advantage of poor, working-class parents' non-involvement, and ignore their children's education. It would be helpful for parents and administrators to consider that most teachers have their own families to care for when they get off work.

Teachers have administrators telling them what to think and how to do every mundane task, and are punished for the perceived infractions even when the evidence is in teacher's favor. Many teachers feel as if they are walking on eggshells be anyone (parents or students) can say anything at any time and it is up to the teacher to prove them wrong. That is a major load on teacher's shoulders; Then a lot of crazy parents' barge in and start making ever-more-unreasonable demands.

Parents, including others who were teachers basically angry because they did not have the time to raise their children, blamed school teachers because their children were not learning. Teachers only have the children from 1 to 6.5 hours a day depending on the grade level. Not only would the subject(s) supposed to be taught, but ethics and discipline also; Areas that should be done at home. When a student did not achieve an acceptable grade, it is always the teacher's fault. Parents could and do bully administrators to have the grade changed for them to an acceptable level. Some students came in everyday fighting with one another, and yelling at their peers and at teacher. Few have any interest in learning, and rarely do 10 per cent complete any assigned homework.

The stress of teaching is often blamed on rowdy students and unrealistic expectations from school officials. But new research suggests that parents may be the real culprit in teacher burnout. Although "burnout" is complex and different for every teacher, it's usually defined as occurring when a teacher feels emotionally exhausted at the end of the day, appears cynical or uncaring about what happens to students and feels as if he or she has reached few personal goals.

Although perfectionism is often linked with job stress, teachers with perfectionist tendencies weren't more likely to have burnout. But teachers who felt pressure to be perfect or experienced criticism for being imperfect were more likely to have burnout. Notably, the highest pressure to be perfect didn't come from students or colleagues but from parents. USA "no child left behind" program is putting added stresses on our teachers.

As parents have become more demanding and more insistently present in their children's daily lives, the pressures on teachers to give high grades, help the precious kids get into the best colleges, and always be positive with and about the kids has become intrusive and unbearable.

However, in too many cases in public schools, it's the parent's failure to be involved in the student's achievement or more accurately, non-achievement. Teachers do not mind answering how she/he arrives at a grade, but those parents who believed Cs were failing and As were the only acceptable grade is not acceptable to them and causes anxiety.

Quite often parents come to school to fight, not for their children, but to win the battles they lost when they were young. The sense of entitlement, joined with self-righteous anger and administrators who fear nothing more than a phone call to their boss leave teachers with little choice but to "try to make overly demanding parents happy.

The most difficult part of teaching in dealing with indulgent parents who don't necessarily want to put in the time to actually be involved with their kids' education, but, blame the teacher when the kid fails to perform.

Low wages and high expectations; this job trains the world of tomorrow with tired, overworked and finally uninterested individuals. Who can stay in a job where everyday brings new problems from anywhere but the curriculum, student or teacher? No one tries to change the low wages or the over time that is not compensated for these teachers. Class disparity is manifested the most transparent way in the academia in U.S. and India, the two countries where the political system is arrogantly pro-rich and pro-powerful.

In short we can say:

children medicated into indifference and incuriosity to subdue their tendencies to be children, leaving only a talented 1/20 willing or able to make the effort to learn –school administrations selling a "product" to "customers" and willing to adjust excellence, content, "curb appeal" to whatever holds market share–teachers so afraid for their own pitiful incomes and second-rate jobs that they gladly abandon integrity in what they teach, and rush to distance themselves should the ax fall on a colleague–the picture is of a system that has lost track of where it is going, who is the captain, why we ever began the trip.

Practical Tips for Teachers Only

1. Teachers are usually in the best position to identify kids who later turn out to be violent. I have had numerous teachers tell me " I knew Johnny was aggressive since he started preschool at the age of three." As you are probably aware, good teachers often have a second sense about their students. These kids are usually the ones slapping other children and teachers and throwing temper tantrums in the classroom at an early age. You might even be astonished by the changes in a child's behavior: cold calculating and aggressive behavior towards others one day and then the next day, they are sweet as can be. It can be exasperating. What can you do?

2. Request that your school have in-service programs for teachers specifically for the purpose of identifying the symptoms of at-risk children. Kids may act in ways that we don't expect. For example, many times boys who are depressed will act aggressively by yelling, bullying etc. If you see a child with signs of

aggressiveness or one that holds everything in and then blows, talk to the parents or school staff about referring the child to the school psychologist or for a psychiatric evaluation.

3. *Teach critical thinking skills*: they can prevent violence. There has been research showing that youthful impulsiveness may be linked to younger teenagers' frenetic brain activity in the amygdala, which is primarily linked with emotions and instinctual reactions. Older teens and adults show more activity in the frontal lobe—the brain tissue involve in planning, insight and organization. Teachers can encourage young teen-agers (and younger) to develop the frontal lobe by teaching them to think more rationally (Yergelun-Todd, 1998). This may translate into integrating more critical thinking skills into school curriculums to teach kids more logical ways to solve problems. Paradoxically, school curricula aimed at helping teens get in touch with their emotions may actually make things worse—given the emotional makeup of many troubled teens—while programs that substitute rational thought for emotion may help them deal with their problems constructively. Star Trek's "Mr. Spock" turns out to be right: cool logic is the enemy of hotheaded violence.

4. *Set a good example*: Use your clout as a teacher to call into question administrative rules in your school that might be leading to misbehavior. These regulations may start out with good intentions, but often create other problems. The Individuals with Disabilities Education Act is one good example. Many kids with behavioral problems are in special education classes. As you know, because of this, there are restrictions on how many days they can be expelled from school even for very serious and violent acts. Meanwhile, the kid in regular education is expelled for misbehavior of a less serious nature. Zero Tolerance works the same way: Kids who are no threat are often expelled from school for bringing a butter knife or model rocketship—getting the same consequences as the kid found with a gun. What is this teaching children about adults' abilities to think critically? Administrators who cannot distinguish between right and wrong teach children that all acts of misbehavior are identical. This sends the message that you might as well commit a serious crime because you'll get the same punishment. Vocalize these concerns to school administrators or even to your legislators. On a smaller scale, provide students in your classroom with consequences that are

comenserate with the misbehavior displayed. Allow your students to see you performing critical thinking in action.

5. If your school does not already have a violence prevention program, talk with administrators about putting one in place. Education is the key in helping students to identify other potentially dangerous students. Several recent school tragedies have been averted by other students telling school officials that someone has a weapon. Get to know your students and establish a trust with them. You might just be the one they turn to if they or their friend is thinking of violence.

The German School System

In research it was found that in the different school systems there is little difference in the violence potential that can take place. The German school system is divided into Grundshule.... almost like a primary school. From there the pupil has the choice of going to either a Gymnasium, a Hauptschule, Realschule or the Gesamtschule. Form the research it seems that in the so called Gymnasien verbal aggression or mobbing is more prevalent where as Hauptschule pupils were not as quick-witted.

Every year, private schools are mushrooming across the country but they lack basic facilities. Most of the schools claim to have computer facilities, CCTV cameras for monitoring the activities of students. However, very few schools talk about providing any teaching for discipline or manners. Parents, school administrators, and mental health workers all can play key roles in protecting children from gun violence and helping them overcome the effects of gun-related trauma. Widespread but erroneous view that is that socially destructive behavior is best discouraged through the criminal justice system". Some measures which might reduce crime by alleviating economic stress and improving the quality of parenting.

Peace Education in Indian Schools

Peace is a way of life; it is not a subject to be taught. Conflict resolution is a major aspect of peace education. Peace education is all about teaching students ways to resolve conflict, both within themselves and with others.

Peace education has two aspects:

1. Ppeace for all and
2. Education for peace.

While the former refers to living in a stress-free environment and learning about values like respecting parents, elders and so on, the latter focuses on learning to maintain peace in social and political aspects.

Stress and anger management also form an important part of peace education in addition to exploring self, quality of life and living in harmony with others. Most teachers say that increasing competition in schools and over expectations of parents and peers tend to create excess burden on students. As a result, students experience anxiety and conflict within themselves. Besides, there has also been an increase in violence in schools as students, today, loses their temper over trivial issues and get into arguments easily. Hence, there is a need to impart moral values. As society evolves, parents are increasingly showing strong emotional dependence on their children and thus their expectations also rise. They associate their child's success with their own and feel let down if the child fails to deliver. In the process, children feel excessively burdened with these high expectations and this leads to increasing stress among them. Schools have chosen to follow an integrated approach so that students aren't burdened with another subject. So, the concepts have been incorporated into mainstream subjects and are being taught simultaneously. While teaching topics like decline of the Mughal Empire, teach our students about religious intolerance, causes of this violence, ways to avoid and solve it and the like. So, in a way, integrate the message of peace and harmony within the subject and impart value-based education. Another important aspect of peace education, is tolerance and introspection, both of which students need to learn.

More over parents should see their child as a child, understand his/her potential and accordingly set their expectations. Schools, on the other hand, should stop glorifying their results and instead of labeling a child with his/her marks should look at him/her holistically.

7

Children and Adults

Today, however, widespread shifts in family and community life have changed the lives of school-age children. Because more parents are working, fewer familiar adults are home or nearby when children are dismissed from school. Neighborhoods seem less safe; they are crisscrossed by traffic, plagued by street violence, and peopled by strangers. School shootings have heightened public concern many forms of trouble that teens and younger children are finding after school—whether it comes in the form of alcohol, drugs, or sexual activity; or takes the shape of vandalism, gang membership, or online relationships with Internet-based hate groups. Americans are becoming increasingly concerned about what the nation's youngsters are doing—and not doing—after school lets out. Familiar activities like sports, piano lessons, religious classes, and scout troops still dot the afternoons and weekends of many children, but other youngsters are adrift after school. Too many fend for themselves in libraries, congregate in subway stations and neighborhood stores, or spend their afternoons behind the locked doors of city apartments and suburban houses.

Growing numbers of children with working parents attend programs in schools or community organizations that provide a range of activities in one place. These programs bear the broad label of "after-school programs" because they offer supervised activities and a safe place to spend time when school is not in session (including holidays and summer vacations).

Decisions about children's activities outside of school have long been a family matter, and many of the activities that occupy children's free time are organized by parents and voluntary organizations. Nevertheless, a consensus is now emerging that the wider society should share with parents the responsibility for providing programs and activities, safe places, and transportation options to make "out-of-school time" productive for children and teens.

> **One in Four Children Admit Crime in U.K.**
>
> ❖ Researchers claim, a quarter of all children have committed a crime in the last year.
>
> ❖ One in four children between the ages of 11 and 16 who were asked, admitted they had taken part in crimes like burglary, stealing cars and vandalism.
>
> ❖ This figure shot up to two thirds among those children who'd been expelled.
>
> ❖ And a quarter of those who had been expelled said they'd stolen a mobile in the last year.
>
> ❖ The research also showed that more young offenders are being punished for their crimes too.
>
> ❖ The only crime which has gone down is shoplifting, but all other types have gone up.
>
> ❖ The 'average' child criminal was also found to be white, between 14-16 years old, and living in London, the south east or the north east.
>
> ❖ More than 5,000 children, and 500 expelled children, were quizzed for the survey.

Children's Reasoning

What Violence Means to Them?

The responses range from being laughed at, not being taken seriously, hitting one another, or not being allowed to be your-self. According to the pupils this includes being afraid to walk in the street or that some one may attack them. Some of the other impressions of what violence means included to feel oppressed, or bullied. These are different forms of situations that can lead to violence. It starts with something as simple as picking on each other, or throwing around pencil cases, pulling hair or taking away another pupils' sandwich....all of these situations have the potential to lead to fighting or physical violence. Sometimes a pupil may even have a knife, but this is very seldom. They make a distinction between a real threat, thus real violence and mere playfulness or teasing.

One assumes that the intensity of physical violence has increased but in the quantitive sense–no. What has increased though is what is referred to as bullying or mobbing ....the sort of verbal violence or insults on the play ground, of which children suffer the most. To understand violence better one has to look beyond the definition and ask what the victim feels in that situation; so violent behavior can start with a simple intimidating glance or the feeling of being excluded. And from this we gather that violence is in reality a very subjective idea.

Children who tend to show aggressive behavior usually seek out weaker children to overpower or intimidate. This creates the feeling of power or of being the winner. In most cases violent behavior stems from a reason or event maybe in the past and yet sometimes not. Violent or aggressive behavior can also be used as an outlet for a situation or feelings the child can not cope with. On the other hand there may simply be no reason at all. It may be possible that one becomes violent to reach a certain aim. Additionally one can ask to what extent children copy violence in what is referred to as the Ellbogeng-gesellschaft or the so-called dog-eat-dog society as a means of gaining or being successful over some-one or a situation.

School yard brawls are mostly associated with young boys but there as been a marked increase in girl or cat fights in the last few years. Girl fights seem to be more intense. For example when they pull each others hair, insult each other it seems to be more serious. This then leads to a fist fight. In general one can not say that boys are more prone to fights than girls, but boys seem to be more direct, in that respect.

Dog-Eat-Dog Society

The dog-eat-dog society has brought a change to the previous image of women as the victim. The rule nowadays is: be strong! In this sense one has the desire to feel accepted. This is a gender neutral emotion felt by everyone. For a boy to achieve this aim it sometimes means to hit another boy. It is a fact that mostly the boys tend get involved in fights, but it has been shown that there is an increase in girl fights. For the girl to be accepted in her gang she will also resort to physical violence if required. There are more serious forms of aggression or violence where the police may be required to step in. One would think that when a situation begins to spiral out of control or where more serious forms of violence has occurred the police are the ones to run to. Pupils have according to the police also from time to time taken various conflicts to their desks, problems which have turned out to be a far cry from what is deemed criminal.

Reality and Fantasy

There is a lot of debate about the influence television; movies, the internet, computer games, music and other media containing violence can have on the psyche and behavior of a child in situations that he or she can not cope with. The problem is on when a child is unable to distinguish between reality and fantasy. The influence media containing violent themes has on a child also depends on the child's family environment and background. Whether open communication exists, what sort of upbringing the child has had and his or her idea of reality. What is of importance is the family structure. A child is more prone to influence by media containing violent themes if the family structures and upbringing is weak. A good upbringing or strong family structure builds a strong „personal immune system"....but where one does not have a firm structure or upbringing one's personal immune system is too weak for the influences the media can have. With a strong system one can then distinguish between what is real or false, and what is wrong or right on the screen.

Reality is felt through your body. One experiences reality through pain and through this one knows that you have a body. One has a sense of existence, a sense of self and this is normal. The aim is to let children realize what the borders of reality are.

School Attendance

For many students, the fear of gun violence is strong enough to interfere with the quality of their lives and their performance in school; they also may suffer from increased absentee, truancy, and dropout rates. Voluntaries who work with children explained the importance of getting them to talk about their fears. They are hungry for information and may distort facts and think they could have prevented the shooting. They need to understand that the school shootings on the evening news are rare events and that schools are safe places. Task Force on Adolescent Assault Victim Needs, convened by the American Academy of Pediatrics, recommends addressing the psychosocial needs of young victims along with their physical injuries. To do this effectively, the task force noted that health care providers must acknowledge and address three myths:

1. That all adolescent victims are "bad" kids who probably deserve what they got,
2. That it is dangerous to care for adolescent victims who may be members of a gang, and
3. That it is hopeless to help them because of the high risk of re-injury and subsequent acts of violence by the victim.

Elementary school-age children also are frequent witnesses to gun violence and often display trauma-related disorders. Some children are afraid of school, and many become fatalistic. Some engage in aggressive play and perform poorly in school, while others become desensitized to violence and lose the ability to recognize and avoid dangerous situations.

Witnessing gun violence affects children in many different ways, depending on the type of wound, the proximity to the shooter, the relationship of the shooter and victim, and whether the shooting took place in a context generally considered safe, among other things. Different reactions can be expected from boys and girls. Child witnesses who have been raised in a subculture of violence in the home may have additional risk factors for long-term psychosocial consequences. The growing cost of gun violence can affect the trauma care available for all community members.

Today's children are pretty bright; they realize that since both of their parents work if they do something wrong at school it will be very hard to contact their parents. They also probably believe that even if the school gets in touch with their parents that they will be too busy to respond to the school other than by just answering the phone. Compounding these problems even further, when children repeatedly get into trouble, parents may still refuse to deal with the situation and have their sitters or housekeepers take care of the problem. Some parents may even believe there is nothing they can do to control their children, or that the school itself is the one to fault and not their children. Why can't the school do more to control the actions of the students? After all, they see them more than we do. This thought process along with the student violence itself poses serious problems to our schools and the future of our society in general. Studies in USA have shown that children as young as seven (7) years old have demonstrated that they can pick or break trigger locks, or operate a gun with a trigger lock in place.

Zero per cent of children that get guns from their parents commit gun-related crimes while 21 per cent of those that get them illegally do. Children that acquire guns illegally are twice as likely to commit street crimes (24%) than are those given guns by their parents (14%).

Almost three times as many children (41%) take drugs if they also obtain guns illegally, as compared to children given guns by their parents (13%). In the 1950's, children routinely played cops and robbers, had toy guns, were given BB rifles and small caliber hunting rifles before puberty. Yet the homicide rate in the 1950's was almost half of that in the 1980's.

Fewer than 2 per cent of all unintentional injury deaths for children in the U.S. between ages 0-14 are from firearms.

Parent's Reaction

Everyone who loves their kids worries about them, but at this point, parents are pushed by the media to OVER-worry. It's not healthy for the kids, either, to have the adults running around in hysterics, reacting to threats that aren't there. What kind of childhoods are we giving them, if we teach them such statistically absurd paranoia?

Students Stop School Violence

1. Refuse to bring a weapon to school, refuse to carry a weapon for someone else, and refuse to keep silent about those who carry weapons.
2. Report any crime immediately to school authorities or police.
3. Report suspicious behavior or talk by other students to a teacher or counselor at your school. You may save someone's life.
4. Learn how to manage your own anger effectively. Find out ways to settle arguments by talking it out, working it out, or walking away rather than fighting.
5. Help others settle disputes peaceably. Start or join a peer mediation program, in which trained students help classmates find ways to settle arguments without fists or weapons.
6. Set up a teen court, in which youths serve as judge, prosecutor, jury, and defense counsel. Courts can hear cases, make findings, and impose sentences, or they may establish sentences in cases where teens plead guilty. Teens feel more involved in the process than in an adult-run juvenile justice system.
7. Become a peer counselor, working with classmates who need support and help with problems.
8. Mentor a younger student. As a role model and friend, you can make it easier for a younger person to adjust to school and ask for help.
9. Start a school crime watch. Consider including a student patrol that helps keep an eye on corridors, parking lots, and groups, and a way for students to report concerns anonymously.
10. Ask each student activity or club to adopt an anti-violence theme. The newspaper could run how-to stories on violence prevention; the art club could illustrate the costs of violence. Career clubs could investigate how violence affects their occupational goals.

Sports teams could address ways to reduce violence that's not part of the game plan.

11. Welcome new students and help them feel at home in your school. Introduce them to other students. Get to know at least one student unfamiliar to you each week.

12. Start (or sign up for) a "peace pledge" campaign, in which students promise to settle disagreements without violence, to reject weapons, and to work toward a safe campus for all. Try for 100 per cent participation.

If they heard a student talking about shooting someone at school, only about half the students would tell an adult.In a study of USA only Fifty-four per cent of the respondents said they would tell an adult, but there were some variations in the likelihood they would report such an incident:

❖ Younger students are more significantly more likely to tell someone than older students.

❖ African-American, Hispanic and other minority students are less likely to tell than white students.

❖ 61 per cent of those who get mostly A's would tell, compared only 42 per cent of those who get mostly D's and F's.

❖ Students with a high quality of life index are more likely to tell an adult than those with a low quality of life index (63% cf. 46%).

❖ Media usage seems to have somewhat of an impact; 59 per cent of those whose media usage is low would tell, but only 51 per cent of those whose media usage is high would.

❖ 65 per cent of those with a low alienation index would report to an adult, compared to only 42 per cent of those with a high alienation index.

Those who perceive their schools to be extremely safe or very safe are far more likely to confide in an adult than those who believe their schools are not safe.

What You can do if Someone You Know Shows Violence Warning Signs

When you recognize violence warning signs in someone else, there are things you can do. Hoping that someone else will deal with the situation is the easy way out. Above all, be safe. Don't spend time alone with people who show warning signs. If possible without putting yourself in danger, remove the person from the situation that's setting them off.

Tell someone you trust and respect about your concerns and ask for help. This could be a family member, guidance counselor, teacher, school psychologist, coach, clergy, school resource officer or friend.

If you are worried about being a victim of violence, get someone in authority to protect you. Do not resort to violence or use a weapon to protect yourself. The key to really preventing violent behavior is asking an experienced professional for help. The most important thing to remember is don't do it alone.

There are many reasons why you should never touch a gun that you find outside your house. It is likely that the gun was used in a crime and then thrown away. The fingerprints on the gun could be very important in solving a crime and touching the gun could destroy them.

The exact place that the gun was found might also be important evidence in an investigation. There could be other evidence in the area such as blood and footprints, you should leave the area immediately.

The gun is very possibly loaded and ready to fire. Never try to pull a gun away from anyone. This is the most common cause of a serious accident. For the above reasons, it is also very important that even a parent or adult who knows all about gun safety, does not touch the gun either.

If a gun is found outside the house, it should never be touched, except by a police officer. As soon as possible, a police officer should be brought to the scene. NEVER TRY TO BRING A GUN THAT YOU FOUND TO A PARENT, ADULT OR POLICE OFFICER. You should instead, bring the police officer to the gun. This is the right thing to do.

Is the Gun Loaded?

On nearly every model of firearm, there is no way you can tell if the gun is loaded just by looking at it.

If you have proper adult supervision and you have been invited to a gun club or shooting range by a parent, grandparent, aunt or uncle, you should NEVER be handed a loaded gun by them until you are taught proper gun safety procedures with an unloaded gun first.

You should always be allowed to practice the basic gun safety procedures with an unloaded gun before you actually are allowed to fire the gun at a target.

These are the proper steps to check and see if a gun is loaded or not:

- ❖ Always point the gun's barrel in a safe direction. At a gun club, this is always what is called "downrange" or at the targets.
- ❖ Always keep your finger alongside the gun and not inside the trigger guard.
- ❖ If it is a revolver, you must activate the cylinder release latch and swing out the cylinder. If it is loaded, there will be cartridges in the cylinder.
- ❖ If it is a semi-automatic, you should pull out the magazine first. By activating the magazine release button, then pull out the magazine from the bottom of the grip.
- ❖ After the magazine is removed, pull back the slide. If it is loaded, the ejector which is part of the slide will eject the cartridge.
- ❖ If there is no cartridge in the chamber, lock the slide back in its rearmost position. It is then unloaded.

Please be aware that these steps are for when you are at the range and under proper adult supervision. If you are bullied at school, be sure to tell your teacher, your principal and your parents. You should then insist on a meeting between your principal, a teacher, your parents, the bully's parents and a student representative. In this meeting, you should discuss the bullying incident and how it affected you. You should also arrange with the principal and the teacher to have witnesses available. Each participant in the meeting should have at least one (1) minute to discuss how this bullying event has affected them and give their thoughts and feelings about it. Don't be ashamed about being bullied by someone. There is nothing to be ashamed about. A bully is really someone who feels bad about their own self worth and picks on someone to make themselves feel better.

Much of the violence that occurs in school comes from students who belong in gangs.Street gangs are merely replacement families for a lost generation of young people. There is no easy solution to getting rid of gangs, but the real solution lies in fathers raising their children according to the precepts and rules laid out for him by God in the Bible.

Communicate

Recently there have been quite a few highly publicized tragic events of kids bringing guns and sometimes bombs to school.

It is very important for you to realize that schools are still a very safe place to be. Incidents such as these are still rare, but they are a problem that must be addressed and addressed soon.

It is extremely important that if you hear another student say that they are going to bring a gun to school and hurt people, that you tell your teacher, your school principal and your parents. The police should also be notified because this type of threat is a crime all by itself.

Make sure you take these threats seriously and make sure you tell your parents at the very least.

It is up to your parents, teachers, school administration and the police to decide if the threats were serious. It is not your responsibility to determine if the student was serious or not.

In 75 per cent of school shootings, other students knew about the shootings before they happened, but said nothing, did not take it seriously or was not taken seriously by people in authority.

In 80 per cent of school shootings, the student who does the shooting had been bullied in the past. Bullying in school has always been a big problem.

What are Learning Difficulties?

A child with learning difficulties is likely to have problems with reading, writing, spelling and mathematics. More subtle and harder to pinpoint are problems in paying attention, following directions, remembering, organising, managing time, dealing with sequences, and distinguishing right from left.

	Area of Difficulty	Symptoms	Examples
Dyslexia	Processing Language	Reading, writing and spelling	Letters and words may be written or pronounced backwards
Dyscalculia	Math's skills	Computation, remembering math facts, concepts of time and money	Difficulty learning to count by 2s, 3s or 4s.
Dysgraphia	Written expression	Handwriting, spelling, composition	Illegible handwriting, difficulty organizing ideas
Dyspraxia	Fine motor skills	Coordination, manual dexterity	Trouble with scissors, buttons, drawing

INFORMATION PROCESSING DISORDERS			
Auditory Processing Disorder	Interpreting auditory information	Language development, reading	Difficulty anticipating how a speaker will end a sentence
Visual Processing Disorder	Interpreting visual information	Reading, wri-ting and math's	Difficulty distinguishing letters like 'h' and 'n'
Attention deficit Hyperactivity Disorder	Concentration and focus	Over-activity, distractibility and impulsivity	Can't sit still, loses interest quickly

It may be that exhausted parents of very active and inattentive children resort to using the television as a 'babysitter' more commonly than do parents of less active and more attentive children, it said. Thus, the relationship between early television viewing and later attention problems may be linked to child temperament as much as or more than television causing children to be inattentive it concluded.

Children between the ages of two and eleven spend an average of one full day every week watching television. With both parents away at work, the urban, middle-class Indian is increasingly seeing children being brought up with television as the new baby-sitter; even when parents are at home; watching television is still the favoured family pastimes.

Children and adults remain completely immobile while viewing the idiot box. Most viewing experiences are both quiet and non-interactive. Children absorb millions of images from the television set in just one afternoon's viewing session. And what are they watching? If the child's television has access to cable, his choice can range from 10 to 70 different channels; all of them showing different programmes.

Researches warn that the risks of viewing the most common depiction of television violence includes learning to behave violently, becoming more desensitized to the harmful consequences of violence and becoming more fearful of being attacked.

Viewing a lot of violence on television does not necessarily cause a child to act more violently, but it can contribute to promoting a view that violence is common place in everyday life. It could also create a heightened fear of being assaulted on the street.

A moderate amount of television may be beneficial for young children, depending entirely on the type of programmes the child is watching and the kind of supervision it is getting from the parents. Quality television can teach children about the world around and the different people that they may not have access to by other means. There are quite a few interesting as well as informative programmes on history, literature, Nature, current affairs, art and culture of various countries and so on.

Well-guided television viewing also increases the general vocabulary of your child and provides opportunities for him to learn about various things, which help him in making choices regarding his areas of interest.

Television, when viewed selectively, along with parents can provide immense scope for learning. Channels like Animal Planet, Discovery Channel, Splash and others have interesting programmes which can be beneficial even for young children. Parents can discuss the subject with their children while they watch these programmes together so that the child finds it more interesting and learns better.

When children watch television, they are not playing with shapes and blocks, or getting fresh air, or feeling the three-dimensional figures, or listening to the sounds of the neighbourhood.

Kids need parents. They need your time and attention. They also need to interact with you and require that you read out to them. They need time to explore and have no time to be bored. The best way for kids to develop physically, mentally and emotionally is for a caring adult or sibling to hold them, talk to them, play with them, and provide a rich interactive experience.

Cultivating intelligent viewing implies that you encourage your child to carefully choose the programmes, restrict viewing time and help them to find fun things to do when the set is turned off.

Growing Child and Parents

Children Need to Feel Safe and Loved

First and foremost, a child needs to feel safe at home. There is no surer way to start children on the right path in life than to provide consistent, reliable, loving care. How you relate to the children inside your home is perhaps the most powerful tool for protecting them from violence outside the home.

Children are People Watchers

Children learn how to behave by watching people around them. Your child learns by watching characters on television, in videos, and in movies. And, above all, your child learns by watching you. Think for a moment about how you react to difficult situations. How do you act toward your spouse? Your friends? Your neighbors? Other family members? You are teaching your child, by example, how to get along in the world. When you and others come together to solve your problems peacefully, your child learns how to deal with people in a positive way. But when you or someone close to your child is aggressive and destructive, the child learns to act the same way.

Just being Exposed to Violence is Harmful

When children, even very young children, see a violent act, they are deeply affected by it. This is especially true if the violence involves a family member or someone they know in the neighborhood. What can you do to help? First, allow the children plenty of time to talk about violence they have seen at school, in the neighborhood, or on TV. Encourage them to express their feelings about it. Second, make sure your children get to see many more examples of people dealing with each other in a spirit of friendly cooperation rather than by threatening violence or hurting each other. The children will gradually realize that there are many ways to deal with people and resolve conflicts peacefully, and that violence is not the best way to get what they want.

Handling Anger

Everyone gets angry at times—it's part of being human. Anger is a normal feeling that can be helpful, because it signals that change is needed. But anger also can get out of control. Helping children learn to manage anger is a very important part of early violence prevention.

It is hard for very young children to understand and manage their anger. As your young child grows, gradually teach these principles:

1. It's okay to be angry.
2. There are "okay" ways and "not okay" ways to show your anger.
3. It's not okay to hurt anyone, to break things, or to hurt pets when you are angry.
4. It's okay to tell someone that you are angry.
5. There are ways to calm yourself when you are angry.

Young Children Get Angry for Many Reasons

Several things stir young children's anger, and they show it in different ways. Here are some typical examples:

❖ When infants, birth to about 9 or 10 months, feel bad because they are hungry, sick, or in pain, or when they are startled by a loud noise—they show their anger by crying and thrashing their arms and legs.

❖ Older babies, up to about 18 months, still show anger with crying and fussing, but the reasons may be different. This tends to occur when they don't get an appealing object, when they can't be with the person they want to be near, when they are frightened, or when they feel bad because of illness.

❖ From about age 18 months to 4 years, children are easily frustrated and will aggressively try to get or to keep what they want. They may grab a toy or take a cookie away from a friend, push a child away from the place they want to stand, or hit someone who takes something away from them.

❖ Children from about ages 4 to 8 years old gradually understand more, and they get angry about what people say, as well as what they do. They get better and better at expressing themselves with words, and their understanding of the world expands dramatically. Their aggression often is aimed at hurting another person— perhaps directly, by hitting or fighting, perhaps indirectly by damaging something the other person cares about.

Children can Learn to Manage Anger

Young children who learn to manage angry feelings are more likely to make and keep friends. Also this skill can help prevent and resolve conflicts at home. Schoolchildren who are constantly arguing and fighting are the ones most likely to have problems in school and to have trouble making friends. And these issues can later lead to quitting school, having problems with the law, and abusing alcohol and drugs.

Importantly, helping a child to control angry feelings begins when you respond to the child's anger in a calm, respectful manner:

❖ Calm an infant by holding and comforting the infant, as well as removing or changing what caused the fussing.

❖ Encourage a toddler to use words to tell you what he or she feels, even in simple language. "I mad," or "Want doll," is a reasonable response from a little boy or girl.

❖ Help preschoolers begin to learn and practice a self-calming method—taking a few deep breaths, sitting down, counting to 10, or repeating, "Be cool, be calm," for example.

❖ Encourage kindergarten and elementary school youngsters to explain what happened and how they feel. After a child is calm, ask what is wrong and LISTEN to the explanation, without interrupting. Help the child think about and tell ways to change the situation that caused the anger.

Social Problem Solving

Problem solving doesn't just mean doing arithmetic or figuring out how to fix a leaky faucet. Many of the toughest problems, some-times involving strong feelings, occur between people. Adults and children who can manage the strong feelings and resolve conflicts reasonably, without hurting someone, have good skills for social problem solving.

Start early to help young children STOP and THINK about different ways to solve a problem. Help them choose to act in a way that is nonviolent, safe, and fair. Around age 3, children are usually ready to begin simple steps of thinking and making choices which are part of social problem solving. As children grow, they get better at solving problems. Around age 4 or 5, children can think of more than one way to solve a problem, and they can predict how people will react to their actions. ("If I hit George when he wants my truck, he will hit me back. If we take turns, he won't grab it any more.") They also learn to name their own feelings and those of others. ("I am mad because Sandra won't let me on the swing." "Carlos is sad because his balloon popped.") Further, they begin to care about other people's feelings and well-being ("Mark, I'm sorry you hurt your knee." "Grandma will be happy when she sees the picture I colored for her."). Children aged 6 to 8 can understand how others might see a problem differently, and they can talk about a situation more clearly. They also develop a conscience and worry about rules and fairness.

Be sure to praise a child who does any of these things:

❖ Calms down,
❖ Tells how he or she feels,
❖ Describes a problem,
❖ Thinks of solutions to a problem, and
❖ Acts in a way that is safe, fair, and nonviolent.

Make sure that your children understand that it's okay to make mistakes trying to solve problems and that we can learn from our mistakes. Always encourage children to seek help from trusted adults when a problem is too hard for them to handle. Most of all, remember that children learn by watching you solve problems with respectful words and nonviolent actions.

Discipline

No child's behavior is perfect all of the time and some kids are harder to deal with than others. When you must act to stop a child's bad behavior, your goal should always be to do it with self-control and without violence. The goal of discipline is to teach children self-control, not to punish them.

The best way to get children to behave the way you want is to pay attention to them when things are calm and comment on their good behavior. Praise children for sharing a toy with a playmate without being told to do so or for putting their toys away when they are finished with them or for avoiding conflicts with other children. If children get attention only when they misbehave, they repeat the bad behavior.

Discipline is an important job—a young child's constant out-of-control behavior can:

- ❖ Hurt that child or others
- ❖ Interfere with the child's learning and making friends
- ❖ Damage property
- ❖ Lead to school failure
- ❖ Create tension and stress at home
- ❖ Set the stage for serious problems as the child grows older

You can teach a child self-control by:

- ❖ Setting reasonable limits and rules
- ❖ Having consistent, age-appropriate standards for behavior
- ❖ Showing consistent consequences for misbehaving
- ❖ Letting the child see good behavior by your example

When Young Children "Act Up"

- ❖ Let children know what you expect, with simple statements. "Please put away your toys right now."
- ❖ Give warnings and reminders, without threats. "When you put away your toys, then you can go outside with your friends."
- ❖ Tell a child what to do rather than what not to do. "Please use a soft voice," instead of "Stop yelling!"

❖ Follow through with praise for following instructions or consequences for disobeying.

Sometimes a youngster's bad behavior can be so frustrating that a parent or caregiver strikes the child without stopping to think. Yet children become confused, scared, and angry when adults hurt them—especially the adults whom they depend on to love and protect them. And continual, harsh punishment can lead a child to become aggressive and out of control—just the opposite of what you want to accomplish.

Some Discipline Methods to Try

Ignore some behavior that is irritating but not dangerous—for example, whining, swearing, or having tantrums. It may be hard to do this, but paying attention to such behavior may just encourage more of it.

Taking away a privilege can help to stop bad behavior. Once children are old enough to understand, tell them that something they like (riding a bike, playing at a friend's house, watching a favorite TV show) will be taken away if they continue to misbehave. This set up a choice: With self-control, they get what they like; if they continue to behave badly, they don't. This kind of approach teaches that actions have consequences.

When young children are fighting or arguing, place yourself between them. If possible, kneel to get to the children's eye level. Let them know you understand that they are upset. If they are fighting over a toy or object, hold the object until the problem is settled. Ask each child to tell you what is wrong and listen to what they say. Ask both children to think of ways they might resolve the problem. Help them think about consequences ("If we do this, then what will happen?"). Help them choose a solution that is fair and nonviolent. Watch what happens: If it works, praise them; if not, have them choose another solution and try again.

If one child clearly has been hitting or picking on another, speak to the victim first, allowing him to say what he wants and how he feels. Encourage the victim to face the bully and say how he feels—perhaps something like this: "I don't like it when you push me. It hurts and makes me mad!" Be sure that the bully doesn't get more attention than the victim gets. *Timeout* is a method that some families use to give children (and adults) a short cooling off period. If you use it, keep the time short and follow these guidelines:

❖ Choose a safe, supervised place where the child can be quiet and undisturbed.

❖ Tell the child that at the end of the timeout, the two of you will talk about the troublesome behavior.

❖ Tell the child to sit quietly, without talking to anyone, until he or she is calm and ready to have a discussion.

❖ When timeout is over, keep your promise and talk with the child about what happened.

About Spanking

People have a variety of opinions about spanking, but the reality is that hitting or spanking your child sends a confusing message. It says it's okay to hurt someone you love in order to control them or solve a problem. Repeated harshly, over time, it will train children to punish others with force—the same way that they were punished.

Caution about Weapons

A child's curiosity about weapons can be deadly. It is heart-breaking to hear of accidental shootings and serious injuries by children who handle guns or play with them. Teach children to never touch a gun, bullet, or knife. Let them know that if they find one, they should not touch it, but should tell a trusted adult about it.

If you own a gun, never leave it out where a child might get it. Always lock your unloaded guns and bullets separately, in secure places that children cannot reach.

At Home and in Your Community

The daily experiences you provide for young children are powerful, not only for preventing violence, but also for increasing their chances to have a productive, happy life. If you stay at home with your children, have a schedule and plan activities for them and with them. If your children are in a child-care program while you work outside of home, make sure that it offers chances for constructive play and learning opportunities, with well-qualified staff who promote positive social behavior. Research shows that high quality child-care programs can reduce behavior problems in later childhood. Teach your child a sense of community by being part of the community yourself. Participate in activities to keep your neighborhood safe and to prevent violence.

Give your children opportunities to play with other children and to interact with people of all ages.

Give children your time—play together, eat together, watch their activities, work on projects together, just hang out and share everyday experiences. As part of a young child's family, you have a critical influence on that young child's development. What you teach children today will make a difference in who they are tomorrow. You are the best person to show a path to nonviolence for the children, for your family, and for your community. Reasons for Punishment A Categorical Imperative (4) B Natural Moral Law (4) C Intuitionism (4) Punishment, in the context of law, is "a penalty inflicted by a court of justice on a convicted offender as a just retribution, and incidentally for the purposes of reformation and prevention". In this definition, three possible understandings of punishment are stated, but there are several more. Some of the theories or reasons for punishment include retribution, vengeance, rehabilitation (or reform) and deterrence. Retribution and vengeance are backward-looking theories, insofar as they understand punishment to be inflicted as a direct consequence of an offence committed in the past, whereas forward-looking theories such as deterrence, rehabilitation and reconciliation are based on the notion that punishment can change the offender and improve society.

Nature of Personal Disorganization

Personal disorganization represents the behavior of the individual which deviates from the social norms. It results in social disapproval which may express itself in a wide variety of degree. The individual may also react in different ways. Social reality presents an endless confusion of social disapproval from time to time. It may be mild or violent. Accordingly individuals respond either positively or negatively to social disapproval. The most visible aspect of personal disorganization in complex societies is that in which there is mild social disapproval to which the individual responds positively. This kind of personal disorganization does not deeply disturb the social order.

The second aspect of social disorganization is that in which there is violent social disapproval and yet the individual responds positively. In the third aspect in which the individual's response to social disapproval is subjective the person retreats into an individually defined inner world. His innovations lose their social character. He becomes enmeshed in the development of mechanisms which further isolate him from the normal influences of group life. This type of personal disorganization results in psychosis through which the individual tries to escape from the web of social relations and in suicide.

Causes of Social Disorganization

According to Maclver and Page five main factors such as psychological, biological, physical, technological and culture bring about social change. When the changes brought about these factors in the social structure are so disturbing that the present institution and other means of social control are no longer able to control them by adjusting themselves to the new situations there arise social disorganization. Factors of social disorganization at a particular period are so interrelated that it is difficult to find which factor is predominant.

Elliott and Merrill observe that in order to understand the full implications of a study of social disorganization we must keep in mind the complex nature of all social phenomena. Out of man's fruitless search for unique causes has come recognition of the multiple factors which account for such characteristics of modern society as the decline in the acceptance of revealed religion the changing structure of the family, the increasing importance of the central government, and the lowering standards of morality. Others would rely on a re-constructuction of the fundamental economic institutions to bring about the changes. Still another group insists that the basis of all human woe lies in the biological field. Each of these groups however ignore the selective nature of the interpretation while on the other hand any realistic social understanding must consider all the factors related to the particular manifestation of social disorganization which is under investigation.

Social disorganization consists of the co-ordination of individual responses as a result of the operation of consensus and control. Personal organization refers to the coordination and integration of the attitude systems within the personality. A change in the cultural context which destroys the functioning of coordination that constitutes the social order represents social disorganization. Similarly any variant behavior which disturbs the integration of the attitude systems within the personality represents personal disorganization.

Social Disorganization in a Simple Society

The social change, social disorganization and personal disorganization have their genesis in the variant behavior of the individuals. In simple societies, however deviations in behavior are minimum. Therefore there is a little awareness of their existence by the group. New coordination is made both for the society and for the individual with a minimum of stress and strain.

Social Disorganization in a Complex Society

The functioning of three important factors is commonly held responsible for spontaneous variations in behaviour. They are—the specialized functioning inherent in complex society. The family as a culture defining agency and cultural participation outside the particular social order. The result is the emergence of a wide variety of various response patterns out of which develops disorganization both in society and individual. Some innovations find ready acceptance because they are related to those aspect of culture which are found outside institutional pattern. Innovations in mores, ideas and beliefs often meet with social disapproval because they vary from the accepted pattern. In simple society people revamp the discordant elements to the degree that their variance is no longer apparent. Innovations which meet with organized resistance tend to result in marked social disorganization. All positive response to social disapproval does not result in attempts to explain the variant behavior in terms of the welfare of the group.

Social disorganization is the inevitable result until such time as the new behavior pattern loses group support or becomes incorporated into the social order. When however social disapproval of variations is met negatively by retreat into a world of fantasy there is no corresponding social disorganization except to the extent to which the individual becomes a threat to the safety of society and its members. This point of view does not deny the causative role of social organization in the production of personal disorganization.

All social change involves some social disorganization. It is important to think of social disorganization related to those aspects of social change which result in the disturbance and revamping of social institutions and of the patterns of interrelationship between them. In the same way the social responses of the individual are always in flux. But only when changes take place in the individual's pattern of adjustment to social situations which arouse social disapproval that one may speak of personal disorganization.

Social Actions

social actions refer to any action that takes into account actions and reactions of other individuals and is modified based on those events. Social action is a concept developed by Max Weber that explores interaction between humans in society. The concept of social action is used to observe how certain behaviors are modified in certain environments. The impact of social action is clearly seen in norms and everyday interaction between people.

Weber differentiated between several types of social actions:

1. *Rational actions* (also known as value-rational ones, *wertrational*): actions which are taken because it leads to a valued goal, but with no thought of its consequences and often without consideration of the appropriateness of the means chosen to achieve it ('the end sanctifies the means') Value rational or Instrumentally rational social action is divided into two groups: rational consideration and rational orientation. Rational Orientation comes into account when secondary results are taken into account rationally. This is also considered alternative means when secondary consequences have ended. Determining this mean of action is quite hard and even incompatible. Rational orientation is being able to recognize and understand certain mediums under common conditions. According to Weber, heterogeneous actors and groups that are competing, find it hard to settle on a certain medium and understand the common social action;

2. *Instrumental action* (also known as value relation, goal-instrumental ones, *zweckrational*): actions which are planned and taken after evaluating the goal in relation to other goals, and after thorough consideration of various means (and consequences) to achieve it. An example would be most economic transactions. Value Relation is divided into the subgroups commands and demands. According to the law, people are given commands and must use the whole system of private laws to break down the central government or domination in the legal rights in which a citizen possess. Demands can be based on justice or human dignity just for morality. These demands have posed several problems even legal formalism has been put to the test. These demands seem to weigh on the society and at times can make them feel immoral;

3. *Affectional action* (also known as **emotional actions**): actions which are taken due to one's emotions, to express personal feelings. For examples, cheering after a victory, crying at a funeral would be affectional actions. Affectual is divided into two subgroups: uncontrolled reaction and emotional tension. In uncontrolled reaction there is no restraint and there is lack of

discretion. A person with an uncontrolled reaction becomes less inclined to consider other peoples' feelings as much as their own. Emotional tension comes from a basic belief that a person is unworthy or powerless to obtain his/her deepest aspirations. When aspirations are not fulfilled there is internal unrest. It is often times difficult to be productive in society because of the unfulfilled life;

l   *Traditional actions*: actions which are carried out due to tradition, because they are always carried out in such a situation. An example would be putting on clothes or relaxing on Sundays. Some traditional actions can become a cultural artifact Traditional is divided into two subgroups: customs and habit. A custom is a practice that rests among familiarity. It is continually perpetuated and is ingrained in a culture. Customs usually last for generations. A habit is a series of steps learned gradually and sometimes without conscious awareness. As the old cliché goes, "old habits are hard to break" and new habits are difficult to form.

Social Justice

The requirements of justice applied to the framework of social existence. Social justice is the quality of a society's generalized right-ness. Social justice is both a philosophical problem and an important issue in politics, religion and civil society. Most individuals wish to live in a just society, but different political ideologies have different conceptions of what a 'just society' actually is. The basic liberties according to Rawls:

❖   freedom of thought;
❖   liberty of conscience as it affects social relationships on the grounds of religion, philosophy, and morality;
❖   political liberties (e.g. representative democratic institutions, freedom of speech and the press, and freedom of assembly);
❖   freedom of association;
❖   freedoms necessary for the liberty and integrity of the person (viz: freedom from slavery, freedom of movement and a reasonable degree of freedom to choose one's occupation); and
❖   rights and liberties covered by the rule of law.

Social Injustice is a concept relating to the perceived unfairness or injustice of a society in its divisions of rewards and burdens. The concept is distinct from those of justice in law, which may or may not be considered moral in practice.

There are several main issues in teaching for social justice.

Peer Relationships

Peer relationships among learners are largely determinant of the outcomes of schools.

Teacher Relationships

The relationships teachers have with students also affect teaching for social justice.

Classrooms

The number of specific classroom issues that affect teaching for social justice are almost countless. Understanding the affects of teachers on student learning is vital, and a teacher cannot teach under the assumption that "equal means the same." Students come from numerous cultures, languages, lifestyles and values and a monocultural framework will not suit all student needs.

Additionally, teachers need to be critically conscious and offer students well-planned units and lessons that develop knowledge of a wide range of groups. Curriculum building on acknowledgment rather than neglect the experiences of students. Educators can also match students' cultures to the curriculum and instructional practices

Student Voice

Student voice describes the distinct perspectives and actions of young people throughout schools focused on education.

Definition

Student voice is the individual and collective perspective and actions of young people within the context of learning and education. It is identified in schools as both a metaphorical practice and as a pragmatic concern.

Practice

Student voice work is premised on the following convictions:

- ❖ Young people have unique perspectives on learning, teaching, and schooling;

❖ Their insights warrant not only the attention but also the responses of adults; and

❖ They should be afforded opportunities to actively shape their education.

Several typologies differentiate the practices that identify as student voice. One identifies multiple roles for students throughout the education system, including education planning, research, teaching, evaluating, decision-making and advocacy.

Administrative Approaches

The presence and engagement of student voice has been seen as essential to the educational process since at least the time of John Dewey, if not long before. In 1916 Dewey wrote extensively about the necessity of engaging student experience and perspectives in the curriculum of schools, summarizing his support by saying,:

> The essence of the demand for freedom is the need of conditions which will enable an individual to make his own special contribution to a group interest, and to partake of its activities in such ways that social guidance shall be a matter of his own mental attitude, and not a mere authoritative dictation of his acts.

Today student voice is seeing a resurgence of importance as a growing body of literature increasingly identifies student voice as necessary throughout the educational process. Areas where advocates encourage actively acknowledging student voice include curriculum design and instructional methods, Educational leadership and general school reform activities, including research and evaluation.

Curricular Approaches

Specific types of activities that can specifically engage student voice include teaching , education decision-making, school planning, participatory action research, learning and teaching evaluations, educational advocacy, and student advisories for principals and superintendents.

Service Learning

Engaging student voice is a primary objective of service learning, which commonly seeks to entwine classroom learning objectives with community service opportunities. Student voice is also present in student government programs, experiential education activities, and other forms of student-centered learning.

8

Government Responsibility

What is the Function of Punishment? "Justice must not only be done but seen to be done". Most would agree with this statement—the wicked must surely be punished (or should they?—do two wrongs make a right?) but why is it so important that the punishment must be seen to be done? To the utilitarian the answer is simple—punishment must be witnessed in order to deter others from committing the same act. Thus, to a utilitarian the perception of punishment is seen as the main, or even the sole, justification for punishment. Of course, if the wrongdoer is sent to prison for any length of time he is incapacitated, and thus excluded from doing further harm. Further, while being punished there may be at least the hope that the wrongdoer repents and reforms.

Lord Justice Denning wrote that, "Ever since the time of Henry I, in order that an act should be punishable, it must be morally blameworthy. It must be a sin." The Evolution of Punishment "Durkheim (1858-1917) is widely regarded as one of the 'founding fathers' of sociology and was a leading light among the Année Sociologique group" 1 Durkheim wrote about different varieties of topics but based his main issue on the nature of social order and social solidarity. Law and crime was seen as a main term to reveal development of the solidarity in society. The developments of different forms of punishment are discussed in this essay. Durkheim identified 'two laws' 1) The Law of Quantitative Change The intensity of punishment is the greater the more closely societies approximate to a less developed type—and the more the central power assumes an absolute character.2 2) The Law of Qualitative Change Deprivations of liberty, and of liberty alone, varying in time according to the seriousness of the crime, tend to become more and more the normal means of social control.

Informal Social Control

If you had a problem, who would you turn to first? A friend? Family? It is quite likely that you would seek solace in someone you knew well…someone who you saw regularly—someone who plays a very important part in your life. This is what we mean by informal social control. This form of control is therefore based on the approval or disapproval of those around us whose review of us we regard as important.

Hence, the three main groups that fall into this category are;

Family

Our basic learning of norms and values (what is regarded as desirable and achievable, often dictating how we should live) are learned in the realm of the family. The family therefore plays a very important role on socialising us and therefore giving us our own identity. It is in this realm that we learn the basic morality of society (*note for A2 students—which political perspective, however, argues that this is under threat? Why?*) and we learn to develop a conscience. The family controls us in a very subtle way—unless we do very wrong perhaps where punishment is obvious and pronounced.

Friends

In Sociology, the term "peer group" is often used as an alternative to the term "friends". A peer group is a group of people of a similar age to us who we relate to. Often peer groups can teach us informally (i.e. often in a very "piece meal" and subtle way—much like the family) how to behave correctly and properly, but sometimes they do the opposite as we shall see later!

Work Colleagues

Very similar to peer groups but perhaps work colleagues are less likely to abuse the way they can control us!

Formal Social Control

The second form of control is formal social control. In Sociology, these institutions are referred to as organisations or systems that exercise rigid rules, ideologies and morals that we are often compelled to obey.

However, it may also be more useful to look at those who exercise formal social control us people in suits—people or institutions that we don't always come into every day contact with and when we do it is in a very rigid and timetabled way.

Hence, in formal social control we can include:

Religion

Historically, the church was one of the major forms of social control. However, perhaps its degree of social control has waned a little now (*note for A2 students—see the argument of post-modernists for example; although also look at the counter argument by the Functionalists—see Parsons, Malinowski etc.*). Its significance as a form of social control, however, may still exist in the way it has influenced the legal system, the family and education.

Education

Education has often been cited as a form of control in the way morality and citizenship are taught to pupils. Often, this has been referred to as the *Hidden Curriculum* (Bowles and Gintis); a curriculum that you learn without really thinking about it.

The Mass Media

The mass media (radio, television, cinema, arts etc) influence us by providing models of behaviour that we copy (it is through the mass media that we have role models) while condemning other "deviant" forms of behaviour. This is something we will look at in more depth later on; indeed, it could be argued that the media is playing a more and more crucial role in shaping public opinion that it ever has.

The Health Service

At first it may seem quite strange to suggest that the Health Service is a system of social control; but remember, when talking about social control we are not necessarily talking about negative control (i.e. condemning behaviour that is deviant); social control also describes positive control (i.e. encouraging us to conform to the values of society). The Health Service encourages us to be responsible about our health; think about very subtle things for example like a child getting a lollipop at e dentist—that is a sign that you have done what is expected of you. Some perspectives, however, argue that the Health Service is more likely to be a system of informal social control.

The Legal System

Undoubtedly the most obvious type of social control in society. The Legal system, therefore, is the most powerful institution that deals with social control. Included in this are the police and the courts.

Role of the Police to Society

Conflict Policing

This model of policing has been suggested by Scraton (1985) who argues that the police can be seen as an occupying force, imposed, particularly upon working class and ethnic minority communities this model argues that the police are influenced by powerful groups in society (such as the upper class) and powerful forces in society (such as the mass media) Young (1984) describes this style of policing as a "military style"; Large numbers of police officers patrol designated areas with a maximum use of technology for intelligence gathering.

Consensus Policing

Needless to say, the second role of the police would be a more positive affair. The consensual approach sees the police as having a close relationship with the local area being policed. The role of the police force is seen to be representing the interests of the community.

Indeed, the consensual approach believes that the police "hold" the community together; in a way, it is possible to suggest that they actually form the "hub" of the community.

It is also felt among this approach that the majority of law abiding people in the community put great value on the importance of the police in maintaining order—thus, great respect is credited to the police for the work they do.

Social Control

Social control is exercised through the use of sanctions. There are four types of sanctions exercised which ensure we conform to the expectations of society.

Formal Positive Sanctions

These are sanctions that are exercised by a group (or groups) that fall under the concept "formal social control". So, for example, they are sanctions that are exercised by the law or by education for example. However, notice the word "positive"—this means that rather than the sanction being a punishment, it is a reward for good behaviour/achieving something desirable. Let's give some examples:

❖ Winning a medal in a sporting contest,

❖ Receiving a Bible on Confirmation,
❖ Celebrating Bar Mitzvah,
❖ Getting a Certificate after finishing a course, and
❖ Receiving a cash prize for reporting a suspected criminal.

Formal Negative Sanctions

These are sanctions that are again exercised by "people in suits" so to speak. Yet, the sanction this time comes in the form of a punishment for bad behaviour/undesirable behaviour rather than a reward.

Let's give some examples:

❖ Receiving a prison sentence,
❖ Being ordered to pay a fine, and
❖ Being given detention in school.

Informal Positive Sanctions

Informal sanctions are not so severe either way. They are sanctions that are applied by groups in society that we are most likely to turn to for guidance—hence they are groups that fall under the term "informal social control" e.g. family, peer groups. Notice the word positive here; not all sanctions are negative!

Let's give some examples:

❖ A pat on the back by a friend,
❖ A bunch of flowers from a friend for helping her out, and
❖ A present from your family on your birthday.

Informal Negative Sanctions

Agencies of informal social control do, however, also exercise negative sanctions. Hence, agents of informal control also provide punishments as well as rewards;

Let's give some examples:

❖ A friend telling you off for doing wrong,
❖ Parents grounding a child, and
❖ A work colleague telling you to pull your weight.

Sanctions are exercised day in day out—not only are they applied to us—we apply them to other people as well—often sub consciously.

Youth Sub-Cultures and Styles

Youths holding norms and values that were significantly different to the norms and values held by their parents. The idea that "youth" represents a period of "ambivalence"—a distinct phase in human social development that represents a transition period from childhood to full adulthood.

Hall's work focuses upon the relationship between biological/chemical changes and human behavior and represents an attempt to understand youth culture as a form of pathological response (in basic terms, pathology relates to the way in which social behavior is related to biological development. For example, changes in body chemistry during puberty may theoretically produce behavioral changes in the individual—behavioral changes that the individual is relatively powerless to prevent/control). In this respect, Hall noted that the "problems of youth" included:

- ❖ Unbridled sexuality,
- ❖ Rejection of parents/teachers,
- ❖ Lack of concentration,
- ❖ Extremes of emotion/violence, and
- ❖ Unpredictability.

Deviant behavior, therefore, resulted from chemically-based body changes in the transition from child to adulthood (hence the term pathological—youth behavior explained as a "disease" caused by chemical changes in the body).

In addition, social conditions can aggravate this condition (confining children within the family/classroom etc. highlights behavior as deviant when it is really only a case of "growing-up"—a natural process through which all humans supposedly pass). Hall argued that adolescence involved various emotional problems that were associated with such things as:

(a) The break from family life experienced by teenagers.
(b) The development of independent personalities that starts to conflict with parental socialization.

In this respect, Hall placed great emphasis upon adolescence being a time of emotional "storm and stress".

Deviance

Explanations include:

1. Lack of parental responsibility.
2. The breakdown of the family (especially amongst the working class).
3. The breakdown of authority and respect for the law.
4. The breakdown of community values.
5. The lack of discipline in schools.
6. The "permissive society" (at the present, the 1960's represent our permissive society, but this theme reappears from time to time throughout our history).
7. The (bad) influence of the mass media (television and film in particular).

Youth Culture to Social Change

Link the development of specific forms of youth culture to social change (which, as you might expect, involved the implicit use of concepts such as anomie and the more explicit emphasis upon the general socialization process—a traditional Functionalist focus, for example). Thus, taking a selection of these theories, various "causes" of youth cultures were identified as such things as:

1. Consumerism and affluence.
2. The effect on children's socialization.
3. Extension of education into the "teenage years" (youth seen to develop as a "transition phase" between childhood and adulthood).
4. The effect of the mass media on teenage behavior.

"Modern" Phenomenon

Pre-industrial societies did not have the functional requirement of a period of transition between childhood and adulthood because: The family was centre of economic production. People were not geographically mobile. An education system was not required.

The radical psychologist, R.D. Laing has also gone so far as to suggest that the family is actually the source of many of the traumas that we have as individuals in later life—most people find the family such a traumatic, unhappy, experience that they cannot wait to leave it.

Social Distribution of Crime

Social distribution of crime in relation to four main categories:

1. Region,
2. Age,
3. Gender, and
4. Class.

Crime is obviously related to law. As a general rule, more crime takes place in urban than rural areas. A number of possible reasons can be advanced to account for this observation:

1. *There is more opportunity for crime in urban areas*: In this respect, there are more people, more places in which to commit crimes and so forth.
2. *There are more police resources in urban areas*: This tends to increase the possibility that crime will be notified to/by the police, but it is also interesting to note that, in relation to the more visible forms of crime that take place in our society, there is a greater likelihood of detection/police involvement.
3. In rural areas, patterns of association tend to be characterised by informal social controls, whereby in relatively close-knit communities people are able to exercise far higher levels of personal social control over people that they know.

The Rural and Urban Areas

Ferdinand Tonnies expressed this difference in the basic form of social relationships by arguing that rural areas tended to be characterised by "Gemeinschaft" type arrangements:

These are defined as small-scale, close-knit "community" types where "everyone knows everyone else" and people make it their business to know what is going-on in their community.

He contrasted this with "Gesellschaft" type arrangements that he argued tended to exist in urban areas:

These are defined as large-scale, loosely-knit "association" types, whereby people come into contact with large numbers of other people in their everyday lives on a relatively impersonal basis.

The Age and Sex Distribution of Crime

Statistically, most crime in Britain is committed by young males (those between the ages of 14—21). For example—In 1983, of those found guilty/ cautioned for all types of crime there were:

(a) 210,000 males between the ages 14 to 21
     225, 000 males aged 21+
(b) 37,000 females aged 14 to 21
     47,000 females aged 21+

Thus, for both males and females roughly 50 per cent of those found guilty/cautioned were between the ages 14-21. The ration of male—female offenders, however, was approximately 5 : 1 in favour of males.... In terms of longitudinal studies of crime (that is, surveys which aim to build-up a comparative study of crime over a period of time), for people born in 1953:

❖ 30 per cent of these males had a criminal record.
❖ 6 per cent of these females had a criminal record.

Social Class and the Social Distribution of Crime

In relation to age and sex, in relation to conviction rates there is a clear relationship between crime and class, insofar as the majority of convicted offenders are drawn from the working classes. As might also be expected, there is a clear correlation between type of crime and social class. For example:

❖ Crimes involving violence, theft from property, etc. are mainly associated with the working class.
❖ Fraud, embezzlement and so forth are mainly middle class crimes.
❖ Corporate crime (involving such things as insider trading, environmental crimes, market-rigging and the like) is mainly an upper class phenomenon.
❖ This relationship is hardly surprising given the idea of different opportunity structures in our society (working class males and females, for example, are not, by definition, in positions of sufficient power to allow them to carry-out elaborate company frauds). However, simply because more members of the working class are convicted of crimes than the members of other social classes doesn't mean that we can automatically assume that the working classes are somehow "more criminal" than the middle/ upper classes. In this respect, a number of ideas are significant:

The type of crime committed is an important factor:

The working class, for example, tend to be involved in crimes that are highly visible (crimes of violence, for example). In situations where there are clear victims and little attempt to hide criminal behaviour (for whatever reason), it follows that detection/arrest and conviction rates are likely to be higher.

Crimes such as fraud, insider dealing and so forth tend to be much less visible to the police, general public and so forth. Since the police do not routinely involve themselves in companies, offices and so forth, greater opportunity exists for this type of crime.

"Age of Accountability"

The law and order in the late 19th century The law and order in the late 19th century was very different to the law and order at the present time. The criminals and murderers in the 19th century could escape with the crime easier because there was no finger printing and they did not have DNA in that time. They did not have the scientific knowledge as scientists have today. The criminal intelligence department (CID) was set up in 1878 and this led to considerable improvement in detective methods and began to use forensic science, even though the forensic science they used was not as advanced as the ones we use now. They did not have DNA or finger printing, in actual fact they did not even know the difference between animal blood and human blood.

In USA after a 1992 shooting in a Brooklyn high school left two students dead, New York's board of education ordered the installation of metal detectors in the city's schools.

Murders committed by children in USA raise the question, how old must a child be to be held accountable for his or her actions in the eyes of the court system? One may also question how old a child must be to discern "right" from "wrong."

Police were also brought in to patrol 130 of the toughest schools. Teachers got special training, and students were taught conflict resolution. New York City also made it mandatory that anyone bringing a gun, knife or other weapon to school be expelled. But there is a big loophole in the mandate: you have to be 17 or older before you can be expelled.

Recognize that keeping firearms in your home may put you at legal risk as well as expose you and your family to physical risk. In many states, parents can be held liable for their children's actions, including inappropriate use of firearms. If you do choose to keep firearms at home, ensure that they are securely locked, that ammunition is locked and stored separately, and that children know weapons are never to be touched without your express permission and supervision.

Gun control laws do not prevent little kids from using guns and harming people. Violent video games help children with their marksmanship and to get over their fear of shooting someone. Video simulation is the best way to help overcome the natural resistance that most people have about shooting someone. One main difference between military training and video games is that military instructions are constantly pausing the action and where the video game is in constant action.

While citizens worry about protecting themselves from criminals, it has now been shown that they must also keep a watchful eye on those who are supposed to protect and serve. Most countries has made form filling mandatory. Here is a sample:

The legal kind requires a permit that you acquire through special classes and testing. For example, from my city/county government's website on gun permits:

Quote: Concealed Handgun Permit Requirements

Applicant Must:

* ❖ be twenty-one (21) years of age; be a resident of Mecklenburg County and a resident of North Carolina for thirty (30) days;
* ❖ be a citizen or naturalized citizen of the United States of America; not suffer from any mental or physical infirmity which would prevent safe handgun handling and operation;
* ❖ provide a valid N.C. driver's license or other picture ID with current address provided by the state of North Carolina;
* ❖ successfully complete a firearms training and safety course that has been designed by the North Carolina Criminal Justice Standards Commission (See Yellow Pages or a firearms dealer for businesses that provide training).

A criminal background check that takes about 90 days must be performed before granting of permit. Applicant must make an appointment to apply for permit.

Applicant must apply in person and have a verifiable training certificate and a valid picture ID in hand (NC driver's license or other picture ID with current address provided by the state of North Carolina). A Concealed Weapon Permit requires a $90.00 non-refundable fee (which includes a $10.00 fingerprint fee) payable by cash, money order or certified check. If paying with cash, please bring exact amount since we have very little cash on hand. Personal checks are not accepted. Ineligibility for Concealed Handgun Permit Persons not eligible include anyone:

- ❖ found guilty or received a prayer for judgment continued or suspended sentence for any crimes of violence or misdemeanor assaults as defined by General Statutes;
- ❖ under indictment or against whom a finding of probable cause exists for a felony; found guilty in any court for a felony;
- ❖ receiving a prayer for judgment continued for any criminal offense which disqualifies a person from receiving a Concealed Handgun Permit;
- ❖ who is a fugitive from justice;
- ❖ who is an unlawful user of or addicted to illegal drugs;
- ❖ discharged from the armed forces for other than honorable reasons;
- ❖ who has been ruled mentally ill; ineligible to own, possess or receive a firearm under the provisions of state or federal law;
- ❖ free on bond or personal recognizance pending trial, appeal or sentencing for a crime which disqualifies a person from receiving a Concealed Handgun Permit; and
- ❖ convicted of an impaired driving offense within three years prior to application date.

Rules For Carrying a Concealed Handgun

You must notify the sheriff issuing the permit of any change of address within thirty (30) days of the change. You may not carry a concealed handgun while consuming or after having consumed alcohol or other controlled substance which alters judgment or physical control.

Handgun may be concealed in purse or pocket. Permit and a valid North Carolina issued picture ID must be on your person when carrying a concealed handgun. You must tell any approaching law enforcement officer that you are carrying a concealed handgun. Failure to carry permit or to notify approaching law enforcement officer is an infraction for the first offense, a misdemeanor in subsequent instances. Permits can be revoked for lying on application, lending your permit to another person or being charged with a crime. Renewing of Concealed Handgun Permits If a permit expires, an individual may not carry his or her weapon concealed until a new application has been approved and issued.

The renewal process will be similar to the original application except the Sheriff has waived the necessity for existing permit holders to re-take the firearms safety course. However, if a permit holder allows a permit to expire, he or she will be treated as a new applicant and will be required to take the firearms safety class again. Renewal applicants must apply in person by calling the Sheriff's Office Gun Permits Bureau at 704-336-3664 to schedule an appointment. Appointments will be available Monday to Thursday from 8 a.m. to 3:00 p.m. and on Fridays from 8 to 11:00 a.m. At the appointment, applicants will fill out a concealed handgun renewal form, sign a notarized affidavit stating they remain qualified under the concealed handgun law, have a new set of fingerprints taken, sign mental health release forms and pay a non-refundable renewal fee of $85—payable only in cash, money order or certified check. Personal checks are not accepted. An applicant also must bring to the appointment a valid picture ID (NC driver's license or other picture ID with current address provided by the state of North Carolina).

The Sheriff's Office Permit Bureau is located at 715 E. 4th St., behind the historic Courthouse and across the street from the Criminal Courthouse at 720 E 4th St. Once issued, the permit is valid throughout the state for a period of five years, unless it is revoked.

If you are certified to carry a concealed weapon and do so, you must have your permit on your person when you're carrying. Otherwise, it's like driving without a license. The rule on where you can and can't carry varies by jurisdiction, but from what I can remember, it's so restrictive in a lot of places that it's almost not worth even trying.

Educators should never underestimate the importance of social and emotional education; a student who doesn't feel part of the mainstream is more likely to create his or her own agenda.

The Studies

Shooter's Pre-attack Behaviors and Communications

In 2002, the U.S. Secret Service completed the Safe School Initiative, a study of school shootings and other school-based attacks that were conducted in collaboration with the U.S. Department of Education. The study examined school shootings in the United States as far back as 1974, through the end of the school year in 2000, analyzing a total of 37 incidents involving 41 student attackers. The study involved extensive review of police records, school records, court documents, and other source materials, and included interviews with 10 school shooters. The focus of the study was on developing information about the school shooter's pre-attack behaviors and communications. The goal was to identify information about a school shooting that may be identifiable or noticeable before the shooting occurs, to help inform efforts to prevent school-based attacks.

The study found that school shootings are rarely impulsive acts. Rather, they are typically thought out and planned out in advance. In addition, prior to most shootings other kids knew the shooting was to occur—but did not alert an adult. Very few of the attackers, however, ever directed threats to their targets before the attack. The study findings also revealed that there is no "profile" of a school shooter; instead, the students who carried out the attacks differed from one another in numerous ways. However, almost every attacker had engaged in behavior before the shooting that seriously concerned at least one adult—and for many had concerned three or more different adults. Most attackers had no history of prior violent or criminal behavior.

Most attackers appeared to have difficulty coping with losses, personal failures or other difficult circumstances. Almost all of the attackers had experienced or perceived some major loss prior to the attack. These losses included a perceived failure or loss of status; loss of a loved one or of a significant relationship, including a romantic relationship; and a major illness experienced by the attacker or someone significant to him. For most attackers, their outward behaviors suggested difficulty in coping with loss. Several findings of the Safe School Initiative indicate clearly that the school-based attacks studied were rarely impulsive. Rather, these attacks typically were thought out beforehand and involved some degree of advance planning. In many cases, the attacker's observable behavior prior to the attack suggested he might be planning or preparing for a school attack. In nearly all of the incidents for which information concerning the attacker's conceptualization of the attack was available. The attacker had developed his idea to harm the target(s) before the attack. The length of time that attackers held this idea prior to the actual attack varied considerably. Some attackers conceived of the attack as few as one or two days prior to advancing that attack; other attackers had held the idea of the attack for as long as a year prior to carrying it out. Moreover, there was evidence from the attacker's behavior prior to the attack that the attacker had a plan or was preparing to harm the target(s) For example, one attacker asked his friends to help him get ammunition for one of his weapons; sawed off the end of a rifle to make it easier to conceal beneath his clothes; shopped for a long trench coat with his mother; and cut the pockets out of the coat so that he could conceal the weapon within the coat while holding the weapon through one of the cut-out pockets. That attacker had a well known fascination with weapons and had told his friends on several occasions that he thought about killing certain students at school. In most cases, other people knew about the attack before it took place. Most attackers did not threaten their targets directly prior to advancing the attack. Most attackers engaged in some behavior, prior to the incident that caused others concern or indicated a need for help.

Although most attackers carried out their attacks on their own, many attackers were influenced or encouraged by others to engage in the attacks. In other cases, friends assisted the attacker in his efforts to acquire a weapon or ammunition, discussed tactics for getting a weapon into school undetected, or helped gather information about the whereabouts of a target at a particular time during the school day. Most school-based attacks were stopped through intervention by school administrators, educators and students-or by the attacker stopping on his own.

The findings from the study suggest that some school attacks may be preventable, and that students can play an important role in prevention efforts. Using the study findings, the Secret Service and Department of Education have modified the Secret Service threat assessment approach for use in schools—to give school and law enforcement professionals tools for investigating threats in school, managing situations of concern, and creating safe school climates.

The 10 key findings that the authors believe may have implications for the developments of strategies to address the problem of targeted school violence are as follows:

- ❖ Incidents of targeted violence at school rarely are sudden, impulsive acts.
- ❖ Prior to most incidents, other people knew about the attacker's idea and/or plan to attack.
- ❖ Most attackers did not threaten their targets directly prior to advancing the attack.
- ❖ There is no accurate or useful profile of students who engaged in targeted school violence.
- ❖ Most attackers engaged in some behavior prior to the incident that caused others concern or indicated a need for help.
- ❖ Most attackers had difficulty coping with significant losses or personal failures. Moreover, many had considered or attempted suicide.
- ❖ Many attackers felt bullied, persecuted or injured by others prior to the attack.

❖ Most attackers had access to and had used weapons prior to the attack.
❖ In many cases, other students were involved in some capacity.
❖ Despite prompt law enforcement responses, most shooting incidents were stopped by means other than law enforcement intervention.

Educators and other adults can learn how to pick up on these signals and make appropriate referrals

The Psychologists

In a disturbing laboratory experiment in which a gun was hidden in a drawer, many boys found the weapon, played with it and even pulled the trigger without knowing whether it was loaded.

"They did everything from point it at each other to look down the barrel themselves," said Dr. Geoffrey Jackman, who led the study. "The scariest thing is when the children picked up that gun and looked straight down the barrel."

But psychologist Kevin Dwyer, a child-violence expert who was not involved in the research, called the results "extremely important." They suggest, he said, that just telling kids that they should not handle a gun is often not good enough.

"It means that we must have external control rather than education control, such as gun locks and reduced availability of firearms in situations where children can access them," Dwyer said.

More than 90 per cent of the boys who handled the gun or pulled the trigger reported having received some sort of gun safety instruction, ranging from an informal talk with their parents to formal instruction from a teacher or a police officer at school.

A sizable number of parents were college-educated, and parents of most of the boys who handled the gun had believed their sons had a low interest in guns.

Police Role

Police exist to uphold the law. Although cops try to protect people from criminal predation, it is an incidental part of their job. Numerous court decisions have absolved police from liability for failure to protect individuals. Even with the best intentions, police officers are too few to be everywhere they are needed at once.

Police Confessions Style

Juvenile crime is now a product we heartily consume if not entirely fathom. Events like the shooting at Columbine High have created a new model of the murderer. No longer do the maniacal faces of Manson and Gacy define fear. The faces we demonize are those of children, and it has become all too easy for adults to believe children are capable of the most heinous crimes. The trash talk that has dominated school cafeterias and playgrounds from the beginning of time can now get kids expelled, if not land them in jail. And once accused—be it of plotting a school shooting or of murdering the neighbor girl—the police employ the same interrogation techniques used on adults in order to get the conviction that will quell heightened fears of violent youths run amok. Using techniques designed to get confessions from adults seems to be producing a flood of false confessions from children.

Police see nothing wrong with using the same interrogation techniques with juveniles that they use on accused adults, both legal and psychological experts agree that such techniques, designed to break down a suspect's will, are inappropriate and damaging to children. They also say that a juvenile's ability to understand Miranda rights—such as the right not to answer questions or to ask for an attorney—is lacking, making it impossible for a child to knowingly waive them.

Suggestive questioning, repetition, hints of rewards and punishments—make the likelihood of a false confession greater when the person being interrogated is a child. Juveniles simply don't have the psychological resources to withstand such questioning. Under the age of 14 are unable to understand the abstractions much less the potential long-term consequences they could face by waiving them. There are cases where children have confessed to crimes simply because they wanted to go home. Police should be required to keep an attorney on hand for all youth questioning, since even parents might not have their child's best legal interest at heart unless they are aware of the intentions of the police.

9

Case Study

The Only Exception

Oregon's Thurston High School in Springfield in May, 1998 is the only case where the shooter was arrested the previous day for having a gun in his school locker, and released. Kip Kinkel, then 15, shot to death both his teacher parents at home, before the next day killing two classmates and wounding 25, the largest number in the history of such shootings. When terrifying reality hits close to us—society needs to study warning signs it ignored for many years. School shootings that preceded Springfield's indicate they are something more than copycat coincidences. It can involve a thinking mode that causes them to see only one solution to their problems, an option that for a troubled child can become violent. Such a thinking pattern can cause the child to see people as targets, especially if fueled by years of playing video games with violent themes. Research reveals a seasonal pattern in school shootings that should make teachers and administrators especially alert at this time of year. The Thurston shooting in May was one of a national series of eight successive shootings that occurred in the season when the school year comes to a close.

The Inside Story

In home videos made in the final weeks before their deadly attack on Columbine High School, two teen-age gunmen said they hoped to kill hundreds in the assault and speculated about which Hollywood director might make a movie about it. Both Eric Harris and Dylan Klebold expressed concern about the effect their murderous assault would have on their parents. "I hope we will kill 250 of you," Klebold said on one tape. Harris said the moment of the attack would be the most "nerve-wracking of my life.... Seconds will be like hours. I can't wait."

Five videos found in Harris' bedroom after the shootings. They were recorded in the weeks before the April 20 massacre, in which the two seniors killed 12 students and a teacher at the Littleton school before committing suicide. While they showed little or no remorse toward their future victims, both Harris and Klebold came close to apologizing to their parents in the videos. "They're going to be put through hell once we do this," Harris, 18, said at one point. He then addressed his parents directly, saying, "There's nothing you guys could do about this."

Klebold, 17, told his mother and father they were "great parents" and that he appreciated their teaching him "self- awareness, self-reliance." He told them, "I'm sorry I have so much rage." After the shootings, there was much public debate about whether the gunmen's parents, Wayne and Katherine Harris and Thomas and Susan Klebold, should be held responsible for their sons' actions. The carnage might not have happened had a phone call been handled differently. An employee of Green Mountain Guns called Harris' house and told his father, "Hey, your clips are in."

Harris' father said he had not ordered any clips, as recounted by Eric Harris on one tape. Had either party on the phone checked further, the massacre plans would have been ruined, the younger Harris said on tape.

While the videos reinforce the idea that Harris and Klebold were motivated in part by a desire for what they saw as revenge, they also indicate that the two wanted notoriety. The killers made their final tape on the morning of the massacre. "It's a half-hour before judgment day," Klebold said into the camera. "I didn't like life very much. Just know I'm going to a better place than here."

Second Case

Just hours after he killed his parents and two classmates and wounded 25 others, a visibly stunned Kip Kinkel returned with detectives to the scene of the carnage at Thurston High School in Springfield, Oregon.

"Can you tell us what happened," police ask on May 21, 1998.

In videotapes released by police Thursday, Kinkel is nearly inaudible. "I just started shooting," he says.

His hands shackled at his waist and with a police jacket draped over his slumping shoulders, Kinkel is walked through the cafeteria.

"Are you still shooting the .22 rifle at this point?" police ask at one spot in the room.

"Yes," he answers

Did he know who he was shooting? No, the teen-ager said.

In nine minutes of tape, Kinkel is disconsolate, with no outward sign of the demons he said drove him to kill four people.

Detective Al Warthen points to some of Kinkel's weapons, including a semiautomatic rifle and a pistol.

"Is this stuff you brought?" the detective asks.

"Yes," the teen-ager says.

"Is that your backpack?"

"Yes."

His demeanor is a sharp contrast to the deadly violence Kinkel had perpetrated.

Warthen asks, "Why did you do this?"

"I had no other choice," said Kinkel.

"You had no other choice, OK," said the detective. "Did any of these students upset you?"

Police say the 15-year-old had been read his Miranda rights, but Kinkel did not yet have an attorney.

A lawyer hired later fought to keep the tape from being used in court, but lost.

Took Gun to School the Day Before

The day before the tape was shot, Warthen had dealt with Kinkel when the youngster brought a gun to school.

Later that day, Warthen released Kinkel to his father, Bill Kinkel, who scolded the boy on how he had embarrassed the family.

In a tearful, ranting confession conducted before the videotape, Kinkel told police he killed his parents to spare them the shame.

"I didn't want to. I love my dad; that's why I had to," Kinkel says in an audiotape of the police interview.

"You love him, so that's why you had to kill him?" he is asked.

"Yes," he answered.

"Goddamn these voice inside my head!" Kinkel screams on the tape.

Kinkel's family had wrestled for several years with the boy's obsession with guns and explosives. They put him in therapy at one time.

Paranoid Schizophrenia Diagnosed

Doctors called by Kinkel's defense team testified at his sentencing hearing that they found Kinkel to be a paranoid schizophrenic driven to kill by hallucinations. They said he could be treated, but there was no certainty he could be cured.

Now at age 17, he is serving a 112-year sentence at a state juvenile facility near Portland, Oregon.

Jokela High School, Tuusula Finland, November 7, 2007—Class A Event

- ❖ *Who*: Pekka-Eric Auvinen (18), dubbed the You-Tube killer by mass-media for his videos posted on that website under multiple aliases such as Sturmgeist89 and naturalselector89 (account banned).
- ❖ *Where*: Jokela High School in Tuusula with 400 students between ages 12 and 18, located in a small town 30-40 miles from Helsinki.
- ❖ *When*: Wednesday November 7, 2007 at approximately 11:45 am. The shooting was probably timed to coincide with the anniversary of the Bolshevik revolution.
- ❖ *Weapon(s)*: Semi-automatic .22 Sig Sauer Mosquito pistol named Catherine by Auvinen, 69 bullets fired, police reportedly found 320 more bullets with him, also he had an flammable liquid that he tried set fire to a second floor corridor with.
- ❖ *Killed*: School principal Helena Kalmi (61), nurse (42), five boys aged between 16 and 18, and a 25-year-old single mother. Twelve others injured. Except for the principal, the targets appear to be random. Eyewitness claims Auvinen forced Kalmi onto her knees and then shot her. "Helsingin Sanomat has been told that there had been an argument between Auvinen and the principal before Wednesday."
- ❖ *Event*: Much of the event timeline remains undisclosed at this time. We know that Pekka-Eric Auvinen used his .22 caliber pistol to shoot multiple people and after about twenty minutes he shot himself in the head in a toilet stall beside the school cafeteria. About 90 minutes later police found him and took him to the hospital where he died eight hours later.
- ❖ *Background*: Very little has been published on Pekka-Eric Auvinen's background but we have been told that he has a younger brother and that Auvinen's father worked on the Finnish railways for decades, is also a guitarist, and his wife is a vocalist.

Depressed in Finland

Pekka-Eric Auvinen was taking anti-depressant medications. "In a video that he placed on YouTube, Sturmgeist89 displays packages of Cipralex,

Zoloft, Luvox, and Prozac pills." The drugs were prescribed for depression. "The National Agency for Medicines recommends against prescribing SSRIs for people under the age of 18, because of the self-destructive or hostile emotions that they have been known to provoke." Fellow student Tuomas Hulkkonen states the he knew the gunman well and that he had been acting strange lately, "He withdrew into his shell. I had noticed a change in him just recently, and I thought that perhaps he was a bit depressed, or something. But I couldn't imagine that in reality he would do anything like this."

His 18 year-old (or 20 depending on source) girlfriend Tana Scheel recently left him, "He was my boyfriend. I have received many emails and phone calls claiming it is my fault and that I am a murderer because I rejected him. But many people are rejected without going out and murdering." She also claims that banning his YouTube accounts, ".... would have done nothing but take away his ability to express himself through his videos, one thing which made him happy and curbed his homicidal tendencies."

Gun Culture

"People using guns are hunters. They live in rural areas. It's part of the life over there." Auvinen had no previous criminal record and had no difficulty legally obtaining his handgun. He was a member of a hunting club and was practiced enough to direct most of his shots at the head and upper body of his victims during his 20-minute rampage. "With 1.6 million firearms in private hands, the Nordic nation is an anomaly in Europe, lagging behind only the US and Yemen in civilian gun ownership. According to a government study in 2002, only 14 per cent of homicides in Finland are gun-related. Finland has a strong history of armed self-defense, most notable in the collective Finnish effort to repel the invading Soviet Army over 60 years ago.

Misanthropic Malcontent

"Name: Pekka-Eric Auvinen Age: 18 Male from Finland. I am a cynical existentialist, antihuman humanist, antisocial socialdarwinist, realistic idealist and godlike atheist." Pekka-Eric's own words were decidedly aggressive yet equally unfocused.

He wrote of his rampage in advance, "Targets: Jokelan Lukio (High School Of Jokela), students and faculty, society, humanity, human race." It seems that, online at least, Pekka-Eric was a hyper-aggressive and often bullying person that made more enemies than friends. He fixated upon weakness and believed that they should be killed by the strong. "This is my war: one man war against humanity, governments and weak-minded masses of the world! No mercy for the scum of the earth! HUMANITY IS OVERRATED! It's time to put NATURAL SELECTION & SURVIVAL OF THE FITTEST back on tracks!"—Pekka from his 'Manifesto.doc' Pekka is clearly angry but *why* is less clear particularly because his expression doesn't explain the problems he rails against nor do they explain how killing students and faculty at his High School will resolve the issues he is most concerned about. He reportedly admired Stalin and Hitler indicating limited Ideological and historical understanding but rather a craving for power and desire to be a dictator. And now we are beginning to see the source of Pekka's discontent, he felt powerless and/or controlled by others and his sudden, violent outburst was a desperate, and probably delusional, effort to express himself as a potent authority, hence his personal statement, "I am the law, judge and executioner. There is no higher authority than me."

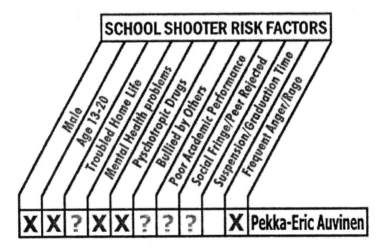

This is your teenage brain on drugs, any questions?

Witnesses describe him as running through the school hallways shouting "Revolution!" and shooting people. Indeed, despite his pleas to the contrary Pekka-Eric is convincing as being mentally unstable. He did take anti-depressant drugs, probably more than one kind, but we don't know the quantities or the timing.

Unfortunately many key details on this event remain unknown, for instance, how well was the shooter doing at his school work? What kind of home-life did he have? What did friends and other students see and think of him? Was he really bullied by other students and if so, why? Lacking these important pieces of information drawing any substantive conclusions remains difficult for this school shooting event.

Success Tech Academy in Cleveland, Ohio, October 11, 2007— Class A Event

- ❖ *Who*: Asa H. Coon, age 14
- ❖ *Where*: Success Tech Academy (High School) in Cleveland, Ohio. With an academic emphasis on technology and entrepreneurship, the school is a five-story converted office building with about 240 students, 85 per cent are black, the remainder mostly Hispanic or white, and all are considered poor according to federal poverty guidelines. Although the school is equipped with metal detectors and 26 cameras, security was intermittent and, apparently, easily defeated.
- ❖ *When*: Wednesday Afternoon, October 10, 2007
- ❖ *Weapons*: One .22 caliber revolver, one .38 caliber revolver, one box of ammunition for each pistol, and three folding knives.
- ❖ *Killed*: Asa H. Coon (suicide) Injured: The first person shot by Coon was Michael Peek, age 14, who had punched Coon in the face right before the shootings began. Darnell Rodgers, 18, black, was grazed by a bullet on the right elbow. David Kachadourian, age 57, white, math teacher, was shot in the back. Michael Grassie, 42, a multicultural studies teacher, was the most seriously injured victim having been shot in the chest.
- ❖ *Event*: Coon had been suspended for fighting on Monday and the same day his older brother, Stephen Coon, age 19, was arrested in connection with an armed robbery. The week before Asa had made threats to blow up the school and stab students but no one paid attention.

  Coon began on the ground floor after changing clothes in a bathroom. The first shooting happened immediately after Coon left the bathroom when another student punched him in the face and he shot back. Coon went up through the first two floors of administrative offices to the third and fourth floor of classrooms. Coon proceeded to shoot one other student, grazing his elbow, and two teachers but only the teacher Michael Grassie seems to have been sought out by Coon. Coon fired eight shots, and shot himself in the head when the police arrived at the school.

❖   *Background*: Even though the school was small it was nonetheless overcrowded and the teaching was impersonal. "I had him since the start of the school year. So that's been about a month and a half. So not a real long time. And the class is real large, so it's hard to know students individually very well or interact with them very much one-on-one."—David Kachadourian, math teacher shot by Coon.

Asa Coon is a poster child for the dysfunctional family, coming from a single parent household with troubled siblings and a father that is nowhere to be found.

"His probation officer described the relationship between Coon and his mother as extremely poor, with both using foul and abusive language toward each other."

Mr. Coon's troubles started early. In 1997, he was 3 and living with his family in Cortland, N.Y., in a house strewn with garbage, according to a report by a caseworker for the Cortland County Social Services Department.

His older brothers, Stephen and Daniel, threatened neighbors with weapons, including rocks, knives and a fake bomb, the caseworker reported.

Mr. Coon's mother, Lori Looney, was found guilty of neglect by the county juvenile court. His father, Thomas Coon, was not involved with the family, the caseworker reported.

Coon was new at SuccessTech Academy and was constantly being bullied and harassed by other students, often for his unkempt and disheveled appearance. In an attempt to belong and develop his personal identity he adopted the 'goth' look and told others that he worshipped musician Marilyn Manson as God. He was reportedly wearing black clothing, black-painted fingernails, and a Marilyn Manson t-shirt at the time of the shooting.

"He was chubby and short, and he was the only kid in school who dressed like a Goth," said LaToya Sparks, 15, a sophomore.

Asa appeared to have potential for academic success but struggled to focus on his work. At one point he was prescribed medication for his psychological stress/mental health problems, suspected to be bipolar disorder, but one source reported that he refused to take them, at least at that time.

Why: If *anybody* was going to crack and go on a shooting spree it was Asa. How many warning signs and telegraphed signals does a kid have to make to get help and attention?! In this case one really has to put much of the blame on the school administration for allowing so much bullying to occur and failing to recognize so many obvious signs of trouble in one of their students. It's remarkable the lack of accountability and responsibility in these situations. I don't remember ever reading of a school administrator being fired after a school shooting; well, Columbine HS had some turmoil afterwards, but that's the exception really. If a Navy submarine captain has a sailor get killed, even in a training accident, the commander will probably not just lose their job but their career too. Yet if students get beat-up and assaulted on a daily basis, and even killed at a public school, it's still just the usual paycheck for the Principal and the rest of the administration who are supposed to be providing a safe and educational environment. This kind of situation means that public school administrators have little personal incentive to really do something of substance to address the root of the problem and prevent school shootings before they happen, and so they keep happening.

"Coon was a new student at the school, but the district has a dossier on past problems. He had mental health problems, spent time in two juvenile facilities and was suspended from school last year for attempting to harm a student, according to juvenile court records."

It's interesting to note that most of the people Asa shot were not hurt very badly except for the multicultural studies teacher Michael Grassie. In a school that was almost entirely black it's doubtful that the multicultural lessons being taught did anything to improve the self-image and self-esteem of the white Asa and it's quite plausible that they magnified his sense of alienation and persecution.

"That child was tormented from his classmates every single day. Everybody's making him out to be a devil, a demon, but nobody knows what was going on with this kid."—Christina Burns, a volunteered at one of the schools Coon attended.

Although the attack was planned in advance, sometime between Monday's suspension and Wednesday's shooting, Coon left no suicide note at the scene and reporting has not indicted the existence of any similar statements elsewhere from Asa.

Mount Vernon Elementary, Newark New Jersey, August 4, 2007—Class B Event (Killed by outsider)

❖ *Who*: Jose Carranza, 28, from Peru; Rodolfo Godinez, 24, and his half-brother, Alexander Alfaro, 16, both from Nicaragua;

Melvin Jovel, 18, from Honduras; and two unnamed 15-year-old boys, all under arrest for murder. "Six people, including three juveniles, have been arrested and charged with multiple counts of murder and robbery in the shootings that horrified Newark and fueled national debate on illegal immigration. One of the suspects was in the country illegally, prompting New Jersey Attorney General Anne Milgram last week to order local police officers to check the immigration status of all suspects charged with serious crimes."

- ❖ *Where*: Mount Vernon Elementary School, Newark New Jersey
- ❖ *When*: August 4, 2007
- ❖ *Killed*: Iofemi Hightower, 19; Terrance Aeriel, 18; and Dashon Harvey, 20. Injured: Natasha Aerial, 19.
  All four of them were current or soon-to-be students at Delaware State University.
- ❖ *Event*: The shooting victims were lined up against a wall behind the elementary school and shot 'execution-style' in the back of the head.
- ❖ *Why*: Likely gang related, the victims were black and the attackers Hispanic and probably members of the MS-13 gang judging from the style of the crime. Reasons beyond that are under investigation by the police.

Note: Although it did involve students the school in this case was merely the venue for a criminal event. The persons involved did not attend the school where the shooting occurred and the crime doesn't appear to have anything to do with school work, academic trouble or social pressures, and therefore this is categorized as a Class B event.

Geschwister School in Emsdetten, Germany—Class A Event

- ❖ *Who*: 18-year-old Sebastian Bosse
- ❖ *Where*: Geschwister Scholl in Emsdetten, near the Dutch border in North Rhine-Westphalia, Germany. The school is reported to have about 700 pupils aged between 11 and 16.
- ❖ *When*: 9:30 a.m. on Monday, November 20, 2006
- ❖ *Weapons*: Volkmann said officers could see two sawed-off guns lying near his body and a knife strapped to his leg. Several home-made pipe bombs also were lying nearby and the man appeared to be carrying other explosive devices on his body. he also used

smoke bombs. The "sawed-off" rifles that he had were actually antique reproductions of muzzle loaders purchased off the Internet!

❖ *Killed*: Sebastian Bosse (suicide)
❖ *Injured*: Three students aged 12 to 15, a female teacher and the head caretaker suffered serious but not life-threatening injuries. Approximately 32 were injured, most from smoke inhalation.
❖ *Event*: The young man, wearing an all-black outfit with explosives attached to his body, entered the Geschwister-Scholl school in Emsdetten near the Dutch border on Monday morning and randomly opened fire at students. He injured at least 32 people, two of them seriously, before he raced off for the school's second floor after he ignited smoke bombs. Police arrived six minutes later, or thirty minutes depending on source, and found the gunman dead from a self-inflicted gunshot wound.
❖ *Background*: Bosse was not currently a student at Geschwister Scholl. He had reportedly worked part-time in a warehouse after leaving school.

He also said the man had been due to go trial tomorrow for weapons offences after being caught with a loaded pistol several months earlier.

Students at the school said the assailant was an aggressive and aloof individual who played violent computer games and had said he wanted to join the army. Katja Weber, a 17-year-old student at the school, said he always wore a black hat and coat. Bosse had repeated classes three times, graduating last year among children three years his junior.

Bosse felt ignored and alienated by his peers and this sense of rejection coupled with his poor academic performance created a perception of injustices being perpetuated against him by the people around him. "The only thing I really learned at school was that I'm a loser," the youth wrote in a letter posted on his Web site that was later removed by police. "I hate people .... I'm gone."

Sebastian Bosse played video games, particularly first person shooters. Eventually he became so engrossed in his shooting games that they became a method of practice and mental conditioning to exact his revenge against school and peers. Completely ignoring the issues of mental health politicians in Germany, like so many other countries, look for the cheapest shot they can take and beat it for every point they can score from voters. Not surprisingly they identify video games and the source of the problem. The shooting has caused German politicians to call for stricter regulations against violent computer games and the need for school psychologists, who would be able to help outsiders at school. Does anyone really believe that 'stricter regulations on video games would have prevented this school shooting? Last time I checked, and this is hard to believe I know, many people play video games and very, very few of them shoot up their schools. Yes it is true that playing violent games repeatedly, to the point of obsession, can be a conditioning factor that can eventually lead to a mental acceptance of violent behavior as a means of rectifying serious internal problems when the individual descends into a debilitated psychological state, but this just demonstrates that the problem is with the mind (and society), not in the game console.

Josef Kraus, president of one of Germany's teachers' unions, the Lehrerverband, charged that German politicians, schools, the media and entertainment industry were too busy blaming one another to take any effective action to re-integrate loner youths like Bosse. "We have a fundamental culture here of looking away if there is a problem," he told N-TV.

In remarks to the newspaper Bild, he said, "Brutal computer games and videos con youths into the idea that the strong win. They don't show the losers any way out. Drugs, consumerism and fun are the sole values that today's pop and TV stars propagate."

Weston School Cazenovia, Wisconsin—Class A Event

- ❖ *Who*: 15 year old Eric Hainstock, a "special-education student" with a history of threatening people.
- ❖ *Where*: In a hallway at Weston School Cazenovia, Wisconsin. The school is reported to have 370 students. "[This] small prekindergarten-through-12th-grade school is near Cazenovia, a community of about 300 people about 60 miles northwest of Madison."
- ❖ *When*: Friday September 29, 2006 before classes were to start, around 8 am.
- ❖ *Weapons*: 20-gauge shotgun and a .22 cal revolver handgun
- ❖ *Killed*: Principal John Klang, 49. "He was really nice," she said, choking back tears. "If we had a problem he'd listen to us. He never raised his voice or anything to any of the students."
- ❖ *Event*: On Friday morning Hainstock pried open his family's gun cabinet, took out a shotgun, retrieved the key to his parents' locked bedroom and took a .22-caliber revolver, according to a criminal complaint.

He entered Weston School with the shotgun before classes began and pointed the gun at a social studies teacher, but custodian Dave Thompson wrested it from him, the complaint said. When Hainstock reached for the handgun, Thompson and the teacher ran for cover.

Headmaster John Klang confronted Hainstock. A teacher said that after the shots were fired, Klang, already wounded, managed to wrestle the shooter to the ground and sweep away the gun, the complaint said. Students and staff detained Hainstock until police arrived, District Attorney Patricia Barrett said.

School officials said Klang had given Hainstock a disciplinary notice Thursday for taking tobacco to school, and the student faced a likely in-school suspension, the complaint said.

Janitor Dave Thompson said he saw the student come out of his truck carrying a shotgun. As the student entered the school, Thompson said he confronted Hainstock. According to Thompson, Hainstock told him, "I'm here to kill somebody."

"The heroics of the people involved in this can never be (overstated)," Sauk County Sheriff Randy Stamen said. "The custodian who initially saw and acted has to be commended for his bravery. The people who subdued him, they're heroes."

❖ *Background*: Sophomore Shelly Rupp, 16, described the boy as a freshman with few friends and said he was "just weird in the head."

"At this time it would appear he acted independently," Sauk County District Attorney Patricia Barrett said of the gunman.

"He did not disclose his plans to anybody else," she said, though the boy had confided to a friend at least two days earlier "that he didn't believe Mr. Klang would make it through homecoming."

The school canceled its homecoming ceremony and football game scheduled for Friday afternoon.

Barrett said the suspect would be charged with murder and faces a maximum penalty of life in prison.

Witnesses told local media the unidentified boy had reputation for behaving strangely and threatening violence.

No comments from Eric's parents or relatives were available or reported. Eric Hainstock has been charged with first-degree intentional homicide with a potential penalty of life in prison. This event was immediately eclipsed in the news media by another one in Amish country...

Update April 2007: Eric Hainstock in court

Eric Hainstock, 16, also told investigators in the same interview hours after John Klang was fatally wounded that he had been in anger management classes for years but found them useless.

Hainstock told detectives he was upset with school chiefs because they did not stop other pupils from picking on him and calling him names.

Going to school with guns occurred to him just that morning, he said, and he just wanted officials to listen to him.

When Klang grabbed him from behind and put him in a bear hug, he put the revolver under his left armpit and shot the principal, he said. He said he did not mean to kill him, but "I just freaked out".

Update August 2007: Eric Hainstock convicted of murder

Eric Hainstock was sentenced to life in prison with the possibility of parole after 30 years for shooting and killing his principle John Klang in 2006. In his trial Eric claimed that he brought the guns to school in order to get the attention of his principle and make him stop kids from teasing him. His attorneys argued that Hainstock is emotional and immature, suffers from attention deficit disorder, and was repeatedly harassed at school and abused at home. "There is very little thought to anything he does," said Hainstock's attorney Rhoda Ricciardi.

Orange High School in Hillsborough, North Carolina— Class A Event

- ❖ *Who*: Alvaro Rafael Castillo, age 19. Castillo has been charged with murder and 10 other charges.
- ❖ *Where*: The Orange High School parking lot in Hillsborough, North Carolina. Orange High School is reported to have about 1,000 students. Two unarmed guards at the school did not stop Castillo from entering because, "Our purpose is to just see that the children go in and out, and make sure nobody scratches up the students' cars or anything like that."
- ❖ *When*: August 30, 2006 during the school lunch break around 1 pm.
- ❖ *Weapons*: Multiple shots fired, with a 9 mm rifle and a 12-gauge shotgun with a shortened barrel found at the scene of the crime. "...police found two pipe bombs and two rifles in the van he was driving and four additional pipe bombs at his home."
Alvaro used a 'smoke bomb' before firing, apparently at random.
Killed/Injured: High School senior Tiffaney Utsman grazed by

bullet. Unnamed student injured by flying glass. Alvaro's father, Rafael Huezo Castillo (reportedly from El Salvador), was killed just before the school attack.

❖ *Why*: The reason for the school shooting is unclear. the intent was not to kill anyone but instead to create a scene and gain attention for the shooter.

❖ *Background*: Alvaro was not a student in school but was a graduate. Castillo joined the North Carolina National Guard in 2004 and had finished basic training in August 2005. However he was being processed out for medical reasons, likely related to court records indicating that he was involuntarily sent to a state psychiatric hospital after telling his family he planned to kill himself with a shotgun. "He stated that he was not going to go back into the Army and was going to kill himself," he was released eight days later, according to court records. No mention is made of medication or drugs, but in this case the use of psychotropic medication seems very likely, we just don't have any information yet one way or the other.

Myspace webpage (still active as this was being written) lists God, Mom, Dad and his younger sister Victoria, at the top of his list of heroes. Interviews with other students did not describe any remarkable behavior on the part of Castillo. Yet Castillo sent a letter and video to the *Chapel Hill News* where he describes a verbally and physically abusive father. The letter ends with, "I will die. I have wanted to die for years. I'm sorry." It's possible that he was trying to present a false image of normalcy and stability to others, and perhaps even to himself, that was at odds with the inner turmoil that was really going on.

Of note, just like Jeff Weise in Red Lake High School, Alvaro also is reported to have fixated upon violent scenes in violent films.

Most of the hour-plus video shows Castillo aiming the camera at a small television playing violent movies. They include "Scarface," "Predator," "The Shining," "Natural Born Killers" and a documentary, "Zero Hour: Massacre at Columbine High." Castillo narrates the violence, sometimes chiming in word-for-word with actors. He repeatedly used the mute button to silence profanity. Grisly scenes are met with a throaty laugh.

He also had a keen interest, perhaps even an obsession, with other school shootings widely reported by the mass media.

When asked why he fixated on the 1999 attack, in which two students wearing trench coats killed 13 people before committing suicide, Castillo said he didn't know. "He was obsessed with Columbine, the (Kip) Kinkel shooting in Oregon, the (Jonesboro) Arkansas high school shooting," the sheriff said. He said Castillo even traveled last year to Colorado to drive by the school and the homes of the two teenagers who carried out the shootings."

AP news reported that as he was being walked to jail and asked why he killed his father Alvaro replied: "We all have to sacrifice. Somebody had to put him out of his misery. He abused all of us."

He definitely had a need for public recognition of his actions as evidenced by at least three factors: the fact he did not kill himself, the letter and video sent to the newspaper, and immediately confessing to killing his father while using the media attention to (vaguely) explain his actions.

All evidence so far indicates this school shooting was planned in advance. However the injured students do not appear to have any connection to the shooter. Although he had pipe bombs and plenty of ammunition there is no reporting he resisted arrest after a school attack that seems half-hearted at best! This aspect is especially striking when considering that Castillo had been trained to kill by the U.S. military, he had just committed murder that day (his father), and there was no one around that had the force to stop him during his attack. Thus it appears that Alvaro's primary intent was to achieve notoriety; perhaps this is a new phenomenon in the history of school shootings: the effort to achieve infamy through imitation.

The trial should bring more facts to light in this case but in the meantime the real motivation and intent behind this incident resides in the mind and family history of Alvaro Rafael Castillo.

Roseburg High School, Oregon—Class A Event

- ❖ *Where*: The shooting occurred in a courtyard on the Roseburg High School campus.
- ❖ *When*: 7:45 am Thursday, Feb. 23, 2006
- ❖ *Who*: Vincent Wayne Leodoro
- ❖ *Why*: The motive remains unclear and is still under investigation.
- ❖ *Event*: "After the shooting, two students followed Leodoro and flagged down a police car as he walked away from school. Police confronted him at a nearby restaurant parking lot, where Leodoro put a gun to his head before surrendering, police and witnesses said."

❖ *Shot*: Joseph Monti (age 16) in the back. Three shots hit his torso and the fourth grazed his elbow.

❖ *Weapon*: "10 mm pistol"

❖ *Trial*: Leodoro is charged with felony counts of "attempted murder, first-degree assault, possession of a weapon in a public building, unlawful use of a weapon and unlawful possession of a firearm. .... If found guilty, Leodoro would face a maximum sentence of commitment to a youth correctional facility until age 25."

"Police have said Monti was cited earlier this month on a misdemeanor harassment charge of spitting on a school bus rider, but that investigators had not found any obvious connection with the shooting." Teenagers who commit these extreme forms of school violence typically have an undeveloped sense of proportion, inadequate self-control and an inability to conceptualize the future consequences of drastic personal actions. This is how Vincent Wayne Leodoro can go from spitting on a bus rider one day to shooting a classmate the next—these kids can't distinguish between degrees of severity or form an appropriate response to the actions of those around them.

Drug use, prescription or otherwise, remains an unknown factor in this shooting, as does the security situation at the school.

Campbell County High School, Tennessee—Class A Event

❖ *Where*: Campbell County Comprehensive High School. Student body: 1,400, located about 35 miles northwest of Knoxville.

❖ *When*: November 8, 2005

❖ *Who*: Ken Bartley Jr., 15 years old.

❖ *Why*: The motive for the shooting remains unclear but at this point it seems likely it was simply the opportunity of the situation coupled with student rage.

❖ *How*: Ken Bartley Jr. brought a .22 caliber handgun to school, reportedly hidden under a napkin. After showing off the gun to other students, school authorities became suspicious and called the freshman into the principal's office where Ken shot the principal and two assistant principals, killing one and seriously injuring the others as well as himself in the melee.

❖ *Killed and Injured*: Assistant Principal Ken Bruce was killed while principal Gary Seale was shot in the lower abdomen, and assistant principal Jim Pierce was shot in the chest.

❖ *Weapon*: One .22 caliber handgun

Bartley was a known trouble-maker. "He has been in trouble before, but I just wouldn't expect something like this out of him," said classmate Courtney Ward, 17. "He is a big jokester. He is rowdy. But I just couldn't see him doing this." "At the age of 12, Bartley was placed by his parents at Kingswood School, a residential counseling program in Grainger County, for treatment for drug and alcohol abuse, Kingswood administrator Darrell Helton told WBIR-TV on Thursday." Security at the school was sufficient to identify the boy with the gun but it did not prevent him from using it. "Campbell County High has one unarmed school resource officer, a woman who also acts as a hall monitor. The school has video surveillance, though it apparently did not cover principals' offices. It has one handheld metal detector."

Apparently, all of the official reporting for this story has been conducted by one source: the Associated Press.

Update 2007: Ken Bartley Jr. Sentenced to 45 Years of Prison in Plea Bargain

Deputy Sheriff Darrell Mongar testified during a February hearing that Bartley told him the pistol was his father's and he planned to trade it for OxyContin, a powerful painkiller.

Pierce testified at that hearing that he told Bartley he wanted the gun the boy had in his pocket. "Kenny stood up with the gun waving it at all of us," Pierce said. "Mr. Seale asked him if it was real. He said 'Yes, it's real. I'll show you. I never liked you anyway."

Pierce said Bartley pulled out an ammunition clip, loaded the gun and fired. Seale was shot first, in the lower abdomen. Bruce was shot in the chest. Pierce was hit in the chest as he struggled to disarm the youth, he testified.

Bartley had been indicted on charges of first-degree murder and felony murder, both of which could have carried a life sentence—meaning a minimum of 51 years in prison. He also was charged with attempted murder, taking a gun to school grounds and possession of controlled substances, which could have added to his sentence if he were convicted. Jury selection was wrapping up when the agreement was reached

Red Lake High School, Minnesota—Class A Event

❖ *Where*: Red Lake High School, Red Lake Indian Reservation in the northern part of Minnesota, approximate school population:

300 students. "According to the 2000 census, 5,162 people lived on the reservation, and all but 91 were Indians."

- ❖ *When*: Approximately 3 pm on March 22, 2005.
- ❖ *Who*: Jeff Weise, age 16, 6 feet, 250 pounds.
- ❖ *Why*: At the time of writing Weise's motive remains unclear in the official record.
- ❖ *How*: One 22 caliber and two police handguns as well as a police shotgun.
- ❖ *Killed*: Weise shot his grandfather Daryl Lusierage, age 58, a tribal police sergeant, and his grandfather's companion Michelle Sigana, age 32, with a .22-caliber handgun. Weise then took his grandfather's police weapons including two handguns and a shotgun and drove his grandfather's squad car to his school, shot the unarmed security guard Derrick Brun, age 28, and then proceeded to shoot students at random and at close range for approximately ten minutes, killing five students including Alicia White (15), Thurlene Stillday (15), Chase Lussier (15). Neva Rogers (62) a teacher, while seven other students were also wounded in the attack. Reportedly, after police responded to the scene and began to fire back, Weise then shot himself. The shooting appeared to be pre-meditated in Weise's mind even if the targets were not, Weise likely having gone over the routine multiple times in his daydreams.

Troubled Childhood

About five weeks before the shooting Jeff Weise was ejected from Red Lake High School due to a violation of school policy and was in a special program for off-campus education. Weise had a troubled childhood and a family history of alcohol abuse.

"The administrator of one Internet site told The New York Times that Weise wrote that his mother, with whom he lived in the Twin Cities before returning to Red Lake, "would hit me with anything she could get her hands on" and "would tell me I was a mistake, and she would say so many things that it is hard to deal with them or think of them without crying." In another message, the administrator said, Weise wrote that "I have friends, but I'm basically a loner inside a group of loners. I'm excluded from anything and everything they do. I'm never invited. I don't even know why they consider me a friend or I them."

Psychotropic Drug Use

Given the family situation Weise came from it's not too surprising that he dealt with issues of depression and had suicidal thoughts.

"Relatives told the newspaper his father committed suicide four years ago, and that his mother was living in a Minneapolis nursing home because she suffered brain injuries in a [alcohol related] car accident. " "In his 16 years, Weise had lost many relatives. He was estranged from other family members and had a strained relationship with Daryl Lussier, the grandfather. … He was taking the antidepressant Prozac and at least once was hospitalized for suicidal tendencies." "[Sky] Grant said he himself was taking 20 milligrams a day of Zoloft, another antidepressant, and the boys talked in detail about their medication. He said Weise told him he was taking 40 milligrams a day of Prozac: 20 in the morning, 20 at night. "Everybody changes when they start taking antidepressants," Grant said. "He was a lot more quiet. I wouldn't say any better."

The shooting at Red Lake High School is one of the more useful ones from an analytical perspective because of the quantity of detailed information that is often lacking in other school shooting events, but not all of it was particularly useful. The mass-media outlets, especially outside the United States, were immediate in describing Weise as some kind of crazed neo-Nazi due to online messages attributed to him and his apparent belief in racial separation. However, since his targets were random it's difficult to make his beliefs out to be the reason for his shooting spree. It seems more likely that his ideas were simply another source of alienation since he lacked anyone to connect with or talk about his views, other than impersonal Internet message groups. This sense of disconnection from the people around him eventually drove him to act out in desperation to gain recognition and a sense of power over a personal situation he saw as extremely bleak and hopeless.

Jeff Weise displayed the psychological elements of a stereotypical school shooter. Suicide is an act of desperation—Weise felt desperate because he couldn't see any way out of his troubles while anger, alienation and resentment pushed him to act out. "Weise hated his mother and had a tendency to skip ahead to violent parts in movies they rented." The culmination of events in his external action took the form it did because, by immersing himself in thoughts and games of killing and retribution, he conditioned himself to view violence as an acceptable means of finally solving his troubles.

10

Media

The media specially TV reports stirring scenes: students crying in each other's arms, parents frantically looking for their children after each shoot-out. How influential is the media in shaping public understanding of crime? With the rise of the mass media throughout the world, predominantly the Western world, the issue of media influence has become a serious one. Due to media's primary obsession with crime and violence, it definitely has a negative influence on shaping peoples understanding of crime by exaggerating it. A branch of media which always exaggerates on some crime e.g. terrorist attacks then other crimes is TV news this is basically an oxymoron; giving us the skin of the truth stuffed with a lie. TV news broadcasts use dramatic, usually violent stories and images to capture and maintain an audience, under the pretence of keeping it informed. What we see and hear on the news affects us both consciously and subconsciously, and sends us about our lives unnecessarily fearing the remote dangers that we see excessively portrayed on the evening news.

The public's fascination with crime lies at the heart of popular culture and crime occupies a large proportion of space in the public's discussion and imagination. Crime reports form an integral part of the daily media consumption. Some see the media as a cause of crime, others see it not as a cause but as "an exaggerated public alarm" (Maguire et al 1997.) There are various genres of media that discuss crime. The most obvious are tabloid newspapers and broadsheets, news reports on the television. However crime can also be discussed in academic journals, true crime magazines and books, crime fiction, television, films and music. Tabloids, broadsheets and television news are the most widely available accounts of crime to the general public.

Mass Media

Mass media is communication—whether written, broadcast, or spoken—that reaches a large audience. This includes television, radio, advertising, movies, the Internet, newspapers, magazines, and so forth.

As an example of the relationship between technological development and the individual, we can note that a car is a form of technology that can be used to transport people from somewhere like Bury to Ipswich. It can also be used to injure people. It's not designed to do the latter, of course, but technology frequently has "hidden" or "unintended consequences".

Functionalist sociologists call this the difference between:

(a) The manifest function of something and
(b) The latent (or hidden) function of something.

The manifest function of a car might be to get you to work. Its latent function might be as a status symbol.... Electronic media and print media include:

❖ Broadcasting, in the narrow sense, for radio and television.
❖ Various types of discs or tape. In the 20th century, these were mainly used for music. Video and computer uses followed.
❖ Film, most often used for entertainment, but also for documentaries.
❖ Internet, which has many uses and presents both opportunities and challenges. Blogs and podcasts, such as news, music, pre-recorded speech and video)
❖ Publishing, in the narrow sense, meaning on paper, mainly via books, magazines, and newspapers.

Computer games, which have developed into a mass form of media since devices such as the PlayStation 2, Xbox, and the GameCube broadened their use.

Moral Promise and Threat

From its post–World War II appearance, the promise of TV has been at once praised and criticized. As a new, more vivid and pervasive form of mass communication than anything that had preceded it (magazines, newspapers, radio, and movies) it was subject to intensified versions of both the hype of modernity, which sees technological innovation as inherently beneficial, and mass culture criticism, which argues technology's dangers and debasements. A love–hate relationship was manifest in tensions between promises of increased democratic enlightenment and worries about the commercialization of culture.

Media influence refers to the way in which the mass media in all their forms (television, film, advertising and similar forms) affect the way we, as an audience, behave and act in our everyday lives.

The media and its approach to the sensitive issue of law and order has come in for some criticism from crime experts recently who say that media spin on crime is driving populist law and order policies that don't work. But perceptions appear to be almost as important as crime itself these days as it plays a vital role in the way police operate. The community judges law enforcement personnel by what appears in the media. Very few citizens have direct contact with police officers; so, they make decisions on the police department's effectiveness based on what they read, see, or hear.

Audience Engages with Media Text

the media exaggerate and distort facts to produce sensationalised articles causing an increase in the publics fear of crime. Today, perhaps never as vividly before, crime stands at the centre of public consciousness. The mass media serve up a regular diet of stories of rising crime, vulnerable victims and callous offenders. The public persistently voice their fears and anxieties about crime in opinion surveys and in official government studies prioritising their concern with the issue. The success of the police in dealing with the crime problem in general comes under ever more scrutiny, and the effectiveness and rigor of the criminal justice and penal systems generate never-ending controversy.

The extent to which an audience engages with a media text can be roughly split into three degrees. The first of these is primary involvement, in which the audience is solely concentrating on consuming the media text. For example, they are sitting down solely to watch their favorite programme on television.

Secondary involvement is when an audience's concentration is split between the media text and another distraction. For example, working on the computer while watching television.

Tertiary involvement is when the media text is merely in the background, with no real concentration upon it at all. For example, glancing at a newspaper on a crowded train. While this theory is somewhat simplistic, it provides a clear and probable explanation as to the changes in audience reception.

Video Games

"Fourteen-year-old Michael Carneal steals a gun from a neighbor's house, brings it to school, and fires eight shots into a student prayer meeting that is breaking up. Prior to stealing the gun, he had never shot a real handgun in his life. The FBI says that the average experienced law enforcement officer, in the average shootout, at an average range of seven yards, hits with approximately one bullet in five. So how many hits did Michael Carneal make? He fired eight shots; he got eight hits, on eight different kids.... Nowhere in the annals of law enforcement or military or criminal history can we find an equivalent achievement. And this from a boy on his first try.

"How did Michael Carneal acquire this kind of killing ability? Simple: practice. At the tender age of fourteen he had practiced killing literally thousands of people. His simulators were point-and-shoot video games he played for hundreds of hours in video arcades and in the comfort of his own home." Playing some types of video games can help you identify and respond to targets quickly.

Linking video games to the supposedly precise aim of the shooters in school shooting cases misses some critical factors. The first is that hitting a large target, such as a person, is not difficult at all. It takes little more than the ability to point, especially if the victims are not moving quickly and are close by, as was the case at the schools.

Television Habits

Definition

Television habits consist of patterns of behavior determined by the amount of time and importance individuals give to watching television broadcasts and recorded videos and DVDs.

Description

Ever since the late 1940s when television first became available, social scientists have been interested in its effect on behavior. Originally seen as entertainment for adults and older children, television in the twenty-first century is watched by all age groups, including infants. More than 98 per cent of homes in the United States have at least one television set. Many have more. One study found that 32 per cent of children ages two to seven had television sets in their bedroom. This number increased to 65 per cent for children ages eight to 18.

Relationships and Media

The mass media influence our sexual knowledge, attitudes and behaviors. They shape how we view males and females, relationships, sexual performance, procreation, and marriage. The media play an important role in adolescent sexual socialization. Today, we live in a more conservative political environment that emphasizes family and religious values. Parents, pressure groups, and lawmakers soundly criticize the media for their portrayals of sex; Yet the outlets for and diversity of sexual fare continue to grow along with the toleration of sexual imagery. We love our media sex, and we hate it too.

Along with the proliferation of and changes in sexual media, there are numerous concerns. Primary among them are the lack of attention to risks and responsibilities in depictions of sexual behavior, the mixture of sex and violence in pornography, and the ready availability of porn on the Internet. Western societies have been more tolerant of media violence and experimentation with violent stimulus materials on younger viewers.

Risky Behaviors

A television station that bores its viewers is unlikely to achieve large audiences; hence, the majority of programmes are made with entertainment and interest (rather than education) in mind. This, therefore, is a significant constraint on the media. TV is chock full of programs and commercials that often depict risky behaviors such as sex and substance abuse as cool, fun, and exciting. And often, there's no discussion about the consequences of drinking alcohol, doing drugs, smoking cigarettes, and having premarital sex. And although they've banned cigarette ads on television, kids and teens can still see plenty of people smoking on programs and movies airing on TV. This kind of "product placement" makes behaviors like smoking and drinking alcohol seem acceptable. In fact, kids who watch 5 or more hours of TV per day are far more likely to begin smoking cigarettes than those who watch less than the recommended 2 hours a day.

Audience Reception

Perhaps the most widely accepted theory on audience reception is Dennis McQuail's Uses and Gratifications model. This places emphasis on why audiences consume media.

The first reasons outlined in the model are the need to reinforce your own behavior by identifying with roles and values presented in the media.

Secondly, we need to feel some kind of interaction with other people; this is offered by text such as soap operas and lifestyle magazines.

The third reason is the need for security in our life.

Media offer us a window to the world that allows education and the acquisition of information. The final reason is the need for entertainment through both escapism and the need for emotional release, such as laughter. Strength of this theory is the emphasis on the audience as active in the reception of media. However, this would suggest no passivity within the audience whatsoever. A person may, for example, be too lazy to turn off their television and so consume any media that is available. This theory also pays little attention to the short term and long term effects of media on the audience.

TV Guns Reflects Reality

Is the media attention conditioning angry people that this is the platform or means to express their anger? All kids and adults have issues that are troubling and disturbing. Sometimes you have to take your losses and move on. The enormous prevalence of guns on TV makes the problem worse, because *nothing about* TV guns reflects reality, and it usually encourages an attitude that guns are fun, desirable playthings that only hurt bad guys. On TV, people shoot guns and then talk. In reality, guns are so loud that after a single shot you can hardly hear anything for a while. On TV someone gets shot and then continues to play a role. In reality, if you even stub your toe you stop. On TV, bullets stay put. In reality even small bullets travel over a mile. Gun fights on the tube take forever. In reality it's typically over in about two seconds. Clearly, you need better information than what you get from your TV. Today the major concern for youth modeling is the media. The media presents today's youth with coverage on war, crime and violence that can alter the way a child acts towards his or her peers, however, life was not always this way. The history of youth crime relates back to direct contact and interaction with peers and role models. When media was not available, social learning was presented through direct contact with observational learning in one's environment. Delinquency is related to social class.

Over Dose of TV

Too much television can be detrimental:

❖ Research has shown that children who consistently spend more than 4 hours per day watching TV are more likely to be overweight.

❖ Kids who view violent events, such as a kidnapping or murder, are also more likely to believe that the world is scary and that something bad will happen to them.

❖ Research also indicates that TV consistently reinforces gender-role and racial stereotypes.

Mass media is a significant force in modern culture, particularly in America. Sociologists refer to this as a mediated culture where media reflects and creates the culture. Communities and individuals are bombarded constantly with messages from a multitude of sources including TV, billboards, and magazines, to name a few. These messages promote not only products, but moods, attitudes, and a sense of what is and is not important. Mass media makes possible the concept of celebrity: without the ability of movies, magazines, and news media to reach across thousands of miles, people could not become famous. In fact, only political and business leaders, as well as the few notorious outlaws, were famous in the past. Only in recent times have actors, singers, and other social elites become celebrities or "stars."

The current level of media saturation has not always existed. As recently as the 1960s and 1970s, television, for example, consisted of primarily three networks, public broadcasting, and a few local independent stations. These channels aimed their programming primarily at two-parent, middle-class families. Even so, some middle-class households did not even own a television. Today, one can find a television in the poorest of homes, and multiple TVs in most middle-class homes. Not only has availability increased, but programming is increasingly diverse with shows aimed to please all ages, incomes, backgrounds, and attitudes. This widespread availability and exposure makes television the primary focus of most mass-media discussions. More recently, the Internet has increased its role exponentially as more businesses and households "sign on." Although TV and the Internet have dominated the mass media, movies and magazines—particularly those lining the aisles at grocery checkout stands—also play a powerful role in culture, as do other forms of media.

What role does mass media play? Legislatures, media executives, local school officials, and sociologists have all debated this controversial question. While opinions vary as to the extent and type of influence the mass media wields, all sides agree that mass media is a permanent part of modern culture. Three main sociological perspectives on the role of media exist: the limited-effects theory, the class-dominant theory, and the culturalist theory.

Limited-effects Theory

The limited-effects theory argues that because people generally choose what to watch or read based on what they already believe, media exerts a negligible influence. This theory originated and was tested in the 1940s and 1950s. Studies that examined the ability of media to influence voting found that well-informed people relied more on personal experience, prior knowledge, and their own reasoning. However, media "experts" more likely swayed those who were less informed. Critics point to two problems with this perspective. First, they claim that limited-effects theory ignores the media's role in framing and limiting the discussion and debate of issues. How media frames the debate and what questions members of the media ask change the outcome of the discussion and the possible conclusions people may draw. Second, this theory came into existence when the availability and dominance of media was far less widespread.

Class-dominant Theory

The class-dominant theory argues that the media reflects and projects the view of a minority elite, which controls it. Those people who own and control the corporations that produce media comprise this elite. Advocates of this view concern themselves particularly with massive corporate mergers of media organizations, which limit competition and put big business at the reins of media—especially news media. Their concern is that when ownership is restricted, a few people then have the ability to manipulate what people can see or hear. For example, owners can easily avoid or silence stories that expose unethical corporate behavior or hold corporations responsible for their actions.

The issue of sponsorship adds to this problem. Advertising dollars fund most media. Networks aim programming at the largest possible audience because the broader the appeal, the greater the potential purchasing audience and the easier selling air time to advertisers becomes. Thus, news organizations may shy away from negative stories about corporations (especially parent corporations) that finance large advertising campaigns in their newspaper or on their stations. Television networks receiving millions of dollars in advertising from companies like Nike and other textile manufacturers were slow to run stories on their news shows about possible human-rights violations by these companies in foreign countries. Media watchers identify the same problem at the local level where city newspapers will not give new cars poor reviews or run stories on selling a home without an agent because the majority of their funding comes from auto and real estate advertising. This influence also extends to programming. In the 1990s a network cancelled a short-run drama with clear religious sentiments, *Christy,* because, although highly popular and beloved in rural America, the program did not rate well among young city dwellers that advertisers were targeting in ads.

Critics of this theory counter these arguments by saying that local control of news media largely lies beyond the reach of large corporate offices elsewhere, and that the quality of news depends upon good journalists. They contend that those less powerful and not in control of media have often received full media coverage and subsequent support. As examples they name numerous environmental causes, the anti-nuclear movement, the anti-Vietnam movement, and the pro-Gulf War movement.

While most people argue that a corporate elite controls media, a variation on this approach argues that a politically "liberal" elite controls media. They point to the fact that journalists, being more highly educated than the general population, hold more liberal political views, consider themselves "left of center," and are more likely to register as Democrats. They further point to examples from the media itself and the statistical reality that the media more often labels conservative commentators or politicians as "conservative" than liberals as "liberal."

Media language can be revealing, too. Media uses the terms "arch" or "ultra" conservative, but rarely or never the terms "arch" or "ultra" liberal. Those who argue that a political elite controls media also point out that the movements that have gained media attention—the environment, anti-nuclear, and anti-Vietnam—generally support liberal political issues. Predominantly conservative political issues have yet to gain prominent media attention, or have been opposed by the media. Advocates of this view point to the Strategic Arms Initiative of the 1980s Reagan administration. Media quickly characterized the defense program as "Star Wars," linking it to an expensive fantasy. The public failed to support it, and the program did not get funding or congressional support.

Culturalist Theory

The culturalist theory, developed in the 1980s and 1990s, combines the other two theories and claims that people interact with media to create their own meanings out of the images and messages they receive. This theory sees audiences as playing an active rather than passive role in relation to mass media. One strand of research focuses on the audiences and how they interact with media; the other strand of research focuses on those who produce the media, particularly the news.

Theorists emphasize that audiences choose what to watch among a wide range of options, choose how much to watch, and may choose the mute button or the VCR remote over the programming selected by the network or cable station. Studies of mass media done by sociologists parallel text-reading and interpretation research completed by linguists (people who study language). Both groups of researchers find that when people approach material, whether written text or media images and messages, they interpret that material based on their own knowledge and experience. Thus, when researchers ask different groups to explain the meaning of a particular song or video, the groups produce widely divergent interpretations based on age, gender, race, ethnicity, and religious background. Therefore, culturalist theorists claim that, while a few elite in large corporations may exert significant control over what information media produces and distributes, personal perspective plays a more powerful role in how the audience members interpret those messages.

Rampage to Express Feelings

Unfortunately, there is implied cultural support for the idea of going on a rampage to express your feelings. The Columbine boys have been the subject of too much glorification. Similarly angry and alienated youth identify with them.

How do you go about determining which maladjusted person (out of millions) is the one who's going to off on a homicidal rampage?

Mass Media and School Shootings

Mass media play an integral role in the public perception of school shootings as a social problem, and social scientists have examined the media framing of school shooting incidents. When it comes to understanding the mass media dynamic related to social problems, it is worth pointing out that the profit motive behind news production may obfuscate a deep understanding of social problems and constructive generation of solutions.

Frequently, journalists are caught between the need to garner attention for a profit-oriented industry and the need to maintain the ethical standard of their profession. At times, journalists highlighted the dramatic elements of school shootings, thereby undermining a sober, longer-term examination of school shooting phenomena as a whole.

The media dynamic of the *Rashomon effect* surrounding school shootings stems from the fact that most people experience school shootings as a mass-mediated phenomenon, rather than directly. While the problem of school-related shootings occurred across history, it was the intense media coverage of the famous incidents, including West Paducah, Kentucky; Jonesboro, Arkansas; and Littleton that created the public perception of school shootings as an emergent and increasing social problem. Thus, the school shooting problem as broadly recognized had more to do with the media coverage of recent incidents than actual changes in levels of violence in schools. Much of this attention concentrated on rampage-type incidents.

To understand the rise of the perceived school shooting problem, it is important to understand the broader social discourse surrounding youth and delinquency in the decade before rampage shootings became widely discussed. David Altheide (2002a) discussed the emergence in the 1980s of the connected discourses of childhood and fear that peaked in 1994, an important historical context regarding the problem of school-related violence that garnered attention in the late 1990s and early 2000s. These concerns reflected public anxiety over crime and disaster, and public outcry surrounding school shootings was a permutation of this calculus of fear (Burns and Crawford 1999; Glassner 1999). Muschert and Carr (2006) tracked the emergence of the school shooting as an issue of national significance in the USA, and found that school shootings first became recognized as a social problem in 1997. Prior to that time, incidents were largely characterized as local in their relevance and impact. The analysis revealed that the socially constructed rampage shooting problem peaked around 1999, roughly coinciding with the 1999 Columbine shootings in Colorado.

At the peak of public interest in school shootings as a social problem, news media coverage was intense. Readers wishing to understand the media coverage of school shootings might begin with the summative, non-technical study on the media content of school violence published by the Center for Media and Public Affairs (1999), which examined the media's characterization of the shooters, communities, causes, and suggested solutions for the problem of school shootings. In addition, Bonilla (2000) produced an edited work, including articles from news media and popular magazines, in which readers can examine the news discourse firsthand. Starting in 2001, the school shooting problem began its decline as a national concern, and incidents were once again most strongly characterized as relevant to the communities in which they occurred (Muschert and Carr 2006). Although school shootings are still newsworthy and do garner media attention, they are somewhat less intensely discussed and the duration of discussion tends to be brief. In the US terrorism, the economy, and foreign military involvement have displaced school shootings as a social problem on the public agenda. When compared with the 1997– 2001 period in which the media characterized school shootings as a social problem of national concern, between 2001 and 2006 school shooting events no longer attracted the intense interest from the media. Following the 2007 shootings at Virginia Tech, it is possible that we will see resurgence in the media focus on issues related to campus crime and safety.

Scholars from a variety of disciplines have examined aspects of the media dynamic evident in the phenomenon of school shootings. For example, Maguire et al. (2002) examined the relative levels of media attention garnered by various shooting incidents. Two studies (Haider-Markel and Joslyn 2001; Lawrence and Birkland 2004) found that the mass media tended to characterize school shootings as a problem emerging from inadequate gun control legislation, while Samuels (2000) argued that the Columbine shooters' actions were guided by the logic of contemporary entertainment media. Lawrence and Birkland (2004) found that political discourse identified mass media as the catalyst for shooting incidents, but Scharrer *et al.* (2003) demonstrated that the news media tends to absolve itself from responsibility for school shooting incidents. Because of its status as the best-known and most intensely discussed school shooting incident to occur in recent decades, Columbine has been the subject of numerous media studies. Two studies (Chyi and McCombs 2004; Muschert forthcoming) examined the framing of Columbine as an event of national import, while Lawrence (2001) argued that Columbine was so powerful that it defines the problem of school shootings. Muschert (2007) examined the media's coverage of the Columbine victims, and Ogle *et al.* (2003) examined the role of clothing and style in the Columbine coverage. Smit (2001) examined Columbine in the media as an example of spectacle, while Gunn and Beard (2003) found that coverage of events like Columbine was taking on an increasingly apocalyptic tone. Other scholars focused on specific social issues in the media coverage of school shootings, including race (Aitken 2001), masculinity (Aitken 2001; Consalvo 2003), and religion (Muschert 2007; Watson 2002). Media studies of other incidents are notably absent from the literature, although Eglin and Hester (2003) and Muschert and Carr (2006) are exceptions. Another interesting variation is Daniels *et al.* (2007), which examines the media coverage of averted school rampages

Advertisement

When looking at an advertisement of a doll with a bullet hole in her forehead, one is immediately struck with a feeling of sadness for the brutality the picture represents. It is disturbing to see such cruelty. The advertisement emphasizes innocence and shows how violence destroys.

Through the picture of the doll, the advertisement gives the reader the impression of an innocent baby. The color pink is usually associated with innocence. By using pink on her dress and her lips, the advertisement is emphasizing innocence to its viewers. Her crystal blue eyes are widely open. Her little smile is welcoming and trusts everyone. She is innocent to the world and everything in it.

Media is often blamed for inciting and glorifying violence. While common sense tells us that media violence is desensitizing and may also inspire the forms violence can take, it is difficult to say that there is a causal relationship between violence portrayed in the media and real violence perpetrated by children, especially since most people who are exposed to violence in the media never become violent. Perhaps the backlash against particular *forms* of media is mostly a reactionary way for many of us to safely characterize the killers as being different from us, a conclusion that is far more comforting than what we subconsciously fear to be true, that such killers are really *not* so different from us and our own children, and we are all subject to (and even part of) the same societal forces that pathologize our troubled youth.

Media and new Postmodern Reality

The sad thing about shootings is that they appear to occur in a cycle. The shooting takes place, the 24-hour news channels feed off the violence for a week, and the usual tired arguments about gun control are trotted out. The weeks go and, memories fade, and nothing happens as a result. Then the whole thing starts up again. Why has so little been done to address this issue? Is it just something we have to accept in an open society?

TV Parental Guidelines: Modeled after the movie rating system, this is an age-group rating system developed for TV programs. These ratings are listed in television guides, TV listings in your local newspaper, and on the screen in your cable program guide. They also appear in the upper left-hand corner of the screen during the first 15 seconds of TV programs. But not all channels offer the rating system. For those that do, the ratings are:

TV-Y: suitable for all children

TV-Y7: directed toward kids 7 years and older (children who are able to distinguish between make-believe and reality); may contain "mild fantasy violence or comedic violence" that may scare younger kids

TV-Y7-FV: fantasy violence may be more intense in these programs than others in the TV-Y7 rating

TVG: suitable for a general audience; not directed specifically toward children, but contains little to no violence, sexual dialogue or content, or strong language

TV-PG: parental guidance suggested; may contain an inappropriate theme for younger children and contains one or more of the following: moderate violence (V), some sexual situations (S), occasional strong language (L), and some suggestive dialogue (D)

TV-14: parents strongly cautioned—suitable for only children over the age of 14; contains one or more of the following: intense violence (V), intense sexual situations (S), strong language (L), and intensely suggestive dialogue

TV-MA: designed for adults and may be unsuitable for kids under 17; contains one or more of the following: graphic violence (V), strong sexual activity (S), and/and crude language (L)

V-chip (V is for "violence"). This technology was designed to enable you to block television programs and movies you don't want your child to see. All new TV sets that have screens of 13" or more now have internal V-chips, but set-top boxes are available for TVs made before 2000. So how exactly does the V-chip work? It allows you to program your TV to display only the appropriately-rated shows—blocking out any other, more mature shows.

For many, the rating system and V-chip may be valuable tools. But there is some concern that the system may be worse than no system at all. For example, research shows that preteen and teen boys are more likely to want to see a program if it's rated MA (mature audience) than if it's PG (parental guidance suggested). And parents may rely too heavily on these tools and stop monitoring what their children are watching.

Also, broadcast news, sports, and commercials aren't rated, although they often present depictions of violence and sexuality. The rating system also doesn't satisfy some family advocates who complain that they fail to give enough information about a program's content to allow parents to make informed decisions about whether a show is appropriate for their child.

Teaching Your Child Good TV Habits

Here are some practical ways you can make TV-viewing more productive in your home:

Limit the number of TV-watching hours:

* Stock the room in which you have your TV with plenty of other non-screen entertainment (books, kids' magazines, toys, puzzles, board games, etc.) to encourage your child to do something other than watch the tube.
* Keep TVs out of your child's bedroom.
* Turn the TV off during meals.
* Don't allow your child to watch TV while doing homework.
* Treat TV as a privilege that your child needs to earn—not a right to which he or she is entitled. Tell your child that TV-viewing is allowed only after chores and homework are completed.
* Try a weekday ban. Schoolwork, sports activities, and job responsibilities make it tough to find extra family time during the week. Record weekday shows or save TV time for weekends, and you'll have more family togetherness time to spend on meals, games, physical activity, and reading during the week.
* Set a good example by limiting your own television viewing.
* Check the TV listings and program reviews ahead of time for programs your family can watch together (i.e., developmentally appropriate and nonviolent programs that reinforce your family's values). Choose shows, says the AAP, that foster interest and learning in hobbies and education (reading, science, etc.).
* Preview programs before your child watches them.
* Come up with a family TV schedule that you all agree upon each week. Then, post the schedule in a visible area (i.e., on the refrigerator) somewhere around the house so that everyone knows which programs are OK to watch and when. And make sure to turn off the TV when the "scheduled" program is over, instead of channel surfing until something gets your or your child's interest.
* Watch TV with your child. If you can't sit through the whole program, at least watch the first few minutes to assess the tone and appropriateness, then check in throughout the show.

Talk to your child about what he or she sees on TV and share your own beliefs and values. If something you don't approve of appears on the screen, you can turn off the TV, then use the opportunity to ask your child thought-provoking questions such as, "Do you think it was OK when those men got in that fight? What else could they have done? What would you have done?" Or, "What do you think about how those teenagers were acting at that party? Do you think what they were doing was wrong?" If certain people or characters are mistreated or discriminated against, talk about why it's important to treat everyone equal, despite their differences. You can use TV to explain confusing situations and express your feelings about difficult topics (sex, love, drugs, alcohol, smoking, work, behavior, family life). Teach your child to question and learn from what he or she views on TV. Talk to other parents, your child's doctor, and your child's teachers about their TV-watching policies and kid-friendly programs they'd recommend.

Offer fun alternatives to television. If your child wants to watch TV, but you want him or her to turn off the tube, suggest that you and your child play a board game, start a game of hide and seek, play outside, read, work on crafts or hobbies, or listen and dance to music. The possibilities for fun without the tube are endless—so turn off the TV and enjoy the quality time you'll have to spend with your child.

Tips for Picking Good TV Shows

What's the difference between good TV and the bad stuff? Kids' TV expert Karen Jaffe says there are five questions parents should ask before their kids pick up the remote:

Value

Is the message a valuable one—one that is important and beneficial for the target audience? You know your child and his/her taste. Make recommendations that are consistent with these interests. You can match up genres like science fiction or history or even sports. If your child is a bibliophile, look for shows with literary connections. Then consider whether the objective of the show is worthwhile.

Clarity

Is the message clearly laid out so that it can be easily comprehended by the target audience? Make sure that the show is appropriate for the age of your child. If the material is age-appropriate, the language and subjects should be clearly und⸱   ⸱d. Then check to see if the information is presented effectively. S ⸱. ⸱times the format of the show will dictate whether your child can pick up the messages. Magazine-style shows usually include many different stories with separate lessons for each one. Some children will be challenged by too much information while others will thrive on the diversity. Some children will be enchanted by a drama, others fascinated by a documentary.

Salience

Is the message consistently conveyed and/or an integral element of the program as a whole? There are two ways to look at issue. If you are only interested in exposing your child to an educational show that is specifically designed to inform, then the main thrust of the show—the premise—should have a message that is developed and resolved at the conclusion of the program or series. This is different from a show that is developed primarily for entertainment but which carries educational messages as a sidebar or, as they say in Hollywood, as the secondary story line. These are often important lessons—but they're clearly ancillary to the main topic of the program.

Another example of educational "nuggets" are shows that embed a lesson at the end of the show or even as a short message after the conclusion of the show. With guidance, parents can reinforce these "secondary" lessons and turn these briefer programming messages into an instructional experience.

Involvement

Is the message presented in such a way that it is engaging and challenging for the target audience? Some shows have terrific content that falls flat in the presentation. Again, some of this depends on your child's response to the material. An animated science lesson will work for some children, while the live-action version makes sense to others. However, the show won't work at all if the format does not present the information in an entertaining manner.

Relevance

Is the message conveyed in such a way that the target audience can see its usefulness in his/her own life? This is perhaps the most important criteria for parents who want to make television an enriching experience. It's also the most global in scope. A newscast or newsmagazine or even a talk show (which you have determined is age-appropriate) can provide valuable information and place issues affecting your child's life and community in perspective. Any lesson offered in a program designed for kids should be relevant to the child. Even certain sitcoms can do this if an adult is there to help make the connection.

Media Influences Children

Media—especially television, but also videos, movies, comic books, music lyrics, and computer games—have a strong influence on children. On the one hand, such media offer powerful tools for learning and entertainment; on the other hand, violence in the media is damaging for young children.

Research shows that violence in the media has the following effects on children:

- ❖ It gives children violent heroes to imitate.
- ❖ It increases mean-spirited, aggressive behavior.
- ❖ It shows children that violence is all right as a way to handle conflict.
- ❖ It makes it easy for children to ignore suffering and the bad effects of violence.
- ❖ It causes fear, mistrust, and worry (sometimes including nightmares).
- ❖ It whets their appetite for viewing more violence, in more extreme forms.

And, bear in mind that even when the "good guys" win, the effects are the same.

As children get older, those who watch a lot of television also have lower grades, especially in reading. After all, they are substituting TV for homework, study time, reading practice, using their imagination, and interacting with others. Start limiting children's TV viewing while they are young to help prevent later problems in school.

The extent of children's exposure to television violence is stunning. Violence also is a theme in many popular video and computer games for children, and new research suggests that those games may be more harmful than television and movies.

It is true that news comes in cycles, but that does not mean there are not many individuals and organizations who are working all the time on this problem. For the past five years we have been training schools in threat assessment. Hundreds of schools are responding.

The CCTV

The general purpose of the CCTV is to prevent and reduce crime. In theory, this happens because of one or more of these reasons: 1. Deterrence: potential burglars and thieves may see the camera and decide that a store in question is too much of a risk and therefore not a good target. 2. Prosecution: thieves and shoplifters may be caught on camera and this can help catch and prosecute them. 3. Fear reduction: if everyone knows that there is a camera, they may feel safer in or around your business, thus preventing potential criminals from attacking. 4. Monitoring and intervention: if there is a security guard monitoring the area through CCTV system, he or she may act on any suspicious behavior and thus prevent a crime from occurring. Security guards may also deploy employees to a suspicious spot or near a person detected on the monitors. Is CCTV effective in tackling crime?

'CCTV is a wonderful technological supplement to the police...cctv catches criminals. It spots crimes, identifies law breakers and helps convict the guilty. The innocent have nothing to fear. 'Closed circuit cameras have proved that they can work.

11

Basic Human Nature

Social Role

It is the expected behavior of an individual occupying a particular social position. The idea of social role originally comes from the theatre, referring to the parts which actors play in a stage production. In every society individuals play a number of different social roles, according to the varying contexts of their activities.

Inequality in Society

- ❖ *Social Stratification*: the division of people socioeconomic ally into layers or strata. When we talk of social stratification, we draw attention into the unequal positions occupied by individuals in society. In the larger traditional societies and in industrialized countries today there is stratification in terms of wealth, property, and access to material goods and cultural products.
- ❖ *Race*: a human group that defines itself and/or is defined by other groups as different... by virtue of innate and immutable physical characteristics. It is a group that is socially defined on the bases of physical criteria.
- ❖ *Ethnicity*: cultural practices and outlooks of a given community of people that set them apart from others. Members of ethnic groups see themselves as culturally distinct from other groups in a society, and are seen by those others to be so in return. Many different characteristics may distinguish ethnic groups from one another but the most usual are language, history or ancestry— real or imagined, religion, and styles of dress of adornment. Ethnic differences are wholly learned.

Definition of Role

Role can be defined as the actual and tangible forms which the self takes. We thus define the role as the functioning form the individual assumes in the specific moment he reacts to a specific situation in which other persons or objects are involved. The symbolic representation of this functioning form, perceived by the individual and others, is called the role. The form is created by past experiences and the cultural patterns of the society in which the individual lives, and may be satisfied by the specific type of his productivity—Every role is a fusion of private and collective elements. Every role has two sides, a private and a collective side.

It begins at birth and continues throughout the lifetime of the individual and the social.

Function of the Role

The function of the role is to enter the unconscious from the social world and bring shape and order into it. The relationship of roles to the situations in which the individual operates (status) and the relation of role as significantly related to ego has been emphasized by Moreno.

Everybody is expected to live up to his official role in life; a teacher is to act as a teacher, a pupil as a pupil, and so forth. But the individual craves to embody far more roles than those he is allowed to act out in life and even within the same role one or more varieties of it. Every individual is filled with different roles in which he wants to become active and that are present in him in different stages of development. It is from the active pressure which these multiple individual units exert upon the manifest official role that feeling of anxiety is often produced. Every individual- just as he has at all times a set of friends and a set of enemies-has a range of roles in which he seems himself and faces a range of counter-roles in which he sees others around him. They are in various stages of development. The tangible aspects of what is known as "ego" are the roles in which he operates, the pattern of role-relations around an individual as their focus—We consider roles and relationships between roles as the most significant development within any specific culture. Role is the unit of culture; ego and role are in continuous interaction.

Role Playing, Role Perception and Role Enactment

Role perception is cognitive and anticipates forthcoming responses. Role enactment is a skill of performance. A high degree of role perception can be accompanied by a low skill for role enactment and *vice versa.* Role playing is a function of both role perception and role enactment. Role training, in contrast to role playing is an effort, through the rehearsal of roles, to perform adequately in future situations.

Role Pathology

Regressive behavior is not a true regression but a form of role playing. In paranoiac behavior, the repertory of roles is reduced to distort acting in a single role. The deviate is unable to carry out a role *in situ.* He either overplays or underplays the part; inadequate perception is combined with distorted enactment. Histrionic neurosis of actors is due to the intervention of role fragments "alien" to the personality of the actor.

Co-unconscious States and the "Inter-Psyche"

By means of "role reversing" one actor tries to identify with another, but reversal of roles can not take place in a vacuum. Individuals who are intimately acquainted reverse roles more easily than individuals who are separated by a wide psychological or ethnic distance. The cause for these great variations is the developments of co-conscious and co-unconscious states. Neither the concept of unconscious states (Freud) nor that of collective unconscious states (Jung) can be easily applied to these problems without stretching the meaning of the terms. The free associations of A may be a path to the unconscious states of A; the free associations of B may be a path to the unconscious states of B; but can the unconscious material of A link naturally and directly with the unconscious material of B unless they share in unconscious states? The concept of individual unconscious states becomes unsatisfactory for explaining both movements, from the present situation of A, and in reverse to the present situation of B. We must look for a concept which is so constructed that the objective indication for the existence of this two-way process does not come from a single psyche but from a still deeper reality in which the unconscious states of two or several individuals are interlocked with a system of co-unconscious states. They play a great role in the life of people who live in intimate ensembles like father and son, husband and wife, mother and daughter, siblings and twins, but also in other intimate ensembles as in work teams, combat teams in war and revolution, in concentration camps or charismatic religious groups. Marriage and family therapy, for instance, has to be so conducted that the "inter-psyche" of the entire group is re-enacted so that all their tale-relations, their coconscious and co-unconscious states are brought to life. Co-conscious and co-unconscious states are, by definition, such states which the partners have experienced and produced jointly and which can, there therefore be only jointly reproduced or re-enacted. A co-conscious or a co-unconscious state can not be the property of *one in*dividual only. It is always a *common* property and cannot be reproduced but by a combined effort. If a re-enactment of such coconscious or co-unconscious state is desired or necessary, that re-enactment has to take place with the help of all partners involved in the episode. The logical method of such re-enactment a *deux* is psychodrama. However great a genius of perception one partner of the ensemble might have, he can not produce that episode alone because they have in common their co-conscious and unconscious states which are the matrix from which they drew their inspiration and knowledge.

Measurement of Roles

As a general rule, a role can be:

1. Rudimentarily developed, normally developed, or over developed;
2. Aimost or totally absent in a person (indifference);
3. Perverted into a hostile function.

A role in any of the above categories can also be classified from the point of view of its development in time:

1. It was never present;.
2. It is present towards one person but not present towards another;
3. It was once present towards a person but is now extinguished.

A simple method of measuring roles is to use as a norm permanently established processes which do not permit any change, role conserves like Shakespeare's Hamlet or Othello, Goethe's Faust or Byron's Don Juan. Another method of measurement uses as norms social roles which are rigidly prescribed by social and legalistic customs and forms. Illustrations for this are social roles as the policeman, the judge, the physician and so forth. Another method of measurement is to let a subject develop a role in *statu nascendi,* placing him into a situation which is little structured, up to situations which are highly organized. The productions of different subjects will differ greatly and will provide us with a yardstick for role measurement.

Another method of measurement is to place a number of subjects unacquainted with each other into a situation which they have to meet in common. **Illustration:** six men of equal military rank are camping. Suddenly they see an enemy parachutist landing in the nearby forest. They have to act on the spur of the moment. A jury watches to see how the group grows in *statu nascendi;* it may discern what relationships develop between the six men; who is taking the initiative in the first phase, in the intermediate phases, in the final phase of their interaction.

Sexuality

Sexuality is not the same as sex. Sex is a biological component associated with procreation & growth in human-beings as in animals. Sexuality connotes psychological reactions associated with "maleness" & "femaleness" and determines behavioural responses. These sex-related behavioural responses are further conditioned by cultural heritage and social norms. Cultural heritage is sum total of religious precepts and traditional concepts. Social norms are the product of compromise between bio-emotional needs of the individual and existing socio-cultural patterns in the society.

Role

In sociology, the behaviour expected of an individual who occupies a given social position or status. A role is a comprehensive pattern of behaviour that is socially recognized, providing a means of identifying and placing an individual in a society.

Social behavior conforms to norms, values, and rules that direct behavior in specific situations. These norms vary according to the positions of the individual actors: they define different roles, such as various occupational roles or the roles of husband-father and wife-mother. Moreover, these norms vary among different spheres of life.

Adolescence

....unsure about who they are, society begins to ask them related questions. For instance, adolescents are expected to make the first steps toward career objectives. Society asks adolescents, then, what roles they will play as adults—that is, what socially prescribed set of behaviors they will choose to adopt.

Role Conflict

Conflict is goal-oriented, just as cooperation and competition are, but, there is a difference, in conflict, one seeks deliberately to harm and/or destroy one's antagonists. The rules of competition always include restrictions upon the injury that may be done to a foe. But in conflict these rules break down; one seeks to win at any cost. Conflict also tends to be more or less personal, just as is the case with cooperation and competition. First, fights and 'shoot-out' illustrate highly personal conflicts.

Probably the most striking thing about conflict is its destructive potential. The word 'conflict' itself often conjures up images of heads being broken, of buildings burning, and of deaths and destruction. Conflict is an abnormal and universal form of social interaction as are any of the others. The more roles one serves, the more often this role conflict happens, and it causes various problems. Role conflict can be stressful. Trying to manage the demands of different roles takes energy and time, and it can be overwhelming. People often get sick when they have too many roles to fulfill. For example, it's a common sight during finals to see students sniffling away with a tissue box next to their bluebook. Another consequence of role conflict is deviance. The expectations of any given role can be thought of as norms—like the laws of our country—and violating these norms can lead to punishment. If you show up late for work because of class, you can be fired. If you neglect your boyfriend/girlfriend to play intramurals, you might be dumped. If you go home to your parents' house instead of going out with your friends, they might not invite you next time.

Usually we think of deviance as a part of who a person is. "This person likes to break rules," "That person is a criminal;" but from the perspective of role theory, deviance is a function of the roles we serve, not of who we are. So, put anyone into incompatible roles, and the resulting role conflict will turn them into deviants of a sort. Take a nun in a convent, give her contradictory role expectations, and you have someone violating norms—a deviant. This is not to say that people are helpless against role conflict; in fact, we do lots of things to successfully manage role expectations. We make detailed plans for out days and write them down in little books or PDAs—as a way of fitting everything in. We change one role make it fit with another. We read books and take seminars on how to manage our lives.

Status and Role

Status is simply a position in a social system, such as child or parent.

Status refers to what a person is, whereas the closely linked notion of role refers to the behavior expected of people in a status.

Status is also used as a synonym for honor or prestige, when social status denotes the relative position of a person on a publicly recognized scale or hierarchy of social worth.

A status is simply a rank or position that one holds in a group. One occupies the status of son or daughter, playmate, pupil, radical, militant and so on. Eventually one occupies the statuses of husband, mother bread-winner, cricket fan, and so on, one has as many statuses as there are groups of which one is a member.

Columbine as a Metaphor

Modernization has affected rates and forms of criminality in the past two hundred years in both capitalist and socialist societies. The relationship between industrialization and urbanization and changes in levels and forms of criminality is never a simple linear one. Complex social changes accompanying these two major manifestations of development that contributes to the observed patterns of criminal behavior.

Crime is any act that violates written criminal law. Society sees most crimes, such as robbery, assault, battery, rape, murder, burglary, and embezzlement, as deviant. A society's criminal justice system punishes crimes.

The types of crimes committed are as varied as the types of criminals who commit them. Most crimes fall into one of two categories:

- ❖ Crimes against people or
- ❖ Crimes against property.

Recent theories on criminology have said that there are really two distinct tracks in explaining crime. The first track states that there is a difference between offenders and non offenders—that criminals have such characteristics as feeblemindedness, emotional instability, physical and mental deficiency, and an antisocial personality. The other track argues that offenders and non offenders are not that different—that they do not differ in terms of personality traits. Criminals commit crime based on the situation at hand. Most all of these new theories on crime can be categorized into these two tracks.

Studies of school shootings have been conducted in a variety of disciplines, including sociology, psychology, and media studies. However, to date there is no unified body of knowledge about such events. School-related shootings, particularly those that are dramatic in nature, evoke strong public outcry, and justifiably so. Following an apparent spate of incidents occurring between 1997 and 2001, it seemed as if the USA was on the brink of a moral panic concerning delinquency and nihilistic youth culture. Since then, '*Columbine* has become a keyword for a complex set of emotions surrounding youth, risk, fear, and delinquency in 21st century America' (Muschert 2007). One alarmist (Stein 2000) went so far as to label Columbine as a metaphor for a contemporary crisis of youth culture. The high level of attention given to school shootings, compared to other forms of victimization in schools, is potentially misleading.

Human Species

We, humans, have the enviable position at the top of the food chain. Although individuals occasionally fall prey to wild beasts, as a species we are safe, except from ourselves. Being an omnivore of modest size, we got to this privileged position through our use of tools. Tools we use are not limited to guns: as a species, we are defined as tool makers and tool users. It is also fortunate that most humans are disposed to cooperate with each other. However, the exceptions to that "most" are sufficient to make weapons ownership a necessity for the rest. Human aggression happens on two levels: individual and organized. Let's consider them separately.

Becoming an adult involves learning to respect others and to take responsibility for our own actions. Most people learn those skills and appreciate the values on which peaceful coexistence is predicated; unfortunately, a minority of people, fewer than 2 per cent, decline to behave in a civilized manner. Civilized behavior, for the purpose of our discussion, could be described as acting humanely towards others even if no punishment would be incurred by acting meanly.

Some of the mean humans are not deterred from harming others by any considerations. Such people are, thankfully, very rare and generally make the news eventually. However, most mean individuals, including those we might consider crazy, behave rationally even if in pursuit of irrational goals. Such people weigh the costs and benefits of their actions and so try to pick victims who cannot fight back.

Here we come to the first benefit of weapons ownership. You may not be armed, but those who would harm you for wanton gratification or for profit have no way of knowing that. Over time, they run a real risk of accidentally attacking an armed person. In that way, general tradition of being able to resist evil affords you some protection by protective mimicry. In nature, a harmless animal would imitate a more formidable species and thus give pause to the would-be predators

Similarly, predators who select victims based on the expected inability to resist, often desist when even a small number of the expected easy marks give them trouble. For example, where even a few women are known to be armed, all women benefit from the reduction in attempted rapes and other violent crimes. That no external differences indicate which person is defenseless and which isn't makes all of us safer.

No one in their right mind, be they peaceful humans or predators, would enjoy a firefight. Safety of the humans is much improved whenever the predators have to endure combat in order to get what they want, with no guarantee of victory but with a serious risk to their hides. The concept of peace through ability to win a war might sound flippant, but the sentiment is based on reason.

Being safe does not mean that we should all string barbed wire around our homes, mine the front lawn and sit behind sandbagged windows in anticipation of hostile hordes. Leading righteous, peaceful lives, being good to others, working to improve ourselves and the world would do much to improve our safety. Yet, just as good health doesn't depend on plenty of exercise or a good diet, safety does not depend only on being armed or on being a decent human. Each is an essential component of the whole. Being armed doesn't mean that we fear our environment. Simply put, being prepared reduces criminal predation to a solved problem. After all, having soap in a bathroom doesn't indicate a paranoid fear of germs, only the recognition of a problem and a ready solution to it. Similarly, carrying a handgun just in case is reasonable. Towing cannon behind your car would be excessive effort relative to the moderate risks we face Conditioning by television or newspapers makes some view every gun as a tragedy in the making. Evening news often show a picture of a gun even when talking about a beating which involved feet and fists. Without a real-world basis for comparison, it is easy to assume that firearms are possessed of supernatural powers. After all, if our understanding of computers was based on Hollywood, wouldn't we all live in fear of killer robots and rogue mainframes?

Judicious use of complex tools separates humans from all other species. To throw away one of our main evolutionary accomplishments out of misguided fear would be akin to wishing away the well-developed brain to make births easier. The loss of functionality to us as human beings would far exceed any potential gain from such a trade.

Difference in Mind Set

Some people wouldn't pick up arms to defend themselves even if presented with such a choice in the hour of need. They do not wish to use force because they feel that it makes them into barbarians just like the attackers. In my view, they are missing the difference between initiation of violence and using force to stop violence,

Some of the people who would be willing to perish rather than fight change their minds when the lives of other innocents are at stake. Parents have an obligation to their children, spouses and friends to each other. Yet efforts to protect family members are likely to fail if the protectors have neither tools nor training with which to save lives.

Some say: "I would not use a weapon even to protect my family." These same people have no problem with calling in police officers who carry guns; and who would shoot criminals to terminate attacks against innocent people. For some reason, they have no objection to deadly force so long as it is used by a uniformed agent of the state.

How many times have you heard: "If accosted by criminals, give them what they want and be a good witness"? Do you think you can be an observant, impassive witness if your family or friends are under attack? Wouldn't you rather have an option to render assistance?

Ironically, some people who loudly proclaim their self-sufficiency deliberately avoid being able to protect themselves. They regard that ability as a trait peculiar to their oppressors, weapons as a hallmark of uncivilized savages. Some even state that they consider being a mangled, abused corpse a more dignified state than resisting with a gun. Do you think that is a logical position?

Giving up, surrendering to evil is not a guarantee of safety. On the contrary, it encourages criminals to attack again. It is like throwing hamburger into shark-infested waters: conditioning predators to expect easy pickings at your expense

Monopoly on Force

Back in the 50's to 70's schools and kids were not classified as ?violent? Like they are now, instead they were considered to be delinquent. The number of violent acts have been increasing and getting worse for the past decades for several reasons. In present society students are less willing to let an argument go and more likely to hold a grudge against a person until they gain revenge. A fistfight seems prehistoric when compared to what happens in fights now. Instead of punching each other and leaving it at that, if they are losing they will most likely use and weapon they can get their hands on, as in a knife or gun. If they don't have a weapon on them they will go get one looking to settle the score.

In the late 1990s, it seemed like an epidemic had hit American schools: Children were acquiring guns and bombs, and then going to school to kill teachers and classmates. Various cultural influences were targeted for blame, such as Stephen King's novel, *Rage*, a film, *The Basketball Diaries*, and the Pearl Jam video, "Jeremy." Violent videogames also entered the discussions, as did the influences of cults like Satanism. Yet a look back reveals some of the earlier incidents as well.

'Violent Culture'

Important factors contributing to school shootings and other deadly:

Very large schools have more problems than small one due to the *alienation* factor and because of the greater personal distance between faculty and students.

Psycho-tropic drugs (like Ritalin) factor into most of the junior and senior high school cases but medical records are notoriously difficult to obtain to link all of them one way or the other.

Contributory Factors—Behavior-Modifying Drugs

The causes are myriad: violent video games, absentee and self-indulgent parents, graphic depictions in slasher films, less participation in sports and scouting, the wholesome activities that earlier generations viewed as standard fare. There is an absurd preoccupation with notions of self-esteem, appallingly unaccompanied by sufficient attention to instilling a sense of responsibility. Factor in the grievous lack of on-site fathers in the lives of far too many children. On varying levels, all of these are contributory factors. However, the most menacing culprit is the alarming rise in medication of children.

On March 21, 2005, 16-year old shooter, Jeff Wiese, murdered his grandfather and the man's girlfriend on Minnesota's Red Lake Indian Reservation, near the Canadian border. He then embarked on a killing frenzy at his high school where he shot five classmates, a teacher and an unarmed school guard, before turning the gun on himself. Wiese was being medicated with Prozac.

Linking violence to psychiatric drugs isn't much of a leap. Since 1997, the evidence has mounted. In the last half of that year alone, there were three notorious crimes in which the young killers were taking prescribed mood altering drugs.

16-year-old, Luke Woodham, savagely beat his mother with a baseball bat and then stabbed her to death before killing two female classmates at his high school. Seven others were wounded by the hail of gunfire. He was medicated with Prozac.

Before the end of that year, Michael Carneal, a 14-year-old on Ritalin, opened fire on students participating in a prayer meeting at Heath High School in West Paducah, Ky. Three teenagers were killed and five others seriously wounded, one of whom was paralyzed.

Spring of 1998, in Jonesboro, Ark., camouflage-clad 11-year-old Andrew Golden and 14-year-old Mitchell Johnson pulled a fire alarm at their middle school. As the students and teachers filed out of the buildings, the shooters, concealed in a wooded area behind the school, targeted and killed four students, one teacher and severely wounded 10 others. Reports indicated the boys were on Ritalin.

15-year-old Shawn Cooper, of Notus, Idaho took a 12-gauge shotgun to school, holding his terrified classmates hostage. One student was wounded while Cooper repeatedly fired rounds. Cooper was on Ritalin.

The grisly and premeditated carnage at Columbine High School also provides a connective link to behavior-modifying drugs. Overindulged and under-supervised, black trench-coat wearing teenagers Eric Harris and Dylan Klebold killed 12 students and a teacher in Littleton, Colo., before taking their own lives. Harris was on the anti-depressant Luvox. Posting their contempt for fellow classmates on websites and detailing their violent plans in journals, they built pipe bombs in hopes of killing hundreds of students.

T.J. Solomon, a 15-year-old high school student in Conyers, Ga., taking prescribed Ritalin, opened fire at his school, wounding six of his classmates. These crimes are not related to inner-city gang violence. In fact, the majority took place in rural settings. The murderers share the distinct commonality of being medicated with behavior-altering pharmaceuticals. Scant information detailing the severity of the side effects of these drugs appears to be available to parents. The FDA has acknowledged that Prozac enhances mental instability, especially in children, causing homicidal and psychotically delusional responses.

The school shooters nearly always have an inability to grasp the gravity of their drastic actions, that of their own situation or the repercussions that follow.

Targets include:

❖   Video games and a 'violent culture'
❖   Immorality (lack of God and religion)
❖   Lack of security (metal detectors, security guards etc.)
❖   Guns

The guns in these cases are almost always stolen anyway. The schools are increasingly heavily guarded but no connection can be found that this decreases violence; on the contrary it increases the sense of alienation and oppression which actually increases school violence. And finally if video games and a 'violent culture' are really to blame then someone has to answer why the vast majority of kids that are immersed in this *don't* act out.

The New Cultural Symbol

School shootings have become so common that these events have achieved a level of cultural symbolism all their own. And it isn't very surprising that they do continue to occur since the source of the problem has not gone away—a society that generates large scale economic redundancy as well as personal isolation and alienation amidst an artificial and extremely hostile environment towards mental health. All of this is occurring amidst a mainstream culture that has its language and symbols defined by a commercial mass-media that perpetuates false expectations to motivate rampant consumerism. Fear, insecurity, and inadequacy are powerful marketing forces that have unintended psychological consequences on the unsuspecting public.

The homogenization of culture means that it doesn't matter whether the school shooting occurs in Canada, Australia or the United States because it is the same mental-cultural environment with similar symbols and expectations being perpetuated by the same profit-motivated commercial forces.

The Revenge Motivation

Revenge seems to be a common thread that runs through all of these events. School shootings are primarily acts of revenge. Revenge is rooted in a sense of real or perceived injustice towards the perpetrator of the shooting and injustice is the feeling that 'I should have something that I don't'. Many school shootings are fomented by a desire for revenge against society and a simmering anger over being denied an entitlement such as respect or personal recognition.

Extensive research has shown that the teenage brain is not nearly as developed as an adult brain and because of this emotion, reason, and a proper sense of self and others are often in an acute state of imbalance. A sense of personal injustice to a teenager may stem from what an adult would consider to be a minor or inconsequential event, yet to a teenager this situation could be of extreme significance. Similarly, the way teenagers respond to violence is also of notable difference to the way adults respond to it. Put these two things together and mix them with the ever present general state of confusion and angst as the young person struggles to construct and define their sense of personal identity, and a very volatile cocktail is formed.

Teenagers are more selfish than adults because they use a different part of their brain to make decisions compared to adults, new research suggests.

The work has implications for the types of responsibility given to adolescents, Blakemore says: "Teenager's brains are a work in progress and profoundly different from adults. If you're making decisions about how to treat teenagers in terms of the law, you need to take this new research into account."

The psychological motivation for acting out in a violent way, such as through a shooting at school, is rooted in more than just the struggle to form an identity amidst a hostile culture of commercialized consumerism and social atomization. The reason it requires more is because even when these young people achieve a sense of acceptance and belonging in a clique it's still not enough to stop them, as in the Montreal case in September 2006.

If they already have a group to belong to and a semblance of unique personal identity then does this new separate identity exaggerate their opposition mentality and drive them to attack a society seen as hostile towards them? Or is it all just a selfish and desperate attempt to sate a bruised ego by gaining attention and personal recognition even if they have to die to get it? Or maybe they are just so apathetic about existence and future prospects that they lack interest and concern for life in general and those around them. Lacking any sense of continuity and historical context, cut adrift and alienated, this seems a plausible explanation.

All of the teenage school shooters have been deeply influenced by mass media, usually in the form of video games and movies—and both media forms tend to be very vivid, intense and increasingly photo-realistic. As the artificial media increasingly comes to define the public's sense of natural reality the negative consequences of this will only become more apparent and deadly. Teenagers growing up in the late 20th century and today in the 21st are immersed in an extremely hostile environment for the mind. This mental environment is especially hazardous for the young mind that is not fully developed and also lacking in the experience needed for balance and proportional decision-making. 16.09.06

Two categories of school shootings: Class A/Class B

At this point I think it is important to distinguish between two categories of school shootings. The first class of school shootings is the ones perpetrated by students at their own school and against other students of faculty.

The second category are the school shootings done by outsiders (non-students or faculty) who come to a school ground, for various reasons, with the intent of perpetrate a crime.

Risk Factors

Post-event interviews of students and faculty regularly express stunned surprise that a shooting occurred at their school with typical statements like 'we thought it was a joke' or, 'it didn't seem real'. school shooting events cut across most all social boundaries transcending race, class, religion and age, and have occurred across the globe from Australia to Finland. A student shooting *can* occur at your school—don't expect that it won't and don't wait for it to happen!

Although Class A school shootings have many elements in common several critical factors significantly increase the likelihood of a violent outburst at school. After studying numerous examples of these events I, Freydis, have developed these ten primary risk factors useful in identifying a potential school shooter:

1. Male
2. Age 14-20
3. Troubled Home Life
4. Mental Health Problems
5. Psycho-tropic Drugs
6. Bullied by Others
7. Poor Academic Performance
8. Social Fringe/Rejected by Peers
9. Suspension/Graduation Timeframe
10. Frequent Anger/Rage

New Virus in Rural and Urban Areas

In recent shootings in USA could represent a new strain of the violence virus one they know little about. While youth homicide rates in major urban areas have dropped in recent years, rates in rural and suburban areas are constant or even rising. These incidents have caught behavioral scientists off guard, psychologists posit. After years of study, behavioral scientists have developed a fairly reliable profile of urban juvenile murderers, who are driven by such risk factors as poverty, the crack trade and a thriving black market for handguns. But those scientists understand far less about the rising number of homicidal boys from seemingly sleepy towns. Few psychologists reject the idea that the risk factors that plague inner-city youth have seeped into the suburbs and beyond. Youth are exposed to a growing amount of violent images on television, in movies, in video games and in popular music. Guns are more widely available than they were a generation ago. Drug abuse remains a problem among teen-agers everywhere. And street gangs even have satellite chapters in the suburbs and rural areas.

Although they have minimal empirical data to go on, psychologists have noticed some distinguishing characteristics among the rural youth murderers who have made headlines in recent months. These adolescents tend to:

- ❖ Kill and injure multiple victims in a single incident. The perpetrators don't target only an individual as part of some interpersonal dispute (although sometimes an ex-girlfriend is among those killed), but seem to launch a shooting spree that results in many deaths and injuries
- ❖ Have no secondary criminal motive, such as robbery. The primary goal is to kill or harm others.
- ❖ Be younger. Statistically, most youth murderers are 15 or older. But the last six incidents involving shootings at small-town schools have involved youths no older than 14,.
- ❖ Have a history of social problems. The phenomenon of rejection contributes to their increased aggressiveness over time, so, they're more inclined to think that people are out to get them. And it's that kind of reactivity that makes them more at risk for doing this.

Other psychologists believe extreme narcissism, rather than despair or self-loathing, may make youth more violent. Narcissists mainly want to punish or defeat someone who has threatened their highly favorable views of themselves.

The youths also seem to be driven by an intense need for attention, psychologists say. While urban youth tend to carry and use guns to wage power, to seek revenge on a rival or to simply protect themselves on the vicious streets, the murderers in these recent, rural incidents seem to be more interested in gaining national notoriety. In fact, many psychologists agree that the intense media attention devoted to these incidents creates a 'copycat' effect. These are kids who feel very isolated in their emotional pain and use aggressive behavior in an attempt to let people know how distressed they are! When they see the kind of attention that comes to people who commit these crimes, they think, Oh my God, that's what I'm looking for?

Urban school officials and law enforcers have taken concrete steps to stamp out violence. Students have to pass through metal detectors when they enter the school, for example. And in cities like Boston, police and civic activists have beefed up community policing and antiviolence education programs in recent years and have dramatically reduced the rate of juvenile crime. But the rural and suburban schools just aren't savvy about this.

Personality Disorders and Traits

Personality traits and disorders have recently become essential in the diagnosis of individuals with antisocial or criminal behavior. These traits and disorders do not first become evident when an individual is an adult, rather these can be seen in children. For that reason it seems logical to discuss those personality disorders that first appear in childhood. Attention Deficit Hyperactivity Disorder (ADHD), Conduct Disorder (CD), and Oppositional Defiance Disorder (ODD) are three of the more prominent disorders that have been shown to have a relationship with later adult behavior (Holmes, Slaughter, & Kashani, 2001).

ODD is characterized by argumentativeness, noncompliance, and irritability, which can be found in early childhood (Holmes *et al.*, 2001). When a child with ODD grows older, the characteristics of their behavior also change and more often for the worse. They start to lie and steal, engage in vandalism, substance abuse, and show aggression towards peers (Holmes *et al.*, 2001). Frequently ODD is the first disorder that is identified in children and if sustained can lead to the diagnosis of CD (Morley &

Hall, 2003). It is important to note however that not all children who are diagnosed with ODD will develop CD. ADHD is associated with hyperactivity-impulsivity and the inability to keep attention focused on one thing (Morley & Hall, 2003). Holmes *et al.* (2001) state that, "impulse control dysfunction and the presence of hyperactivity and inattention are the most highly related predisposing factors for presentation of antisocial behavior" (p.184). They also point to the fact that children diagnosed with ADHD have the inability to analyze and anticipate consequences or learn from their past behavior. Children with this disorder are at risk of developing ODD and CD, unless the child is only diagnosed with Attention Deficit Disorder (ADD), in which case their chances of developing ODD or CD are limited. The future for some children is made worse when ADHD and CD are co-occurring because they will be more likely to continue their antisocial tendencies into adulthood (Holmes *et al.*, 2001).

Conduct Disorder is characterized with an individual's violation of societal rules and norms (Morley & Hall, 2003). As the tendencies or behaviors of those children who are diagnosed with ODD or ADHD worsen and become more prevalent, the next logical diagnosis is CD. What is even more significant is the fact that ODD, ADHD, and CD are risk factors for developing Antisocial Personality Disorder (ASPD). This disorder can only be diagnosed when an individual is over the age of eighteen and at which point an individual shows persistent disregard for the rights of others (Morley & Hall, 2003). ASPD has been shown to be associated with an increased risk of criminal activity. Therefore, it is of great importance that these early childhood disorders are correctly diagnosed and effectively treated to prevent future problems.

Another critical aspect that must be examined regarding antisocial or criminal behavior is the personality characteristics of individuals. Two of the most cited personality traits that can be shown to have an association with antisocial or criminal behavior are impulsivity and aggression (Morley & Hall, 2003). According to the article written by Holmes *et al.* (2001), antisocial behavior between the ages of nine and fifteen can be correlated strongly with impulsivity and that aggression in early childhood can predict antisocial acts and delinquency. One statistic shows that between seventy and ninety per cent of violent offenders had been highly aggressive as young children (Holmes *et al.*, 2001). These personality traits have, in some research, been shown to be heritable.

Environmental Influences

Thus far it has been established through research and various studies that genetics do influence criminal or antisocial behavior. Researchers agree on the point that genes influence personality traits and disorders, such as the ones just mentioned. However, researchers also agree that there is an environmental component that needs to be examined. Environmental influences such as family and peers will be discussed, as well as a look into the social learning theory.

The family environment is critical to the upbringing of a child and if problems exist then the child is most likely to suffer the consequences. We have seen the problems associated with a child who is diagnosed with ADHD and how that can influence antisocial or criminal behavior. In relation to that, some researchers have claimed that it is the family environment that influences the hyperactivity of children (Schmitz, 2003). The researchers in this article specifically identify family risk factors as poverty, education, parenting practices, and family structure. Prior research on the relationship between family environment and child behavior characterizes a child's well being with a positive and caring parent-child relationship, a stimulating home environment, and consistent disciplinary techniques (Schmitz, 2003). Families with poor communication and weak family bonds have been shown to have a correlation with children's development of aggressive/criminal behavior (Garnefski & Okma, 1996). Therefore it seems obvious to conclude that those families who are less financially sound, perhaps have more children, and who are unable to consistently punish their children will have a greater likelihood of promoting an environment that will influence antisocial or delinquent behavior. Another indicator of future antisocial or criminal behavior is that of abuse or neglect in childhood. A statistic shows that children are at a fifty per cent greater risk of engaging in criminal acts, if they were neglected or abused (Holmes *et al.*, 2001). This has been one of the most popular arguments as to why children develop antisocial or delinquent behaviors. One additional research finding in the debate between genetic and environmental influences on antisocial or criminal behavior has to deal with the age of the individual. Research seems consistent in recognizing that heritability influences adult behavior more than environmental influences, but that for children and adolescents the environment is the most significant factor influencing their behavior (Rhee & Waldman, 2002). As an adult, we have the ability to choose the environment in which to live and this will either positively or negatively reinforce our personality traits, such as aggressiveness. However, children and adolescents are limited to the extent of choosing an environment, which accounts for the greater influence of environmental factors in childhood behaviors.

Another significant factor in the development of antisocial or delinquent behavior in adolescence is peer groups. Garnefski and Okma (1996) state that there is a correlation between the involvement in an antisocial or delinquent peer group and problem behavior. One of the primary causes as to why this occurs can be traced back to aggressive behavior in young children. When children are in preschool and show aggressive tendencies towards their peers, they will likely be deemed as an outcast. This creates poor peer relationships and relegates those children to be with others who share similar behaviors. A relationship like this would most likely continue into adolescence and maybe even further into adulthood. The similar tendencies of these individuals create an environment in which they influence one another and push the problem towards criminal or violent behavior (Holmes *et al.*, 2001).

Social learning theory has been cited as way to explain how the environment can influence a child's behavior. Using this theory to explain the aggressive or antisocial behavior of a child means that a child observes aggressive behavior between parents, siblings, or both. As a result, the children believes that this aggressive behavior is normal and can therefore use it themselves because they do not see the harm in acting similar to their parents (Miles & Carey, 1997). As stated earlier, interaction between family members and disciplinary techniques are influential in creating antisocial behavior. Using the social learning theory these two factors are also critical in the development of aggression. Children who are raised in an aggressive family environment would most likely be susceptible to experiencing a lack of parental monitoring, permissiveness or inconsistency in punishment, parental rejection and aggression. The exposure to such high levels of aggression and other environmental factors greatly influences and reinforces a child's behavior. A significant point that should be known however is the fact that other research has supported the notion that genetics do influence levels of aggression, which stands in opposition to the social learning theory (Miles & Carey, 1997).

Gene-Environment Interactions

There are theories, however, concerning genetic and environmental influences, which seem to suggest an interaction between the two and one such theory is the general arousal theory of criminality. Personality psychologist Eysenck created a model based on three factors known as psychoticism, extraversion, and neuroticism, or what is referred to as the PEN model (Eysenck, 1996). Psychoticism was associated with the traits of aggressive, impersonal, impulsive, cold, antisocial, and un-empathetic.

Extraversion was correlated with the traits of sociable, lively, active, sensation-seeking, carefree, dominant, and assertive. Finally, neuroticism was associated with anxious, depressed, low self-esteem, irrational, moody, emotional, and tense (Eysenck, 1996). Through research and surveys, Eysenck found that these three factors could be used as predictors of criminal behavior. He believed this to be especially true of the psychoticism factor and that measuring it could predict the difference between criminals and non-criminals. Extraversion was a better predictor for young individuals, while neuroticism was a better predictor for older individuals (Eysenck, 1996). An important point about these factors and the personality traits associated with them is that most of them have already been found to be heritable (Miles & Carey, 1997).

Understanding Eysenck's original model is critical to assessing the general arousal theory of criminality, which suggests an interaction between factors. Research has shown that criminality is strongly correlated with low arousal levels in the brain. Characteristics related to low arousal levels include lack of interest, sleepiness, lack of attention, and loss of vigilance. Eysenck (1996) believed that these characteristics were similar to the personality factor of extraversion. Individuals with low arousal levels and those who are extraverts need to seek out stimulation because they do not have enough already in their brains. Therefore, the premise of the general arousal theory of criminality is that individuals inherit a nervous system that is unresponsive to low levels of stimulation and as a consequence, these individuals have to seek out the proper stimulation to increase their arousal. Under this theory, the proper stimulation includes high-risk activities associated with antisocial behavior, which consists of sexual promiscuity, substance abuse, and crime (Miles & Carey, 1997). A significant fact that must be pointed out though is that not every individual with low arousal levels or those who are extraverts will seek those high risk activities just mentioned. It takes the right environment and personality to create an individual with antisocial or criminal tendencies and that is why this theory can be considered to take into account both factors of genetic and environmental influences.

Conclusion

There cannot be enough possible evidence to conclude the point that genetics play the most important role in the outcome or behavior of an individual. The opposing viewpoint of environmental factors is not without its doubts either as to being the prominent factor influencing antisocial or criminal behavior of an individual. In this paper, there is more evidence supporting the genetics viewpoint, but that does not mean it is more important. With the research and studies having numerous flaws and the inability to adequately separate nature and nurture, there is still a great debate between genetic and environmental factors.

Researchers, however, have certainly come far in their progression, to the point where there is a large consensus of the fact that genes do influence behavior to a certain extent. Although not as widely publicized, it is the belief of the author that these same researchers also believe that environmental factors account for what cannot be explained by genes. Therefore it seems obvious to reach the conclusion that an individual's antisocial or criminal behavior can be the result of both their genetic background and the environment in which they were raised.

One researcher has proposed a theory relating to sociopaths and their antisocial behavior. According to the theory, a primary sociopath is lacking in moral development and does not feel socially responsible for their actions. This type of sociopath is a product of the individual's personality, physiotype, and genotype. A secondary sociopath develops in response to his or her environment because of the disadvantages of social competition. Living in an urban residence, having a low socioeconomic status, or poor social skills can lead an individual to being unsuccessful in reaching their needs in a socially desirable way, which can turn into antisocial or criminal behavior. The first type of sociopath is dependent on their genetic makeup and personality, while certain factors of the second type can also be heritable. Notwithstanding, the second type has a greater dependence on environmental factors (Miles & Carey, 1997). Perhaps from this review of both genetic and environmental factors, it seems clear to support the idea of the secondary sociopath type. An individual can inherit certain genes and when combined with the right environmental factors can lead them to engage in antisocial or criminal behavior.

Although not mentioned extensively in the text of the paper, there is a great need to try and identify those individuals, especially children, who may become susceptible to certain disorders or personality traits that can lead into antisocial, delinquent, or criminal behavior. Society should not try to imitate the era of controlled breeding, but rather focus on the treatment and rehabilitation of those individuals in need. Certain educational, environment enrichment programs have been shown to have a lasting effect on children if given by a certain age (Raine, Mellingen, Liu, Venables, & Mednick, 2003). If more of these programs could be developed, society could help prevent the future antisocial or criminal behavior of children.

Psychology of School Shootings

Every Class A school shooting (the ones perpetrated by students at their own school and against other students of faculty) is basically about two things: power and revenge—the gun grants power to those that feel powerless, while pulling the trigger on someone confers revenge.

When kids suffer abuse at home from parents and siblings, then they go to school and suffer bullying from peers and an endless series of dictates from teachers, they begin to feel trapped because no matter where they are they can't avoid abuse. And when they see that the authority at home is part of the problem and authority at school is either unconcerned or inept at helping them they gradually realize that authority is fundamentally hypocritical since it is not based on benevolent guidance as officially stated but is instead based on controlling and exploiting the less powerful. Consequently these kids begin to perceive the world as the 'strong' towering over and abusing the 'weak'.

Feeling trapped and powerless they naturally search for a way out. The easiest and most effective way to acquire power is to get a gun. Kids easily believe that using a gun is an effective method for resolving their problems because every movie and television show they watch depicts the world through this foolish one-dimensional lens of power expression and problem resolution via deadly violence. And these kids believe that it's acceptable to act-out their drama as a school shooting because that's what other students have done before.

This is the psychological basis for a school shooting. The only piece remaining is a sufficient triggering event to push them over the edge.

Effects of School Shootings

An aspect of the research that is greatly underemphasized is the effects of school shootings. In rare cases, such as one study that examines the psychological effect of a school shooting on students (Curry 2003), studies may examine the direct effect of such tragedies on their community and its members. However, most research focuses on the wider cultural impact of school shootings. Sociologists have examined the cultural and symbolic importance of school shootings, which have been a source of great public fear (e.g. Altheide 2002b; Burns and Crawford 1999). Empirical studies of students' fear of victimization in school have produced mixed results. For example, Addington (2003) found that the fear of victimization reported by US students aged 12–17 did not significantly change following the 1999 Columbine shootings. Other studies revealed an increased fear of victimization among secondary school students in Texas (Snell *et al.* 2002) and among female university students (Stretesky and Hogan 2001). A nuanced recent study of fear in 1500 schools revealed that students typically felt that their own schools were safer than average (Chapin and Coleman 2006).

Highly publicized school shooting incidents also had an impact on school crime policy decisions, where these decisions were more frequently biased toward punitive policies. Frequently, school antiviolence policies were developed after school administrators received calls from parents (Snell *et al.* 2002), and these calls may be interpreted as evidence of public concern about school shootings generated by intense media coverage (Chenault 2004). In general, the USA takes a punitive response to juvenile offenders, but the USA might benefit from observing more restorative policies in Europe (Klein 2005a). One scholar (Webber 2003b) argues that the punitive approach adopted in the USA to combat school violence follows the military model of containment historically used to fight Communism. In this sense, youth are treated as a foreign enemy within domestic borders. At times, it appears that students in the USA are increasingly subject to surveillance programs instituted in the name of security, but which may increase the sense that schools are more analogous to correctional facilities, rather than nurturing institutions concerned with youth development (Dimitriadis and McCarthy 2003). In an attempt to cut through the hype surrounding the knee-jerk responses to violence in schools, Brooks *et al.* (2000) offered the following concrete policy recommendations: adding more contexts to media coverage, encouraging the use of punitive and meditative practices inside schools to maintain safety, and increased regulation of the gun industry.

Another interpretation of school-related shootings and violence is that these events are a threat to the public health and welfare (Elliott *et al.* 1998). Many studies concentrate on the mental health needs of the communities in which school shootings occur (Fast 2003; Fein 2003; Martin 2001; Weintraub *et al.* 2001; Windham *et al.* 2005). Another study in this tradition adopts a pragmatic approach that the emphasis should be on weapons-free schools, which might be achieved through entry-based weapons screening (Mawson *et al.* 2002).

Another variety of effect stems from the strong mass media dynamic present in school shootings, and this has sparked a number of studies. In a case study of the Dunblane shootings in Scotland, Jemphrey and Berrington (2000) demonstrated that mass media presence in communities following disastrous events may exacerbate the trauma experienced by the communities. However, the findings also indicate that many journalists are self-reflexive regarding their professional responsibilities toward the victims and communities where school shootings occur. This is especially important where the subjects of media attention are young. Some scholars have criticized the news media for their irresponsible handling of school shooting events (e.g. Muschert and Larkin forthcoming); however, journalists have reflected on their lessons learned by covering school shootings (Shepard 2003; Simpson and Coté 2006). Clearly it is psychologically difficult for media personnel to cover school shootings, especially when they occur in their own communities. One scholar examined the immediate challenges experienced by *Denver Post* journalists when they covered Columbine (Shepard 1999), and a related study demonstrated that the Columbine story had a long-lasting traumatic effect on the media personnel who covered it, especially those in the Denver area (Simpson and Coté 2006, 193–200).

How to Help Kids in Times of Crisis and Stress

- ❖ Try and keep routines as normal as possible. Kids gain security from the predictability of routine, including attending school.
- ❖ Limit exposure to television and the news.
- ❖ Be honest with kids and share with them as much information as they are developmentally able to handle.
- ❖ Listen to kids' fears and concerns.
- ❖ Reassure kids that the world is a good place to be, but that there are people who do bad things.
- ❖ Parents and adults need to first deal with and assess their own responses to crisis and stress.
- ❖ Rebuild and reaffirm attachments and relationships

Sociological Causes

In some communities, particularly those, "where disorder and crime are conflated with poverty and socioeconomic disadvantage," social norms against violence have broken- down, fostering conditions where youth gun violence can thrive. In these environments, many youth feel the need to arm themselves for self-protection. The economic and social factors that underlie youth gun violence must be addressed.

Diverse Causes

There are diverse factors that cause such things to happen—sociological, psychological and societal tectonic shifts and adjustments. But let us examine the boomtown phenomenon first.

The gradual expansion of cities along the fringes has spawned a new phenomenon that has to be taken note of and that needs to be re-examined. It is the acquisition of land, often farmland, and the pauperisation of those who have been living on that land for generations. After getting their compensation, they have been disposed off in every sense of the word—their land as well as their livelihood. They have to come to terms with their loss of land and adjust to the new status of the dispossessed. If the compensation is sufficient or above prevailing prices, it creates another problem. This new bounty can cause other undesirable effects.

In the present case, the parents of both the victim and the ones who committed the crime come from more or less similar backgrounds. They had just moved into the city and admitted their children into this elite school so that they could have the education that they themselves had been deprived of. But they had also come into sudden riches and one way is through real estate. One father runs a transport business, another avenue for making it big. This newfound status and way of life, we assume, led to other pressures. May be they perceived new forms of "domination" and "exclusion".

Social Differences

Then there are social differences that are sometimes manifested in remarks or attitude that cause hurt or feelings of inferiority or oppression. These feelings can suddenly burst out in aggressive behaviour or spurts of violence in otherwise docile children. In this case, the children owned up to the killing and felt no "remorse" about the act. They were handed over to the police and subsequently moved to the juvenile home. However the parents remained untraceable until they surrendered to the police later.

It is unnerving that these youngsters thought the best way to resolve the issue was to kill their classmate. Ostensibly, there was no room for negotiation or talking over the issue. We are dealing with a disturbing level of anger and frustration that resulted in two children taking the drastic step of killing a classmate. The parents and teachers were oblivious of what the children were going through.

However, the reality is more complex than what appears on the face of it. In fact, the boys had approached the Principal on the trouble they were facing but it was treated as a casual, everyday tiff part of the usual one-upmanship when young boys try to settle scores with each other. In the media, the Principal has been quoted as saying that, when the boys approached her, she made them talk to each other, patched things up, made them shake hands. She imagined all was well. Evidently the adults were too busy to understand the young minds.

The children, of course, not only knew how to use the gun but also planned out how to go about killing their classmate. Now they are lodged at the Juvenile Home in Faridabad. One wonders who is responsible for their present plight. Ever since the incident, they have been treated as outcasts by their parents, school, friends and society at large. Are we in a position to disown our children, especially when we are all struggling to understand this phenomenon?

Periodically, when such an incident happens, educationists, parents, sociologists and even the police discuss measures to prevent future outbreaks. But very rarely are there follow ups with the result that when something like this happens, they are taken aback.

What About Values?

As adults, especially those shaping the lives of children, as parents, caregivers, teachers and members of civil society, we need to stop and rethink about the way we are treating our children. Are we providing them the right kind of education or passing on the correct values? Are we able to provide them with good role models? We all know that, with no proper anchoring in values or role models, they tend to sway to any trend that catches their fancy. Imagined wrongs can drive them to violence. Ridicule, taunts or bullying by bigger boys (as is supposed to have happened in the Gurgaon case) can result in retaliatory measures.

So, as parents, the question we need to ask ourselves is whether we have imparted to our children right values like respect, love and tolerance? Have we taught children to function within boundaries? As adults, do we mix up firmness with inflexibility or feel that by being firm we are being uncaring and undemocratic?

It is high time schools taught their wards that, apart from competition and grades, it is also necessary to learn camaraderie, bonding and qualities such as compassion and goodwill and the need to go out of one's way to help others. Do they not need to do more to foster outdoor activities like sports or excursions or even working with craftspeople? Incidents like the

Gurgaon shootout point towards the fact that we are somewhere failing in our roles and responsibilities as adults. As a young nation, we need to shape our future. We need to take the first step so that our children can inherit a better tomorrow.

Rashomon Effect

School-related shootings, particularly those that are dramatic in nature, evoke strong public outcry, and justifiably so. Following an apparent spate of incidents occurring between 1997 and 2001, it seemed as if the USA was on the brink of a moral panic concerning delinquency and nihilistic youth culture. Since then, '*Columbine* has become a keyword for a complex set of emotions surrounding youth, risk, fear, and delinquency in 21st century America' (Muschert 2007). One alarmist (Stein 2000) went so far as to label Columbine as a metaphor for a contemporary crisis of youth culture. It seems that perceptions about school shootings are an example of the Rashomon effect, which refers to the subjective construction of reality in which observers of a single event perceive incompatible, yet plausible versions of what happened. First suggested by Heider (1988), the term *Rashomon effect* is derived from the title of a 1951 film by the Japanese director Akira Kurosawa in which four characters who witnessed a crime later describe the event in different and contradictory ways. Unlike more traditional detective films, in which a single unified truth ultimately emerges, the complex message of *Rashomon* emerges when viewers are left to decide for themselves which, if any, of the four characters is telling the truth. Alternately, viewers may choose to construct their own truth by synthesizing the divergent accounts (Kurosawa 1969).

A similar *Rashomon effect* occurs when school shootings are discussed, in that those seeking to understand such incidents hear varying claims about what occurs. Certainly, there is a strong mass media dynamic occurring, and the characteristics of school shootings reported in the media are frequently different than those reported in social science research. At the turn of the millennium, school shootings were an ascendant social problem, often because the events garnered public interest, which contributed to the perception that school shootings were a new form of violence occurring with increased frequency and intensity.

Definition and Typology

An initial requirement is to define the phenomenon of school shootings and the subcategories of incidents, teasing out the varying motives and identities of the perpetrators of school shootings. While rampage attacks are the variety of school shooting incidents that have captured the lion's share of mass media attention in the last decade, a broader historical perspective reveals a variety of school-related shooting incidents. Five varieties of school-related shooting incidents:

1. *rampage* shootings,
2. school-related *mass murders*,
3. *terrorist* attacks on schools or school children,
4. school-related *targeted* shootings, and
5. *government* shootings taking place at schools.

Key operational elements of the typology include the in-group/out-group status of the perpetrator(s), and whether victims were specifically targets or selected for symbolic reasons. For each type, exemplary cases are offered, more because they are well known, than because they necessarily epitomize the type. In most cases, the examples are well known because they were severe.

Rampage shootings are among those that have recently attracted the most public attention. These are expressive, non-targeted attacks on a school institution. 'An institutional attack takes place on a public stage before an audience, is committed by a member of former member of the institution, and involves multiple victims, some chosen for their symbolic significance or at random. This final condition signifies that it is the organization, not the individuals, who are important' (Newman 2004, 231). Frequently, the motivations for rampage shootings are to attain power or to exact revenge on the community or large groups within the community, and the rampage shooter has also been labeled in the literature as the *classroom avenger* (McGee and DeBernardo 1999). Many perpetrators equate their target schools with the communities where they are located, and the rationale of attacking the school can be understood as an attempt to attack the community. The 1999 Columbine shootings in Littleton, Colorado, is the archetypical case occurring in the USA, where two students attempted to blow up their school, ultimately killing 15 (Muschert and Larkin forthcoming). While most rampage shootings studied have occurred in high schools or middle schools, some shootings occurring at universities also fit this category. The 1966 University of Texas tower shootings and the 2007 shootings at Virginia Tech are well recognized examples of rampage incidents that occurred at universities.

A second category is the school-related *mass murder* incident, typically carried out by an individual who targets categories of individuals or the school institution in general. School-related mass murders are a subset of mass murder incidents, where an adult perpetrator, who is not a current or former student or employee, targets a school institution or group of students, selected for their symbolic importance. As in rampage cases, such incidents are sometimes labeled 'postal-type shootings', and are typically carried out by individuals, motivated by desires for power, revenge, or a perverted sense of loyalty (Levin and Fox 1999). Although it is not technically a shooting incident, the worst school violence incident in US history fits the mass murder category. In 1927, a farmer killed his wife, blew up every building on their farm, and then detonated explosives placed under the Bath, Michigan, school building, killing a total of 45 people. The attack seems to have been motivated by the desire for revenge for a newly levied school tax (Ellsworth 1927). Outside the USA, the 1989 shooting at the École Politechnique de Montréal in Canada (also known as Montréal Massacre) also qualifies as a mass murder. Engineering student Marc Lépine entered a classroom, and then separated the male and female students. After claiming that he hated feminists, he shot at the women, killing six (Eglin and Hester 2003).

A third variety of incident involves *terrorist* attacks, in which a school institution or students are selected as a symbolic target in a politically motivated attack. Since children and schools are important institutions in most communities, such a strike is particularly horrific, and may be effective in gaining attention for the terrorist groups. Noteworthy examples include the 1974 incident in Ma'alot, Israel, where three terrorists held students in an elementary school hostage, demanding the release of political prisoners. Before the attack ended, 25 people died, including 21 children (Jacoby 2004). In 2004, terrorists took 1200 people hostage at a school in Beslan, Russia. After 3 days, Russian security stormed the building, and 344 people died, including 186 children (Dunlop 2006).

A fourth variety of school shootings are school-related *targeted* incidents, where a member or former member of the institution specifically attacks an individual or group of individuals in order to exact revenge for some real or perceived mistreatment. Unlike a *rampage* shooting, a *targeted attack* is not a symbolic attack on the entire school. For example, the 1992 incident at Tilden High in Chicago that resulted in the death of a student was gang related (Hagan *et al.* 2002). Another incident that fits this category is the 2003 shooting in Red Lion, Pennsylvania, where a student fatally shot a school administrator (CNN 2003). While many school-related shootings are of the targeted variety, such incidents often fail to garner widespread media attention.

A final variety of school-related shootings are those that involve *government* agents as perpetrators, such as police or military personnel. This category typically involves government agents' use of violence in response top Protest or riot behaviors. Noteworthy incidents in the USA include the 1968 shooting of anti-segregation protesters by South Carolina Highway Patrol officers that occurred at South Carolina State University, also know as the Orangeburg Massacre (Nelson and Bass 1970). Better known is the 1970 shooting of four students by Ohio National Guard troops at Kent State University, as they protested the US invasion of Cambodia during the Vietnam War (Caputo 2005). Such attacks may signal public unrest coupled with a crisis of legitimacy for government institutions as the 1989 Tiananmen Square incident when student-led protesters were gunned down by the Chinese military. In other cases, such incidents may result from government agents' panicked responses to protest behaviors, as in the Kent State shootings.

Of the five varieties of school shootings, much of the recent attention surrounding school-related shootings has focused on the rampage, mass murder, and targeted varieties of attacks. Although the school-related terrorist attacks and government attacks do occur, it was the perceived wave of rampage school shootings occurring in the late 1990s and early 2000s that motivated much of the recent social science research.

Social Science Research

In a brief article that appeared in the wake of the Columbine shootings, Kleck (1999) argued that the attention garnered by such cases is counterproductive to the sober, generalizable study of crime and delinquency.

Although the relatively brief attention given by the media and public to the social problem of school shootings may have served as an impediment to the sociological study of more common forms of youth offense and victimization, the notoriety of Columbine-type events has spurred a number of studies in school shootings. However, once again there is an apparent *Rashomon effect* that might confound those seeking to understand the causes of such events. Scholars have studied a variety of cases from a variety of academic perspectives, and there is a lack of integration across disciplines.

A variety of causes may contribute to school shootings, and therefore no single dynamic is sufficient to explain all, or even a subset, of such events. The causes may emerge from a variety of levels, ranging from the individual causes, community contexts, and social/cultural contexts in which the events occur. The reader might understand the individual factors and community contexts as being among the more proximate causes for school shooting events, while the social/cultural contexts may less directly cause individual school shootings. Nonetheless, the culture serves as a general backdrop for school shooting incidents, even if direct causality may not be established.

Among the causes only one of the causes is necessary for a school shooting to occur: the availability of guns. All other causes may be understood as frequently contributing to the problem of school shootings, but none of them alone is sufficient to cause a school shooting to occur. Individual causes may be present with varying intensity in some cases, but may be absent in other cases. Indeed, some of the causes suggested may be exclusive of others, as in the cases there tightly knit communities are identified as a context conducive to school shootings (Newman 2004) versus another case where a deracinated community setting is identified (Larkin 2007). School shooting incidents need to be understood as resulting from a constellation of contributing causes, none of which is sufficient in itself to explain a shooting. The fact that many researchers have focused on a single causal dynamic has contributed to the lack of integration in the field.

Concluding Reflections

Public and academic understanding of the phenomenon of school shootings is challenging, because there is a *Rashomon effect* derived from the varying sources of information. This article has attempted to clarify the distinction between the images of school shootings derived from two sources:

First, social science studies paint the picture of school shootings as occurring at a relatively steady rate over recent decades.

Second, news media accounts tended to concentrate on the apparent spate of school shootings occurring during the late 1990s and early 2000s.

This purported wave of school shooting incidents contributed to the general impression that there was an emergent and increasing social problem of school shootings. As a problem on the public agenda, school shootings recently seem to have been supplanted by other social problems, which now seem more pressing. However, if we believe the social scientists, the status of school shootings has not changed much at all. In this article,

Continued research conducted by social scientists contributing to a more organized field of knowledge about school shootings would be most likely to contribute to effective public policy responses to respond to such incidents, or prevent them from occurring.

Mind

The most startling idea of the 20th century was the idea that man is a composite being. He is not just a body, he is not just 206 bones, he is not just mortal. He has a mind that helps him survive and to create. The mind is made up of images, mental image pictures or impressions. The sound you hear in your mind when you "listen" to how a song was sung is an example of a mental image or impression. Recall a memory of a happy time, or a sad time and you will have at least an inkling of where you were, who was there. It is recorded as a mental picture. The mind is also made up of "machinery" that you have built in order to learn subjects, such as your times tables. It is made up of copies you have made of other people doing things, so that you can learn by mimicry. It also is made up of unknown times, where impact and pain caused you to lose consciousness, and you were vulnerable to suggestions. Many strange behavioral patterns can be traced directly to such traumatic events, accompanied by relief when a person recognizes the source of his difficulties.

The mind contains entities, which are like personalities you may have adopted. You have seen it in yourself when you caught yourself doing and saying the things mother did, even though you decided you wouldn't be like that. It is a bit like something else takes over for a moment. The mind can contain opposing entities, so that you become like the person you hate the most, and hate yourself for it.

The composite human being is not only a body, with all its parts, a mind, with all its parts (and significances), but more importantly, there is you, the awareness of awareness, the control center for the body. The you that perceives your mind, changes your mind, and moves your body.

Your body may eventually die, your memories may become forgotten, but you will still be aware. There is more than one life possible. What's the difference between mental health and mental illness? Sometimes the answer is pretty clear. People who hear voices in their heads may have schizophrenia, for instance. And those with such grandiose ideas as becoming the secretary-general of the United Nations without any experience may have a form of bipolar disorder.

But more often, the distinction between mental health and mental illness isn't as clear-cut. If you're afraid of giving a speech in public, does it mean you have a disease or simply a run-of-the-mill case of nerves? If you feel sad and discouraged, are you just experiencing a passing case of the blues, or is it full-fledged depression requiring medication?

Just what is normal mental health, anyway?

What's normal is often determined by who's defining it. Normalcy is ambiguous and often tied to value judgments particular to a certain culture or society. And even within cultures, concepts of normal mental health may evolve over time if societal values or expectations change One thing that makes it so difficult to distinguish normal mental health and abnormal mental health is that there's no easy test to show if something's wrong. There's no blood test for obsessive-compulsive disorder, no ultrasound for depression and no X-ray for bipolar disorder, for example. That's not to say mental disorders aren't biologically based. Most mental health experts do believe that some mental disorders are linked to chemical changes within the brain, and they're beginning to map these changes visually using imaging studies. But for now, there's no physiological diagnostic test for mental illness.

Distinguishing Mental Health from Mental Illness

Mental health providers define mental disorders by signs, symptoms and functional impairments. Signs are what objective observers can document, such as agitation or rapid breathing. Symptoms are subjective, or what you feel, such as euphoria or hopelessness. Functional impairment is the inability to perform certain routine or basic daily tasks, such as bathing or going to work.

In mental illness, signs and symptoms commonly show up as:

- ❖ Behaviors, such as repeated hand washing
- ❖ Feelings, such as sadness
- ❖ Thoughts, such as delusions that the television is controlling your mind
- ❖ Physiological responses, such as sweating

How do mental health providers determine whether the signs, symptoms and dysfunctions you're experiencing are normal or abnormal? Experts often use a combination of the following approaches:

- ❖ *Your Own Perceptions*: How you perceive your own thoughts, behaviors and functioning can help determine what's normal for you. You may realize that you aren't coping well or that you aren't able to or don't care to do routine activities or the things you used to enjoy. If you have depression, the dishes may go unwashed for days, you may stop bathing or you may lose interest in hobbies. You may feel sad, hopeless or discouraged and realize that something's amiss, that you don't enjoy life anymore. Or you may not be able to pinpoint what's wrong.

❖ *Others' Perceptions*: Your own perceptions are subjective and may not give you an accurate assessment of your behavior, thoughts or functioning. Objective observers, on the other hand, might be able to do so. To you, your life may seem perfectly normal or typical. Yet to those around you, it may seem odd or abnormal. This is often the case with schizophrenia. If you have schizophrenia, you may have auditory hallucinations—you hear voices and carry on conversations with them, believing it's a normal interaction with another person. To witnesses who observe this behavior, it may seem abnormal.

❖ *Cultural and Ethnic Norms*: Many times what's normal behavior or thinking is defined by your culture. But that means what's normal within the bounds of one culture may be labeled abnormal within another. Conversing with voices only you can hear may be an indicator of schizophrenia in Western cultures. But these kinds of hallucinations may be a normal part of religious experience in other cultures.

❖ *Statistical Values*: Normal is often defined by what's statistically average. Most people fall in the middle ground, the average, while others fall to one extreme or the other. Those in the extremes are often labeled abnormal because they aren't average, or the same as most others.

Evaluating Your Mental Health

In evaluating your mental health, all four of these approaches—your own perceptions, others' perceptions, cultural and ethnic norms, and statistical values—are typically taken into consideration. Mental health experts may ask how you feel, whether others have noticed a difference in your behavior or mood, and what your cultural background is. They also may ask you to fill out psychological questionnaires.

Other factors also are considered. Among them:

❖ How long you've had symptoms?
❖ How severe your symptoms are?

❖ How upsetting the symptoms are to you?
❖ How the symptoms disrupt your life?

It's normal to feel sad after a valued relationship ends. But if you feel intensely sad and upset for several weeks and you lose interest in daily activities, you may have depression. Similarly, if you get anxious before a presentation to a big client but manage the signs and symptoms, such as sweating or rapid breathing, you may just have a case of normal stage fright, and not social anxiety disorder. And if you cut someone off in traffic or yell at a store clerk, you may just be having a bad day or be a generally ornery person. But if you're abusive, violent, manipulative, exploitive and disregard the law, you may have antisocial personality disorder, sometimes known as sociopathy.

12

Delinquency

All human life is governed by norms and values. Some of these are formally enforced by the criminal justice system (police, courts, probation service, and prisons) and others are enforced through informal social controls. (Family, friends, work colleagues and how they see themselves as individual). The informal control stops most people from stealing; only a few have to be subjected to formal controls, for some even this doesn't work. What is deviance? Deviance is to stray from the accepted path which most follow. In some cases this may involve criminal behavior but on many occasions it is just not conforming to what most people do.

No matter which country we live in, what culture we belong to, whether we are black, white, rich, poor, etc. every individual is aware that some criminal activity is going on around them. You do not have study crime to understand it's existence, many people live their lives in environments where crime is clearly visible, and in turn make their own judgments and assumptions of what is acceptable or not.

It is the reaction of society that determines how deviant an act is, if at all. Becker's labeling theory suggests that deviance is actually created by the social groups which create and promote norms and values which are deviated from, rather than the act itself. He says that by applying these rules to outsiders and labeling them as deviant, deviance is created—therefore deviance is not created by the individual who carries out the act, it is created by the labels which are attached by others to that act. Deviance could be identified as a form of social classification which is a sociological concept concerning "things" which offend a cultures expectance and social norms. Thus deviance can change over time and differ from societies, what is not accepted in one decade or society can be in another. This change of viewpoint could be due to time and the society's values changing. Downs and Rode defined deviance "As banned or controlled behavior which is likely to attract punishment or disapproval." Thus suggesting that all forms of "anti social" behavior are included, when considering deviance. As commonly understood, crime includes many different kinds of activities such as theft, robbery, corruption, assault, fraud, rape and murder. So the simplest way of defining it is to see it as "an act or omission prohibited and punished by law."

Over the years, criminologists have put forth a wide variety of theories as to what causes crime in adolescent males. In most cases, crimes by adolescent males have always appeared to lack motive, to be sometimes filled with a hatefulness that defies reason, to be part of senseless "exploratory" adolescent behavior. Most simply, juvenile crime is an umbrella term for different types of punishable conduct of young people up to the age of 18. An example of a serious crime is murder. "You must obey the authorities, not just because of God's punishment but also as a matter of conscience." To have peace within a society, there must be laws and regulations, which exist to establish that harmony to bring, maintain and promote peace. Laws are those principles, which human beings living in society have learned from experience to be essential for the survival and prosperity of the society; without laws, society would dissolve into chaos. One way in which a state promotes law and order is through the punishment of crime. A crime is an offence against a law of the state and a punishment is a suffering inflicted on a person because of a crime, which this person has committed. Murder is a serious crime.

Sociologists believe that studying theories of deviance are of "tremendous importance to anyone concerned with gaining a valid understanding of deviance in our society" (JD Douglas, 1970). It is important to note that deviance is a general concept that can cover a range of factors, including sexual behavior and mental illness.

The concept of adolescence was first found in the late nineteenth and early twentieth centuries to describe the period in between childhood and adulthood—a period containing a large amount of emotional and physical stress. The teenage years of a young person, starts off a whole new lifestyle, some get through them without any trouble while others can find it more difficult. They become more self dependent and can start to act very different due to the changes that are occurring within their body, both mental and physically. The adolescent male may start to have large mood swings, which can affect his behavior in a big way. A great many new influences come into their lives, such as alcohol, relationships with girls, which can lead to distress and violence. Violence is not a gene it is learnt either in the home or the community, some adolescents can become aggressive.

Genes come from our parents and are the cause and blueprint for every (mal) function within us. But when it comes to the function of emotions, reactions and even the rational thinking within people, how much of this influence is purely genetic? Can family shape us in anyway or is something else entirely responsible for us being different. Some of the genetic abnormalities that would make someone pre-determined would be the XYY chromosomal structure (Not effective in women, just men). A chromosomal test in prisons had an outcome of 27Y.

Historically crime causation was deemed as a form of illness, suggesting individuals were not able to control their behavior, considered mad. The early study of Phrenology was proposed by Gall who decided the brain was responsible for crime his theory was based on different parts of the brain determined individual differences. Some of these differences being lumps and bumps on our head growing differently. These theories were developed and led to those responsible for criminal behavior. Sheldon proposed Somatotyping, 3 different body shapes/build, one being indicative to aggressive criminal behavior, 'mesomorphs'. All these arguments have long since been discredited. The argument always being nature v nurture, asking if criminals are born or made? When looking to evaluate biological theories of criminality one needs to take into consideration that there are 4 factors which are explanations, Constitutional, Genetic, Biochemical and Neurological.

Are juvenile prisons there just their to punish or to reform. Also are juvenile prisons worth the tax payers' money,? Children who break the law are not supposed to be treated as adults, since they are regarded as more amenable to change then adults. Children are regarded to have less responsibility for their actions. Juvenile prisons are there to hold juveniles who have broken the law. Fundamentally as a punishment so the crime they have committed.

'Orwellian Response to Prejudice'

It has been claimed that hate crimes are an 'Orwellian response to prejudice'. How convincing are the justifications provided for such laws and what are the chief objections against them? George Orwell's novel '1984' is a fictional story in which the government attempts to control the speech, actions and even the thoughts of the public. Unacceptable thoughts are a breach of the law and are called 'thought crimes'. An 'Orwellian response to prejudice' is therefore one in which the state regulates every aspect of social life including controlling the thoughts of individuals in an attempt to wipe out the opportunity for prejudice thoughts and actions to exist. Hate crimes are like messages to members of a certain group that they are unwelcome in a particular neighborhood, community, school, or workplace. Hate crimes are criminal offenses, usually involving violence, intimidation or vandalism, in which the victim is targeted because of race, sexual orientation, religion, ethnicity, sex or political affiliation. Hate crimes can occur at home, at school, at places of worship, at work, on the street—virtually anywhere. A hate crime has many victims as it not only victimizes the immediate victim, but also impacts the larger community by creating fear and insecurity among all members of the group that the victim represents.

Social Inequalities in a Child's Life

Crime and the family Crime is sometimes popularly blamed on the family, with poor parenting, lack of discipline and family breakdown often associated with youth crime. A recurrent theme in academic research has been to investigate the relationship between delinquency and a range of family related factors. Early studies explored child-rearing behavior, parental discipline, the criminal histories of parents and family size and income. Popular theories in the 1950s and 1960s related juvenile delinquency to material deprivation, broken homes and to the growing number of 'latch key' children who were left unsupervised after school while their mothers went to work. All of these presaged current concerns with discipline and the role of single-parent families. What has emerged from this research is that some family factors are related to the likelihood of delinquency but that they must be considered in the context of the socio-economic circumstances of the family

Poor parental supervision was a powerful predictor of involvement in juvenile crime, especially for families residing in crime-prone neighborhoods. Areas with high levels of economic stress tended to have a higher incidence of child neglect, and a higher rate of juvenile and adult offending

There are many factors that influence the development and social inequalities in a child's life. These include:

- ❖ biological,
- ❖ family,
- ❖ social,
- ❖ parenting factors,

- ❖ attachment, and
- ❖ The way non-maternal care is influenced.

Social status can alter the way we perceive things and the opportunities that are presented to certain individuals. Being assigned a particular social class based on the amount of money you have, the location and size of your home, your health, and how educated you are shouldn't contribute to the problems in society. These factors play a significant role in the way youth and adults are treated.

The nature/nurture debate is considered. Youth of all ages and social class are known to commit crimes. When children and teens are treated with discrimination of any form they tend to give back what they are getting. Observational learning is one of the major issues that contribute to youth crime. High social class youth are also associated with crime and delinquency. Society does not look at high social class in the same respect as middle and low classes. lower class and upper class youth live in the same society and share the same needs and wants, but their social class makes this economically difficult to achieve. This lead to strain theory which believes people steal out of frustrated needs and wants. One theory that was studied was the Millus theory. This theory was based on social disorganization and described urban poverty areas. This theory states that these parents did not fail in teaching some values to their children; however, on the contrary, the values that were taught to the children were delinquent types of values. Another study done by Short and Strodtbeck was that poverty creates socially disabled male youths who feel comfortable only with their fellow gang members. And going a little further, Klein argued that the reactions of middle class institutions to the poor, lead the poor to criminal behavior because they are labeled as such.

There are many other factors which may cause a youth to commit deviant acts. Many people believe that it is not social class that determines this. There have been many studies attributing the crime and deviance in youth to other factors. Some of these factors include the ways of parenting, the amount of attention a child gets or the sized of a family. It has not actually proven that social class attributes to the amount of delinquency one would commit, but it does prove that there is a large number of crimes and deviant behaviors which are evident in the lower class.

Country Comparisons

When looking at different countries it was difficult to define such things as juvenile, crime and social class because all had different ways to classify such things. Therefore when looking at Japan, Scotland and Israel, I generally looked at trends involving youth and delinquency.

Japan, the land renowned for the friendly nature of its people is suddenly faced with mindless crime by its youth. Today, teenage crime is one of the country's pressing problems. The bizarre motives of the Japanese teens have been unpredictable and often deadly. Society, beset as it is with stress, tension, and impatience on everyone and the pressure faced by the youth with years of pent up anger has resulted in frightening acts. Japanese teens are sometimes the victims of bullying and end up shutting themselves together in isolated rooms for days at a time. They are known as HIKIKOMORIS and are estimated to be between half and one million youth. The government's is working hard to eliminate this problem.

Juvenile crime in Japan is characterized by the relatively young age of most of those involved. Of all juvenile's (defined in Japan as under 20 years old), charged with violating the penal code, 16 year olds account for the largest single age group, followed by 15 and 14 year olds. Most of these juveniles come from the lower class. Also, together these three groups make up 2/3 of all juvenile violators in Japan.

In Scotland, youth crime is seen as being related to such factors as low family income, low IQ and low school achievement. Youth crime is on the up rise in many parts of Scotland. Substance abuse is high, particularly in males of the middle class. In 1996 a study was completed by Hegall and Newburn. In this study they interviewed youth and asked them why they got involved in criminal activities. Most stated that it was because of boredom, lack of entertainment and "for the fun of it". Also, many youth in lower classes had a need for money (as they lacked it greatly). In their homes money was desperately needed to feed themselves and other family members; therefore they felt the hungry need to steal. Like youth in Western countries many committed delinquent acts for the thrill; irregardless of their social background.

In Israel there is a relatively low rate of crime, social deviance and violence among its youth. Despite such social strengths, there are a number of social forces that may be contributing to the problems of youth in particular. An important issue is the high rate of poverty among youth in Israel. The rates of youth poverty have risen significantly since the 1970's. Poverty is not only a problem in itself but is a major factor influencing educational achievement. Youth do not have a desire to complete school, and become bored. Because of this boredom youth have a tendency to become involved with crime and deviant acts. It is also very difficult to achieve equality of opportunity against the background of large gaps in economic circumstances among youth. Along, with increased poverty in Israeli society there has also been an increasing gap between the rich and the poor. Within Israeli society an underclass is beginning to develop as a third generation of youth is growing up to severely disadvantaged families. These families are mostly families who arrived in Israel during the period of massive immigration in the 1950's and who failed to integrate successfully into Israeli society. This group is subjected to poverty and disadvantage and the youth from this class commonly engage in deviant behavior leading to crime. In addition to its growing underclass, Israeli youth is undergoing social changes that are common to other Western countries such as substance abuse. More and more Israeli youth are drinking and using "light" drugs. Substance abuse among youth is much more common than in the past: and must less common than in other Western countries. Though crime and delinquency are probably less common in Israel than other Western countries, there are indications that these problems may be becoming more widespread.

There are no definitive answers to eliminating class in our society. And class can not solely eliminate crime. In this past this is what many criminologists believed. Class seems to have little influence over delinquency. People of all classes tend to commit the same amount of crime, it only differs in what types of crimes are being committed.

Almost all youth are deviant; it just deviates by what types of offences are being committed and how they are enforced. Lower class youth would be more prone to fighting on the streets, stealing and rug offences. They would spend more time on the street where they are in full view of the public. Upper class youth would have the ability to shield themselves from the prying eyes of the public

Personality Disorders and Traits

Personality traits and disorders have recently become essential in the diagnosis of individuals with antisocial or criminal behavior. These traits and disorders do not first become evident when an individual is an adult, rather these can be seen in children. For that reason it seems logical to discuss those personality disorders that first appear in childhood. Attention Deficit Hyperactivity Disorder (ADHD), Conduct Disorder (CD), and Oppositional Defiance Disorder (ODD) are three of the more prominent disorders that have been shown to have a relationship with later adult behavior (Holmes, Slaughter, & Kashani, 2001).

ODD is characterized by argumentativeness, noncompliance, and irritability, which can be found in early childhood (Holmes *et al.*, 2001). When a child with ODD grows older, the characteristics of their behavior also change and more often for the worse. They start to lie and steal, engage in vandalism, substance abuse, and show aggression towards peers (Holmes *et al.*, 2001). Frequently ODD is the first disorder that is identified in children and if sustained can lead to the diagnosis of CD (Morley & Hall, 2003). It is important to note however that not all children who are diagnosed with ODD will develop CD.

ADHD is associated with hyperactivity-impulsivity and the inability to keep attention focused on one thing (Morley & Hall, 2003). Holmes *et al.* (2001) state that, "impulse control dysfunction and the presence of hyperactivity and inattention are the most highly related predisposing factors for presentation of antisocial behavior" (p.184). They also point to the fact that children diagnosed with ADHD have the inability to analyze and anticipate consequences or learn from their past behavior. Children with this disorder are at risk of developing ODD and CD, unless the child is only diagnosed with Attention Deficit Disorder (ADD), in which case their chances of developing ODD or CD are limited. The future for some children is made worse when ADHD and CD are co-occurring because they will be more likely to continue their antisocial tendencies into adulthood (Holmes *et al.* 2001).

Conduct Disorder is characterized with an individual's violation of societal rules and norms (Morley & Hall, 2003). As the tendencies or behaviors of those children who are diagnosed with ODD or ADHD worsen and become more prevalent, the next logical diagnosis is CD. What is even more significant is the fact that ODD, ADHD, and CD are risk factors for developing Antisocial Personality Disorder (ASPD). This disorder can only be diagnosed when an individual is over the age of eighteen and at which point an individual shows persistent disregard for the rights of others (Morley & Hall, 2003). ASPD has been shown to be associated with an increased risk of criminal activity. Therefore, it is of great importance that these early childhood disorders are correctly diagnosed and effectively treated to prevent future problems.

Another critical aspect that must be examined regarding antisocial or criminal behavior is the personality characteristics of individuals. Two of the most cited personality traits that can be shown to have an association with antisocial or criminal behavior are impulsivity and aggression (Morley & Hall, 2003). According to the article written by Holmes *et al.* (2001), antisocial behavior between the ages of nine and fifteen can be correlated strongly with impulsivity and that aggression in early childhood can predict antisocial acts and delinquency. One statistic shows that between seventy and ninety per cent of violent offenders had been highly aggressive as young children (Holmes *et al.*, 2001). These personality traits have, in some research, been shown to be heritable.

Environmental Influences

Thus far it has been established through research and various studies that genetics do influence criminal or antisocial behavior. Researchers agree on the point that genes influence personality traits and disorders, such as the ones just mentioned. However, researchers also agree that there is an environmental component that needs to be examined. Environmental influences such as family and peers will be discussed, as well as a look into the social learning theory.

The family environment is critical to the upbringing of a child and if problems exist then the child is most likely to suffer the consequences. We have seen the problems associated with a child who is diagnosed with ADHD and how that can influence antisocial or criminal behavior. In relation to that, some researchers have claimed that it is the family environment that influences the hyperactivity of children (Schmitz, 2003). The researchers in this article specifically identify family risk factors as poverty, education, parenting practices, and family structure. Prior research on the relationship between family environment and child behavior characterizes a child's well being with a positive and caring parent-child relationship, a stimulating home environment, and consistent disciplinary techniques (Schmitz, 2003). Families with poor communication and weak family bonds have been shown to have a correlation with children's development of aggressive/criminal behavior (Garnefski & Okma 1996). Therefore it seems obvious to conclude that those families who are less financially sound, perhaps have more children, and who are unable to consistently punish their children will have a greater likelihood of promoting an environment that will influence antisocial or delinquent behavior. Another indicator of future antisocial or criminal behavior is that of abuse or neglect in childhood. A statistic shows that children are at a fifty per cent greater risk of engaging in criminal acts, if they were neglected or abused (Holmes *et al.* 2001). This has been one of the most popular arguments as to why children develop antisocial or delinquent behaviors.

One additional research finding in the debate between genetic and environmental influences on antisocial or criminal behavior has to deal with the age of the individual. Research seems consistent in recognizing that heritability influences adult behavior more than environmental influences, but that for children and adolescents the environment is the most significant factor influencing their behavior (Rhee & Waldman, 2002). As an adult, we have the ability to choose the environment in which to live and this will either positively or negatively reinforce our personality traits, such as aggressiveness. However, children and adolescents are limited to the extent of choosing an environment, which accounts for the greater influence of environmental factors in childhood behaviors.

Another significant factor in the development of antisocial or delinquent behavior in adolescence is peer groups. Garnefski and Okma (1996) state that there is a correlation between the involvement in an antisocial or delinquent peer group and problem behavior. One of the primary causes as to why this occurs can be traced back to aggressive behavior in young children. When children are in preschool and show aggressive tendencies towards their peers, they will likely be deemed as an outcast. This creates poor peer relationships and relegates those children to be with others who share similar behaviors. A relationship like this would most likely continue into adolescence and maybe even further into adulthood. The similar tendencies of these individuals create an environment in which they influence one another and push the problem towards criminal or violent behavior (Holmes *et al.*, 2001).

Social learning theory has been cited as way to explain how the environment can influence a child's behavior. Using this theory to explain the aggressive or antisocial behavior of a child means that a child observes aggressive behavior between parents, siblings, or both. As a result, the children believes that this aggressive behavior is normal and can therefore use it themselves because they do not see the harm in acting similar to their parents (Miles, & Carey, 1997). As stated earlier, interaction between family members and disciplinary techniques are influential in creating antisocial behavior. Using the social learning theory these two factors are also critical in the development of aggression. Children who are raised in an aggressive family environment would most likely be susceptible to experiencing a lack of parental monitoring, permissiveness or inconsistency in punishment, parental rejection and aggression. The exposure to such high levels of aggression and other environmental factors greatly influences and reinforces a child's behavior. A significant point that should be known however is the fact that other research has supported the notion that genetics do influence levels of aggression, which stands in opposition to the social learning theory (Miles & Carey, 1997).

Gene-Environment Interactions

There are theories, however, concerning genetic and environmental influences, which seem to suggest an interaction between the two and one such theory is the general arousal theory of criminality. Personality psychologist Eysenck created a model based on three factors known as psychoticism, extraversion, and neuroticism, or what is referred to as the PEN model (Eysenck, 1996). Psychoticism was associated with the traits of aggressive, impersonal, impulsive, cold, antisocial, and un-empathetic. Extraversion was correlated with the traits of sociable, lively, active, sensation-seeking, carefree, dominant, and assertive. Finally, neuroticism was associated with anxious, depressed, low self-esteem, irrational, moody, emotional, and tense (Eysenck, 1996). Through research and surveys, Eysenck found that these three factors could be used as predictors of criminal behavior. He believed this to be especially true of the psychoticism factor and that measuring it could predict the difference between criminals and non-criminals. Extraversion was a better predictor for young individuals, while neuroticism was a better predictor for older individuals (Eysenck, 1996). An important point about these factors and the personality traits associated with them is that most of them have already been found to be heritable (Miles & Carey, 1997).

Understanding Eysenck's original model is critical to assessing the general arousal theory of criminality, which suggests an interaction between factors. Research has shown that criminality is strongly correlated with low arousal levels in the brain. Characteristics related to low arousal levels include lack of interest, sleepiness, lack of attention, and loss of vigilance. Eysenck (1996) believed that these characteristics were similar to the personality factor of extraversion. Individuals with low arousal levels and those who are extraverts need to seek out stimulation because they do not have enough already in their brains. Therefore, the premise of the general arousal theory of criminality is that individuals inherit a nervous system that is unresponsive to low levels of stimulation and as a consequence, these individuals have to seek out the proper stimulation to increase their arousal. Under this theory, the proper stimulation includes high-risk activities associated with antisocial behavior, which consists of sexual promiscuity, substance abuse, and crime (Miles & Carey, 1997). A significant fact that must be pointed out though is that not every individual with low arousal levels or those who are extraverts will seek those high risk activities just mentioned. It takes the right environment and personality to create an individual with antisocial or criminal tendencies and that is why this theory can be considered to take into account both factors of genetic and environmental influences.

Conclusion

There cannot be enough possible evidence to conclude the point that genetics play the most important role in the outcome or behavior of an individual. The opposing viewpoint of environmental factors is not without its doubts either as to being the prominent factor influencing antisocial or criminal behavior of an individual. In this paper, there is more evidence supporting the genetics viewpoint, but that does not mean it is more important. With the research and studies having numerous flaws and the inability to adequately separate nature and nurture, there is still a great debate between genetic and environmental factors.

Researchers, however, have certainly come far in their progression, to the point where there is a large consensus of the fact that genes do influence behavior to a certain extent. Although not as widely publicized, it is the belief of the author that these same researchers also believe that environmental factors account for what cannot be explained by genes. Therefore it seems obvious to reach the conclusion that an individual's antisocial or criminal behavior can be the result of both their genetic background and the environment in which they were raised.

One researcher has proposed a theory relating to sociopaths and their antisocial behavior. According to the theory, a primary sociopath is lacking in moral development and does not feel socially responsible for their actions. This type of sociopath is a product of the individual's personality, physiotype, and genotype. A secondary sociopath develops in response to his or her environment because of the disadvantages of social competition. Living in an urban residence, having a low socioeconomic status, or poor social skills can lead an individual to being unsuccessful in reaching their needs in a socially desirable way, which can turn into antisocial or criminal behavior. The first type of sociopath is dependent on their genetic makeup and personality, while certain factors of the second type can also be heritable. Notwithstanding, the second type has a greater dependence on environmental factors (Miles & Carey, 1997). Perhaps from this review of both genetic and environmental factors, it seems clear to support the idea of the secondary sociopath type. An individual can inherit certain genes and when combined with the right environmental factors can lead them to engage in antisocial or criminal behavior.

Although not mentioned extensively in the text of the paper, there is a great need to try and identify those individuals, especially children, who may become susceptible to certain disorders or personality traits that can lead into antisocial, delinquent, or criminal behavior. Society should not try to imitate the era of controlled breeding, but rather focus on the treatment and rehabilitation of those individuals in need. Certain educational, environment enrichment programs have been shown to have a lasting effect on children if given by a certain age (Raine, Mellingen, Liu, Venables, & Mednick, 2003). If more of these programs could be developed, society could help prevent the future antisocial or criminal behavior of children.

Criminality is a Product of Genes and Environment

In considering the roles of genetics and environment on criminal behavior, or any behavior for that matter, the best explanation is that there is a complex interaction between one's inherited traits and the environment in which he or she lives. Although the idea of environmental influences seems rather intuitive, regardless of knowledge regarding heredity and biological factors, it is surprising that some may have considered criminal behavior to be solely a result of genetics.

Despite the relative lack of reliability and validity in twin, adoption, and family studies, they still provide valuable insight into the roles of heredity and environment in criminal behavior. However, it seems that most studies of this kind focus on the role of heredity in influencing behavior. It would be interesting to see whether any studies with adopted children have examined the role of environment in criminal behavior. Most adoption studies examine the correlation between criminality in the biological parents of adopted children, but what about the correlation between the children and their adopted parents who are crucial to their environment?

The influence of neuro-chemicals on criminal and antisocial behavior is indicative of a genetic component to such behaviors. However, they reflect the complex interactions between genetics and environment. There is evidence that the expression of genes is influenced by a wide variety of environmental factors. Therefore, it is very possible that disorders relating to such chemicals as serotonin and dopamine could be caused by stressful environmental situations. If environment affects the regulation of gene expression and, in turn, the activity of neurotransmitters that modulate behavior, this kind of interaction may be a significant factor in the development of criminal and antisocial behavior.

Inherited traits provide the foundation by which people are able to learn and respond to their environment. An adult's personality is the combination of traits and learned behavior patterns that have been established throughout childhood. Thus, although it is true that adults have more control over their current environment, they are still heavily influenced by both their current environment and by past exposure to environmental factors.

The social learning theory is a good way to explain the influence of environment on antisocial behavior in children, and does not necessarily have to oppose the notion of genetic influence on behavior as well. Rather, it should be considered part of a larger theory or model that could describe how environment and genetics interact. Eysenck's general arousal theory, which suggests such an interaction, could be modified to encompass the social learning theory, providing a more complete model to explain how upbringing and inherited traits interact to influence criminal behavior.

Secondary sociopath type; Genetics and environmental factors are so intertwined, that it seems impossible to separate them in explaining how people are caused to engage in criminal acts. it is important for society as a whole to take responsibility in preventing the advent of criminal and antisocial behavior in children via programs to provide children with healthy, enriching environments. A eugenic approach to preventing antisocial behavior is immoral and impinges on human rights, but taking an active approach to ensure positive environmental influences would be appropriate.

In India

Juvenile Justice (Care and Protection of Children) Act, 2006

Section 21 of the Juvenile Justice (Care and Protection of Children) Act, 2006 enacted by the Government of India which prohibits publication of the name, address or any other particulars calculated to lead to the identification of the juvenile(s) involved in the incident. In India, this is not the first time media has taken the law of the land for a ride in such instances. The legal position in this context as follows: Section 21 of the Juvenile Justice (Care and Protection of Children) Act, 2000 (56 of 2000) as amended by the Juvenile Justice (Care and Protection of Children) Amendment Act, 2006 (33 of 2006)., states that: "Prohibition of publication of name, etc., of juvenile or child in need of care and protection involved in any proceeding under the Act-(1) No report in any newspaper, magazine, news-sheet or visual media of any inquiry regarding a juvenile in conflict with law or a child in need of care and protection under this Act shall disclose the name, address or school or any other particulars calculated to lead to the identification of the juvenile or child shall nor shall any picture of any such juvenile or child shall be published: Provided that for any reason to be recorded in writing, the authority holding the inquiry may permit such disclosure, if in its opinion such disclosure is in the interest of the juvenile or the child. (2) Any person who contravenes the provisions of sub-section (1), shall be liable to a penalty which may extend to twenty-five thousand rupees".

In India, the National Commission for Protection of Child Rights, as per section 13(1)(a) of the Commission for Protection of Child Rights Act, 2005 can examine the safeguards provided by or under the Juvenile Justice Act (Care and Protection) of Children Act, 2000 and also recommend measures for the effective implementation of the safeguards provided.

Further, as per section 13(1) (c) of the Commission for Protection of Child Rights Act, 2005 this Commission can inquire into violation of child rights and proceedings in such cases. In addition, as per section 13(1)(j) of the Commission for Protection of Child Rights Act, 2005 this Commission can inquire into complaints and take suo motu notice of matters relating to depravation and violation of child rights and non implementation of laws providing for protection and development of children.

The Juvenile Justice (Care And Protection Of Children) Act, 2000

[30th December, 2000]

An Act to consolidate and amend the law relating to juveniles in conflict with law and children in need of care and protection, by providing for proper care, protection and treatment by catering to their development needs, and by adopting a child-friendly approach in the adjudication and disposition of matters in the best interest of children and for their ultimate rehabilitation through various institutions established under this enactment.

WHEREAS the Constitution has, in several provisions, including clause (3) of article 15, clauses (e) and (f) of article 39, articles 45 and 47, impose on the State a primary responsibility of ensuring that all the needs of children are met and that their basic human rights are fully protected;

AND WHEREAS, the General Assembly of the United Nations has

adopted the Convention on the Rights of the Child on the 20th November, 1989;

AND WHEREAS, the Convention on the Rights of the Child has prescribed a set of standards to be adhered to by all State parties in securing the best interests of the child;

AND WHEREAS, the Convention on the Rights of the Child emphasises social reintegration of child victims, to the extent possible, without resorting to judicial proceedings;

AND WHEREAS, the Government of India has ratified the Convention on the 11th December, 1992.

AND WHEREAS, it is expedient to re-enact the existing law relating to juveniles bearing in mind the standards prescribed in the Convention on the Rights of the Child, the United Nations Standard Minimum Rules for the Administration of Juvenile Justice, 1985 (the Beijing rules), the United Nations Rules for the Protection of Juveniles Deprived of their Liberty (1990), and all other relevant international instruments.

BE it enacted by Parliament in the Fifty-first Year of the Republic of India as follows:

CHAPTER I
Preliminary

1. Short title, extent and commencement—(1) This Act may be called the Juvenile Justice (Care and Protection of Children) Act, 2000.

(2) It extends to the Whole of India except the State of Jammu and Kashmir.

(3) It shall come into force on such date as the Central Government may, by notification in the Official Gazette, appoint.

2. Definitions—In this Act, unless the context otherwise requires—
(a) "advisory board" means a Central or a state advisory board or a district and city level advisory board, as the case may be, constituted under section 62; (b) "begging" means—

(i) soliciting or receiving alms in a public place or entering into any private premises for the purpose of soliciting or receiving alms, whether under any pretence;

(ii) exposing or exhibiting with the object of obtaining or extorting alms, any sore, wound, injury, deformity or disease, whether of himself or of any other person or of an animal;

(c) "Board" means a Juvenile Justice Board constituted under section 4;

(d) "child in need of care and protection" means a child—

(i) who is found without any home or settled place or abode and without any ostensible means of subsistence,

(ii) who resides with a person (whether a guardian of the child or not) and such person-

(a) has threatened to kill or injure the child and there is a reasonable likelihood of the threat being carried out, or

(b) has killed, abused or neglected some other child or children and there is a reasonable likelihood of the child in question being killed, abused or neglected by that person,

(ii) who is mentally or physically challenged or ill children or children suffering from terminal diseases or incurable diseases having no one to support or look after,

(iv) who has a parent or guardian and such parent or guardian is unfit or incapacitated to exercise control over the child,

(v) who does not have parent and no one is willing to take care of or whose parents have abandoned him or who is missing and run away child and whose parents cannot be found after reasonable injury,

(vi) who is being or is likely to be grossly abused, tortured or exploited for the purpose of sexual abuse or illegal acts,

(vii) who is found vulnerable and is likely to be inducted into drug abuse or trafficking,

(viii) who is being or is likely to be abused for unconscionable gains,

(ix) who is victim of any armed conflict, civil commotion or natural calamity;

(e) "children's home" means an institution established by a State Government or by voluntary organisation and certified by that Government under section 34;

(f) "Committee" means a Child Welfare Committee constituted under section 29;

(g) "competent authority" means in relation to children in need of care and protection a Committee and in relation to juveniles in conflict with law a Board;

(h) "fit institution" means a governmental or a registered non-governmental organisation or a voluntary organisation prepared to own the responsibility of a child and such organisation is found fit by the competent authority;

(i) "fit person" means a person, being a social worker or any other person, who is prepared to own the responsibility of a child and is found fit by the competent authority to receive and take care of the child;

(j) "guardian", in relation to a child, means his natural guardian or any other person having the actual charge or control over the child and recognised by the competent authority as a guardian in course of proceedings before that authority;

(k) "juvenile" or "child" means a person who has not completed eighteenth year of age;

(l) "juvenile in conflict with law" means a juvenile who is alleged to have committed an offence;

(m) "local authority" means Panchayats at the village and Zila Parishad at the district level and shall also include a Municipal Committee or Corporation or a Cantonment Board or such other body legally entitled to function as local authority by the Government;

(n) "narcotic drug" and "psychotropic substance" shall have the meanings respectively assigned to them in the Narcotic Drugs and Psychotropic Substances Act, 1985 (61 of 1985);

(o) "observation home" means a home established by a State Government or by a voluntary organisation and certified by that State Government under section 8 as an observation home for the juvenile in conflict with law;

(p) "offence" means an offence punishable under any law for the time being in force;

(q) "place of safety" means any place or institution (not being a police lock-up or jail), the person incharge of which is willing temporarily to receive and take care of the juvenile and which, in the opinion of the competent authority, may be a place of safety for the juvenile;

(r) "prescribed" means prescribed by rules made under this act;

(s) "Probation officer" means an officer appointed by the State Government as a probation officer under the Probation of Offenders Act, 1958 (20 of 1958);

(t) "public place" shall have the meaning assigned to it in the Immoral Traffic (Prevention) Act, 1956 (104 of 1956);

(u) "shelter home" means a home or a drop-in-centre set up under section 37;

(v) "special home" means an institution established by a State Government or by a voluntary organisation and certified by that Government under section 9;

(w) "special juvenile police unit" means a unit of the police force of a State designated for handling of juveniles or children under section 63;

(x) "State Government", in relation to a Union territory, means the Administrator of that Union territory appointed by the President under article 239 of the Constitution;

(y) all words and expressions used but not defined in this Act and defined in the Code of Criminal Procedure, 1973 (2 of 1974), shall have the meanings respectively assigned to them in that code.

3. Continuation of Inquiry in respect of juvenile who has ceased to be a juvenile—Where an inquiry has been initiated against a juvenile in conflict with law or a child in need of care and protection and during the course of such inquiry the juvenile or the child ceases to be such, then, notwithstanding anything contained in this Act or in any other law for the time being in force, the inquiry may be continued and orders may be made in respect of such person as if such person had continued to be a juvenile or a child.

Juvenile in Conflict with Law

4. Juvenile Justice Board—1. Notwithstanding anything contained in the Code of Criminal Procedure, 1973 (2 of 1974), the State Government may, by notification in the Official Gazette, constitute for a district or a group of districts specified in the notification, one or more Juvenile Justice Boards for exercising the powers and discharging the duties conferred or imposed on such Boards in relation to juveniles in conflict with law under this act.

2. A Board shall consist of a Metropolitan Magistrate or a Judicial Magistrate of the first class, as the case may be, and two social workers of whom at least one shall be a woman, forming a Bench and every such Bench shall have the powers conferred by the Code of Criminal Procedure, 1973 (2 of 1974), on a Metropolitan Magistrate or, as the case may be, a Judicial Magistrate of the first class and the Magistrate on the Board shall be designated as the principal Magistrate.

3. No Magistrate shall be appointed as a member of the Board unless he has special knowledge or training in child psychology or child welfare and no social worker shall be appointed as a member of the Board unless he has been actively involved in health,

education, or welfare activities pertaining to children for at least seven years.

4. The term of office of the members of the Board and the manner in which such member may resign shall be such as may be prescribed.

5. The appointment of any member of the Board may be terminated after holding inquiry, by the State Government, if -

    i) he has been found guilty of misuse of power vested under this act,

    ii) he has been convicted of an offence involving moral turpitude, and such conviction has not been reversed or he has not been granted full pardon in respect of such offence,

    iii) he fails to attend the proceedings of the Board foe consecutive three months without any valid reason or he fails to attend less than three-fourth of the sittings in a year.

Comments

The State Government has been authorised to constitute for a district or a group of districts one or more Juvenile Boards for exercising the powers and discharging the duties, conferred or imposed on such Boards in relation to Juveniles in conflict with the law under this act. The Board shall consist of a Metropolitan Magistrate or a Judicial Magistrate of the first class, as the case may be, and two social workers of whom at least one shall be a woman.

5. Procedure, etc. in relation to Board—(1) The Board shall meet at such times and shall, observe such rules of procedure in regard to the transaction of business at its meetings, as may be prescribed.

(2) A child in conflict with law may be produced before an individual member of the Board, when the Board is not sitting.

(3) A Board may act notwithstanding the absence of any member of the Board, and no order made by the Board shall be invalid by reason only of the absence of any member during any stage of proceedings:

Provided that there shall be at least two members including the principal Magistrate present at the time of final disposal of the case.

(4) In the event of any difference of opinion among the members of the Board in the interim or final disposition, the opinion of the majority shall prevail, but where there is no such majority, the opinion of the principal Magistrate, shall prevail.

Comments

A child in conflict with law can be produced before an individual member of the Board, when the Board is not sitting.

6. Powers of Juvenile Justice Board—(1) Where a Board has been constituted for any district or a group of districts, such Board shall, notwithstanding anything contained in any other law for the time being in force but save as otherwise expressly provided in this Act, have power to deal exclusively with all proceedings under this Act, relating to juvenile in conflict with law.

(2) The powers conferred on the Board by or under this Act may also be exercised by the High Court and the Court of Session, when the proceedings comes before them in appeal, revision or otherwise.

7. Procedure to be followed by a Magistrate not empowered under the Act—(1) When any Magistrate not empowered to exercise the powers of a Board under this Act is of the opinion that a person brought before him under any of the provisions of this Act (other than for the purpose of giving evidence), is a juvenile or the child, he shall without any delay record such opinion and forward the juvenile or the child, and the record of the proceeding to the competent authority having jurisdiction over the proceeding.

(2) The competent authority to which the proceeding is forwarded under sub-section (1) shall hold the inquiry as if the juvenile or the child had originally been brought before it.

8. Observation homes—(1) Any State Government may establish and maintain either by itself or under an agreement with voluntary organisations, observation homes in every district or a group of districts, as may be required for the temporary reception of any juvenile in conflict with law during the pendency of any inquiry regarding them under this Act.

(2) Where the State Government is of opinion that any institution other than a home established or maintained under sub-section (1), is fit for the temporary reception of juvenile in conflict with law during the pendency of any inquiry regarding them under this Act, it may certify such substitution as an observation home for purposes of this Act.

(3) The State Government may, by rules made under this Act, provide for the management of observation homes, including the standards and various types of services to be provided by them for rehabilitation and social integration of a juvenile, and the

circumstances under which, and the manner in which, the certification of an observation home may be granted or withdrawn.

(4) Every juvenile who is not placed under the charge of parent or guardian and is sent to an observation home shall be initially kept in a reception unit of the observation home for preliminary inquiries, care and classification for juveniles according to his age group, such as seven to twelve years, twelve to sixteen years and sixteen to eighteen years, giving due considerations to physical and mental status and degree of the offence committed, for further induction into observation home.

Comments

State Governments have been empowered to establish and maintain either by themselves or under an agreement with voluntary organisations, observation homes in every district or a group of districts as may be required for the temporary reception of any juvenile in conflict with law during the pendency of any inquiry regarding them. State Governments have also been empowered to certify any institution, other than a home established or maintained by themselves or under an agreement with voluntary organisations, as an observation home for this purposes of this Act.

9. Special Homes—(1) Any State Government may establish and maintain either by itself or under an agreement with voluntary organisations, special homes in every district or a group of districts, as may be required for reception and rehabilitation of juvenile in conflict with law under this Act.

(2) Where the State Government is of opinion that any institution other than a home established or maintained under sub-section (1), is fit for the reception of juvenile in conflict with law to be sent there under this Act, it may certify such institution as a special home for the purposes of this Act.

(3) The State Government may, by rules made under this Act, provide for the management of special homes, including the standards and various types of services to be provided by them which are necessary for re-socialisation of a juvenile, and the circumstances under which and the manner in which, the certification of a special home may be granted or withdrawn.

(4) The rules made under sub-section (3) may also provide for the classification and separation of juvenile in conflict with law on

the basis of age and the nature of offences committed by them and his mental and physical status.

Comments

State Governments have been empowered to establish and maintain, either by themselves or under an agreement with voluntary organisations, special homes in every district or a group of districts for the reception and rehabilitation of juvenile in conflict with law. State Governments have also been empowered to certify any institution, other than a home established or maintained by themselves or under an agreement with voluntary organisations, that it is fit for the reception of juvenile in conflict with law.

10. Apprehension of juvenile in conflict with law—(1) As soon as a juvenile in conflict with law is apprehended by police, he shall be placed under the charge of the special juvenile police unit or the designated police officer who shall immediately report the matter to a member of the Board.

(2) The State Government may make rules consistent with this Act,— to provide for persons through whom (including registered voluntary organisations) any juvenile in conflict with law may be produced before the Board; to provide the manner in which such juvenile may be sent to an observation home.

Comments

When a juvenile in conflict with law is apprehended by police, he has to be placed under the charge of the special juvenile police unit or the designated police officer who shall immediately report the matter to a member of the Board.

11. Control of custodian over juvenile—Any person in whose charge a juvenile is placed in pursuance of this Act shall, while the order is in force have the control over the juvenile as he would have if he were his parents, and shall be responsible for his maintenance, and the juvenile shall continue in his charge for the period stated by competent authority, notwithstanding that he is claimed by his parents or any other person.

Comments

When any juvenile is placed in the charge of a person he shall have the control over the juvenile as he would have if he were his parents, and shall be responsible for his maintenance and the juvenile shall continue in his charge for the period stated by the competent authority.

12. Bail of juvenile (1) When any person accused of a bailable or non-bailable offence, and apparently a juvenile, is arrested or detained or appears or is brought before a Board, such person shall, notwithstanding anything contained in the Code of Criminal Procedure, 1973 (2 of 1974) or in any other law for the time being in force, be released on bail with or without surety but he shall not be so released if there appear reasonable grounds for believing that the release is likely to bring him into association with any known criminal or expose him to moral, physical or psychological danger or that his release would defeat the ends of justice.

(2) When such person having been arrested is not released on bail under sub-section (1) by the officer incharge of the police station, such officer shall cause him to be kept only in an observation home in the prescribed manner until he can brought before a Board.

(3) When such person is not released on bail under sub-section (1) by the Board it shall, instead of committing him to prison, make an order sending him to an observation home or a place of safety for such period during the pendency of the inquiry regarding him as may be specified in the order.

13. Information to parent, guardian or probation officer—Where a juvenile is arrested, the officer incharge of the police station or the special juvenile police unit to which the juvenile is brought shall, as soon as may be after the arrest, inform—

(a) the parent or guardian of the juvenile, if he can be found, of such arrest and direct him to be present at the Board before which the juvenile will appear; and

(b) the probation officer of such arrest to enable him to obtain information regarding the antecedents and family background of the juvenile and other material circumstances likely to be of assistance to the Board for making the inquiry.

Comments

When any juvenile is arrested, the officer in charge of the police station or the special juvenile police unit to which the juvenile is brought, as soon as may be after the arrest, has to inform the parent or guardian of the juvenile about his arrest and direct him to be present at the Board before which the juvenile will appear and he has also to inform the probation officer of such arrest to enable him to obtain information regarding the antecedents and family background of the juvenile.

14. Inquiry by Board regarding juvenile—Where a juvenile having been charged with the offence is produced before a Board, the Board shall hold the inquiry in accordance with the provisions of this Act and may make such order in relation to the juvenile as it deems fit:

Provided that an inquiry under this section shall be completed within a period of four months from the date of its commencement, unless the period is extended by the Board having regard to the circumstances of the case and in special cases after recording the reasons in writing for such extension.

15. Order that may be passed regarding juvenile—(1) Where a Board is satisfied on inquiry that a juvenile has committed an offence, then notwithstanding anything to the contrary contained in any other law for the time being in force, the Board may, if it thinks so fit,—

(a) allow the juvenile to go home after advice or admonition following appropriate inquiry against and counselling to the parent or the guardian and the juvenile;

(b) direct the juvenile to participate in group counselling and similar activities;

(c) order the juvenile to perform community service;

(d) order the parent of the juvenile or the juvenile himself to pay a fine, if he is over fourteen years of age and earns money;

(e) direct the juvenile to be released on probation of good conduct and placed under the care of any parent, guardian or other fit person, on such parent, guardian or other fit person executing a bond, with or without surety, as the Board may require, for the good behaviour and well-being of the juvenile for any period not exceeding three years;

(f) direct the juvenile to be released on probation of good conduct and placed under the care of any fit institution for the good behaviour and well-being of the juvenile for any period not exceeding three years;

(g) make an order directing the juvenile to be sent to a special home,—

(i) in the case of juvenile, over seventeen years but less than eighteen years of age for a period of not less than two years;

(ii) in case of any other juvenile for the period until he ceases to be a juvenile:

(2) Provided that the Board may, if it is satisfied that having regard to the nature of the offence and the circumstances of the case it is expedient so to do, for reasons to be recorded, reduce the period of stay to such period as it thinks fit.

(3) The Board shall obtain the social investigation report on juvenile either through a probation officer or a recognised voluntary organisation or otherwise, and shall take into consideration the findings of such report before passing an order.

Where an order under clause (d), clause (e) or clause (f) of sub-section (1) is made, the Board may, if it is of opinion that in the interests of the juvenile and of the public, it is expedient so to do, in addition make an order that the juvenile in conflict with law shall remain under the supervision of a probation officer named in the order during such period, not exceeding three years as may be specified therein, and may in such supervision order impose such conditions as it deems necessary for the due supervision of the juvenile in conflict with law:

Provided that if at any time afterwards it appears to the Board on receiving a report from the probation officer or otherwise, that the juvenile in conflict with law has not been of good behaviour during the period of supervision or that the fit institution under whose care the juvenile was placed is no longer able or willing to ensure the good behaviour and well-being of the juvenile it may, after making such inquiry as it deems fit, order the juvenile in conflict with law to be sent to a special home.

(4) The Board shall while making a supervision order under sub-section (3), explain to the juvenile and the parent, guardian or other fit person or fit institution, as the case may be, under whose care the juvenile has been placed, the terms and conditions of the order shall forthwith furnish one copy of the supervision order to the juvenile, the parent, guardian or other fit person or fit institution, as the case may be, the sureties, if any, and the probation officer.

16. Order that may not be passed against juvenile—(1) Notwithstanding anything to the contrary contained in any other law for the time being in force, no juvenile in conflict with law shall be sentenced to death or life imprisonment, or committed to prison in default of payment of fine or in default of furnishing security:

Provided that where a juvenile who has attained the age of sixteen years has committed an offence and the Board is satisfied that the offence committed is of so serious in nature or that his conduct and behaviour have been such that it would not be in his interest or in the interest of other juvenile in a special home to send him to such special home and that none of the other measures provided under this Act is suitable or sufficient, the Board may order the juvenile in conflict with law to be kept in such place of safety and in such manner as it thinks fit and shall report the case for the order of the State Government.

(2) On receipt of a report from a Board under sub-section (1), the State Government may make such arrangement in respect of the juvenile as it deems proper and may order such juvenile to be kept under protective custody at such place and on such conditions as it thinks fit:

Provided that the period of detention so ordered shall not exceed the maximum period of imprisonment to which the juvenile could have been sentenced for the offence committed.

17. Proceeding under Chapter VIII of the Code of Criminal Procedure not component against juvenile—Notwithstanding anything to the contrary contained in the Code of Criminal Procedure, 1973 (2 of 1974) no proceeding shall be instituted and no order shall be passed against the juvenile under Chapter VIII of the said Code.

18. No joint proceeding of juvenile and person not a juvenile— (1) Notwithstanding anything contained in section 223 of the Code of Criminal Procedure, 1973 (2 of 1974) or in any other law for the time being in force, no juvenile shall be charged with or tried for any offence together with a person who is not a juvenile.

(2) If a juvenile is accused of an offence for which under section 223 of the Code of Criminal Procedure, 1973 (2 of 1974) or any other law for the time being in force, such juvenile and any person who is not a juvenile would, but for the prohibition contained in sub-section (1), have been charged and tried together, the Board taking cognizance of that offence shall direct separate trials of the juvenile and the other person.

Comments

No juvenile can be charged with or tried for any offence together with a person who is not a juvenile.

19. Removal of disqualification attaching to conviction—(1) Notwithstanding anything contained in any other law, a juvenile who has committed an offence and has been dealt with under the provisions of this Act shall not suffer disqualification, if any, attaching to a conviction of an offence under such law.

(2) The Board shall make an order directing that the relevant records of such conviction shall be removed after the expiry of the period of appeal or a reasonable period as prescribed under the rules, as the case may be.

20. Special provision in respect of pending cases—Notwithstanding anything contained in this Act, all proceedings in respect of a juvenile pending in any court in any area on the date on which this Act comes into force in that area, shall be continued in that court as if this Act had not been passed and if the court finds that the juvenile has committed an offence, it shall record such finding and instead of passing any sentence in respect of the juvenile, forward the juvenile to the Board which shall pass orders in respect of that juvenile in accordance with the provisions of this Act as if it had been satisfied on inquiry under this Act that a juvenile has committed the offence.

21. Prohibition of publication of name, etc., of juvenile involved in any proceeding under the Act—(1) No report in any newspaper, magazine, news-sheet or visual media of any inquiry regarding a juvenile in conflict with law under this Act shall disclose the name, address or school or any other particulars calculated to lead to the identification of the juvenile nor shall any picture of any such juvenile be published:

Provided that for reasons to be recorded in writing the authority holding the inquiry may permit such disclosure, if in its opinion such disclosure is in interest of the juvenile.

(2) Any person contravening the provisions of sub-section (1) shall be punishable with fine, which may extend to one thousand rupees.

Comments

Newspapers, magazines, news-sheet or visual media have been prohibited to disclose the name, address or school or any other particulars calculated to lead to the identification of the juvenile in conflict with law nor they can publish any picture of such juvenile. Any person who contravenes this provision shall be punishable with fine upto one thousand rupees.

22. Provision in Respect of Escaped Juveniles—Notwithstanding anything to the contrary contained in any other law for the time being in force, any police officer may take charge without warrant of a juvenile in conflict with law who has escaped from a special home or an observation home or from the care of a person under whom he was placed under this Act, and shall be sent back to the special home or the observation home or that person, as the case may be; and no proceeding shall be instituted in respect of the juvenile by reason of such escape, but the special home, or the observation home or the person may, after giving the information to the Board which passed the order in respect of the juvenile, take such steps in respect of the juvenile as may be deemed necessary under the provisions of this Act.

23. Punishment for cruelty to juvenile or child—Whoever, having the actual charge of, or control over, a juvenile or the child, assaults, abandons, exposes or willfully neglects the juvenile or causes or procures him to be assaulted, abandoned, exposed or neglected in a manner likely to cause such juvenile or the child unnecessary mental or physical suffering shall be punishable with imprisonment for a team which may extend to six months, or fine, or with both.

Comments

If any person having the actual charge of, or control over, a juvenile or the child, assaults, abandons, exposes or willfully neglects the juvenile or causes or procures him to be assaulted, abandoned, exposed or neglected in any manner likely to cause such juvenile or the child unnecessary mental or physical suffering, he shall be punishable with imprisonment upto six months, or fine, or with both.

24. Employment of juvenile or child for begging—(1) Whoever employs or uses any juvenile or the child for the purpose or causes any juvenile to beg shall be punishable with imprisonment for a term which may extend to three years and shall also be liable to fine.

(2) Whoever, having the actual charge of, or control over, a juvenile or the child abets the commission of the offence punishable under subsection (1), shall be punishable with imprisonment for a term which may extend to one year and shall also be liable to fine.

25. Penalty for giving intoxicating liquor or narcotic drug or psychotropic substance to juvenile or child—Whoever gives, or causes to be given, to any juvenile or the child any intoxicating liquor in a public place or any narcotic drug or psychotropic substance except upon the order of duly qualified medical practitioner or in case of sickness shall be punishable with imprisonment for a term which may extend to three years and shall be liable to fine.

26. Exploitation of juvenile or child employee—Whoever ostensibly procures a juvenile or the child for the purpose of any hazardous employment keeps him in bondage and withholds his earnings or uses such earning for his own purposes shall be punishable with imprisonment for a term which may extend to three years and shall be liable to fine.

27. Special offences—The offences punishable under sections 23, 24, 25 and 26 shall be cognizable.

28. Alternative punishment—Where an act or omission constitute an offence punishable under this Act and also under any other Central or State Act, then, notwithstanding anything contained in any law for the time being in force, the offender found guilty of such offences shall be liable to punishment only under such Act as provides for punishment which is greater in degree.

Child in Need of Care and Protection

29. Child Welfare Committee—(1) The State Government may, by notification in Official Gazette, constitute for every district or group of districts, specified in the notification, one or more Child Welfare Committees for exercising the powers and discharge the duties conferred on such Committees in relation to child in need of care and protection under this Act.

(2) The Committee shall consist of a Chairperson and four other members as the State Government may think fit to appoint, of whom at least one shall be a woman and another, an expert on matters concerning children.

(3) The qualifications of the Chairperson and the members, and the tenure for which they may be appointed shall be such as may be prescribed.

(4) The appointment of any member of the Committee may be terminated, after holding inquiry, by the State Government, if-

    (i) he has been found guilty of misuse of power vested under this Act;

    (ii) he has been convicted of an offence involving moral turpitude, and such conviction has not been reversed or he has not been granted full pardon in respect of such offence;

    (iii) he fails to attend the proceedings of the Committee for consecutive three months without any valid reason or he fails to attend less than three-fourth of the sittings in a year.

(5) The Committee shall function as a Bench of Magistrates and shall have the powers conferred by the Code of Criminal Procedure, 1973 (2 of 1974) on a Metropolitan Magistrate or, as the case may be, a Judicial Magistrate of the first class.

Comments

State Governments have been empowered to constitute for every district or group of districts one or more Child Welfare Committees for exercising the powers and discharge the duties in relation to child in need of care and protection under the Act. The Committee shall consist of a Chairperson and four other members, of whom at least one shall be a woman and another an expert on matters concerning children.

30. Procedure, etc., in relation to Committee—(1) The Committee shall meet at such times and shall observe such rules of procedure in regard to the transaction of business at its meetings, as may be prescribed.

(2) A child in need of care and protection may be produced before an individual member for being placed in safe custody or otherwise when the Committee is not in session.

(3) In the event of any difference of opinion among the members of

the Committee at the time of any interim decision, the opinion of the majority shall prevail but where there is no such majority the opinion of the Chairperson shall prevail.

(4) Subject to the provisions of sub-section (1), the Committee may act, notwithstanding the absence of any member of the Committee, and no order made by the Committee shall be invalid by reason only of the absence of any member during any stage of the proceeding.

31. Powers of Committee—(1) The Committee shall have the final authority to dispose of cases for the care, protection, treatment, development and rehabilitation of the children as well as to provide for their basic needs and protection of human rights.

(2) Where a Committee has been constituted for any area, such Committee shall, notwithstanding anything contained in any other law for the time being in force but save as otherwise expressly provided in this Act, have the power to deal exclusively with all proceedings under this Act relating to children in need of care and protection.

32. Production before Committee—(1) Any child in need of care and protection may be produced before the Committee by one of the following persons:

(i) any police officer or special juvenile police unit or a designated police officer;

(ii) any public servant;

(iii) childline, a registered voluntary organisation or by such other voluntary organisation or an agency as may be recognised by the State Government;

(iv) any social worker or a public spirited citizen authorised by the State Government; or

(v) by the child himself.

(2) The State Government may make rules consistent with this Act to provide for the manner of making the report to the police and to the Committee and the manner of sending and entrusting the child to children's home pending the inquiry.

33. Inquiry—(1) On receipt of a report under section 32, the Committee or any police officer or special juvenile police unit or the designated police officer shall hold an inquiry in the prescribed manner and the Committee, on its own or on the report from any person or agency as mentioned in sub-section (1) of section 32, may pass an order to send the child to the children's home for speedy inquiry by a social worker or child welfare officer.

(2) The inquiry under this section shall be completed within four

months of the receipt of the order or within such shorter period as may be fixed by the Committee: Provided that the time for the submission of the inquiry report may be extended by such period as the Committee may, having regard to the circumstances and for the reasons recorded in writing, determine.

(3) After the completion of the inquiry if the Committee is of the opinion that the said child has no family or ostensible support, it may allow the child to remain in the children's home or shelter home till suitable rehabilitation is found for him or till he attains the age of eighteen years.

34. Children's homes—(1) The State Government may establish and maintain either by itself or in association with voluntary organisations, children's homes, in every district or group of districts, as the case may be, for the reception of child in need of care and protection during the pendency of any inquiry and subsequently for their care, treatment, education, training, development and rehabilitation.

(2) The State Government may, by rules made under this Act, provide for the management of children's homes including the standards and the nature of services to be provided by them, and the circumstances under which, and the manner in which, the certification of a children's home or recognition to a voluntary organisation may be granted or withdrawn.

Comments

State Governments have been empowered to establish and maintain either by themselves or in association with the voluntary organisations, children's homes in every district or a group of districts for the reception of child in need of care and protection during the pendency of any inquiry and subsequently for their care, treatment, education, training, development and rehabilitation.

35. Inspection—(1) The State Government may appoint inspection committees for the children's homes (hereinafter referred to as the inspection committees) for the State, a district and city, as the case may be, for such period and for such purposes as may be prescribed.

(2) The inspection committee of a State, district or of a city shall consist of such number of representatives from the State Government, Local Authority, Committee, voluntary organisations and such other medical experts and social workers as may be prescribed.

36. Social auditing—The Central Government or State Government may monitor and evaluate the functioning of the children's homes at such period and through such persons and institutions as may be specified by that Government.

37. Shelter homes—(1) The State Government may recognise, reputed and capable voluntary organisations and provide them assistance to set up and administer as many shelter homes for juveniles or children as may be required.

(2) The shelter homes referred in sub-section—(1) shall function as drop-in-centres for the children in the need of urgent support who have been brought to such homes through such persons as are referred to in sub-section (1) of section 32.

(3) As far as possible, the shelter homes shall have such facilities as may be prescribed by the rules.

COMMENTS

State Governments have been empowered to recognise reputed and capable voluntary organisations and provide them assistance to set up and administer shelter homes for juveniles or children. These shelter homes shall function as drop-in-centres for the children in the need of urgent support.

38. Transfer—(1) If during the inquiry it is found that the child hails from the place outside the jurisdiction of the Committee, the Committee shall order the transfer of the child to the competent authority having jurisdiction over the place of residence of the child.

(2) Such juvenile or the child shall be escorted by the staff of the home in which he is lodged originally.

(3) The State Government may make rules to provide for the travelling allowance to be paid to the child.

39. Restoration—(1) Restoration of and protection to a child shall be the prime objective of any children's home or the shelter home.

(2) The children's home or a shelter home, as the case may be, shall take such steps as are considered necessary for the restoration of and protection to a child deprived of his family environment temporarily or permanently where such child is under the care and protection of a children's home or a shelter home, as the case may be.

(3) The Committee shall have the powers to restore any child in need of care and protection to his parent, guardian, fit person or fit institution, as the case may be, and give them suitable directions.

Explanation—For the purposes of this section "restoration of child" means restoration to—

(a) parents;
(b) adopted parents;
(c) foster parents.

CHAPTER IV
Rehabilitation and Social Reintegration

40. Process of rehabilitation and social reintegration—The rehabilitation and social reintegration of a child shall begin during the stay of the child in a children's home or special home and the rehabilitation and social reintegration of children shall be carried out alternatively by (i) adoption, (ii) foster care, (iii) sponsorship, and (iv) sending the child to an after-care organisation.

41. Adoption—(1) The primary responsibility for providing care and protection to children shall be that of his family.

(2) Adoption shall be resorted to for the rehabilitation of such children as are orphaned, abandoned, neglected and abused through institutional and non-institutional methods.

(3) In keeping with the provisions of the various guidelines for adoption issued from time to time by the State Government, the Board shall be empowered to give children in adoption and carry out such investigations as are required or giving children in adoption in accordance with the guidelines issued by the State Government from time to time in this regard.

(4) The children's homes or the State Government run institutions for orphans shall be recognised as an adoption agencies both for scrutiny and placement of such children for adoption in accordance with the guidelines issued under sub-section (3).

(5) No child shall be offered for adoption—

— until two members of the Committee declare the child legally free for placement in the case of abandoned children,
— till the two months period for reconsideration by the parent is over in the case of surrendered children, and
— without his consent in the case of a child who can understand and express his consent.

(6) The Board may allow a child to be given in adoption—

to a single parent, and

to parents to adopt a child of same sex irrespective of the number of living biological sons or daughters.

42. Foster care—(1) The foster care may be used for temporary placement of those infants who are ultimately to be given for adoption.

(2) In foster care, the child may be placed in another family for a short or extended period of time, depending upon the circumstances where the child's own parent usually visit regularly and eventually after the rehabilitation, where the children may return to their own homes.

(3) The State Government may make rules for the purposes of carrying out the scheme of foster care programme of children.

43. Sponsorship—(1) The sponsorship programme may provide supplementary support to families, to children's homes and to special homes to meet medical, nutritional, educational and other needs of the children with a view to improving their quality of life.

(2) The State Government may make rules for the purposes of carrying out various schemes of sponsorship of children, such as individual to individual sponsorship, group sponsorship or community sponsorship.

44. After-care organisation—The State Government may, by rules made under this Act, provide-

(a) for the establishment or recognition of after-care organisations and the functions that may be performed by them under this Act;

(b) for a scheme of after-care programme to be followed by such after-care organisations for the purpose of taking care of juveniles or the children after they leave special homes, children homes and for the purpose of enabling them to lead an honest, industrious and useful life;

(c) for the preparation or submission of a report by the probation officer or any other officer appointed by that Government in respect of each juvenile or the child prior to his discharge from a special home, children's home, regarding the necessity and nature of after-care of such juvenile or of a child, the period of such after-care, supervision thereof and for the submission of report by the probation officer or any other officer appointed for the purpose, on the progress of each juvenile or the child;

(d) for the standards and the nature of services to be maintained by such after care organisations;

(e) for such other matters as may be necessary for the purpose of carrying out the scheme of after-care programme for the juvenile or the child:

Provided that any rule made under this section shall not provide for such juvenile or child to stay in the after-care organisation for more than three years:

Provided further that a juvenile or child over seventeen years of age but less than eighteen years of age would stay in the after-care organisation till he attains the age of twenty years.

45. Linkages and co-ordination—The State Government may make rules to ensure effective linkages between various governmental, non-governmental, corporate and other community agencies for facilitating the rehabilitation and social reintegration of the child.

Miscellaneous

46. Attendance of parent or guardian of juvenile or child—Any competent authority before which a juvenile or the child is brought under any of the provisions of this Act, may, whenever it so thinks fit, require any parent or guardian having the actual charge of or control over the juvenile or the child to be present at any proceeding in respect of the juvenile or the child.

47. Dispensing with attendance of juvenile or child—If, at any stage during the course of an inquiry, a competent authority is satisfied that the attendance of the juvenile or the child is not essential for the purpose of inquiry, the competent authority may dispense with his attendance and proceed with the inquiry in the absence of the juvenile or the child.

48. Committal to approved place of juvenile or child suffering from dangerous diseases and his future disposal—(1) When a juvenile or the child who has been brought before a competent authority under this Act, is found to be suffering from a disease requiring prolonged medical treatment or physical or mental complaint that will respond to treatment, the competent authority may send the juvenile or the child to any place recognised to be an approved place in accordance with the rules made under this Act for such period as it may think necessary for the required treatment.

(2) Where a juvenile or the child is found to be suffering from leprosy, sexually transmitted disease, Hepatitis B, open cases of Tuberculosis and such other diseases or is of unsound mind, he shall be dealt with separately through various specialised referral services or under the relevant laws as such.

49. Presumption and determination of age—(1) Where it appears to a competent authority that person brought before it under any of the provisions of this Act (otherwise than for the purpose of giving evidence) is a juvenile or the child, the competent authority shall make due inquiry so as to the age of that person and for that purpose shall take such evidence as may be necessary (but not an affidavit) and shall record a finding whether the person is a juvenile or the child or not, stating his age as nearly as may be.

(2) No order of a competent authority shall be deemed to have become invalid merely by any subsequent proof that the person in respect of whom the order has been made is not a juvenile or the child, and the age recorded by the competent authority to be the age of person so brought before it, shall for the purpose of this Act, be deemed to be the true age of that person.

50. Sending a juvenile or child outside jurisdiction—In the case of a juvenile or the child, whose ordinary place of residence lies outside the jurisdiction of the competent authority before which he is brought, the competent authority may, if satisfied after due inquiry that it is expedient so to do, send the juvenile or the child back to a relative or other person who is fit and willing to receive him at his ordinary place of residence and exercise proper care and control over him, notwithstanding that such place of residence is outside the jurisdiction of the competent authority; and the competent authority exercising jurisdiction over the place to which the juvenile or the child is sent shall in respect of any matter arising subsequently have the same powers in relation to the juvenile or the child as if the original order had been passed by itself.

51. Reports to be treated as confidential—The report of the probation officer or social worker considered by the competent authority shall be treated as confidential:

— Provided that the competent authority may, if it so thinks fit, communicate the substance thereof to the juvenile or the child or his parent or guardian and may give such juvenile or the child, parent or guardian an opportunity of producing such evidence as may be relevant to the matter stated in the report.

52. Appeals—(1) Subject to the provisions of this section, any person aggrieved by an order made by a competent authority under this Act may, within thirty days from the date of such order, prefer an appeal to the Court of Session:

Provided that the Court of Session may entertain the appeal after the expiry of the said period of thirty days if it is satisfied that the appellant was prevented by sufficient cause from filing the appeal in time.

(2) No appeal shall lie from—

(a) Any order of acquittal made by the Board in respect of a juvenile alleged to have committed an offence; or

(b) Any order made by a Committee in respect of a finding that a person is not a neglected juvenile.

(3) No second appeal shall lie from any order of the Court of Session passed in appeal under this section.

53. Revision—The High Court may, at any time, either of its own motion or on an application received in this behalf, call for the record of any proceeding in which any competent authority or Court of Session has passed an order for the purpose of satisfying itself as to the legality or propriety of any such order and may pass such order in relation thereto as it thinks fit:

Provided that the High Court shall not pass an order under this section prejudicial to any person without giving him a reasonable opportunity of being heard.

54. Procedure in inquiries, appeals and revision proceedings—(1) Save as otherwise expressly provided by this Act, a competent authority while holding any inquiry under any of the provisions of this Act, shall follow such procedure as may be prescribed and subject thereto, shall follow, as far as may be, the procedure laid down in the Code of Criminal Procedure, 1973 (2 of 1974) for trials in summons cases.

(2) Save as otherwise expressly provided by or under this Act, the procedure to be followed in hearing appeals or revision proceedings under this Act shall be, as far as practicable, in accordance with the provisions of the Code of Criminal Procedure, 1973 (2 of 1974).

55. Power to amend orders—(1) Without prejudice to the provisions for appeal and revision under this Act, any competent authority may, on an application received in this behalf, amend any order as to the institution to which a juvenile or the child is to be sent or as to the person under whose care or supervision a juvenile or the child is to be placed under this Act:

Provided that there shall be at least two members and the parties or its defence present during the course of hearing for passing an amendment in relation to any of its order.

(2) Clerical mistakes in orders passed by a competent authority or errors arising therein from any accidental slip or omission may, at any time, be corrected by the competent authority either on its own motion or on an application received in this behalf.

56. Power of competent authority to discharge and transfer juvenile or child—The competent authority or the local authority may, notwithstanding anything contained in this Act, at any time, order a child in need of care and protection or a juvenile in conflict with law to be discharged or transferred from one children's home or special home to another, as the case may be, keeping in view the best interest of the child or the juvenile, and his natural place of stay, either absolutely or on such conditions as it may think fit to impose:

Provided that the total period of stay of the juvenile or the child in a children's home or a special home or a fit institution or under a fit person shall not be increased by such transfer.

57. Transfer between children's homes, under the Act, and juvenile homes, of like nature in different parts of India—The State Government or the local authority may direct any child or the juvenile to be transferred from any children's home or special home outside the State to any other children's home, special home or institution of a like nature with the prior intimation to the local Committee or the Board, as the case may be, and such order shall be deemed to be operative for the competent authority of the area to which the child or the juvenile is sent.

58. Transfer of juvenile or child of unsound mind or suffering from leprosy or addicted to drugs—Where it appears to the competent authority that any juvenile or the child kept in a special home or a children's home or shelter home or in an institution in pursuance of this Act, is suffering from leprosy or is of unsound mind or is addicted to any narcotic drug or psychotropic substance, the competent authority may order his removal to a leper asylum or mental hospital or treatment centre for drug addicts or to a place of safety for being kept there for such period not exceeding the period for which he is required to be kept under the order of the competent authority or for such further period as may be certified by the medical officer necessary for the proper treatment of the juvenile or the child.

Comments

If any juvenile or the child kept in a special home or children's home or shelter home or in an institution, is suffering from leprosy or is of unsound mind or is addicted to any narcotic drug or psychotropic substance, the competent authority can order his removal to a leper asylum or mental hospital or treatment centre for drug addicts or to a place of safety for being kept there.

59. Release and absence of juvenile or child on placement—(1) When a juvenile or the child is kept in a children's home or special home and on a report of a probation officer or social worker or of Government or a voluntary organisation, as the case may be, the competent authority may consider, the release of such juvenile or the child permitting him to live with his parent or guardian or under the supervision of any authorised person named in the order, willing to receive and take charge of the juvenile or the child to educate and train him for some useful trade or calling or to look after him for rehabilitation.

(2) The competent authority may also permit leave of absence to any juvenile or the child, to allow him, on special occasions like examination, marriage of relatives, death of kith and kin or the accident or serious illness of parent or any emergency of like nature, to go on leave under supervision, for maximum seven days, excluding the time taken in journey.

(3) Where a permission has been revoked or forfeited and the juvenile or the child refuses or fails to return to the home concerned or juvenile to which he was directed so to return, the Board may, if necessary, cause him to be taken charge of and to be taken back to the concerned home.

(4) The time during which a juvenile or the child is absent from a concerned home in pursuance of such permission granted under this section shall be deemed to be part of the time foe which he is liable to be kept in the special home:

Provided that when a juvenile has failed to return to the special home on the permission being revoked or forfeited, the time which lapses after his failure so to return shall be excluded in computing the time during which he is liable to be kept in the institution.

60. Contribution by parents—(1) The competent authority which makes an order for sending a juvenile or the child to a children's home or to a special home or placing the juvenile under the care of a fit person or fit institution may make an order requiring the parent or other person liable to maintain the juvenile or the child to contribute to his maintenance, if able to do so, in the prescribed manner according to income.

(2) The competent authority may direct, if necessary, the payment to be made to poor parent or guardian by the Superintendent or the Project Manager of the home to pay such expenses for the journey of the inmate or parent or guardian or both, from the home to his ordinary place of residence at the time of sending the juvenile as may be prescribed.

61. Fund—(1) The State Government or local authority may create a Fund under such name as it thinks fit for the welfare and rehabilitation of the juvenile or the child dealt with under this Act.

(2) There shall be credited to the Fund such voluntary donations, contributions or subscriptions as may be made by any individual or organisation.

(3) The Fund created under sub-section (1) shall be administered by the State advisory board in such manner and for such purposes as may be prescribed.

Comments

State Governments or local authorities have been empowered to create Funds for the welfare and rehabilitation of the juvenile or the child. Such funds may be created with voluntary donations, contributions or subscriptions as may be made by any individual or organisation. Such funds are to be administered by the State Advisory Boards.

62. Central, State, district and city advisory boards—(1) The Central Government or a State Government may constitute a Central or State Advisory board, as the case may be, to advise that Government on matter relating to the establishment and maintenance of the homes, mobilisation of resources, provision of facilities for education, training and rehabilitation of child in need of care and protection and juvenile in conflict with law and co-ordination among the various official and non-official agencies concerned.

(2) The Central or State advisory board shall consist of such persons as the Central Government or the State Government, as the case may be, may think fit and shall include eminent social workers, representatives of voluntary organisations in the field of the child welfare corporate sector, academicians, medical professionals and the concerned Department of the State Government.

(3) The district or city level inspection committee constituted under section 35 of this Act shall also function as the district or city advisory board.

63. Special juvenile police unit—(1) In order to enable the police officers who frequently or exclusively deal with juveniles or are primarily engaged in the prevention of juvenile crime or handling of the juveniles or children under this Act to perform their functions more effectively, they shall be specially instructed and trained.

(2) In every police station at least one officer with aptitude and appropriate training and orientation may be designated as the 'juvenile or the child welfare officer' who will handle the juvenile or the child in co-ordination with the police.

(3) Special juvenile police unit, of which all police officers designated as above, to handle juveniles or children will be members, may be created in every district and city to co-ordinate and to upgrade the police treatment of the juveniles and the children.

64. Juvenile in conflict with law undergoing sentence at commencement of this Act—In any area in which this Act is brought into force, the State Government or the local authority may direct that a juvenile in conflict with law who is undergoing any sentence of imprisonment at the commencement of this Act, shall, in lieu of undergoing such sentence, be sent to a special home or kept in fit institution in such manner as the State Government or the local authority thinks fit for the remainder of the period of the sentence; and the provisions of this Act shall apply to the juvenile as if he had been ordered by the Board to be sent to such special home or institution or, as the case may be, ordered to be kept under protective care under sub-section (2) of section 16 of this Act.

65. Procedure in respect of bonds—Provisions of Chapter XXXIII of the Code of Criminal Procedure, 1973 (2 of 1974) shall, as far as nay be, apply to bonds taken under this Act.

66. Delegation of powers—The State Government may, by the general order, direct that any power exercisable by it under this Act shall, in such circumstances and under such conditions, if any, as may be prescribed in the order, be exercisable also by an officer subordinate to that Government or the local authority.

67. Protection of action taken in good faith—No suit or legal proceedings shall lie against the State Government or voluntary organisation running the home or any officer and the staff appointed in pursuance of this Act in respect of anything which is in good faith done or intended to be done in pursuance of this Act or of any rules or order made thereunder.

68. Power to make rules—(1) The State Government may, by notification in the Official Gazette, make rules to carry out the purposes of this Act.

(2) In particular, and without prejudice to the generality of the foregoing powers, such rules may provide for all or any of the following matters, namely:

i) the term of office of the members of the Board, and the manner in which such member may resign under sub-section (4) of section (4);

ii) the time of the meetings of the Board and the rules of procedure in regard to the transaction of business at its meeting under sub-section (1) of section 5;

iii) the management of observation homes including the standards and various types of services to be provided by them and the circumstances in which and the manner in which, the certification of the observation home may be granted or withdrawn and such other matters as are referred to in section 8;

iv) the management of special home including the standards and various types of services to be provided by them and the circumstances in which and the manner in which, the certification of the special home may be granted or withdrawn and such other matters as are referred to in section 9;

v) persons by whom any juvenile in conflict with law may be produced before the Board and the manner of sending such juvenile to an observation home under sub-section (2) of section 10;

vi) matters relating to removal of disqualifications attaching to conviction of a juvenile under section 19;

vii) the qualifications of the Chairperson and members, and the tenure for which they may be appointed under sub-section (3) of section 29;

viii) the time of the meetings of the Committee and the rules of procedure in regard to the transaction of business at its meeting under sub-section (1) of section 30;

ix) the manner of making the report to the police and to the Committee and the manner of sending and entrusting the child to children's home pending the inquiry under sub-section (2) of section 32;

x) the management of children's homes including the standards and nature of services to be provided by them, and the manner in which certification of a children's home or recognition to a voluntary organisation may be granted or withdrawn under sub-section (2) of section 34;

xi) appointment of inspection committees for children's homes, their tenure and purposes for which inspection committees may be appointed and such other matters as are referred to in section 35;

xii) facilities to be provided by the shelter homes under sub-section (3) of section 37;

xiii) for carrying out the scheme of foster care programme of children under sub-section (3) of section 42;

xiv) for carrying out various schemes of sponsorship of children under sub-section (2) of section 43;

xv) matters relating to after-care organisation under section 44;

xvi) for ensuring effective linkages between various agencies for facilitating rehabilitation and social integration of the child under section 45;

xvii) the purposes and the manner in which the Fund shall be administered under sub-section (3) of section 61;

xviii) any other matter which is required to be or may be, prescribed.

(3) Every rule made by a State Government under this Act shall be laid, as soon as may be after it is made, before the Legislature of that State.

69. Repeal and savings—(1) The Juvenile Justice Act, 1986 (53 of 1986) is hereby repealed.

(2) Notwithstanding such repeal, anything done or any action taken under the said Act shall be deemed to have been done or taken under the corresponding provisions of this Act.

70. Power to remove difficulties—(1) If any difficulty arises in giving effect to the provisions of this Act, the Central Government may, by order, not inconsistent with the provisions of this Act, remove the difficulty:

Provided that no such order shall be made after the expiry of the period of two years from the commencement of this Act.

(2) However, order made under the section shall be laid, as soon as may be after it is made, before each House of Parliament.

Report of the National Commission for Protection of Child Rights

Rebellion against standards set up for the child by those in authority may lead to delinquent behavior when adults do not live up to their own demands

A report released by the National Commission for Protection of Child Rights (NCPCR) throws light on the pitiful condition of juvenile delinquents languishing in reform homes in India.

Around 5,000 cases against juveniles are pending in courts.

Apart from delayed justice, these children are victims of improper care by reform homes.

Over 50 per cent of the juvenile homes do not provide any counseling services to juvenile delinquents, besides more than 80 per cent of caretakers at these homes are not trained.

The report was compiled after a detailed study of various juvenile care-centres across the country. The report has suggested that reforms should be undertaken at juvenile homes.

Terming the juvenile care-centres as jails, child-rights activists have suggested that foster care-centres should be set up, where children would lead better lives.

"All children call them (juvenile homes) as jails. They are worse than adult jails. Prisons at least have enough space. For girls, the situation is even worse. A hundred girls are made to spend their entire day inside one small room in name of protection," said Harsh Mander, a child-rights activist.

In 70 per cent of the juvenile care-centres, physical punishment is a dominant method to discipline children.

The juveniles recounted the horrors meted out at the centres.

"We used to be locked up 24 hours. We were not allowed to go out. Even if we tried to peep outside the compound, the police would beat us up. We didn't like the place at all," said Vijay, a juvenile delinquent.

The Juvenile Justice Act was introduced in 1986 to establish the basis for a national uniform juvenile justice system, addressing care, protection and treatment of neglected and delinquent juveniles.

In 2006, the Juvenile Justice (Care and Protection) Act was revised in order to strengthen the previous act and instill a child-centric rehabilitation and family restoration focused system.

Probation Service

The roots of the probation service go back to the nineteenth century where clergy members took responsibility for young offenders to prevent them entering the prison system. Many changes have been made over the years, moving from the 'advise, assist and befriend' notion to the present day position of enforcement. Prison has an important role to play in protecting the community against the most dangerous offenders and in punishing the most serious crimes. But research and experience have shown the many disadvantages of over using imprisonment. Imprisonment can harm the chances people have to make amends.

13

Contributing Factors

In the New Globalised Economy in which multinational corporations enjoy more power and far more financial resources than many governments, the story of judicial constraints on corporate governance ultimately impacts on everyone's lives.

What is Morality?

Morality can be defined as principles we use to distinguish right from wrong. According to Shaffer (1993; see PIP p.580), human morality has three components.

The Components of Morality

1. *Cognition*: Thoughts and decisions about moral issues. Emphasised by Piaget and Kohlberg.
2. *Emotions*: Feelings, such as guilt, connected to moral issues. Emphasised by Freud.
3. *Behaviour*: How we behave, and the extent to which we behave honourably or not. Emphasised by social learning theorists.

Theories of Moral Development

Freud

Basic ideas:

❖ Freudian theory concentrates on the emotional component.
❖ Moral issues are based on the superego, which consists of two components (conscience and ego ideal).
❖ The superego forms as result of identification with same-sex parent when resolving Oedipus/Electra complex around age 5/6.

❖ According to Freud, girls have weaker superegos because they have less anxiety in the Electra complex.
❖ The moral level of the child therefore depends on the parents.

Research Evidence

❖ Brody and Shaffer (1982; *see* PIP p.582) determined that parental style does affect moral development (but the child's behaviour may affect choice of style).

Style	Improvement in Morality (% of studies)
Induction (explaining)	86
Power assertion (punishing)	18
Love withdrawal	42

❖ Freud's work is based on retrospective case studies.
❖ The theory about early events cannot be refuted, as lack of memory for them is taken as evidence of repression.
❖ More fear (i.e., punishing parents) doesn't lead to stronger superego (Hoffman, 1988;).
❖ Girls are not morally weaker (Hoffman, 1975;).
❖ Children aged 26–41 months show some evidence of conscience (Kochanska *et al.*, 1994;).

Piaget

Basic ideas:

❖ This is a cognitive-developmental theory, which concentrates on the cognitive component.
❖ It is based on three stages in moral development, which depend on the child's attitude to rules, intentions, and punishment:

— *Stage 1*. Premoral: 0–5 years. Children have very little understanding of rules.
— *Stage 2*. Moral realism: 5–10 years. Children believe in expiatory punishment and immanent justice.
— *Stage 3*. Moral relativism: 10 years upwards. Children recognise the individual's intentions and believe in reciprocal punishment.

❖ Moral reasoning changes during childhood due to decreasing egocentrism, exposure to different views, and disequilibrium (observation of inconsistencies).

Kohlberg

Basic ideas:

❖ Kohlberg focuses on the cognitive element of morality.
❖ The theory recognises three levels (pre-conventional, conventional, and post-conventional morality). Each level has two stages, giving six stages in all.
❖ How morality is regulated moves from external reward-based and social regulation to internal abstract ideas.
❖ Developments in moral reasoning is motivated by disequilibrium.
❖ı Development continues throughout early adulthood.

Warning Signals

There is no claim, however, that media violence is the sole cause or even principal cause, of violent behavior. It is a contributing factor. It does not affect everyone to the same degree. It is like smoking and cancer. Many people smoke but do not get cancer, and many people get cancer who do not smoke. But the correlation between smoking and cancer is about the same as the correlation between exposure to media violence and measures of subsequent aggressive behavior. It is not a perfect analogy, but it makes the point that the effect is real.

In most cases like this, we find out that the attacker was depressed, angry, frustrated, embittered, and disillusioned. There is usually ample warning in the form of threats and desperate statements. Rarely are there no prior indications.

Imaginative Heroic Scenarios

It is always tempting to imagine heroic scenarios where someone with a gun comes to the rescue. We see it on TV every night, but it is not realistic. More things can go wrong than go right. When we look at other nations we see that they have a much, much lower rate of gun violence than we do, yet this is not because their citizens are armed and ready to shoot the shooters. We need a more realistic understanding of the problem and not one that has been produced by all our years of watching television violence.

Research Findings

America is now and has long been a relatively violent nation (Gurr, 1989; NRC, 1993). It has had a particularly notorious history with respect to *lethal* violence (Zimring, 1998). In recent years, the general violence of American society has engulfed the nation's young (Cook and Laub, 1998). From 1985 to 1994, the United States experienced a historically unprecedented epidemic[1] of lethal youth violence that took the lives of young victims, shattered inner-city communities, and ruined the prospects of many young people across the nation (Blumstein, 1995; Moore and Tonry, 1998; Cook and Laub, 1998).

The general violence and the fear it causes have also reached into American schools. Serious violence has always been rare in schools, and it remained so even as society weathered the epidemic of youth violence. Recent figures show that between 1994 and 1999, 220 events of school-associated violent deaths occurred—on average, 36 per year. This is less than 0.3 per cent of all violent deaths that occurred during that time period. Young people are far more likely to be killed or seriously injured when they are out of school rather than in it. The school boundary has continued to create a relatively safe haven for the nation's young.

To say that schools have remained relatively safe compared with other social and geographic communities is not to say that current levels of violence and fear in schools are acceptable. Quite the contrary. The prevalence of violent victimizations in schools has more than doubled since 1989:3 per cent of youths reported violent victimizations at school then, compared with 8 per cent today. And while it is true that most schools are relatively free of violent crime, some schools experience very high rates, especially those in high-crime areas of U.S. cities (Kaufman *et al.*, 1999). During the past 10 years, a spate of multiple-victim shooting incidents in school settings has greatly increased and widened public concern about violence in schools. From 1992 to 2001, 35 incidents occurred in which students showed up at their school or at a school-sponsored event and started shooting at their schoolmates and teachers. These incidents, represented most starkly by the incident at Columbine High School in Littleton, Colorado, left 53 people dead and 144 injured These shootings contributed to a significant increase in homicide rates for students killed in multiple-victim incidents on school grounds between 1992 and 1999 (Anderson *et al.*, 2001).

These events shocked the public partly because so many were killed or injured so quickly in a single incident. It was also particularly frightening that in many instances the victims seemed to have been chosen more or less at random. But the intense public concern was also due to the social location of the shootings. Much of the violence occurred in communities that had, until the time these shootings occurred, been spared the kind of lethal youth violence that beset some of their urban neighbors. Moreover, the shootings took place in schools—the place in communities that is supposed to be protective of children. Finally, the fact that these terrible shootings didn't stop—they kept occurring at an apparently increasing rate in a pattern that suggested an emergent epidemic—pushed the level of concern much higher.

Serious School Violence

Serious school violence involves:

- ❖ incidents of lethal violence
- ❖ that took place in or were associated with schools
- ❖ that were committed by students of the school and
- ❖ that resulted in multiple victimizations in a single incident.
- ❖ "Lethal school violence includes multiple victimizations."

In the 1990s, youth violence, which had reached epidemic levels in the nation's cities beginning in the late 1980s, took an apparently unprecedented form in rural and suburban middle and high schools across the country. Between 1992 and 2001, 35 incidents occurred in which students showed up at their school or at a school-sponsored event and started firing at their schoolmates and teachers. These incidents represented most starkly by the incident at Columbine High School, in Littleton, Colorado, left 53 dead, and 144 injured.

These incidents shocked the public, partly because so many were killed in single incidents and partly because the targets of the shootings seemed so arbitrarily selected. A third reason is that these incidents occurred in such unexpected places. The previous epidemic of deadly youth violence, which peaked in 1993 and then declined, had occurred among black and Hispanic youth in the nation's most disadvantaged urban neighborhoods and schools. In most of these new cases, communities that had previously thought of themselves as insulated from lethal youth violence discovered that they, too, were vulnerable.

Causes

Although the lethal shooting sprees of the 1990s followed closely on and even seemed to emerge from or be influenced by the earlier violence—and may have stemmed from similar underlying factors—it is possible that these events represent a separate strain of violence. While the inner-city epidemic of violence was fueled by well-understood causes—poverty, racial segregation, and the dynamics of the illicit drug trade—the violence in the suburban and rural schools more closely resembles "rampage" shootings that occur in places other than schools, such as workplaces, or in other public spaces.

In these six cases, this idea is supported by the notable differences in the motives of the shooters and the circumstances under which the shootings occurred. In the inner-city cases, the shooting incidents involved specific grievances between individuals that were known in the school community. In contrast, the suburban and rural shooting incidents did not involve specific grievances. These shooters felt aggrieved, but their grievances were a more general and abstract sense of feeling attacked rather than a specific threat by an individual. The grievances of these youth were not understood by those around them. As in rampage shootings involving adults, suburban and rural school shooting cases generally seem to involve youth who have these kinds of exaggerated and somewhat abstract grievances.

Evidence from Trends

Whereas events that could be described as rampage violence are only a small component of all violence and seem to move independently of other forms of violence, the committee found a spike for all kinds of rampage Killings in the late 1990s; this raises the possibility that there may have been some kind of epidemic of rampage shootings in the late 1990s that cut across all ages, including youth. Consistent with this hypothesis is the evidence from the cases that copycat mechanisms, which clearly were at work in at least one of the shootings, also may have influenced two of the other three suburban and rural school shootings examined.

The Shooters

Looking across the cases, we found that the eight shooters exhibited a number of similar traits. While these are consistent with risk factors for serious youthful violence identified in the literature, this study can do no more than claim them as tendencies or propensities. All were boys. Five had recently begun hanging out with delinquent or more troubled friends.

Five had a relatively recent drop in their grades at school. Five had engaged in previous serious delinquent acts and the other three in minor delinquent behavior. Serious mental health problems, including schizophrenia, clinical depression, and personality disorders, surfaced after the shootings for six of the eight boys in these cases. All had easy access to guns. The rural and suburban boys had experience with guns, and one of the urban teens appears to have practiced with the gun he used.

However, there were also some characteristics that are usually thought of as protective. Half of the shooters came from intact and stable two-parent families, and five of the eight were good students, at least until 8th grade. Only three of the shooters struggled with grades or experienced the early school failure that frequently precedes the development of serious delinquent behavior. Only one of the eight shooters was a loner, and only two were gang members. Most had friends, although the quality of the friendships differed. Most of these shooters were not considered to be at high risk for this kind of behavior by the adults around them.

Community and School Environments

The central differences in these cases can be found in community structure. The two urban neighborhoods were characterized by community social and physical conditions that research has shown create a milieu for the development of youth violence. Most of the rural and suburban communities did not demonstrate these structural conditions, and in fact three of the four were demographically the opposite—thriving economically, having a high degree of social capital, and mostly free of crime and violence. The committee notes that five of the six communities in these cases had experienced rapid social change, which may produce instability even where the changes are seen as positive ones.

A common element across school settings was the presence of numerous informal and exclusive student groups. In the urban schools, these were mostly marginal groups—gangs, including criminal gangs, and "crews." In the rural and suburban schools, they were cliques—some mainstream and some marginal. Membership in these groups determined social status in most of these schools, but there were notable differences in relationships in the different school settings. In the urban cases, the boys' friendships were embedded in these marginal groups; in the rural and suburban cases, the boys were marginal members of both mainstream and marginal groups.

An important similarity across all of the cases was the gulf between the communities' youth culture and that of adults. Parents and most teachers had a poor understanding of the children's exposure to changing community conditions, their experiences in social situations including at school, and their interpretations of those experiences. There was an intense concern among these shooters about their social standing in their school and among their peers. This took different forms in the inner-city and the rural and suburban cases, but for this group of offenders it was similar in that it was almost always about shielding themselves from physical victimization, including bullying or other personal humiliation. Although in most cases the youth had hinted at what was to come, parents and teachers were mostly unaware of the status problems they were experiencing and of their almost universal belief that they had nowhere to turn. In the words of one of the case authors, "the social dynamics of adolescence in these communities were almost entirely hidden from adult view." Whether or not this is characteristic of most communities is a question that remains unanswered.

Community Responses

With only one exception, the cases were treated virtually identically in the criminal justice system. Six of the eight shooters were charged with the highest offense that could be supported by the evidence, usually first- or second-degree murder, and tried in the adult (criminal) courts rather than the juvenile courts. Most were sentenced to long terms of incarceration and correctional supervision, with the upper limit of sentences for most ranging from 20 to 60 years. The exception was where state law required the justice system to treat the offenders, ages 11 and 13, as juveniles. Even though there is little room in the adversarial process of the criminal courts for the special problems these boys had to influence the outcome, most residents of that particular community saw adjudication in the juvenile system as unjustifiably lenient treatment, given the nature of the offense.

Instituting or adding to physical security measures was the most common response of the school communities to these shootings in almost every site. In the urban cases, public officials and residents went well beyond security measures to effect improvements in community climate and communication between youth and adults. The rural and suburban communities also took steps to improve communication but did not focus on community climate, tending to explain the incidents as the act of a troubled youth rather than resulting from community-level or social factors that needed attention.

Observations and Research Recommendations

School rampage shootings are rare events that have occurred in middle-class and affluent rural and suburban schools, but they are not found in inner-city schools. They resemble other rampage shootings, especially mass murders, more than other forms of youth violence or urban school shootings. It is virtually impossible to identify the likely offenders in advance; thus, there is no accurate way to develop a profile of students at high risk to commit these kinds of acts.

Little is known about what causes school rampages, so the development of primary prevention mechanisms is difficult. Until more can be learned about causes, case studies such as these can be helpful in identifying some plausible targets of intervention. One approach involves the fact that these young people had such easy access to firearms. Based on these cases—and the fact that all but one of the incidents of lethal school violence involving multiple victims in the United States over the last decade have involved firearms in the hands of children—the committee believes it is necessary to find more effective means than we now have of realizing the nation's long established policy goal of keeping firearms out of the hands of unsupervised children and out of our schools. In addition, there is a need for youth and adults, among themselves and together, to be more sensitive to the often fragile status concerns of young people. Students are often in a position to preempt rampage attacks simply by telling what they know to school authorities, but that requires crossing the gap between the society of youth and that of adults. Specifically, there is a need to develop a strategy for drawing adults and youth closer together in constructing a normative social climate that is committed to keeping the schools safe from lethal incidents.

The committee notes that conducting empirical studies to establish causal processes leading to these rare and heinous outcomes is not the only scientific approach possible in the search for prevention and control. Case studies like those presented here are essential and appropriate scientific tools for use in seeking for causes and effective interventions, especially in the study of important but rare events such as these school shootings. Only by first carefully analyzing the patterns that exist in the unfolding of these occurrences can one gather the information needed to develop studies from which findings can be generalized.

The committee recommends that new research be undertaken to further improve understanding of the factors that might influence school shootings, particularly school rampage shootings, and to develop knowledge on the impact of interventions. Our specific research recommendations cover further exploration of the precursors to these incidents, including nonlethal violence and serious bullying in schools; illegal gun carrying by adolescents; the signs and symptoms of developing mental health problems in youth in grades 6–10; the effects of student attacks on teachers; and the effects of rapid change in increasingly affluent rural and suburban communities on youth development, socialization, and violence. Evaluation studies should include programs targeted at thwarting planned school shootings. Evaluations of security measures and police tactics in responding to school shootings are also needed.

Social Psychology: Causes

Social psychology states that violence is a learned behavior. There are no born criminals. Children observe violence in people around them and imitate them accordingly. They may also assimilate hostile ideas through the media. Destructive lyrics in rap and rock songs may be doing more damage to your teenager than you realise.

These days, violent computer and video games have become immensely popular among youngsters. This may be a cause as well as effect of teen violence. Research studies have proven that the aggression rate in teenagers can rise substantially if they are exposed to the following risk factors:

Subjection to Physical or Sexual Abuse: Even corporal punishment qualifies as physical abuse and studies have shown that it is counter-productive.

Violent Behaviour at Home or in Society: Children from families where wife-beating may occur or from broken families are more likely to be aggressive as adolescents.

Violence in the Media: There is a glut of songs with self-defeating lyrics, movies that depict extreme violence, assassination games, books with violent content, etc. It may be difficult to wean your teenager off these but the effort is worthwhile.

Drug Abuse, Smoking and/or Alcohol Addiction: This is a problem that requires serious and immediate action. If you or your partner smoke or drink regularly, consider quitting for the sake of your teenager. Monitor the company your child keeps. If you suspect drug abuse, check your teenager's bags and pockets. The earlier you act, the more effective it will be.

Guns or Other Firearms at Home: This may well be the most important risk factor. Consider this: If you have a gun in your home, you are five times more likely to have a suicide in your house than homes without a gun. If you must have one, keep it out of reach of your children. Try not to let them know of its presence. Keep it locked at all times.

Finally, socio-economic factors like poverty, severe deprivation, unstable family, single-parent family, unemployment, lack of family support may also play a role in inciting teenage aggression.

Warning Signs

Prevention is always better than cure. Look out for the following signs in your adolescent. Remember, the more signs you perceive, the higher the threat. However, not all teens who exhibit some of these signs may resort to violence.

Verbal or written threats of violence—take everything that your teen says seriously.

History of aggression—this includes uncontrollable angry outbursts at home or other delinquent behaviour.

Taking a weapon to school—do not let your teen carry knives or guns outside, whatever the excuse.

Suicide attempts or threats in the past—the unfortunate truth is that once you have a problem with your adolescent, you will always have to be on your toes.

History of violent behaviour or suicide attempts in the family—family remains the primary unit of socialisation.

Lack of responsibility—be alert if your teen always blames destiny or other people for his mistakes and misfortunes. We all do it at times but to assume such a role persistently, in every situation, can lead to an eventual lack of self-confidence and self-reliance.

An incident causing humiliation, loss, shame, or rejection in recent times—you may believe that your child has moved on but teenagers can be excellent actors. Stay connected to your child to be aware of what is playing in his mind.

Morbidity in conversation, selection of books or movies, artwork, etc.—a preoccupation with death, depression, violence, and other dark themes may indicate mental turmoil.

A mental illness, such as depression, mania, psychosis, or bipolar disorder—such individuals are always at a high risk of aggressive behaviour.

Indiscipline at school or college—this may consist of bullying or beating up, impertinence, stealing, copying answers, vandalising benches or walls, cutting class, etc.

Difficulty in making friends; feeling anchorless—this leads to feeling unfulfilled emotionally, which incites the teenager to seek an outlet in violence. Inability to make friends can tarnish self-esteem as well.

Being part of a gang or cult—as long as it is for harmless or entertainment purposes, this should not be a problem. But if the gang engages in antisocial activities or even if it discusses make-believe plans inspired by dacoit or heist movies, it can act as a precursor to serious violence.

Over-protection or apathy from parents—both can be detrimental to your teen. Over-protection can stifle and retard the development of the child while indifference can make the teenager feel unloved and unwanted.

Irrationality—if you're teen refuses to listen to reason and believes that her every wish should be granted, you have a problem at hand.

14

Prevention

Dealing with It

The best way to deal with serious cases of teen violence is to consult a qualified mental health professional; the treatment will chiefly focus on anger management and on the expression of anger in socially acceptable ways. The therapist will teach your teen to assume responsibility for his actions and cope with the consequences; any issues that your teen has regarding school, friends, or family will be addressed. In an emergency, you may dial the local police or fire station, suicide helpline or hospital, depending on the problem.

At the root of all aggression lies suppressed anger. Adolescents undergo a number of changes—both physical and mental. Frustration and confusion can make the transition more traumatic, leading to persistent anger. As a parent, you may need to change your own behavior in order to help your teen. Do not react. Respond. There is no point in wishing away the anger. It must have an appropriate outlet.

Parents and teens should look within themselves to find the cause of their anger. You may ask yourself or tell your teen to ask questions like, "Where does my anger come from? When do I get angry? What are my expectations from life and people? Are they unreasonable? Do I display physical signs of anger such as clenching fists and shortness of breath? Where is my anger directed? Do my emotions control me or do I control my emotions?" The key is self-awareness.

Ensure that your child feels secure and loved. Just be there for him or her. Do not force them into admitting anything. Refrain from adopting an accusing tone. Look at the problem objectively and coax your teenager to express himself. Do not be judgmental when your teenager tells you something. Listen with empathy and understanding. Eliminate the risk factors and always keep in touch with what is happening in your child's life. Always keep in mind—anger is powerless without accompanying action. Guide your teenager to channel the anger proactively.

Counselling

Treating victims of gun violence involves healing both physical and emotional wounds and mitigating the factors that can perpetuate the cycle of violence. One promising approach is therapeutic group intervention.

Whether you want them to know about it or not, children of all ages are hearing about the shootings in Virginia yesterday. Unfortunately, many are getting inaccurate information from unreliable sources like classmates, kids on the bus and friends' older siblings. There is bound to be plenty of embellishment and inaccuracies. Keeping in mind that children are ego-centric by nature, you can bet that the Number One question in any child's mind is: What about me? Am I safe?

Whenever there's a tragic or scary event in the world it's important for children to have their parents' take on it for two reasons: 1. your own credibility. If they learn they can come for you for truthful, accurate information about this, they are more likely to talk to you truthfully about scary or dangerous things in their own lives; 2. Their emotional health. Children feel safer when they know what we think.

Our job as parents is to convey how awful and sad this is, but also that we think they are safe, that their school is safe, and that you are doing everything you can as their parents to make sure they stay safe. You can even remind them of some of the things you do to keep them safe, including little things like putting on the porch light so no one in the family trips on the steps in the dark. We need to convey this sense of safety even if we don't feel it ourselves.

The best conversation with a child of any age begins with you asking a question: "Have you heard about the shootings in Virginia?" If your child says yes, then follow-up by asking, "Tell me what you heard." That way you are working from her knowledge base. If she says no, tell her, "Well, there were some shootings at a college in Virginia. If you hear about it and you want to talk about it or ask me a question, let me know." That gives them permission to talk to you; some kids shut down when they hear scary things because they don't want to see you upset.

Kids of any age who have a sibling in college are likely to be worried about him/her. Better to bring up the subject in a pro-active way than to let the potential worry fester under the surface: "I've been wondering about the safety on John's campus, have you?" And then remind her what safety precautions there are. Most campuses, for instance, require a magnetic pass to get into a building. Of course, the obvious response is, "Yeah, but this shooter was a student!" Then you can remind her that RAs and college personnel are trained to recognize when students have mental health problems, and to help them get help. Unfortunately, that doesn't seem to have happened at Virginia Tech, and yes, you need to acknowledge that.

Initial Reactions to Loss of Known Person

When someone close to you dies you may feel shock, disbelief, numbness, sadness, anger or loneliness. It may seem like everything has been turned upside down. Everyone reacts differently and it is normal to experience many emotions. It is all part of a grieving process. During this time it is important to take care of yourself.

Shock/Disbelief: It is normal to feel a sense of shock when someone close to you has died. Experiencing shock can mean you have a physical and emotional reaction. You may feel dizzy, nauseous, dazed, numb or empty. As part of feeling shocked you may not believe that the news is real.

Shock may also mean that you feel nothing when you hear of the loss. This is normal and over time you are likely to start to feel different emotions. Shock is different for everyone and may last for a couple of days or weeks.

Shock may cause some people to react in an unusual way when they first hear the news of a death. It may be that some people laugh hysterically. This is often a result of the shock and not necessarily because they find the situation funny.

It is a good idea to take it easy. If you feel like things are building up on top of you may want to see your local doctor.

Numbness/Feeling Nothing: As a way of coping with the news of a loss your feelings may become numb. This may mean you feel like you are dreaming, or the event seems unreal. Sometimes this can make it hard to cry or feel any sort of sadness. Over time you are likely to start feeling emotions.

Grief: As the shock and numbness lessens you are likely to start grieving. Everybody grieves differently and there are different things that may affect the way people grieve. Knowing these may help to understand yours and other people's reactions to the loss. If someone's reaction is different to yours it does not necessarily mean they care any less. Some reasons why people grieve differently may be:

The type of relationship they had with the person.

Other losses they have had may come back and be grieved again with the new loss.

Gender: Males and females may have different ways of managing their grief. Males are more likely to feel restrained and may need to show they are in control of their feelings. They are also more likely to be physically active in their grief. It is not uncommon for men to sort out practical problems or to be focussing on getting stuff done. Females are more likely to want to share their feelings with others. This may mean they talk about what is happening or cry more openingly than males.

Cultural Background: Cultural groups express grief in different ways. The rituals and ceremonies, expressing emotions and the rules around what is considered respectful may vary depending on your cultural background. Crying and showing lots of emotion in public does not necessarily mean that someone is not coping with their grief, instead it may be their way of managing their grief.

❖ *Age*: Children of different ages understand death differently. Younger children may not understand that the person is not coming back. Older children, on the other hand, understand that the person is not coming back, but may not understand why.

Some of the things you may experience after losing someone:

❖ *Physical*: Headaches, feeling tired, achy muscles and nausea.
❖ *Emotional*: Sadness, anger, disbelief, despair, guilt, loneliness.
❖ *Mental*: Forgetfulness, lack of concentration, confusion, and poor memory.
❖ *Behavioural*: Changes to sleeping patterns, dreams or nightmares, changes in appetite, not wanting to go out or to be around too many people, experiencing emotional reactions that are out of the ordinary, and crying.
❖ *Social*: Some friends may avoid you because they do not know what to say or how to help you.
❖ *Spiritual*: Your beliefs may be challenged.

It is normal to grieve after you have lost someone. Everybody should be able to grieve in their own way and time. Sometimes you may feel pressure to be strong for family or friends. It is important to be supportive of others however you shouldn't feel like you have to bottle up what you feel. For more information about the stages of grief you may want to check out the working through your grief fact sheet.

Unexpected Feelings and Reactions

It is not unusual for events in your everyday routine to trigger a strong emotional reaction, as they are often a reminder that your friend or loved one is no longer with you. This may happen through something as simple as setting the table for a family meal or being reminded of the person you lost by the words of a song. Over time these reactions may not be as regular or as painful.

Self Psychology

Weapons have been objects of fascination throughout history and have had highly symbolic meanings for many cultures, including our own. Their significance has been examined from a variety of theoretical orientations and by a number of disciplines. Self psychology provides valuable insights into the importance of weapons. Children exposed to gun violence may experience negative short- and long-term psychological effects, including

- ❖ anger,
- ❖ withdrawal,
- ❖ posttraumatic stress, and
- ❖ Desensitization to violence.

All of these outcomes can feed into a continuing cycle of violence. Certain children may be at higher risk for negative outcomes if they are exposed to gun violence.

Groups at Risk Include children

injured in gun violence, those who witness violent acts at close proximity, those exposed to high levels of violence in their communities or schools, and

Those exposed to violent media.

Parents, school administrators, and mental health workers all can play key roles in protecting children from gun violence and helping them overcome the effects of gun-related trauma.

Gun Free Zones

Prevention must start long before the gunman is at the door. In almost every case of a mass shooting, the perpetrator has spent weeks or months planning the attack, and has expressed threats that we could have detected. In many cases, we have prevented acts of violence by responding to these threats.

Many schools have enacted 'gun free zones' on, and around, campus but signs and rules are not going to stop anyone determined to use a gun in a school. It's quite possible that these kinds of superficial responses to school violence actually make things worse because they just create a false sense of security. The 'drug free zones' around schools don't really stop drug dealing but they do give judges the capacity to grant more severe penalties when the case goes to court. Yet a legal penalty is useless against a gunman that kills himself, or is killed, in the attack. Similarly, security cameras when and if they are in the right position to record events, are great for just that but they can't stop any crime. Security cameras are only useful in prosecuting the crime after it has occurred.

If an effort isn't delivering results it usually means it's time to start doing something different. For instance, what if the teachers carried a firearm and were trained in how to use it? Other methods of self-defense desperately need to be explored and implemented. Personal self-defense classes should be offered in every school for all the students, teachers and administrators. Some kind of mental and physical training is definitely needed here so teachers and students can fight back, or at least increase their chances of surviving a school shooting or other violent event by knowing how to react. It's especially tragic to see students in a class of questionable life-utility totally helpless when attacked and even murdered, when they could have been taking a self-defense course that would have given them the right frame of mind to deal with a violent attack while giving them a useful skill for the rest of their lives.

Difference in the Sexes

Attention Deficit Hyperactivity Disorder (ADHD) is just a slightly exaggerated symptom of normal male behavior. When an increasingly large percentage of the boys have to be drugged-up just to get them to sit through an average school day without causing disruptions then it should be obvious to even a half-wit that something is not right with that educational equation. Boys cannot be expected to sit in an uncomfortable chair for eight hours every school day and listen to droning lectures from teachers without reacting in a negative fashion. Mix in drugs to keep them sedated, violent pop-cultural imagery, plus chronic social pressures, and it's no surprise that kids like Pekka-Eric in Finland flip out lusting for revolution in the classroom.

The girls aren't getting much out of contemporary education methods either but crudely speaking women can be programmed, *read this book and listen to this lecture then take this test,* but men have to be trained, *show then do then test.* Yet it's just so much cheaper and quicker to teach the female way than it is to do it the male way because the school system can buy a few books and hire some hack to talk to the kids all day and they don't have to do any of the necessary but slightly more expensive hands-on, out of the classroom type experience-based education. Consequently school becomes a prison sentence for the boys who just get increasingly angry and agitated as it goes on and a gossip session for the girls waiting for the bell to ring.

Knife Menace

The British government has announced plans to search every student for weapons in order to stop a knife-violence 'epidemic'. The blueprint for tackling knife-related violence will include a radical move to give police hundreds of metal detectors to catch young people carrying hidden weapons in schools, clubs and pubs. It has now emerged that the number of people sentenced for having an article with a blade or point on school premises has risen from just 12 in 1996 to 45 in 2005—peaking at 106 in 2004.

Be Your Own Bodyguard

Protection of persons is the job of bodyguards. Unless you are rich enough to afford them, you may wish to learn how to be your own bodyguard. Considering that most people have learned to be their own chauffeurs, chefs and accountants, learning yet another skill won't be much different.

Protecting Children from the Harmful

Effects of Gun Violence

Parents, school administrators, and mental health workers all have roles to play in protecting children and youth from exposure to gun violence and in helping them overcome the effects of gun-related trauma. Parents can closely monitor their children's behavior, environment, and media use. Schools can identify and target services toward students who may be at risk for perpetrating gun violence, but they must be careful not to create a climate of fear. Finally, mental health workers can develop and implement intervention programs that help youth cope with gun violence.

Ethical Values Teachings

Gun control advocates argue that they curb access by criminals, juveniles, and other "high-risk" individuals. It is indeed a sorry state of devaluation of ethical values, now no longer being taught any where including schools and homes. The parents are themselves captive of materialistic world, devoid of real sense of human values like compassion, love, care of weak, destitute, old and disabled. Everywhere, it is money and status which counts and schools like Euro International Public School are no exception. In such a scenario there is an express need to inculcate ethical values in parents and children as well. For this purpose, in schools, there should be a period when ethical values by way of stories, movies, cartoons and discussions should be taught. There children should be encouraged to express their minds freely and hear others. This should eventually become a platform where once in a month teachers and parents should also participate and attend attentively to their wards views, their worries, concerns, hopes, fears openly being expressed. Thus a safety valve will evolve to clean minds of our children from the very beginning and help them to develop the fine qualities of heart and mind.

Gun License Regulated

Gun license should be regulated properly so irresponsible person could not have it. Blame game is an evasive behaviour of the person who has been groomed in subhuman environment. First we must admit the wrong and take corrective measure for future so recurrence of such kind of shame-full incidents could be prevented. whosoever is guilty must be punished so deterrent effect will prevail gun culture has already entered into India. In Bihar most of the Sena have guns and indulging gun fight between them, sambal robbers use guns as of now school boys using guns it is due to recklessness of parents of the boys involved in this incident

Recognizing Violence Warning Signs In Others

Often people who act violently have trouble controlling their feelings. They may have been hurt by others. Some think that making people fear them through violence or threats of violence will solve their problems or earn them respect. This isn't true.

People who behave violently lose respect. They find themselves isolated or disliked, and they still feel angry and frustrated.

If you see these immediate warning signs, violence is a serious possibility:

- ❖ loss of temper on a daily basis,
- ❖ frequent physical fighting,
- ❖ significant vandalism or property damage,
- ❖ increase in use of drugs or alcohol,
- ❖ increase in risk-taking behavior,
- ❖ detailed plans to commit acts of violence,
- ❖ announcing threats or plans for hurting others,
- ❖ enjoying hurting animals, and
- ❖ carrying a weapon.

If you notice the following signs over a period of time, the potential for violence exists:

- ❖ a history of violent or aggressive behavior,
- ❖ serious drug or alcohol use,
- ❖ gang membership or strong desire to be in a gang,
- ❖ access to or fascination with weapons, especially guns,
- ❖ threatening others regularly,
- ❖ trouble controlling feelings like anger,
- ❖ withdrawal from friends and usual activities,
- ❖ feeling rejected or alone,
- ❖ having been a victim of bullying,
- ❖ poor school performance,
- ❖ history of discipline problems or frequent run-ins with authority,
- ❖ feeling constantly disrespected, and
- ❖ failing to acknowledge the feelings or rights of others.

School Checking: First check out the students while he was entering the school campus, if he had any gun, or any violent instruments. Then their parents should be warned to give more money than his/her normal expenditure. The parents should watch their son/daughter's everyday programs. The TV's should be censored the serials.

Media Ban: stop children's TV showing the violence serials.

Sensor for films should be strict.

This can stop to sum extant of the gun culture.

Spirituality: Gun culture could be brought down in India, only when all educational institutions in India, follows from 1st standard, the complete education of 'Vethathri Maharishi',. It is a package, starts with exercise, meditation, introspection. courses and all about spiritual.

Global India: To know what can we do to stop this we first need to know the cause of the same....which in my opinion are:

1. We are no more Indians....Our global image of being polite and culture centered is gone now!!....Indian are the most misbehaved tourist globally: (Sad but true....so since we are not that cultured we can expect such barbaric actions from our kids....
2. Childs development can be easily questioned here.
3. House policies....how come a child has access to these things at home?....
4. Childs exposure to outer world....
5. His friends circle....

To stop the same I guess all the parents need to become better parents to stop such extreme aggressive moves from a child.... a more psychological and scientific approach to child's care will for sure tackle the root cause of the problem....

Finger Print: An effective measure to ensure children's safety around household guns is to implant a fingerprint chip in the trigger. The gun will not fire unless the print of the index finger that pulls the trigger matches that of the embedded chip. This measure also renders all stolen guns useless.

Some feel Gun locks won't stop adult criminals from firing their own guns, but they will prevent law-abiding citizens from defending themselves.

Private safety efforts coupled with a more responsible set of rules and care is needed to avoid any kind of such incidents. There should be advertisements made so as to educate children, as well as adults against the use of such kind of illegal weapons

International: In July 2001, the first UN Conference of Small Arms produced an agreement called the UN programme of action to prevent, combat and eradicate the illicit trade in small arms and light weapons in all its aspects (UN Programme of Action on SALW).

Gunlocks, which are already in stores and on the shelves, may help keep accidents from happing and somewhat keep guns from the wrong hands. They keep children and all others but the key's owner from getting a hold of the gun and even from firing it. This way only the owner of the gun can use it or allow anyone else to use it.

Clinics that teach people how to operate guns properly would help make owners safer. Not only could they teach the proper way to operate the gun but also, they could demonstrate the proper safety precautions that need to be taken into consideration when handling any sort of fire arm. Police procedure to be strict; the person purchasing the gun has to wait for two week while the government performs a background check. Engage today's youth by engaging them in gun safety programs. This way the kids will know about guns and what will happen to them if they abuse them. Also, by legalizing some guns that are illegal the demand for them will go down and illegal gun sale will drop. But if those illegal guns become legal then there should be longer waiting periods and more thorough background checks.

At some places ban a gun, like most campuses, schools etc.

International Help: Of the many organizations keen on implementing gun control, the UN has been the most active. Like every other government or gang, the UN are after maintaining control.

Warning Signs: The warning signs for violent behavior appear in home life, school life, and personal behavior. There is not an accurate way to determine which young people will become violent.

- ❖ Students coping with dysfunctional families and are unable to deal with stresses of their daily life.
- ❖ Students feeling isolated, friendless and picked on are potential school shooters.
- ❖ If a student is talking about shooting people even if it seems like their joking.
- ❖ If a student talks about plans to kill people.
- ❖ Threats to other students.
- ❖ Cannot handle anger.
- ❖ Sometimes a teen will talk about their plans or leave clues that they are thinking about becoming violent.

School programs: In the Kess-lesson (Germany) a speech-stone is passed along so that children have the opportunity to say what they feel while the others have to listen.

When the children act out being the class clown, the super-macho, being chaotic or aggressive, they, on-stage, often say that they were afraid of being laughed at. And everyone else thus realizes that they too may have felt the same and this creates a little more understanding but also self confidence. Many of the children may also have the secret desire to get on stage, but want to be asked. In this way one can gauge a child's courage. This courage gauging is often sought with children and violence is a form of courage testing. In this case one tries through games to strengthen a child's courage though in a more positive way.

Value Education: 'Value Education in schools'. The schools today are drifting away from its meaning as "Institution" and have moved more towards the structure of a corporate system where ultimately financial growth is taken as measure of success! Hence many new schools in metros have advertisement which are glamorous rather than having a list of masterpieces (students) the school has crafted in different fields in past years. The school authorities including the founders and the franchise should understand the basic difference between "LITERACY" and "EDUCATION". gone are the days where the parents used to send children to schools to become literate and earn a degree to earn bread. Today's parents are equipped enough to earn a professional degree for their ward without sending him/her to any school. still every one tries to find a good school for the ward. Its not for the LITERACY but for the EDUCATION! there are certain values social, national etc which can not be taught at home in a closed family. exactly for this EDUCATION, major section of parents today send their children to school.

Criminals have misused firearms, often with tragic results, a few individuals committed those crimes. We should punish the individuals who commit these crimes, and we should imprison those who pose a threat to society so that they do not have the opportunity to cause harm. Punishing law-abiding citizens by passing restrictive gun laws is wrong. Guns are not the cause of this country's crime problem.

Criminals are. Effective crime control legislation must control criminals, not guns.

Effective crime control legislation should provide more prisons to lock up these criminals, and more police officers to deter crime and capture criminals. Effective crime control legislation should give the law-abiding citizens of our country the means to defend themselves.

Firearms can be dangerous in the wrong hand, that is why firearms training is important. The best training consists of parents passing on our firearms heritage, respect for people and property, and some common sense safety rules to their children.

Society does benefit from firearms in the hands of responsible citizens.

It is our responsibility to use them properly and safely.

Report Threatening Behavior

Project trains school teams to conduct threat assessments. The school educates students and staff to report threatening behavior, and then the team evaluates threats to determine how serious they are and what to do in response. Often there is an interpersonal problem, a bullying situation, academic problems, and other concrete problems that the team can address through counseling and other forms of assistance. It is possible to defuse these situations by acting early, not waiting until someone has a loaded gun and hoping that your security forces will stop them.

Psychologists and careful investigation

❖ Psychologists do a careful investigation and develop a response.
❖ Counseling,
❖ law enforcement involvement,
❖ conflict resolution,
❖ many possible interventions.

This is not hypothetical; it is something that many schools are doing.

Threat Assessment

The FBI and Secret Service both studied the possibility of developing profiles of school shooters and both concluded that it was not feasible or scientifically possible to have a PROFILE. However, both groups recommended threat assessment. Threat assessment involves investigating ONLY those individuals who have communicated or engaged in some kind of threat behavior. This is not profiling, but is a response to a behavior that indicates potential violence. Threat assessment is a widely accepted practice in law enforcement and has been encouraged for schools.

Gun Safety Programs

Gun safety programs, typically administered by local firearms dealers and clubs, are designed to teach older children and adolescents how to properly handle a firearm (typically for hunting). Although no study has systematically evaluated such programs for children, gun safety programs have been found to be ineffective in decreasing the firearm injury and death rate among adults[56] and to have had no positive effect on storage practices by gun owners.[57, 58] Even worse, some researchers suggest that gun safety courses for children are likely to increase children's interest in obtaining and using guns and that children cannot be expected to consistently use guns safely even with training.[59]

Gun Avoidance Programs

Gun avoidance programs are more common than gun safety programs, particularly for young children. The curricula of gun avoidance programs depend upon the age of the targeted audience. For younger children, the focus is on avoiding accidental injury; for older children and adolescents, the focus is on preventing the intentional carrying and use of guns. See Table 1 for an overview of several gun avoidance programs.

"Just Say No" Programs

Perhaps the most popular "Just Say No" curriculum for gun avoidance is the Eddie Eagle Gun Safety Program for prekindergarten children through sixth graders, developed by the National Rifle Association (NRA). According to the NRA, the Eddie Eagle program has reached 12 million children since 1988 and "isn't [intended] to teach whether guns are good or bad, but rather to promote the protection and safety of children."[60] The NRA compares Eddie Eagle, the program's mascot, to Smokey Bear. The program advocates teaching children, "Stop! Don't touch. Leave the area. Tell an adult." The program does not give children a reason for avoiding guns (such as that guns are dangerous), but program developers do emphasize that children should be taught that real guns are not toys.

Peer-Based Programs

A final approach to teaching children, particularly older youth, about firearm violence is the use of peers as educators. Most peer-based programs focus on providing or suggesting alternative activities to gun violence and reducing rates of adolescent gun carrying. Such programs are based on the premise that only peers can convince youth to "put down their weapons." However, most of these programs fail to provide adequate alternatives for solving conflict, and do not confront the other reasons youth have for using or carrying guns, such as attaining status, getting attention, retaliation, or fear for personal safety.[73]

Hands without Guns, developed by the Educational Fund to Stop Gun Violence in Washington, D.C., is perhaps the best-known peer-based program to reduce youth gun violence. Targeting junior high and high school students, Hands without Guns is both a public health and an educational campaign, using theater groups, art centers, video clubs, and other after-school projects to change youth attitudes about gun possession. The program includes an evaluation component: a survey to assess changes in attitude and self-reported behaviors among the youth who participate. The unpublished results of this survey of more than 400 students found that of the 38 per cent of youth who could identify the program, only 1.3 per cent carried a gun. Of the 62 per cent who could not identify the program, 10.3 per cent carried a gun.[78] These results should be interpreted with caution, however, because other more relevant variables may be correlated with being able to identify the program. For example, youth who are frequently truant from school and who may not therefore be able to identify a program presented during the school day may be more likely to carry guns. Moreover, self-reporting may overestimate the success of a program, particularly when individuals are asked to reveal illegal behavior.

Furthermore, similar peer-based programs designed to address other concerns of adolescence have not met with great success. For example, according to an evaluation of Students Against Drunk Driving (SADD), a nationally known peer-based program to reduce the rates of drunken driving among adolescents, students at schools with SADD chapters and those at schools without SADD chapters reported similar rates of driving while intoxicated or of riding with a drunken peer.[79] Evidence regarding the effectiveness of peers in influencing youth to adopt healthy behaviors is limited, however; more research is needed.

Program Levels

Grades K-1

Depending on the comprehension level of the children, some terms may need to be explained. For example, children may not understand what is meant by the phrase, "leave the area." The teacher is asked to discuss the concept of "area." Is it the room, the house, the playground, the street corner?

If the children are not familiar with guns, it may be necessary to explain or show graphically what a gun is. Children may have seen people using guns on television. The teacher is asked to explain that guns on television are toys. People on television shows pretend to be shot and die. It's not real. In real life, in all cases, children must follow the safety practices when they come across a gun. They must understand the potential harm that can occur if these safety practices are not followed. Guns are not toys.

Safety education materials designed especially for the ages and development levels of your students are available. Coloring books, for distribution on the same day as the presentation, are provided, and the students should be asked to show them to their parents. The coloring sheets are provided for follow-up reinforcement. The gun safety poster should be put up in the classroom for permanent display.

Grades 2-3 & 4-6

Young people in grades 2-6 are more prone to be curious about guns. They may have developed varying perceptions of fantasy and reality. Television and movies can distort their perceptions. Students at these grade levels need to understand that gun use on television is fantasy. People on television pretend to be shot and die. This age group needs to know that guns are not toys and that showing off with guns is not "cool."

Some children at this age may own BB and pellet guns. *These guns are not toys* and when handling them, children should treat them accordingly. If BB and pellet guns are not handled properly and with adult supervision, they can cause serious injury.

Activity sheets in the form of word finds, a word game and a crypto word are also available. These activity sheets should be used by the classroom teacher for follow-up reinforcement. The gun safety poster should be put up in the classroom for permanent display.

Parent Determination

Guns in America are a problem as bad as the drug problem. There may be nothing anyone can do to reduce the incidence of gun related crimes, but there is something that can be done to protect the innocents from accidental deaths. Stand up for the rights of your children. Put an end to the madness that allows anyone over the age of 18 to walk into a gun shop and walk out 5 minutes later with a gun in their pocket. Make it a law that to own a gun, you must prove not only a valid reason for its possession, but also prove that the gun can be safely and securely stored.

The most important thing is to get some training for yourself. Get some good books on the subject and read them. Knowledge is power, and you need it in this life or death matter. Many families that keep guns at home try hiding them for safety. Sometimes, for good measure, they forbid touching them. These are noble gestures, but they are flawed. You won't hide a gun so well that it's not available when you need it in an emergency, and anything in your house that can be found will be found by an ambitious youngster with sufficient time. The time frame here is, literally, years.

A few devices are available which may be of some use. Several companies are producing lock boxes which bolt to the floor, and have push button combinations which can be operated quickly in the dark. Certain types of handguns can be modified so that only an authorized person can operate it. These may be of use in homes with youngsters where a defensive firearm is kept available.

They're of no use, however, when your kid goes to play across the street with the neighbor's kid. The forbidden fruit approach may only make matters worse. What's a parent to do?

One of the nation's leading experts in this field suggests *empowerment.*

Guns aren't about to go away, and the threat they pose is real, constant and immediate. Don't wait another moment to bring yourself up to speed. Take a class, read some books, and learn what you need to know. Your kids are too precious to sacrifice up to the evening news

Many agree that gun violence is still a major problem that can be alleviated with gun control measures. "A little thing like a background check can prevent a murder. And a little thing like a waiting period can save a life.

15

Techno-Savvy School

The 'Space of Flows'

An important idea which Castells talks about both in this book and his more recent work is that of 'the space of flows'. What he means by this is that historically 'space' has often referred to places in which power, capital, people etc have been concentrated—such as particular cities. However, the new information technology means that people working together in some kinds of work no longer have to be in the same place.

Postindustrial societies from are moving from industrialism to *informationalism*, or the 'informational mode' which now operates together with the capitalist mode of production. Their economies are not based on services so much as 'information processing as the core, fundamental activity conditioning the effectiveness and productivity of all processes of production, distribution, consumption, and management.' Production now means the production of knowledge, and the companies producing it are typically large corporations, many of which are able to operate internationally thanks to information technology. Collective consumption organized by the state, and private consumption through the market also involve the increasing use of information. The machines and software they use have to be developed and made somewhere, and this is where information technology has an impact on urban development and location.

The Focus on School Safety

A generation ago, safety in the classroom wasn't a high-priority concern for school administrators. While there may have been an occasional theft or fight in school, guns, crime and violence weren't by any means considered a significant threat in educational environments. School administrators now know all too well that those days have passed. School safety has become a priority issue—for school administrators, local communities and the nation as a whole. The focus on school safety has been heightened by numerous tragic incidents that have shocked and saddened school communities Student-on-student and student-on-faculty violence has also become a growing concern. As a result, school administrators have been mobilized to join forces with community leaders, law enforcement officials, faculty, staff, parents and students in a collaborative effort to prevent school violence and make educational institutions safer and more secure. That process seems destined to continue for the foreseeable future. Administrators from elementary, middle and high schools across the United States and Canada are assessing the state of safety at their campuses and developing plans, procedures and programs to reduce crime and violence. According to the 2005 report, in the 1999-2000 school year, 14 per cent of primary schools, 20 per cent of middle schools, and 39 per cent of secondary schools used one or more security cameras to monitor the school. That same year, 1999-2000, during school hours, 75 per cent of schools controlled access to school buildings by locking or monitoring doors, and 34 per cent of schools controlled access to school grounds with locked or monitored gates. The vast majority of public schools required visitors to sign or check in when entering the school building (97 percent), while few schools required either students or visitors to pass through metal detectors regularly (1 per cent each). Many security measures varied by school level, and not surprisingly, primary schools were generally less likely than middle schools and secondary schools to report using most security measures.

Schools, like all other facilities and organizations, should have a comprehensive plan that encompasses all facets of security, including the following:

- ❖ Controlling access to buildings, parking lots and other areas.
- ❖ Appropriate security surveillance measures.
- ❖ Electronic equipment, such as access control, intrusion detection, CCTV and video identification systems, required to meet the needs of your school.
- ❖ Written policies, procedures and programs for handling security issues and incidents, responding to emergencies and operating security equipment and systems.
- ❖ Training of staff, faculty and students on security and emergency procedures. Those involved in operating equipment also need to be trained on its proper use.

❖ Establishment of a security education program for staff, faculty, students, parents and the community at large.

Experts often think of security in terms of concentric rings. In a school, the protection rings, or layers, would be as follows:

❖ Outer perimeter protection (this includes the farthest reaches of the school property). Protection of this layer may consist of fencing, natural barriers, CCTV (closed circuit television), lighting systems, signs and alarm systems.
❖ Building perimeter (this generally includes parking lots and the areas immediately surrounding the school).
❖ The protection of this layer may include lighting systems, alarm systems, locking devices, CCTV, bars or grillwork, signs or additional fencing.
❖ Building interior (this includes the entire interior of the building, i.e. corridors, classrooms, offices, faculty areas, cafeteria, gymnasium, library, etc.) The security design for this layer can include window/door bars, locking devices, barriers, access/intrusion/alarm systems, CCTV, lighting systems, and safes and controlled areas.
❖ Very high security areas (areas that may need especially tight security, such as computer rooms, science laboratories, front offices, etc.). Security here might entail access/intrusion/alarm systems and/or CCTV cameras or systems.

Closed circuit television (CCTV) has become a primary tool in modern security systems.

Technological advances have made video monitoring systems much more effective for security, and much more affordable. As a result, closed circuit television systems represent one of the fastest-growing segments of the electronic security market. And CCTV cameras are most definitely becoming more widely used in schools.

Today's most basic CCTV system consists of cameras, an LCD or flat-screen monitor and a digital video recorder. The more sophisticated systems allow viewing and control of cameras at an on-site workstation. In general, surveillance security systems can provide:

❖ General facility surveillance.
❖ A deterrent to undesirable behavior.

❖ Recorded evidence of security events that can be used to identify individuals involved in a security incident.

With a CCTV systems, any office in the building can have immediate visibility to activity inside or outside the school. Video images can also be directed to any laptop computer.

In school settings, surveillance cameras can be positioned to record events in parking lots, corridors, the library, gymnasium, or cafeteria, or in potential trouble spots in the school. CCTV cameras are also frequently placed in school buses. (It's important to note that in school environments, cameras are not used to directly monitor the activities of students, faculty and staff. Rather, they're used to monitor the environment, ensuring that it remains safe for students, faculty and staff.)

There are two basic types of surveillance cameras. Fixed cameras show a single field of view. Pan—Tilt-Zoom (PTZ) cameras can look around, or zoom in to get a closer look. Schools today typically use fixed cameras in housings. We're also seeing an increase in the use of high-security type housings. In some cases, schools are installing dome enclosures with built-in camera/optics packages. These provide all the capability and control of a PTZ product in smaller, less conspicuous packages.

Advancing technology is bringing larger monitors and higher screen resolution to CCTV applications.

The use of color cameras is also on the rise. With its high resolution and low light sensitivity, current color camera technology provides superior identification capability. Today's advanced digital communications technology provides schools with remote video capability, which allows "live" images from CCTV cameras to be compressed and transmitted to a central station monitoring center.

The use of digital video systems that operate via an IP-based Internet connection is on the rise in schools. In large districts, we're seeing IP-based surveillance systems with 500 or more cameras. With today's technology, these systems can operate on the school's existing network architecture and be implemented in a way that minimizes bandwidth requirements. The systems can also provide immediate retrieval—the ability to retrieve a desired set of still images or motion video clips from specific cameras over a specific time frame. A network-centric system can make current or archived surveillance data quickly and conveniently available anywhere on the network to authorized users.

In K-12 schools, surveillance systems typically are not monitored. It does take an investment of resources on the part of a school in order to monitor CCTV cameras. If there is no live on-site monitoring, the cameras—rather than serving an intervention function—act as an after-incident review tool. Ultimately, CCTV, will only be as good as the monitoring and recovery operations applied to the system by the school. All of these issues related to monitoring should be considered in the security assessment and system design process.

Consideration should also be given to the type and method of image recording and to the desirability of remote monitoring, which can be delivered by a security provider with a central monitoring station. Many schools are beginning to have their CCTV systems monitored by an off-site central monitoring facility during critical situations.

Central station monitoring centers can provide around-the-clock electronic surveillance for schools as well as commercial and industrial facilities. In the event of an intrusion or a detected emergency (or a fire if your fire alarm system is also connected to a central station), a message is transmitted to the central station. The alarm message indicates the nature and location of the incident. Customer service personnel at the Center then notify the appropriate authorities according to your customized emergency response protocol. This arrangement requires a strong partnership between the school and local law enforcement.

Access Control Systems: Access control is the process of determining who is allowed entry to a school building, or to specific areas within it. The use of access control technology, in accordance with clearly defined and carefully implemented security procedures, provides a school with an effective means of managing risk. In school applications, access control systems are used to identify users (students, faculty and frequent authorized visitors) before allowing them to enter the building or in some cases, the school grounds. The intent of an access control system is to let only authorized people in, and do so with a minimum of inconvenience. Access control points like doors or gates are equipped with a card reader or biometric device to authenticate an access request.

System users are typically issued a card with a magnetic stripe or an embedded electronic circuit that enables them to gain access to the building. Cards are swiped through the magnetic stripe reader, or placed next to a proximity reader. Most access cards issued in schools also contain some identifying information that may include a name, ID number, portrait or signature (see Video or Photo Identification Systems below). Many are even worn as identification badges after entry to the building has been granted.

Intrusion Detection and Alarm Systems: Detection and alarm systems provide perimeter and interior protection for school facilities by detecting unauthorized entries into a building, or into a protected area within a building. These systems are typically used to monitor the after-hours status of buildings. An intrusion might trigger a siren or bell, send an alarm message to the security control panel, prompt a surveillance camera to automatically pan to a door, or transmit an alarm message to a remote central station if the school has a monitoring agreement in place.

Video or Photo Identification Systems: Many schools have implemented video or photo identification systems that provide a means to identify students, faculty and staff. Each student, teacher and staff member is issued an identification card, or a badge, that contains his or her picture. In the case of a video identification system, the person's picture is captured on a video camera and stored in conjunction with his or her data record.

A video identification system can operate as a stand-alone badging system or as a component of an access control system. In that application, the badge serves a dual purpose as it also becomes an access control card. One of the benefits of a video or photo identification system is that it provides a school with database from which information, such as video images of students and staff or emergency contact names, can be extracted.

Security Management Systems: The most advanced electronic security systems provide complete coordination of all security activities. With those systems, all aspects of security—access control, intrusion detection, CCTV and video badging—can be linked to a common database and controlled from a single PC workstation. Again, keep in mind that an investment of resources on the part of the school administration is required in order to derive the benefits of a sophisticated security management system.

Metal Detectors: The NCES 2005 school safety report shows that between 3 and 4 per cent of primary schools reported performing random metal detector checks on students. Fifteen per cent of secondary schools reported random metal detector checks. Metal detectors are probably one of the most visible and intrusive types of physical security. They also demand a large amount of personnel time to staff the detector location so as to prevent walk-around and detain for closer inspection any person triggering a detection alarm.

Communication systems can play a significant role in school safety. Telephone, intercom, paging, public address and emergency call systems can enhance school security by making classrooms, parking lots and other areas safer for students and teachers. For example, some digital telephone systems provide for emergency calls to be generated—manually or automatically—from any classroom equipped with a phone. The emergency call is sent to a digital display phone in the main office. When the call is received there, the display screen on the office phone labels it as an **EMERGENCY,** and also identifies its place of origin. The office in turn can contact the adjacent classrooms to warn of the emergency, or to activate a mutual help compact if one has been put in place. A new approach, mandated in some states, is to use the E911 service, whereby the emergency condition and location are automatically transmitted to the phone company, which dispatches the responding personnel.

You need to carefully consider how you will operate, support and maintain the system on a day-to-day basis. Because resources are usually limited, schools sometimes have a tendency to look for 'quick fix' solutions. Security definitely cannot be viewed in that narrow kind of context. Rather, you need to employ a comprehensive, systems approach when thinking about security. As we mentioned earlier, security doesn't begin and end with security equipment. It's essential that you have the personnel, plans and procedures in place to operate and maintain the system and to fulfill the requirements of your security program. Otherwise, you won't get the most out of your system or the investment you make in it. Toward that end, an analysis of the skill levels and capabilities of the people who will be asked to operate the system should be part of your evaluative process. You'll want to make sure they have the skills required to operate today's advanced technology systems.

What all this means is that you need to plan not only for incorporating new electronic equipment into your security program, but also for managing the impact of those technological changes on the people and processes that you currently have in place. Understanding those issues in advance will help ensure that you make a wise investment, and that you avoid after-implementation pitfalls that many security purchasers face.

Schools that have fire alarm systems with voice communications capabilities can use it to help improve emergency notification and evacuation. With the approval of the local AHJ (Authority Having Jurisdiction…typically a fire marshal or fire chief), interactive paging can be employed to evacuate in an emergency or to direct students and staff away from the danger and toward "safe zones." Wireless telephone systems can provide a tie-in to emergency first responders, meaning two-way communications can be established to support the response effort regular service is a critical component of a security program. Your security system represents an important investment in the protection of your students and your staff. To protect that investment, you'll want to be sure the system is properly serviced so that it functions at an optimal level. Periodic inspections, testing and preventive maintenance, as well as 24-hour emergency service, all contribute to the proper operation of your security system and/or CCTV equipment. Because maintenance funds are difficult to procure, some schools incorporate the cost of a service contract into a monthly lease payment.

There are a number of other things you can do. You can forge a partnership with the local police and other law enforcement agencies. If possible, consider having a police officer routinely walk through the school as part of his or her daily patrol. You might think about having an officer on the grounds at peak times in the morning and afternoon, or even about setting up a police substation at the school.

16

Our Troubled Teachers

There was a time when teachers were highly respected in the society and teachers were also dedicated to enlighten the pupil with his knowledge. However with the changing time the concept changed gradually and today the world has become very much professional. Now that rapport between teachers and students is missing.

The teacher of today is gloomy, pessimistic and frustrated. Some of the common types of teachers that one finds in schools are:

- ❖ Insecure teachers.
- ❖ Poorly prepared teachers.
- ❖ Conservative teachers.
- ❖ Experimentally minded teachers.
- ❖ The frustrated teacher.

It is expected of a teacher that he should be a Robot. But all cannot be equally good and great. There are teachers who are good, who are reputed and respected in the society. There are teachers also who are bad, useless, and not even fit for profession.

Some teachers have entered the teaching profession, because nothing else was available. They had to join it without an inner urge. They look upon the work as a means of earning a Hvelihqpd. There is no joy, no self-fulfillment, no self-expression. "A teacher whose soul is dead, whose heart is atrophied, who is devoid of energy and enthusiasm, capacity and character, who simply marks I time, whose eyes are fixed on the calendar is a disgrace and curse to the society". If he finds no joy in his work, how can he be expected to infuse sense of happiness in the child he teaches '. If he is dissatisfied and insecure how can he provide satisfaction and security to the boy whom he guides ? If he lacks sparkling wine within how can he light the lamp in others?

"You cannot pour put into it: and if a teacher is poor out of a vessel except that you have and shallow from within, if there is no sparkling wine in him, he cannot quicken the mind or humanize the emotions of the children, if he is not the lighted candle himself he will not be able to light the flame in others". —*K. G. Saiyidan.*

Below we are giving a discussion on some common types of teachers as we find in our schools, but at the same time we would like to caution that there are still a greater number of successful, invigorating, good teachers even in the high or higher secondary schools.

The teacher of today is gloomy, pessimistic and frustrated. He represents the withered heart of the school whose morale has gone down to the bottom of the sea. He suffers from dry rot. He will chill the fire in a January stove or furrow the brow or a happy, barefoot boy. In the classroom he calls the roll, hears the spelling, reads the book, dictates the notes, and leaves the room in the same spirit in which he brings the necessaries for his home. The Poorly Prepared Teacher. Why does a teacher become low in the eyes of others? It is perhaps because he lacks the mastery of the subject natters; consequently he is unable to control the Class. No teacher can be expected to inspire youth with the love of scholarship if he has no mastery over his field, if he does not himself abreast of the latest developments there, if he not study and make continuous research in his area. A number of teachers who come to school have a self-conceit that they know enough and do not need to know more. There is no type of work where the results of poor planning are so devastating as in teaching. A teacher may be very able and experienced, but he cannot succeed without his preliminary preparation.

A teacher may not be the master of his subject, but he can succeed if he indulges in self-study while he is in service. Attending seminars and refresher courses costs nothing. Such opportunities are offered to all teachers but a teacher who has no fire within cannot take advantage of those facilities. A teacher cannot teach unless he is learning himself.

This broad classification of poorly prepared teachers is always with as and a concrete action can be taken to improve them. Every teacher is to some extent poorly prepared for the specific responsibility he assumes in a school. Each teacher is unprepared in quite a different way. One may feel uncertain as to how to deal with a troublesome child. The other may feel insecure as how to conduct a first grade reading programme. It is the teacher himself who should find his own shortcomings and improve himself.

The Insecure Teacher. To some extent all teachers are insecure as are all human beings in any walk of life. Feelings of insecurity in teachers are especially important because in his work with children the insecurity is transmitted to those with whom he comes in contact. It is therefore being widely realised that we should not allow teaching profession to suffer from insecurity. The economic status of the teacher is uncertain. The financial prospects which teaching profession offers are still so poor that persons with ambition and intelligence are seldom attracted to it and there are only a few who have a genuine call for it. Persons who come to teaching profession are mostly drawn from lower middle and low income groups of the society. We have sons and" daughters of farmers, small businessmen, clerks in abundance who are working as teachers. Those who can afford to pay for higher education go up to the university and try to find more lucrative jobs and rarely think of coming to teaching profession. It is only when they have failed to get good jobs elsewhere, that they enter teaching line and remain always on the lookout for still better jobs elsewhere. This is the real cause of insecurity.

The insecure teacher needs above all to find some source of assurance in his position and his work with boys and girls. If the major source of insecurity lies in a heavy financial burden in maintaining a home it is difficult to see how the administration can help him. Vigorous championing of better salary schedules may help. Therefore, the Education Commission (1964-66) has given top priority to enhancement of salaries and improvement of general service conditions. If, however, the teacher feels insecurity because he lacks status in the group, it may be possible to produce confidence him by recognizing his worth and men and by giving him the responsibility he can shoulder successfully. If he feels insecure because of some personal defect, the Principal can help him to overcome it and thus by improving his classroom practices make him feel more confident.

The Frustrated Teacher: Frustration is caused by blocking of the satisfaction of needs and desires of an individual. Financial problems sometimes may cause frustration in a teacher. Family make a teacher frustrated. Unhappiness on the contributory factor. For certain combination the teachers it may For example, some troubles may job is also a be any one or some of them in teachers become frustrated in the teaching situation which leads them to feel that the Principal docs not believe they are repentant. Such teachers can be helped to increase their effectiveness if their leader shows confidence in them and respects them for their contri-bution So long as a frustrated teacher is faced with serious emotional problems which interfere with his professional competence he is a problem to the headmaster. The minimum that the official leader can do in this case is to make the school climate for him so pleasant and happy that he forgets his frustration during the school day.

The Conservative Teacher: As we have said earlier, many teachers do not feel fire within to know more. They stick to the 'tried and true' and do not adventure with new educational traditional method is the best teachers and "therefore they prefer the conventional one. These should be guaranteed the right of making progress at their own pace and be given assurance arid encouragement to hold what they believe to be right or true until their convictions change, *Use,* we would have frustration again and make such teachers insecure.

The Experimentally Minded Teacher: At the opposite end of the scale lies a teacher who is always ready for change, who is impatient with the old order" and who thinks of any change as an improvement. Such a class of teachers is a rare phenomenon. He loses drive and enthusiasm when he finds himself surrounded by the conservatives. As he is one to be prized; the Principle should help him to fit himself in the framework of the staff values. H» motivations, his desires should be respected and should be guided as to how he can achieve change in the world having firm belief in the status quo.

Presence of Dull Teachers a Challenge to the Headmaster or Principal: When the Principal has dull teachers, pessimistic and gloomy, what can he do? Should he promote team work? Should he give them a sense of satisfaction in work well don? His ability to encourage such teachers to work creatively is taxed. Should he remain businesslike in his relations with them or should he develop a good school climate in which they may get fresher air? The best way is to create a good school climate by giving them a feeling that they belong to the school, that their achievement is being acknowledged, that they will get as much economic security as he can possibly offer them, that they should be free from fear that they have a contribution to make to the school as their powers allow, that they will be respected and regarded as individuals and fellow colleagues.

Such a school climate is directly related to morale and group morale comes when each member is invited to share in making plans, in determining the procedures, and in executing the plans and schemes so decided.

Teachers want security and comfortable living, pleasant working conditions, fair treatment, a sense of achievement and growth, recognition of contribution, participation m deciding policy, opportunity to maintain self-respect. The Principal is required to give them all these.

Role of Teacher

Good people make good schools. The quality of the school can be no better than the people who are responsible for its improvement. If the headmaster is the coping stone in the school structure, the teacher's role is no less important. If the nation's teachers are C$_s$, the nation itself cannot but be C$_3$ and' let there be no "doubt about it: if we wish to be A$_1$. We want a duly equipped living teacher—a teacher who realizes his duties and responsibilities to the child, the parent, the community and the nation itself. Without good teachers the best system is bound to fail, as without a good Principal the best school is wrecked. With good teachers even the defects of a system can be largely overcome.

The teacher's role in the society is vital. He acts as a pivot. He keeps the lamp of civilization burning. He guides the destiny of the nation. He is the architect of the future. He has a specific role to play in the reconstruction of the country.

India which has planned for education reconstruction, is in need of really good teachers. It is the body of good teachers upon which the destiny of the nation depends,

"Of all the different factors which influence the quality of contribution to national development, the quality, competence and character of teachers are undoubtedly the most significant."

❖ *The Role of Teachers in Guiding Learning*: The effective teacher develops broad outlines and objectives to be attained for a subject, selects materials, teaching aids, uses efficient methods, makes judicious use of lectures, discussions, demonstrations, experimentation, projects and field trips; maintains and develops pupil interest in the learning process; develops suitable study habits in children; evaluates the effective evaluation techniques: in short, does all for pupil growth and development in the school.

❖ *He is also Responsible for Judging Pupil Growth Through Evaluation*: He collects evidence of a specific nature about the child, judges it objectively, and makes unbassed interpretation of the mass of data that he so collects regarding the child's intelligence, achievement and aptitude. He gets all information about the child from his health records, anecdotal reports, activity records, his creative writings, his interest inventories, and parent conferences. He attempts to gain the widest and the deepest understanding and knowledge of individual child.

The teacher is also responsible for building character. It is he who can best infuse in the child the respect for what is good, what is right and what is just. It is he who can create leadership qualities in the children he guides. It is he who can encourage desirable traits of personality and character because he alone comes in direct contact with the pupil.

❖ *Role of Teacher in Guidance*: The changing concept of guidance, which associates it with the daily activity of the class-room teacher, gives a greater responsibility to him. It means that the teacher who is dealing with children should be given in service education for discharging his responsibility in personal, educational and vocational guidance. The necessity of such an inservice employ special guidance. The necessity of such an inservice programme is felt because we are at present not in a position to employ special guidance personnel in each school. Many of the non-teacher: and some aspects needing technical knowledge may be developed through inservice education. The functions of the school teacher for guidance include:

Use of tools and techniques for intensive study of children, e.g., intelligence, achievement, aptitude tests, interest inventories.

❖ Establishing and maintenance of records and reports.
❖ Developing a programme of study groups for parents so that they may be able to understand their children's problems

Coordinating the work of special services related to guidance, for example, the work of school doctor, the dentist, the counsellor, and the guidance officer. Role of Teacher in maintaining community relations. A good teacher understands the importance of good parent and community relations. He understands well that however good a proposal or an educational programme may be; unless the public understands and accepts it as good, he cannot hope to succeed. A good teacher therefore tries to make community ready for accepting a desirable change in the programme through parent-teacher associations or parent study councils. He understands that, as the public has a tremendous investment in the public schools, participation of the community is essential in the development of school policies. He also understands well that the role of education is not only confined to serve the needs of children and youth, but in a broader sense education has to contribute much to the community as a whole.

With this philosophy in mind, a good teacher tries to build good parent-community relations. He tells through his children what a good school is doing. He draws the attention of the parents to school's prowess, service and cultural contribution by taking an effective part in the organization of school functions. He impresses the public by showing the achievements of his boys in scholastic field, in cultural programmes, and in games and sports. When parents come to school he welcomes their visits, respects their ideas and gives them help and confidence.

In the Parent Study groups he informs the parents how well they can look after the welfare of their children. The alert school staff can serve a great need in the lives of the ignorant, uneducated, illiterate parents by making it possible for them to come together, to become better acquainted with the needs of children in general, to inform them how well they can nourish, look after their children at home and help the school in achieving its goals. What a teacher can do to help the parent has been explained in detail in section dealing with Parent Teacher Association.

Role of the Teacher in Helping Administration: No administrator can be successful without the active and willing cooperation of the school teacher. The creative Principal knows well the power of cooperative process of using his staff and community resources. The creative headmaster improves an educational institution only through group approach. He believes that there is much greater chance of success when a group turns its creative power to the problem of school policy, making and executing it. He knows well that there is a greater support for confidence and shares with them his responsibility. A good teacher is then one who shares responsibilities with his head, and performs his duties like a disciplined soldier. He helps the headmaster not only in administration but gives him enough support in his organization which involves manifold activities— classification and reclassification of pupils, framing of time table, organization of co-curricular activities, maintenance of building, maintenance of pupil records, management of school business, supervision of other colleagues, organization of public function, building of head-community relations, etc.

When teachers in England talk about their work, their concerns are predictable; They talk about the fact that there doesn't seem to be enough time to cover what is expected, let alone time to follow up interesting lines of thought or explore new ideas with their classes. They feel that their freedom to make decisions about their work has been constricted. They worry about dealing with increasingly difficult behavior from pupils. They are concerned about the image of teachers in the media and an apparently generalized lack of respect for their work. They talk about increased managerialism, paperwork and bureaucracy in schools. They talk about the amount of testing and number of examinations they have to prepare pupils for. They talk about rising levels of stress, reduced leisure time and, often, express a sense that much of the fun or enjoyment has gone from their work.

If we take an even broader frame of reference, it is clear that, in developed societies, the nature of work itself is changing in response to what might be generally termed the processes of globalization—that is, the availability of information technologies and instant communication networks which facilitate the movement of capital around the world to take advantage of local conditions. The processes of globalization have a profound impact on where work is located, the skills required in the workforce and how the workplace is organised. Amongst the changes in work patterns identified by Smyth *et al.* (2000:3) are:

❖ the harnessing of peer pressure and team work
❖ a greater emphasis on customer needs
❖ the promotion of a culture of continuous improvement
❖ reliance on market forces as a form of regulation, rather than rules and centralised bureaucratic forms of organisation
❖ more emphasis on image management
❖ a greater reliance on technology to solve problems
❖ a resort to increasingly technicist ways of responding to uncertainty.

But in school, as in other workplaces, the changes mean that teachers' work has been redesigned, and that the skills teachers need today are different from the skills teachers needed in the past. Lawn (1996:18) offers the example of what counts as a 'good primary teacher,' commenting that this 'has shifted from being an isolated classroom worker with generalist skills to a classroom and school-based team worker with specialist skills.' Coaching, supporting, mentoring and developing other staff have become increasingly important in teachers' work. These processes, viewed from different perspectives, in different contexts and at different historical moments, can be interpreted as participatory and enlightened or part of an apparatus of surveillance and control.

Waters (1995:3) defines globalization as "a social process in which constraints of geography on social and cultural arrangements recede and in which people become increasingly aware that they are receding." On the macro level, the possibilities of immediate communication and transfer of information and ideas, the ease of travel and the sense of a global community can seem exciting, if dangerous, and redolent with potential. But these same possibilities can also seem overwhelming and potentially disempowering, and part of people's response to the removal of geographical and cultural constraints has been an increased focus upon the local. This has resulted in national fragmentation in many parts of the world, and a focus on ethnicity, hybridity and difference which might be seen as staking a claim for individual and group identities in the face of globalising forces. In teachers' work these same tensions can be traced. New technologies, common improvement policies and teaching resources and shared recipes for pedagogic 'best practice' seem, on one level, to efface differences between schools. Yet on another level, differences between schools are becoming more marked; school is signally failing to meet the educational needs of some groups of children, and for some teachers the work environment is proving personally and professionally damaging.

Teaching is complex moral and cultural, as well as intellectual, work. The work is about identity formation, cultural transmission, communication, moral responsibility and caring for children. A reduced view of the teacher's role, which over-emphasises teaching as a technical activity, dis-empowers teachers and diminishes their effectiveness in working with pupils and colleagues. Kevin Harris calls this reduced effectiveness and confidence 'subdued agency':

> ...*discourse surrounding the role of the teacher has tended recently to promote a particular form of disempowerment of teachers, which I would characterize as 'subdued agency'. In starting from a pessimistic view about the potential ineffectiveness of teachers to promote social change (a view ironically spawned by both correspondence and resistance theories of schooling), or from a moral concern over whether teachers have the right to manipulate other people and impose their goals on them, or from a political concern that those targeted for change might have no desire (or need) to be meddled with, or even from simply eschewing conflict theories of the state, this discourse has moved generally towards embracing the language of 'consensus'. It has cast the teacher not as the deliberate promoter of particular ends, but rather as one who lays out options without favour, and who facilitates the process of choice among available options within a context seeking, if not total consensus, then at least a form of social harmony.* (1994:4)

To be effective, schools rely upon the energy, confidence and commitment of individual teachers. Teaching should be optimistic, active work; teachers should consider themselves as 'deliberate promoters of particular ends' rather than neutral channels for providing a range of options. When teachers feel discouraged and disempowered as a group, the problem often becomes individualised and reframed to make individual teachers feel personally guilty or incompetent. The 'solutions' that follow are then also framed in individual terms—rectifying skills deficits, appraisal, putting more accountability measures in place. I am interested here in looking at teachers' work from the other angle—understanding more about the broader context of teaching as work, exploring what societies seem to be demanding of teachers at this particular historical moment—in the belief that teachers can regain some sense of power, and claim back some of the 'subdued' agency, by having an analysis of their current work situation that focuses on the macro level changes currently engulfing the profession.

The development of Labour Process Theory (particularly in the work of Smyth *et al*, 2000) is useful in thinking through recent changes in teachers' work; Braverman's original formulation of the theory in 1974 related to capitalist production processes, so the theory does not immediately seem to be applicable to teachers as public sector workers. But teachers' work can be seen as part of the total production process in that they have their own part to play in educating future labor power, and developing skills and knowledge which increase labor productivity. In this view, schools are seen as producers of human capital needed by the economy, with teachers as a specialized workforce producing the larger workforce (Connell, 1985). Like private sector workers, teachers sell their labor power. The problem for the state as teachers' employer is how to convert their labor power into actual labor. Therefore control is essential, as with private sector workers. Control is therefore a core concept in labour process theory (Smyth *et al.*, 2000:21).

The need for control also relates to the intensely political nature of the work teachers are engaged in. Different stakeholders expect differing 'products' from the education system—for example, parents and employers might have different hopes and expectations of schooling. At any historical point there will be divergent opinions about what should be taught and why. The curriculum—that is, both the formal specification of knowledge to be taught and the informal curriculum, which includes decisions about how knowledge is segmented, how teaching is organized, what are considered to be the right ways of behaving—is the key element that defines teachers' work. The curriculum glues teachers' disparate activities together. The curriculum is therefore the main specification of the labour process of teaching. And this specification is likely to be struggled over by the different groups with an interest in what schooling sets out to achieve. One of the state's roles, then, will be to broker agreements between different groups. To ensure that agreed decisions are implemented, the state will need to be able to control teachers.

In USA

What ails American schools can be traced to a bureaucracy that: a) doesn't pay enough; b) does too little to encourage and reward creativity; c) doesn't give principals authority over who works in their schools; d) makes it nearly impossible to fire bad teachers. No one becomes a teacher to get rich. You become a teacher because you want to give back, you want to shape future generations, you want to change the world. But the reality of educational system and the grimy culture in which it operates is that that prime directive often winds up subordinate to the directives of a creativity-choking bureaucracy that seems less interested in educating disadvantaged kids than in warehousing them.

The new contract between New York City's teachers and the Board of Education is more than just a package of wage increases. It also redefines important elements of a teacher's professional role.

Highlights of the Teachers Pact

Teachers will receive a one-year pay increase of 5.5 per cent and contribution of $100 per member to the welfare fund. The total of $236 million would come from these sources: (chart showing sources as $104 miilion in pension savings; $62 million from city budget and $62 million in state aid). Hearings for teachers charged with policy or rule violations will be quicker. Decisions, under binding arbitration, will be made by a single arbitrator, and there will be no appeal. A school-based management program is incorporated into the contracts official policy.

School principals must respect teachers' judgment on student grades and may not change them without justification.

Teachers may determine the format of their own lesson plans; the principal may no longer dictate lesson plan forms.

A new provision allows teachers to work part-Time at prorated salaries.

17

Conclusion

❖ 74 per cent of Indian population lives in the villages i.e. 1,100 million Population
❖ 794.5 million Rural living in 750,000 villages
❖ 305.5 million Urban

Differences are there between urban and rural areas in their physical characteristics and density of population, utilization of land and habitation.

India has a rich religious and cultural heritage, extending about 5,000 years into the past. The population of India is multi-racial, multi-religious and multi-lingual. This populace lives within extremely diverse geographical conditions. Equally diverse has been their history, due to invasions by various races-dating back to Huns & Greeks in the 2nd and 3rd centuries A.D. (Panikkar, 1955).

For this diverse population Indian religion provides a common base. Indian religion, 'Dharma', is not a narrow term in the Western sense, but is an all encompassing way of life. More than 80 per cent of the population are Hindus, and the rest belong to major religion like Christianity (2.5%) Islam (12%) and Jainism (2%) Christians and Muslims of India are converts from Hinduism. Hence, they follow most of the socio-religious beliefs and practices of Hinduism.

Nature and Beliefs in Hinduism

Hinduism is polytheistic in nature. It also believes in the existence of God in humans, animals, and natural forces. It believes that God exists in the soul of the individual, which ultimately merges into a universal cosmic force called 'Paramatma' meaning 'Universal Soul'.

These beliefs about the nature of God and human beings, was earlier put into writing in the Sanskrit language, through the Vedas, the Smritis and the Dharma Shastras. They were further vividly illustrated in the two most important epics of Indian mythology—the Ramayana and the Mahabharata. From the 10th century onwards these works were re-interpreted and translated into the vernacular by saints of the Bhakti movement and other preachers. They spread these beliefs among the masses through the media of story, drama, dance, Ballads and hymns, and even sculpture.

Polytheistic beliefs were practised through idol worship, the idols, being in human, animal or 'natural' (e.g. the Sun God) forms. Each of these idols has a symbolism, representing knowledge, wealth, strength etc. Every Hindu is believed to be born with Godly and demonic qualities innate in him.

New Urbanism

A late 20th-century movement in planning variously called new urbanism, smart growth, *or* neo-traditionalism, has attracted popular attention through its alternative views of suburban development. Reflecting considerable revulsion against urban sprawl, *suburban* traffic congestion, and long commuting times, this movement has endorsed new construction.

Urban-Rural Community

What does it mean to live in a rural community? It has been said rural life encourages a greater sense of community and perspective on what is important. The health benefits of living out of the urban, or even suburban areas are manifold, as well: clean air and an abundance of foliage are enough to convince many 'urbanites' that country living is for them.

Services such as municipal water and sewage disposal are a rarity in rural areas. Private services, such as wells and septic tanks, which require periodic maintenance, water and ground testing, and the possibility of a dry well in the summer months, come at what can be a greater cost.

In urban areas it is fairly easy to find transportation, with city bus systems and taxis serving the populace. The opposite is the case in rural areas; without your own transportation, it is difficult to get around. With greater distances between houses and commercial outlets, even getting groceries becomes a difficulty. If a person loses their driver's licence or vehicle for any reason, it's a real hardship in a rural area. People can lose their jobs as a consequence of not being able to drive. The whole family will suffer.

That said, when a family faces hardship, often those in a rural community are quick to help wherever they can. If there is a death in the family of a member of the community, neighbours are right there with condolences and casseroles. If a child of a community member falls ill, the community pulls together to raise money for the family. If fire takes your possessions, the community will hold fundraisers and give donations to ensure that the basics are covered, or even more.

The reactions to these kinds of situations are much different in urban areas. Many urbanites don't know their neighbours beyond a 'hello' as they pass each other in the hall. Some not even that much. Maybe they don't need their neighbours, the way people in the rural areas have come to depend on theirs.

Neighbours in rural areas organize more events together than urbanites. From church dinners to fairs, to the community's summer barbecue, most members of the community have their fingers in the pie, in one way or another. It is these types of events that help to bring a community together, because those who attend can claim ownership of the event.

In urban areas, special events are often competing against each other, since there are often many happening at any given time. Many people who attend urban events have no sense of pride in these events, as they are just that, patrons of the event, not co-ordinators.

Rural Network

What makes rural, rural? What is unique about living in a rural community? What changes are taking place that affect the quality of rural living? The density of population and the relative isolation from other people have a distinct effect on the way people view life and the values they espouse.

Density of population doesn't mean more social interactions. In fact the smallest and most remote rural communities have the most social interactions. A "dense" social network means that people in the social network are friends, related, know each other and interact regularly. In terms of quantity of social interactions, rural isolation is a myth. In another sense, rural isolation is not a myth. It is precisely because of the closeness of the social network that rural people generally confide in fewer people about important matters. Friendly doesn't necessarily mean open.

Communitarian and individualistic values. The rural value system is primarily communitarian and relational. These values are found primarily in peasant villages, agricultural communities, ethnic neighborhoods or tribal communities. The dimensions of being rooted in a particular place and having continuous life-long relationships with kin and friends underpin the psychology and sociology of these communities. The dominant value system in the cities is that of individualism. These values flourish in western, industrial, mobile societies where capitalism, material well-being and career identity form the bedrock of personal endeavor. These values are embedded in the economy, schools, media and other institutions. These messages are taught, articulated and advertised.

Rural people adopt these values to survive in the larger economic and social environment they find themselves. Underneath these values are the rules for surviving in a harmonious community.

Rewards in rural life. The rewards of the rural value system are belonging, emotional support, security and predictability. One major contrast between rural and urban living is the type of emotional connections and bonds rural people have with their friends and neighbors. Another is the sense of community and community participation.

The way people relate to one another in rural communities is more personal, emotional, direct and socially supportive. People encounter each other in friendship and social roles as well as formal roles within the community. Everybody knows everybody. There is a feeling of belonging and fellowship, a feeling of genuine affection for each other. Even relationships with authority figures are softened or tempered by social constraints and niceties.

Rural people have more relationships characterized by this direct, personal style of interaction than do urban residents. The social sphere of urban dwellers is limited to a much smaller range of friends and acquaintances.

Conclusion

There are different types of media: teenagers are eager consumers of television, video games, and the Internet. They rarely read the newspapers. There is excessive information. Violence is a fact of life. Physical, psychological, economic, social, or environmental violence is an essential part of humanity and its works.

Guns can become fatal when in the hands of a criminal, someone who is not stable and sane, children, or even someone who has no or very little experience shooting or handling guns. If guns can be controlled there would certainly be a lot less death because of guns and even less death in general.

In a democratic society, there are alternatives to violence that must be pursued. The problem with absolutists is that they cannot lose an argument or admit defeat, and this is an anti-democratic view.

Guns are for cowards. You can kill from a distance. You are detached, removed. You don't get your hands dirty. You don't feel the life draining out of another human being in an eye to eye struggle, face to face, with your hands squeezing or beating soft, human, flesh, one on one.

Exposure to gun violence profoundly affects children and youth—even if they are not the direct victims or perpetrators. Psychologically, exposure to violence can normalize the use of violence to resolve conflicts. Socially, it can limit young people's ability to develop healthy relationships and friendships. Victims of gun violence also may suffer permanent physical damage, both visible (scars) and invisible (altered patterns of brain activity). Finally, children exposed to violence may do poorly in school and stop hoping for a productive and happy future. All of these outcomes can feed into a cycle of continuing violence.

Working together, parents, school administrators, and mental health professionals can help to prevent gun violence and to minimize children's exposure to violence when it does occur. The potential rewards of such efforts are clear: fewer children and youth injured and killed by guns or burdened with the long-term emotional scars that result when young people witness violence.

Educators, law enforcement officials' social scientists and others with public safety responsibilities may be able to prevent some incidents of targeted school violence if they know what information to look for and what to do with such information when it is found.

Index